LA NILSSON

LA NILSSON

My Life In Opera

BIRGIT NILSSON

FOREWORD BY SIR GEORG SOLTI

AFTERWORD BY PEGGY TUELLER

TRANSLATED FROM THE GERMAN BY
DORIS JUNG POPPER

Northeastern University Press
Boston
PUBLISHED BY UNIVERSITY PRESS OF NEW ENGLAND
HANOVER AND LONDON

Northeastern University Press
Published by University Press of New England,
One Court Street, Lebanon, NH 03766
www.upne.com

Printed in the United States of America
5 4 3 2 1

Library of Congress Cataloging-in-Publication Data
Nilsson, Birgit.
[Nilsson. English]
La Nilsson : my life in opera / Birgit Nilsson ; foreword by Sir Georg Solti ; afterword by Peggy Tueller ; translated from the German by Doris Jung Popper.
p. cm.
Includes discography (p.) and index.
ISBN–13: 978–1–55553–670–1 (cloth : alk. paper)
ISBN–10: 1–55553–670–0 (cloth : alk. paper)
1. Nilsson, Birgit. 2. Singers—Biography. I. Popper, Doris Jung. trl. II. Title.
ML420.N697A313 2007
782.1092—dc22
[B] 2006101273

green press INITIATIVE

University Press of New England is a member of the Green Press Initiative. The paper used in this book meets their minimum requirement for recycled paper.

Contents

Foreword

BY GEORG SOLTI

My Dear Birgit,
I want to set down a few personal thoughts for the beginning of your autobiography.

For more than sixty years I have worked closely with singers, and in this time I have had the good fortune to build a storehouse of lovely memories. But there are very, very few singers whose artistry and musicality have impressed me so deeply as yours. Whenever we worked together there were those times, often unexpected, when we created something of lasting value. You are undoubtedly as happy as I that many such moments, through our recordings, have been preserved. To recount all these moments I would need an entire book; therefore, just one small incident will have to serve for your readers. We had just finished a concert performance of *Salome* in Chicago and were waiting backstage to go out and accept the applause of the audience. Suddenly you began vocalizing the Queen of the Night's aria, a piece that your colleagues in their best years and best form feared. And this after singing Salome? I was speechless but your only comment was, "Oh, that is no problem for me." This, for me, explains your long and extraordinary career: no matter what problems—musical or other—you came up against, we, your devoted fans, were never aware.

Again and again I encourage young singers to follow the shining example of your life and your devotion to the art of singing. And I am personally deeply grateful that you have so wonderfully enriched my life.

Fondly,
Georg Solti

Translator's Note

Brigit Nilsson's autobiography not available in English? I was in shock! A major operatic scandal!

Having read *La Nilsson* in German, I was fascinated with the story of her childhood on the farm and the formative years leading to her extraordinary career. There is such a wealth of information, particularly about the voice, which I wanted to share with my students and friends that I felt compelled to translate her story into English.

Nilsson was known for her fearless forthrightness as well as her great sense of humor and her memoirs sparkle with anecdotal gems. I hoped that my own fifteen years of singing in German opera houses would give me some special insight in getting the right "flavor" for an English version. Apparently it was so. I sent Mme. Nilsson a copy of the translation and she acknowledged receipt of it with a handwritten letter saying, in part:

I have "tried" 3 different translations but, alas, none of them were to my liking. So far I have read only part of it, but it is enough to see that this is the translation I like. Thank you!

We are all happy that Mme. Nilsson overcame her reluctance to write her memoirs. It is an important book.

D.J.P.

Preface

Writing memoirs: For some years various publishers have tried to break down my resistance, which I had held to be unshakable.

Writing memoirs: A shiver of respect ran down my spine at the very thought of those authors who, when writing of their life experiences, can hold their readers spellbound from the first to last word.

Writing memoirs: To my amazement I have come to realize that publishers are inundated with egoists, each of whom believes his life *has* to be in print for the benefit of future generations. Heart, kidneys, you-name-it—all are exposed; with unrestrained joy dirty laundry is publicly washed in the hope of writing a best seller.

Writing memoirs: No! Never! I will not be answerable to putting any heavier burden on the environment by adding the noxious chemicals of printer's ink to the air.

And yet! Here I sit, tortured, before the blank sheet of paper to which I will shortly entrust some of my memories.

This is a challenge whose result I have fortunately not fully grasped. What caused me to change my mind about memoirs?

First, for reasons on which I shall not further elaborate, I find myself at a dead end.

Second, I can blame everything on the onset of senility, which has diminished my capacity for self-criticism.

Third, I want to forestall the coming of the day when some nasty little writer will cook up a brew of lies about la Nilsson.

And last, I hope to tell my readers something about my long life, forty years of which were devoted to a career in singing.

Just at this moment I am experiencing almost wonderful expectations and I am filled with happiness. I am enthusiastic, even feverish, and my head is swimming at the thought of letting my life happen all over again by bringing all my experiences back into the present. How exciting!

But how will my whole life fit into one book? Never mind; it is much too soon to worry about that. Now the only thing that counts: "To write! To write!"

At this moment nothing seems to stand in the way of my decision. But I know that soon doubt and what remains of any self-criticism will give me trouble. The sun will disappear behind the clouds, my desire to write will waver, and feelings of inadequacy will plague me. But a challenge it is and I love challenges.

So with God's help! Amen.

MY DEBUT AT THE MET

A horrendous noise filled the room. With a start I awoke to the blaring of a siren. I reached for the lamp to my left on the nightstand. It was not there. Where was I? Slowly I came to my senses. Oh, of course, I was in New York, where sirens from police cars and fire trucks can be heard all day long; after a while one learns to tune them out. The noise of the siren was lost in the distance but I got up and, in spite of the cold weather, threw open the window. The sun was already sending a faint glow over Central Park. I drew in a deep, vitalizing breath of the frosty air, which—for New York—was astonishingly fresh and clear. A smile spread over my sleepy face; I felt at once excited, full of joyful anticipation, and sure of victory. The thrill of singing shot through my veins and I did not even need to test whether I was in voice—I knew it was there!

What good luck on the morning of a premiere to feel so shamelessly well! And this was not for just any premiere. It was Friday, December 18, 1959: in a few hours I would be singing for the first time on the stage of the Metropolitan Opera. I hoped to crown my career with this debut as Isolde in the opera of all operas, *Tristan und Isolde.*

"Wake up, you sleepyhead!" I called to Bertil from the window, "you have to sing Melot tonight at the Met . . . ." Bertil suffered from the recurring nightmare that he would be called upon, fully unprepared, to sing Melot in *Tristan,* and this had become a running joke between us. To befriend his demons, he had talked himself into believing such a performance was possible, even though he could not sing three consecutive notes from "Mary Had a Little Lamb." After all, the role of Melot was very short and he thought somehow he would manage it. He maintained this fiction for quite some time, until he finally heard Melot sung by someone who sounded like a stuck pig. Then he noticed the role was not so short; in fact, it seemed to have no end. Thus ended the dream of the Melot becoming reality.

Bertil rubbed his eyes and looked at me, astonished to see me up so early on the morning of a premiere and in such a good mood. Immediately he started to worry; he believed I gave my best performances when I was especially nervous all day and intolerable.

After breakfast we went for a walk in Central Park and fed acorns to the squirrels, who collected them eagerly for the colder days. We spoke about the impending performance. Ramón Vinay, the famous Chilean tenor, had canceled at the last moment because of illness. That was a shame, as during the three weeks of rehearsal, we had developed such a good rapport. Fortunately Karl Liebl, who was scheduled for a later performance, was able to jump in for the premiere. Liebl was an excellent tenor and I had sung with him in *Tristan* a year ago in Chicago.

On our walk I told Bertil about a strange man who had called me a few days earlier to offer to applaud for me in the premiere. I thought that a very friendly gesture but was curious enough to ask how he knew he was going to be enthusiastic about my performance. "Hmm-ah," he muttered, "I am the head of the claque and I am assuming you will make a contribution to me and my colleagues."

The claque is a strange phenomenon in the opera world. Applause for sale. Have you heard the likes of that? Yes, it happens, according to how much you are willing to pay. It is a widespread unfairness that can become very disagreeable when two singers on the stage are rivals and have each paid a claque. I hope the buying of applause will become less and less evident; it has no place nowadays when we are trying to revive our art form.

In this telephone conversation I recalled what Jussi Björling had once said in a similar situation and I answered quickly, "The day I have to pay for applause is the day I quit singing."

The wind was sharp and we soon returned to our hotel, the Alden, between 82nd and 83rd Streets on Central Park West. Many prominent musicians had lived there, including the conductor Fritz Busch, as well as the present conductor of the *Tristan* performance, Karl Böhm. Singers such as Leonie Rysanek, Inge Borkh, Jon Vickers, Jess Thomas, and countless others chose to make the Alden their home in New York. There were one-two-and three-room apartments, all of which had small kitchens where you could make small meals on a hot plate.

Today the obligatory steak was on the menu, which almost all singers eat before a performance and which had become for me a ritual. The meat in the United States is of very high quality and it is a pleasure to go into the markets to shop. About three in the afternoon it was time to rest awhile and let the meal digest, and around four or five (depending on when the performance began) I drank a cup of strong coffee to brace myself for the challenge ahead. I packed up everything I would need for the evening: my makeup, my dressing gown, hand towels, tea, honey, lemons, and an electric kettle for boiling water (I would not think of asking my dresser to make tea for me!), my Swedish Coryfin throat lozenges, and my little mascot, a black bull with red horns and hooves and a thick mane (my birth sign is that of Taurus). The bestower named him after me, "Krylltoppa" (Curly Top), which is what I was called as a child. Placing two fingers between my lips, a taxi instantly appeared. This whistle I learned from my father and it has saved me hours of waiting time over the years. The taxi driver stops on a dime, thinking the police are after him. To arrive in a limousine, the kind the great prima donnas appeared in, never occurred to me in those days. First I had to prove myself; my motto was "One should never decorate the cake before it is baked!"

The old Metropolitan lay between 39th and 40th Streets between Broadway and Seventh Avenue. It was not an impressive edifice, the inside shabby, the outside dirty and rundown. There was never room enough, and the stage door at 40th Street resembled nothing more than the door of a stable. The floor appeared to be hard, beaten-down earth; wags speculated it hadn't been cleaned since the opening of the house in 1883.

Dark closets functioned as dressing rooms; the office of the general manager was tiny and windowless. The secretaries practically sat on one another's laps. The restroom was often called upon for vocal warm-ups. The painting shop was no more up-to-date: the flats had to lie on the floor and the set designers could work on only a small part at one time. Then the flats had to be stored outside the house leaning on the Broadway wall of the building in the cold wind and rain. There they stood all season long or at least as long as the opera they were needed for was playing. No wonder the sets, after only a few seasons, had a worn and faded look.

In spite of all that, what a feeling of reverence one had upon entering this singers' temple! Here all the great ones sang: Christine Nilsson, Tetrazzini, Lilli Lehmann, Caruso, Chaliapin, Gigli, Jeritza, Flagstad, Melchior, Thorborg, Branzell, Ponselle, Svanholm, Björling, and countless others.

Ah, but the auditorium looked nothing like a stable. On the contrary, it was a wonder of gold, velvet, crystal, and silk—exactly the way an opera house should look! The boxes of the auditorium were shaped like a horseshoe and were given the name "The Golden Horseshoe." I loved the old Metropolitan. Never did I feel the presence of the great singers of the past as I did there. One expected Lilli Lehmann (in 1886, the first Isolde of the Metropolitan) to emerge dramatically and declaim: "In my time we did it better." Thanks to the hall's round form the members of the audience in the loges could see one another perfectly. The view of the stage, however, was not so good from every seat, but that was probably not so important to some of the operagoers, especially at a premiere.

The acoustics were particularly good for big voices. There was sufficient room for standees along the sides of the parquet as well as behind the last rows. After an especially good performance the standees would scream and applaud wildly and run forward to the stage. The ones in front were hanging over the orchestra pit in order to get as close to the singers as possible and the temperature in the hall rose a few degrees. You knew then you had been a success—at least for that evening.

In my tiny dressing room ("the Prima Donna Loge," as it was called), I began with a few scales accompanying myself on the Knabe piano, lent by that company to the Met. A similar one was in my apartment at the Alden. Everything was going well; after a few scales I began to feel the voice vibrating in the forehead, where it should be. It was my habit not to warm up too long for Isolde, as the first part of the role did not pose any special problems. On the other hand, it *is* the longest female role in opera (the first act alone is longer than the entire role of Aida). One must be less concerned about warming up and far more concerned about not being sung out at the end of the opera.

No sooner had I unpacked my makeup and put Krylltoppa in his place than there was a knock at the door. It was Irene Dalis, who was singing Brangäne, Isolde's maidservant. An unusually generous colleague with a wonderful dark mezzo-soprano voice, she wanted to wish me good luck. Irene was born in California of Greek heritage. She has jet-black hair, flashing brown eyes, and sparkling white teeth. She had already sung a few seasons at the Met and felt very much at home here. It was a good feeling for me to have someone to turn to should I need advice. Irene was convinced that I would have a big success on this evening and said, "After Isolde's 'Curse' [in the first act] you will have tremendous applause just as the Isolde two years ago did."

This astonished me: in Wagner operas there is never any applause interrupting the flow of the action. In Vienna it happened a few times that I received applause after Elisabeth's "Dich, teure Halle" but that is a free-standing aria with a wonderful ending and almost invites applause. In *Tristan,* however, the "Curse" of Isolde is more or less narrative, something that just moves the action along. Until now, after sixty-six Isoldes, I had never had any applause during act 1.

But soon my thoughts would be interrupted. Flowers and telegrams from near and far arrived continuously and there was constant knocking at my door. In a long line, stage director, set designer, coaches, assistant conductors, the prompter, and various secretaries appeared to wish me well—and as crowning glory, the general manager himself, the most powerful of the powerful, Rudolf Bing.

Never before had I experienced anything like this. In Europe you feel honored if the head of the opera or his representative greets you before a performance. It is certainly not a routine occurrence. Naturally it was fantastic to have the entire staff, one after the other in tuxedo or evening gown, taking the time to offer me their best wishes and making me feel so welcome.

But there can be too much of a good thing and I always say you can be killed with kindness when the affection is served up in too large a portion.

My nerves were telling me that after the tenth visitor I had had enough and could not smile one more grateful smile. Finally I had to gently move the last well-wisher toward the door. I had to have some time for myself and I was becoming impatient. I had just a few minutes to find my equilibrium and try the voice again before the stage manager, in his tux, came to say it was time to go onstage. One last look in the mirror. With my reddish-blond wig, and blue dress with black velvet appliqué, I hoped to give the impression of an Irish princess—at least from a distance.

All the other singers were already onstage. Karl Liebl, the Tristan, seemed very nervous, which was not surprising, as he was jumping in at the last minute to save the premiere—a predicament that critics seldom take into consideration.

King Marke was also there, Isolde's future spouse, whom she does not want: this was the over six-feet-tall American bass, Jerome Hines. A wonderful voice wrapped up in an ascetic man. Hines was very religious and graced every autograph hunter with a quotation of a Bible verse, for example: "See Matthew, chapter 5, verses 1–13." Many a fan has, upon reaching home, opened his Bible immediately and read the message of the missionary.

Kurwenal, Tristan's servant, was sung by Walter Cassel, likewise an American. He was a superb singer and actor who had already appeared in a number of musicals on Broadway as well as on other stages in the States. A sporty type, he appeared then much younger than his fifty years. For some reason he found no favor in the eyes (or, better said, the ears) of the conductor, Karl Böhm, and was often blamed for the mistakes of others.

And now there appeared in the arena the conductor of the evening, the sixty-five-year-old Karl Böhm. He was brought in by another stage manager, also in a tux. Originally the veteran, Otto Klemperer, was engaged for this production but he had suffered a terrible accident, which made it necessary to cancel his contract. He had fallen asleep with a lighted cigar in his mouth and had suffered severe burns. Luckily they were able to obtain Böhm for this new production of *Tristan,* although he was primarily known for his marvelous conducting of Mozart and Strauss works.

This was Böhm's first Wagner opera at the Metropolitan. He spoke both German and English with a strong Austrian accent, which was often imitated by some of the singers and other talented jokesters. When he was very excited or angry he mixed up the two languages freely.

During a *Tristan* rehearsal of act 2, Brangäne sang her "Warning" as planned, from backstage. Böhm could not hear her clearly enough and called to the assistant conductor who gave her Böhm's tempo, "I want you to have her a bit more pregnant . . . !"* The German coach, who had learned to fathom all of Böhm's wishes from the changes of facial expression, came to the stage apron and said, "With pleasure, Maestro, just a minute." Curtain!

On the evening of the premiere, Dr. Böhm appeared excited indeed. Before he disappeared into the pit he turned once more, pointed to Kurwenal and said loudly, "Bitte, Herr Cassel, look at mich!"

The performance could begin.

My first entrance worried me a bit. The set design represents the deck of a ship and in the staging I had had in all other productions, Isolde is seen onstage as the curtain opens. In this staging she had to come hurtling out of the cabin in the moment she begins to sing.

*In German, prägnant means bring out more or be more precise.

The door of the cabin was very narrow and low so that I had to bend over low to get out. I feared that my very first entrance, with my red wig at knee level, would find me looking more like a cocker spaniel than an Irish princess. Friendly applause for the conductor was heard through the curtain and wings and into the dark spot behind the stage where I waited for my entrance. Then I heard the first long tones of the strings from the prelude. It was unearthly. At this point I always experienced a stomach cramp and this evening it was worse than ever. Never had I heard the prelude so beautifully played.

When Wagner had finished composing *Tristan und Isolde* he feared it could be banned. The music was so strong and moving and so seductive that he feared for the sanity of the singers and the audience. "Good performances of *Tristan* must make the listeners go mad," said Wagner. Ludwig Schnorr von Carolsfeld, who sang Tristan in the first performance in Munich on June 10, 1865, died shortly after the premiere. One speaks of Mozart, Verdi, and Strauss lovers, but of Wagner, fanatics. His music not only strengthens the personality of the singer but raises the standard of his performance and deepens his expressiveness. Wagner himself was addicted to his own musical "drugs."

The prelude ended. The young steersman directed his last mocking words to Isolde. Like an arrow I shot out of the cabin (Hurrah! The entrance went perfectly!) and suddenly stomach cramps and pounding heart were forgotten. Had my hand or foot been cut off, I would not have noticed; I was so concentrated on my role. The voice responded; I had only to open up and let it flow. Irene Dalis was wonderful to interact with: active, alert, but at the same time solicitous, as Isolde's servant must be. I have had colleagues who ceaselessly tried to convince the audience that they should be the one singing Isolde. Then everything goes wrong and nothing in their relationship works. But here, everything ran perfectly and I was able to rise to the intensity of Isolde's "Narration," which ends with the imprecation "Tod, Tod uns beiden."

As required by the staging, I fell, half-fainting, to the ship's deck. It was so still in the auditorium that you could have heard a pin drop. At this moment I was thinking: "This was the place where the last Isolde received applause and my Brangäne had predicted I would bring the house down." Not a hand moved. I had failed and just when I was feeling so vocally and histrionically inspired. I would be lying if I claimed that the absence of applause didn't disturb me, but the show must go on even when you have to swim against the tide.

Kurwenal came on and was simply wonderful; his acting was daring and irreproachable. He did not notice that Karl Böhm's face lost all its color, but everything went well musically.

Theo Otto from Germany had designed the set, stark, bordering on the surreal, but with just enough realism. It was difficult for me in this setting to get into the mood for the "Love Duet" in act 2. We sat under a small, windblown tree whose autumn leaves were, for the most part, lying on the ground. Perhaps contributing more to my discomfort was the bright lighting. It was, after all, night, which affords the opportunity for the lovers' tryst. I had not yet grasped that Met audiences demanded the stage be more brightly lit than did the audiences in Europe. On the one hand, the Met auditorium with its four thousand seats is much larger than most European houses; on the other hand, American audiences "hear" more with their eyes than, say, a German audience. In Germany, many members of the audience know the opera and obviously have no difficulty with the language of the Wagner operas.

The stage director for this *Tristan* was an Austrian, Herbert Graf, the head of the Zurich Opera, an experienced and competent man. He oozed confidence and calmness and the work with him was totally free from conflict. His staging concepts were traditional, no revolutionary ideas that would go against the music—he allowed Wagner to reign.

But after Kurwenal's exit came Tristan's entrance, which began an emotional and highly charged dramatic scene. I love act 1; it is so very complex and multifaceted. But I imagine that most people prefer act 2 with the wonderful "Love Duet" where the beauty of the voices is in the foreground and the complexities of the plot held in abeyance.

The first act was nearing its end. Tristan and Isolde, in passionate embrace, are liberated by the effect of the love potion. The curtain fell and there was a long pause—quiet. The general manager had warned me of the possible reaction of the premiere audience. He said many came to the opening merely to show off their gowns and applaud with only one hand to protect their jewelry. And some of the audience actually leave after the second intermission as there is nothing more of interest to them.

"But," he added as he observed by disbelief, "the following performances find the public much more enthusiastic." Rudolf Bing knew his Met audience.

The act ended and the moment the curtain opened I was greeted with deafening jubilation. An uproar had broken out in the auditorium. The audience had risen to its feet and were screaming, stamping the floor, and applauding wildly. They seemed to have forgotten the champagne and the mutual fashion show awaiting them. They remained standing and it seemed as though they would not leave until they could applaud the Isolde by herself. There is a rule at the Met that there are no solo bows between acts. Bing began to get nervous and glanced at his watch. Two acts to go and the performance must be over by midnight, otherwise tremendous overtime salaries would have to be paid. He saw no way out of the dilemma other than to break his rule and send me out for a solo bow.

The ovation was deafening. Only as Turandot at the opening of a La Scala season have I ever experienced such a storm of applause, such a manifestation of approval.

I sailed on clouds back to my dressing room where I was quickly brought into the real world. Hairstylists and dressers stood ready for my change for act 2. We ended up with only five minutes as the audience had applauded during the entire intermission. There was not time for any rest. I drank a glass of water, which tasted of chlorine, stuck a Coryfin lozenge in my mouth to get rid of the bad taste and hurried back to the stage. After having sung continuously in act 1, which is seventy-nine minutes long, I now had act 2 facing me in which I would be singing much of its seventy-one minutes.

I went onstage for act 2 with unsettled feelings. Since the first act had gone over so overwhelmingly, I doubted whether I could fulfill the listeners' expectations in the next two acts. An audience, I knew, could be very capricious. In Naples, I actually experienced a performance in which after act 1 Maria Callas was cheered and applauded and after act 2 was booed. A hair-raising thought!

The hunting horns began to play, my pulse quickened, and my adrenaline heightened my awareness. I was so inspired I could hardly wait for my entrance. Any fatigue was blown away; the voice reacted to every command and a feeling of great happiness pervaded me.

Karl Liebl's Tristan was particularly good this evening. The "Love Duet" in act 2 can be a real stumbling block for most Wagner tenors, as it has to be sung lyrically, but Liebl had no difficulty since his voice was unusually lyric for a Wagner tenor. The conductor, Karl Böhm, was fantastic. It was as though he could simultaneously fulfill the wish of the orchestra, singers and public. After this act the enthusiasm of the public was just as overwhelming as after the first act and I began to believe I would have a successful debut. Finally, I found a little time to relax and to think about some of the wonderful moments that had happened: my fantastic colleagues, the public and the personnel backstage—everyone had in his way made this performance the high achievement it was.

Act 3 is the longest and most difficult part for the Tristan. Isolde is only onstage for the final twenty minutes when she closes the opera with its crowning glory, the "Liebestod." This is the scene all Wagner lovers wait for. An Isolde can be superb in the first two acts but if she falls short in the "Liebestod," she is not a good Isolde.

While waiting for my act 3 entrance I looked over a few telegrams, letters, and flowers that had arrived, fearing, in so doing, of losing touch with the role. At such times I do not like visits from colleagues or others who only want to pass the time, as I have to preserve my concentration.

But we are all so different. The great Kirsten Flagstad was in the habit of ordering a bottle of cognac from the bar while knitting sweaters and mufflers for her children and grandchildren. When she was called for her entrance, she laid the knitting aside, went onstage, and sang like an angel.

The last note in the "Liebestod," a pianissimo F sharp, was sung. Over the body of my beloved Tristan, I collapsed, still filled with the bewitching, seductive sounds of Wagner's music. There is no coming back to reality yet; the atmosphere must be preserved! No matter how I love to be the object of the audience's acclaim, I am annoyed when the atmosphere is broken by early applause or bravas called out before the end of the music. At least a moment of silence should be granted the universe of music.

The lights were turned off and on—a warning to the audience that it was near midnight and they should be leaving the opera house. Even though they protested, they were given no quarter, and the hangers-on had to feel their way out in the dark.

After I had given my thanks to my colleagues, the conductor, and stage director, I started for my dressing room where an endless line of acquaintances and strangers waited to congratulate me or ask for an autograph. Only now did I begin to feel, after the great exertion, fatigue overcoming me. It took quite some time for us to leave the opera house. I had given away most of the flowers but even for those I took we had to order an extra taxi. When the taxi driver saw the flowers he asked if I was "the girl" in the interview he had read: "who on the evening before her entrance exam for the Music Academy in Stockholm had milked ten cows?" I couldn't deny it, whereupon he replied, "Then you deserve every single one of these flowers!"

And with this performance ended the 282nd *Tristan* at the Metropolitan and the first new production of the opera since 1920.

. . .

I finally fell into bed but found it difficult to sleep. I lay there and thought about how it might have been had I made my debut at the Met earlier.

The Met had made overtures before but a role was offered that I had never sung and I felt that was out of the question for me. Rudolf Bing had not shown any great interest. He had heard me sing twice: once at an audition in Berlin in 1953 and again in 1955 in Munich as Salome. Time passed and I had the impression that the Met was a dead issue. Anyway, I could comfort myself that I was sought after by all the big opera houses of the world: Vienna, Milan, Munich, Bayreuth, London, Buenos Aires, San Francisco, Chicago, and—lest we forget—Stockholm. I could choose my engagements and I told myself I could live very well without Rudolf Bing and his dusty old opera house. Honestly, though, deep down inside it bothered me that I heard nothing from the Met.

In the summer I sang in the Vienna Festival, which was by now almost a tradition. On June 24, *Tristan* was on the program with Wolfgang Windgassen singing the title role; which always pleased me. Someone said Rudolf Bing was attending the performance. That made me wonder as I knew he was not a Wagner fan and Wagner operas were seldom in the Met repertoire.

Windgassen was known to Bing as he had already been engaged at the Met for a season, and I was sure Bing was not interested in me. But I decided anyway to show him what he was missing.

On the same evening there was a soccer match between Sweden and Germany. Windgassen, a great soccer fan, was heartbroken not to be able to follow the game on the radio. But he arrived at a solution. Kurwenal, sung by the unforgettable Paul Schöffler, had little to do in act 1 so Windgassen gave him the responsibility of standing in the wings with a large placard that kept Windgassen informed of the score! This resulted in a rather platonic "Love Duet" as Windgassen could hardly take his eyes off the sign in the wings. In the second act it became more difficult because night had fallen and it was dark and impossible to see the placard. But necessity is the mother of invention. The highly admired bass and actor Ludwig Weber sang King Marke and it was no problem for him to change the staging without disturbing the believability of the scene. Mark was the last to enter in act 2 so he was able to listen to the radio until just before coming onstage. Instead of leaving the stage wounded and offended after learning of Isolde's unfaithfulness, he went broken and inconsolable to Tristan, laid both hands on his shoulders, and whispered, "You lost . . . 4 to 2 Sweden." At the next opportunity Tristan came to me and kissed me with the loving words, "Congratulations . . . 4 to 2 Sweden!"

A few days later I received a telegram from the Metropolitan with an offer to sing Isolde in the new production of *Tristan* opening on December 18, 1959. To my great sadness, Windgassen was not engaged for Tristan. I am sure the soccer game was to blame for this. Ever since, I have had quite ambivalent feelings about soccer, as I know how addictive it can become.

But back to my premiere at the Met.

Obviously, I had at some time fallen asleep because I was suddenly awakened by the ringing of the telephone. On the other end was Sven Åhmen, the legendary correspondent for the Swedish daily paper *Dagens Nyheter.* He congratulated me upon the unbelievably good notices and was surprised that I had not already read all the wonderful things that had been written about me. It was only 9:30 in the morning and I am never very active at that hour. One at a time we got all the five daily papers in New York City; even though I was usually lucky enough to have good reviews, these were above and beyond anything I had ever known. Both the *New York Times* and the *Herald Tribune* had my review under a two-column headline on the first page. The *Times* enthused, "Birgit Nilsson as Isolde Flashes Like New Star in the Met Heavens." Only once before, for Ljuba Welitsch's *Salome* debut, had there been a front-page review. Along with my review on page one, there was a lengthy article with the headline, "President Eisenhower Meets With Heads of Western Powers in Paris." Thus was the news juxtaposed.

The head critic of the *New York Times,* Howard Taubman, wrote among other things, "with a voice of extraordinary size, suppleness, and brilliance she dominated the entire performance. Isolde's fury and passion were as consuming as cataclysms."

The article on the front page of the *Herald Tribune* contained an Isolde photo with the headline: "The Met Has a New Isolde and She is a Real Princess." The critic Paul Henry Lang wrote: "this, ladies and gentlemen, is a real Princess, a magnificent artist and a sensation. With wide-open eyes the dazed listeners half-stumbled from the opera house after the performance. You must go and hear her as you will regret hearing from your friends how it was to have heard Birgit Nilsson at the Met."

Also the *New York World Telegram* did not spare itself with its four-column headline: "The Debut of a New Swedish Nightingale!" and Biancolli closed his praise with "it was a great day for Sweden."

In the *World News* the headline over three columns read: "The Met

Has a Radiant New Isolde" and Douglas Watt wrote that I was "the first really sensational soprano since Kirsten Flagstad. Nilsson possesses a pure and powerful voice, which she uses with dazzling skill. In addition she has a stately bearing."

The *New York Journal American* declared: "A New Star is Risen—Isolde—Nilsson." Miles Kastendick added: "the best Wagner soprano since Kirsten Flagstad and greater praise one cannot give. We were rewarded in waiting for this Isolde. She has a powerful voice with great brilliance in the top register. Seldom can the listener understand the text so clearly and follow the plot."

Harriet Johnson, the *New York Post* critic wrote: "even after the first act, the public honored her with unbelievable ovations. Those who go often to the Metropolitan will feel gratified to hear the entire audience calling "Bravo" instead of the paid claque or fan club members."

The enormous power of the New York critics reaches throughout the entire opera world. Even now I am deeply moved by the outpouring of praise I had then, approbation that laid the foundation of my future career. I knew that a debut at the Met was important but luckily I did not have any idea how important it would be for me. In the end, after I had taken in all the superlatives, I silently thanked Rudolf Bing for waiting so long to engage me.

WHEN THE LITTLE ONE CAME INTO THE WORLD

"More milk! There's another mouth to feed!" cried out the farmhand, Otto, on the morning after I was born.

The seventeenth of May 1918 was a sunny Friday. The cows in the pasture had not yet calved and those who should have had milk had none. There had been a crop failure, there was no more hay, and for some time the main feed for the cattle consisted of weeds. One of Otto's jobs was to fetch milk from the neighboring farm, and he used this as the opportunity to broadcast, "More milk! There's another mouth to feed!"

For my father, Nils, and for the midwife, I was, however, a disappointment. He was hoping to have a son and had promised the midwife fifty extra kronor if a son was delivered, but I squelched the transaction.

Both my parents were from farming families. My father had bought a farm adjoining that of his parents and he hoped that when my grandfather was no longer able to farm he would inherit the land that had been in the family for ten generations. Nils had nine siblings: eight sisters and a much younger brother. My mother, Justina (or Stina, as she was usually called), was born in the same parish as my father, Västra Karup, but three miles away in the village of Faritslöv. She had two brothers. Her family was thought of as well-to-do. Unfortunately my maternal grandmother died suddenly at the age of fifty-two and my mother, who was then eighteen, had to take charge of the household of her father and brothers. All her dreams of studying singing and acting were forever gone! My mother played the accordion with the power of a man and she sang along with an unusually strong, clear, and beautiful voice. She was often asked to sing at village festivities in various localities. She was slim, graceful, and very pretty. I recall hearing that there were more than a few rebuffed suitors who had asked my strict grandfather for her hand.

One day a young man who had been mining for gold in America's West came back to town. He had made his fortune and attempted to awaken my mother's interest in him. The pursuit was futile, as she had already secretly made her choice: my father.

One evening the gold miner asked to speak to my grandfather. After they had spoken for a while, the miner got to the point and asked for Stina's hand in marriage. At the same time he brought forth a leather pouch from his pocket and emptied the contents onto the table. Gold nuggets of various sizes that he had panned "over there" spilled out. With these gold nuggets he intended to buy one of the most beautiful farms in the parish. The heart of my grandfather melted like gold in a crucible, and he promised to bring his influence to bear on his daughter. But nothing came of it, as Stina informed her father at this time that she had already made her choice.

Nils had many siblings, however, and the "pie" had to be divided among them all. Certainly he could not come up with any gold nuggets. It went so far that Stina's aunt and uncle threatened to disinherit her if she did not accept the gold miner. But my mother followed her heart and went to the altar with my father in 1916.

I've been told that I was a ravenous child, always hungry. At my christening I allegedly drowned out both the pastor and the organ. The old pastor, Anders Nilsson, who was born in the 1850s advised my mother to put me on my stomach and let me suck on a pacifier. Stina often told the story of what the pastor said but I was too young to make any sense of her words. Only much later I read in a book of local customs about how crying babies were quieted in the nineteenth century. One made a dummy "thumb" from a piece of cloth (this was before pacifiers could be bought), soaked it in brandy and stuck it in the mouth of the shrieking child. No wonder quiet prevailed, at least as long as the child was sleeping off the booze!

When I was two we moved to the farm of my grandfather, land I still own. Allegedly, I could sing and speak before I could walk; however, I did not walk until I was fifteen months old.

I was totally in love with our farmhand, Otto, who stayed with us for seven years, and I think he was also fond of me. He had thick black hair, which I could comb as much as I wanted. Otto was also the first one who promoted my musical talent. When I was four he bought me a child's piano at the fall fair in Båstad. It was the size of a large cigar box and had the range of an octave in C major. The black half tones were merely painted on. On this little piano I played all the melodies I could and sang within the octave range. What heaven!

I sang and played from morning till night. When I was more proficient I ran over to our neighbors and begged them to let me play their organ. Nils did not want his daughter to be disturbing the neighbors all the time so he bought a house organ for me for seventy-five kronor. (It stands today in the pastor's house in the Boarp Museum of Local History in Båstad.) I shall never forget my father hitching the horses to the wagon to fetch my organ. When he returned with the long-awaited music instrument, I threw myself on the sofa and buried my face in a pillow; for a long time I did not dare to look for fear the whole thing was a dream. When I look back on this event, so significant for me, I can still remember the feeling of happiness I experienced then.

Now there was more music in the house. Stina played diligently and also Karin showed musical talent. She had come from Göteborg during her school vacation and stayed long enough to get married to the son of our neighbor. Otto and Karin were like family, and during cozy winter evenings we played and sang our hearts out. Every issue of the *Every Family's Journal* contained a song in which the chords and melody were indicated by numbers instead of notes—one called this system, I believe, "Aladdin notes"—and I quickly learned how to play these chords.

I was an only child and had to rely on my own dreams and fantasies. Most of the neighbors' children were older than I and often made fun of my not being able to read. One evening, after a day of intense teasing, I asked Stina to teach me the letters in the *Ängelholms Tidning*. First we looked at all the large letters, then we went through the small ones. By the time I had to go to bed I could read.

Now I felt as grown-up and important as the other children. I was five years old. From then on I stood at the door every day waiting for the letter carrier who brought the *Ängelholms Tidning* so I could read the magazine section; it was very interesting—or so I told the neighbors.

I soon learned how to read standard musical notation even though I was not sure of the note value. Besides, I found it more fun to play by ear as I could have a much larger repertoire. If I heard a song whose melody I didn't recognize, I quickly composed one of my own.

Our home was always open to guests and Nils liked to have me sing and play for our visitors. He enjoyed this and was as proud as a Spaniard of me. Many people advised him to take care that I didn't overexert myself, but we never took heed. Singing was not at all strenuous; it was the most wonderful thing in the world.

One of the very first to notice my vocal talent was Ludwig Nobel, the nephew of the great Alfred Nobel. He was a man of few words, modest, and with a great sense of humor. He had, with his fortune and generosity, made his home, the town of Båstad, into a veritable summer paradise, one of Sweden's most beautiful areas. I very gladly granted his wish and I sang one song after another for him and not just because his tips were extremely generous.

Even as a child, I was not supposed to say "father" and "mother," but "Nils" and "Stina." And the child was always to have her way (had my father added, "as long as her way is identical with mine," we would have been nearer the truth). Nils was very friendly, generous, and full of humor, but he was stubborn.

Stina, on the other hand, was impulsive and temperamental even though her outbursts were over as quickly as they had begun. She believed in the "hands-on" method of bringing up children and backed up her belief with a scrub brush, one with a long, sharp-edged, cracked handle. Even today I can see the hated instrument of torture. A few times—totally without reason—she pulled down my drawers and taught me a lesson with the handle of the scrub brush. This humiliation was a thorn in my flesh for my entire childhood. My father never spanked me. He realized that the one who dished out the punishment felt guilty afterward, and was then friendlier than ever.

Stina adored dancing and I was introduced to this fine art. I had to stand on Stina's feet while Nils lay on the floor indicating the dance steps with his hands. One day we had a visit from a Mr. Lindgren, a teacher in the high school in Hov, a neighboring village. He had heard of my unusual voice and wanted to hire me for the school's Christmas pagent. Stina worked with me on the program and I wore a white silk dress, trimmed with swan feathers on the sleeves and neck, and a huge rosette in my dark curls. The older children called me "Curly Top," which greatly annoyed me. In the pageant the organ burst forth with a horrible squeal—but no matter how fast I pounded with my little feet the sound disappeared instantly. I didn't let myself become rattled by this, however. I climbed up on the organ bench, standing a head taller than everyone else and gave the concert a cappella. There was appreciative applause and the ladies found me sweet and pretty. But I had reckoned on greater enthusiasm. Therefore, I decided to change my program and put in "Nickolina," a song Otto had taught me:

> Att vara kär de é en ryslig pina,
> den som försökt, den säger inte nej osv.
>
> (To be in love will cause you pain
> But who ever tries it says no in vain.)

Finally the proper atmosphere was created and I went energetically into "Marriage in Flänga," which I sang to my own melody:

> Petter Johansson i Flänga skulle gifta bort sin tös,
> de va ett släng och slamrande som håken skull' vatt lös osv.
>
> (Peter Johansson in Flänga was to marry a lass
> There was endless pressing and crushing out there in the grass)

That's how it should go, I thought triumphantly as I proudly climbed down from the organ bench. Unfortunately Stina was of another opinion and made it very clear to me when we got home. Once again, I could not understand why she was punishing me.

Often I was allowed to go with Nils when he went to the mill in Båstad. That was exciting and most of the time there was a treat on the way home, as we each had a sweet tooth. I usually stayed with the wagon, holding the horses by the reins while Nils went into the mill and paid. One day, standing before our wagon was another carriage from which the horses were unharnessed and over which a drawbar loomed. A miller's helper came out of the mill toting on his back a large sack, which he tossed onto the wagon. The drawbar fell down on my horse's nose, sending him into a frenzy. Fifteen yards ahead raged the mill's waterfall, over which was a rather narrow bridge. The seat on which I sat was not screwed to the wagon and the chance to survive this mad dash seemed slim. At the last moment a farmer from nearby jumped in. He was known for his daring and, throwing himself toward the horse and grabbing the bit, he brought the animal to a standstill.

This time there were more treats than usual, since I had agreed not to mention the incident to Stina. Nonetheless, through the grapevine she learned of the adventure a few days later, and with that, all future trips to the mill were over for me.

My father kept all kinds of animals: dogs, cats, goats, calves, rabbits, guinea pigs, ducks, geese, turkeys, pheasants, chickens, bantams, parrots, and canaries. Naturally we didn't have all these animals at the same time, but there were always enough that a special person was responsible for their care. When Nils was asked why he owned so many animals he would answer, "The girl likes them." That meant he had decided that the girl liked them. I really liked only the dogs and cats, but my father as a child was not permitted to have so many pets and this was his way of making up for it, and of course the girl went along with him.

For some time I had been longing to have a bicycle but instead I received a wagon. Unfortunately, I had no brothers or sisters to pull me around as my father did with his nine siblings. It wasn't until I was ten that I finally got a bicycle. Nils laid down the following rule: it had to be a Wiklund (that was the most expensive), it had to have yellow fenders (yuk, so ugly, but that was the color of his bicycle) and it was to be purchased at Schmied's in Mäsinge where he had bought his bicycle. So if I wanted a bicycle I had no choice but to travel the eight miles to Mäsinge to fetch this new means of transportation with the yellow fenders. And I surely wanted the bicycle.

I had no difficulty in school. "You read like a pastor," said the teacher and moved me on to the second grade. Stina continually asked me how I was getting along in school. She was quite demanding and insisted that I be the best in everything.

I had a cousin who was one grade behind me. There was no greater carrier of tales than he and he watched me like a hawk. If I didn't recite my lesson with total aplomb or if I made the slightest error, he ran home and blabbed about it, exaggeratedly, to everyone. On the next day Stina would hear from her sister-in-law about the huge mountain that had been made out of a small molehill. Almost every day I had a stomachache as I went home from school just thinking about all the trouble my stupid cousin would make for me.

As long as I can remember, I dreamed of becoming a singer and each time I saw a shooting star I curtsied and made my most fervent wish. I had always heard that wishes were granted when one saw a falling star and since I made the same wish each time I saw a shooting star I was completely convinced that I was heard. (Author's Note: to avoid any misunderstanding it should be clear that *falling star* means the celestial phenomenon and not the earthly "fallen star.")

In grade school we had a clever and friendly teacher named Erik Pamp. He taught more than forty students, five grades in the same room. He was absolutely phenomenal in dividing up the work. It was generally known that the students in his school were the best. This teacher was the one who discovered that I had absolute pitch, an attribute I had assumed everyone had. Pamp had only two fingers on his left hand. I was allowed during my grade school years to accompany the singing classes and sometimes conduct. This continued even after I had finished grade school. The teacher and I were agreed that I should study further because I possessed the qualifications. My parents were also of this opinion—so Pamp and I thought—but they abruptly changed their minds, which canceled out my dreams of further study.

I have never found out why they reversed their decision but I guess that pure provincialism was the cause. For me it was as though the sun had gone out of my world and I knew not where to turn. The duties on the farm did not appeal to me as they were at that time one step from slavery. Nils could not imagine anything better in the entire world, so why shouldn't the girl think the same? He was free and independent and could decide for himself when he wanted to work. He had no need of vacations; the farm gave him relaxation and change of pace. If at times the work was too much there was always additional help available. He refused to be a slave to time and did not even carry a watch every day. Only on special holidays would the "gold piece" be brought out. Nils wished for his daughter the same worry-free existence with which he was so completely satisfied. He would live with a son-in-law whom we would select together. Why should I, the only child, struggle with learning and getting a degree?

I had to help with everything that went on in the operation of the farm, but I actually had a lot of free time. Stina, who didn't find everything about farm life completely to her liking, sacrificed herself gladly so that I would have a comfortable life. I was the apple of her eye and she probably wished her daughter a different existence, a different future. But which one?

When I was fourteen years old I had my first actual piano lesson. For ten years I had been my own teacher and unaided interpreter and it was difficult to learn the ground rules now. My piano teacher was not exactly loaded with energy. He often sat in the next room and read the newspaper while I played "Napoleon's March over the Alps" in waltz-time.

Sometimes I also got a voice lesson and since he was the acting choir-master in Västra Karup I was very soon a member of the church choir. I was very proud and happy as I, the youngest member of the choir, was chosen to sing a solo from Beethoven's "Lobgesang" (Song of praise) at the wedding of my Sunday School teacher. On all holidays we sang in two churches, in Västra Karup and in Torekov. When the celebration of the first day of Christmas was in Torekov, which was the farthest away, I had to get up at five in the morning, but it was well worth it. There was a ceremonial atmosphere with candlelight, wonderful aromatic pine boughs, and psalm singing, with the roaring of the organ and the church full of people.

Among the chorus members there was a lovely camaraderie and it was so wonderful to meet young people with, however limited, an interest in music. The gold miner from my mother's past had two children, a daughter and a son, who were in the choir. The daughter was always especially well dressed. One time when I was invited to her home she suggested that we go dancing in the evening. I was quite torn. I knew that my parents would think I, at sixteen, was too young to go dancing and I had not asked their permission. But the temptation was irresistable and I went with her.

Ah, how much fun it was to dance! The evening flew by and soon the last waltz was being played. This meant that the boy who had asked a girl to dance would accompany her to her door. I, however, got rid of my dance partner as quickly as Cinderella left the ball so I could get home as soon as possible.

Strangely enough I was not punished. Luckily it was the gold miner's daughter who got all the blame. When it had to do with dancing and similar entertainment, Stina had the say. Another time on a Wednesday evening, I had a visit from a girlfriend who wanted to go dancing. Stina forbade my going: for one thing it was during the week and I could only go out Saturday or Sunday; second, she would be alone at home until late in the evening; third, it looked like a storm was brewing. No, I could only accompany my friend a part of the way. The temptation again was so strong that I went all the way to the dance hall. There I made an important discovery: dancing was also wonderful in the middle of the week! When I got back home the door was locked. I was baffled; we never made it a habit to lock the door either day or night. Stina had simply locked me out! My knocking was unsuccessful but I had an idea. I crawled through the cellar window and very quietly sneaked into my room. My goodness, what a dressing-down I got! When Nils got home the story was told and retold and ended with the threat, "And now you will stay home for the rest of the summer!"

The declaration was especially harsh as we were only "In the Wonderful Month of May," as the Schumann song has it. And I was not to go dancing at all! That was a real blow. In the following weeks a friend who was a member of the Young Farmers' Club invited me to a party given by the club. It looked bad but I told Stina anyway about the invitation. "What dress are you going to wear?" she asked. That told me that she had already regretted her hard words.

But life does not consist only of carefree days and dancing. There were also endless days in the vegetable garden where the sun burned you and the wind blew the dusty earth over you, covering your face and clothing with a black layer of grime, while the luxury coaches sped their way back and forth between the modern spas of Båstad and Tarekov. "If only . . ." —oh, I had many dreams that would never become reality unless a miracle happened.

Certainly one can direct one's life with energy and determination. But how? There was no one who could give me advice. My plans and hopes went beyond the understanding of most people. They would simply think, if they could see into my thoughts, that I was arrogant and suffering from delusions of grandeur.

I myself didn't even know what opera was. The little singing I had heard was limited to choir music and a few concerts with vocal soloists. There was an oratorio and concert singer Märta Palm from Ängelholm whom I admired greatly. I wanted to be like her. She sang so beautifully and was otherwise so stylish with her big, wide-brimmed hats and elegant dresses.

In Båstad was one of the best choir directors in Sweden, Albert Runbäck. He directed a church choir with many lovely voices and had engaged a voice teacher, Ragnar Blennow, to work with the members of the choir. This Blennow came from Ästorp and functioned as choir director and organist in the church in Björnekulla. In addition he taught voice in the upper grades in Helsingborg, was himself a well-known concert singer, and gave private lessons. I nosed around like a cat before hot porridge until I finally got up nerve enough to call Runbäck and ask for an audition with Ragnar Blennow. Runbäck said the chances were slim because Blennow had all he could manage with the voices in the Båstad choirs. He was unable to teach every applicant, especially one from another church—and I belonged to the choir in Västra Karup.

Perhaps he noticed my great disappointment because he followed with the suggestion that if someone canceled because of illness I might be able to take that time. That was at least a ray of hope.

For some days I went about hoping that coughs and hoarseness would infect the chorus members of Båstad—and, what do you know, not long after our telephone conversation my wish was granted. Runbäck called and said there was an hour free for me. What did I want to sing? I chose a song from Ivar Widéen, "Serenade." Actually this song was composed for a male voice but it made no difference to me. I would have preferred to sing Wagner but the only music available in the music library in Båstad was Siegmund's aria from *Walküre* and that would have been going too far.

I was early and had to wait in an anteroom. A soprano was having a lesson with Blennow and her voice sounded very beautiful. Her vibrato went to and fro like the lapping of waves. My piano teacher had this kind of vibrato and I presumed this was a sign of good vocal training. Neither Stina nor I or anyone from the choir in Västra Karup sang with this "advanced" technique. I tried to imitate this phenomenon by punching myself in the belly. I was so deep in this musing that I did not notice that her lesson had ended. The soprano, a member of the police force, passed by, commanding my full respect. She shot me a contemptuous glance. Maybe she thought I would make fun of her but that was the farthest thing from my mind.

Soon I was in the room with him, the person who held my fate in his hands. Ragnar Blennow was an imposing figure; tall, strongly built and oozing authority, which made one feel quite small. (Much later in my career the former ambassador Gunnar Jarring, who had had voice lessons with Blennow, told me how free he could be with boxing his pupils' ears). We began with Widéen. When I finished the song, he removed his clouded-over glasses and polished them, lost in thought. Finally he said, "That was very beautiful. You, young lady, will certainly become a great singer."

This went through me like lightning. Certainly I had always dreamed that my discoverer would tell me that I was the wonder the world had been waiting for, but now that I heard it with my own ears the shock was almost too much. The rest of the lesson has escaped my memory, only that Blennow expressed that he wished to work with me again when he was next in Båstad.

Like a madwoman, I cycled my way home up all the hills of Båstad—no mean feat at any time—rushed into the house, and cried out, "I have been discovered! I am going to be a great singer!" Stina was surprised, happy, and proud while Nils continued to believe that what I could do already was quite enough. He did not believe in my future as a singer and he felt I had a good enough life at home on the farm.

Unfortunately I didn't receive many lessons. Blennow became seriously ill and was in a clinic for a long time. My everyday work was harvesting, digging potatoes, pulling weeds, and milking without a glimmer on the horizon of anything Blennow had made me hope for. It made my work even harder to bear.

The new year, 1940, saw me taking a five-month household management course in Ljungskile. The school included also a commercial school, an adult educational institute for about three hundred students. I shared my room with two other girls, Elsa from Blekinge, who was engaged to a pastor of a Free Church, and Evy, a sweet girl from the area of Ängelholm, who looked like Deanna Durbin. Evy and I became very good friends and kept in touch for many, many years. Every week there was a student evening organized by the school members, with singing, music, readings, theater performances, and much more. I was a principal motivator here and was spurred on like a bloodhound when my performance received a lot of applause. I felt like a fish in water. During the day I learned cooking, sewing, and weaving, and everything passed as though I were tipsy.

It was the middle of the Finnish Winter War. After two and a half months we had news that the school would have to close for possible use as a hospital. The situation was not so serious as it was feared and in the next year the school was again opened. In answer to Rector Hellerstedt's letter inviting me back in the autumn of 1941, I wrote, not without pride: "My plans have changed and unfortunately I cannot continue the course. I have been accepted in the class for vocal soloists at the Royal Academy of Music in Stockholm." Rector Hillerstedt and his family shared in my joy and I was later asked to sing at the school's various events, which I did very gladly.

I had been thinking over my uncertain future for some time before I renewed contact with Ragnar Blennow. He began with a dressing-down in which he asked how much longer I was going to put off making a decision. True, I knew what I wanted but I was still as hesitant as before because I had so little self-confidence and no one to really encourage me.

"So Birgit will come to me for six months once a week for voice lessons, and then in the fall I will register her for the entrance examination for the Royal Academy of Music in Stockholm."

And these words were what I needed finally to force me to make a decision. A wonderful time was unfolding. Once a week I took a bus and train for the sixty miles to Åstorp. I worked and practiced and Blennow gave me a solid grounding for my further development. In addition to the technical work we sang romances and arias that I would need for the examination. We did songs by Sibelius, Heise's "Dyveke Songs," "Elisabeth's Prayer" from *Tannhäuser*, and Vaino's songs from the opera *Arnljot* by Petersson Berger.

Nils, who was accustomed to everything going his way, didn't want to yield in battle yet. Although he was the one who had originally got the organ and piano for me and who praised my voice to the skies before his friends and acquaintances, it was he who opposed my decision to become a singer. The last bomb he exploded was that he had no intention of financially supporting any music education in Stockholm for me. This threat, however, did not have the desired success, as Stina promised to come through with an inheritance she had received. Then he began to reproach Stina. Because she was the one who supported my decision, she must hold herself solely responsible for all the evil that would surely come to me in the big city. I felt sorry for Stina who stood between two such determined people and who wanted only the best for me. That Nils wanted also. And as usual, it went according to his prediction.

About a month before I was to leave for Stockholm a couple on bicycles rode into the farm. It was raining buckets and they asked if they could take shelter for a while. We offered them coffee, for which they were very grateful. They appeared uncomplicated and sympathetic and there was a pleasant atmosphere. Nils suggested that I sing something for them and I began without further ado with "Elisabeth's Prayer" from *Tannhäuser*. The two guests sat with their mouths open from astonishment. They had never dreamed of hearing Wagner sung here in the wilds. The most they thought they could hope for was "Lili Marlene," a song very popular at that time.

As I explained my plans to them, they asked where I would be living in Stockholm. I said I knew no one in Stockholm but it would all work out all right. Out of the blue they offered me living quarters in their villa in Stocksund. The housekeeper, Laila, would be there to receive me and they would return a week later. The couple were Lilian and Bertil Lindquist: Bertil was head of research and later the director of the Botanical Gardens in Göteborg.

They were sent from heaven.

The nearer the day of my departure, the more uncertain I became that I had made the right decision. It was not only the unhappy atmosphere at home that made me feel down. I had also fallen in love. But a future together was as good as impossible if I dedicated myself to a singing career. Sometimes I asked myself if it was worth it not only to break with my father but also to sacrifice love on the altar of art. But a strong inner voice convinced me that I should, now that I finally had the chance to go ahead with my plans. If I threw away the chance I had dreamed of for so long, I would regret it the rest of my life.

Nils was nowhere to be seen as I said farewell. In his confusion he had gone out and this weighed on my conscience even more. My dear grade school teacher, Erik Pamp, gave me some good advice. If I could only avoid the two dangerous "Vs"—"Verkühlung and Verliebtheit" (catching cold and falling in love)—then everything would go well for me. That was easier said than done, for soon I would be stricken with both.

After a thousand embraces from Stina I finally found myself sitting in the train and breathed a deep sigh of relief.

Now a page would be turned in the book of my life.

THE ROYAL ACADEMY OF MUSIC AND THE OPERA SCHOOL IN STOCKHOLM, 1941–1946

The dizzying effect of leaving the farm for the city has been described many times before. However, there are not many descriptions of moving from the farm to the city to take the entrance examination for the Royal Academy of Music in Stockholm. Therefore, I should like to give an account of how I survived transplanting myself to this very raw climate.

If my story seems to meander, or moves between past and present in fits and starts, it is only because that is how memories work. My experience in the late summer and autumn of 1941, as well as in the years that followed, are burned into my memory.

The air literally shimmered from the heat and I sweated it out in my felt hat and heavy coat as I got out of the train at the Stockholm station. I took a taxi to Engelbrektsplan; from there I would catch the train to Stocksund where my friends and patrons, Lilian and Bertil Lindquist lived. When I got to Engelbrektsplan I was unable to see where the train came in or where a ticket could be bought. On the corner was a bank. Lugging all my baggage, I crossed the street to ask an employee if there was a train station here. He smiled patronizingly and explained that there was no station there. You simply got on when the train made its brief stop. Again I picked up my two heavy bags and hatbox (I love hats) and was making my way back to the railroad tracks when the handle on the heaviest bag, which weighed a ton, broke! I will never forget how confused, exhausted, and hot I was after the trip to the bank and then back to Engelsbrektsplan, all the while lugging my damaged bags.

As I arrived in Stocksund there was Laila, the housekeeper, awaiting me. She totally dismissed my suggestion to take a taxi, assuring me it was not far to the villa. It seemed miles to me, uphill, downhill, until we finally came to the lake where the villa was. Now I had two days to become acclimated to my new living conditions. The Lindquists, my hosts, would not be coming home from Torekov for another week. I should have felt as though I were resting in these beautiful surroundings but I felt much more as though I were swimming upstream.

Finally the day of the entrance examination came.

Some of my friends held to the idea that a bromide tablet was good in instances where the nerves had to be controlled. No one in my family had ever had to settle their nerves. My father was seventy-five years old before any medicine was prescribed for him. Stina had prudently given me a bottle of port, thinking a swallow when needed would strengthen the throat as well as free it up.

I put the bottle in my music case (genuine imitation leather for four kronor) and made my way to the train. I decided that if I saw a pharmacy on the way from Engelbrektsplan to the music academy, I would get some bromide tablets. If I saw no pharmacy it would mean I would just have to get along without the help of the tablets. I saw no pharmacy. This was the closest I ever came to nerve-calming medication.

There was another need which was in fact more urgent. I was unable to find a restroom. The public toilets had obviously escaped my attention. What to do? Necessity is the mother of invention, they say. In Berzelli Park were many park benches, white and with good space between the slats. I picked one, took out my music as though studying. It was quite simple; the billowy light summer dress easily concealed the necessary arrangements. Wonderful! After a moment I walked away, cheerful and relieved.

There were already a lot of students gathered in the waiting room at the academy and we could hear the singers as they auditioned in the next room. Everyone seemed so advanced and worldly-wise. A few had studied in Rome, some in Paris. When asked where I had studied I answered, "In Sweden."

I had a long wait before it was my turn and had plenty of time to hear through the wall those auditioning before me. They all sounded fantastic to me, unbelievably beautiful. I began to think that I had best not get my expectations too high. But I clenched my teeth and decided to do the best I could—I couldn't ask anything more of myself.

In a corner, out of the view of the others, I secretly calmed myself with a drink from the wine bottle. I went with renewed courage, music under my arm, into the audition room. I started with the aria I did best, "Elisabeth's Prayer" from *Tannhäuser,* pouring my whole soul into the words. Then I sang the "Black Roses" by Sibelius. That was the end of the entrance examination. I looked at the strange expressions on the faces of the jury but could read no reaction. "Well, that was that," thought I, and shoved my music back into the case, pushed the cork tighter in the wine bottle, and left.

Obviously I was the last to audition; when I reached Nybroplan, two gentlemen who had attended the auditions caught up with me. The one was tall with bluish-gray hair and classic profile; the other was somewhat short and dark, with a friendly, inquiring expression. The taller man, who was probably in his midfifties, said, "Miss, your singing moved me, an old opera fox, to tears. Who are you and with whom have you studied?" When I told him I'd studied with music director Ragnar Blennow in Åstorp the questioner grimaced, "Good heavens, with a mere choir director—that is one of the strangest things I've heard of. . . ."

As we spoke further I admitted to him that I had sung no complete roles, only songs and romances. The tall man praised me for my unusually beautiful voice and my mature interpretation; as he looked at his companion he came out with "Verrry, verrry bootiful" in broken Swedish. These gentlemen did not think it necessary to introduce themselves. Perhaps they thought themselves known to everyone. But when I asked with whom I had the honor to speak, the tall one said he was stage director at the opera and teacher at the music academy. His name: Ragnar Hyltén-Cavallius. The other man was Kurt Bendix, conductor at the opera and also teacher at the Opera School.

Hyltén-Cavallius suggested that I go with him to a voice teacher, Andrejeva von Skilondz. She lived on Strandvägen, not far from Nybroplan where we were. I hesitated a bit, which prompted Hyltén-Cavallius to explain that if I got into the solo singers class—and he had no doubt that I would—I would be assigned a voice teacher and the teachers there did not have very good reputations. He felt it would be better if a responsible teacher took me under her wing. I went with him and met a wonderful, friendly, and effervescent little lady whose chest expanse was as wide as she was tall. She was certainly not taller than five feet. In Russia, she was once a celebrated coloratura. I sang something for her (cannot recall what) and she was immediately all fire and flame and said I had no need of a voice teacher, that I had obviously had God for my teacher. Nevertheless she did find that God needed her help on something, so she offered to accept me as a private student. I thanked her but said I felt it necessary to wait and see whether I was accepted at the music academy. There

I would have voice lessons in the curriculum. Also, there were ever so many other subjects I had to study. . . . however, if I were not accepted I said I would gladly seek her out again. We parted great friends.

When all the tests were over it was just a matter of waiting for the results. In the meantime my lovely hosts, Lilian and Bertil Lindquist, had returned and they proved most supportive. On the day the list was put up on the bulletin board denoting which two from the forty-seven applicants would be the lucky ones, they went with me. They let me go in alone. With shaking knees I went up to the bulletin board and—I thought I would faint. There it was—Number One: Birgit Nilsson. (Number Two was Uno Eriksson, later Ebrelius, schoolteacher and choir director from Karlstad, a beautiful lyric tenor who was known above all as a wonderful concert and oratorio singer.) I believe seeing my name there was the happiest moment of my twenty-three years.

But now something new awaited me. It was not necessary for me to find a job as a housekeeper, which I had decided to do in case I was not accepted in the music academy. I would not have liked to return home a failure. The people back home had already made fun of my ambitions and behind my back called me "The Opera Singer." Those pessimists announced that just because I could scream so loud, I shouldn't think I could compete with singers from all over Sweden. In Stockholm they would set me straight.

It was a very proud girl who telephoned Nils and Stina. They were very happy for me and, I think, Nils was especially proud to have his daughter's success to hold over the neighbors' heads.

For almost two weeks I remained out in Stocksund with the Lindquists. Through them I became acquainted with a number of prominent people in music, painting, and writing, all of whom made me feel at home.

At last I found myself a place to live, a place I could afford. The address was quite fashionable: Strandvägen 55. The rest of the address, "Kitchen Entrance East," I covered up. No one has ever seen a smaller maid's room than this. On a long wall was a couch, on the other a piano and between these two pieces of furniture a piano stool was squeezed in. On the short wall across from the window stood the landlady's linen closet, which she seemed to go back and forth to, day and night. (I believe she was actually checking to see whether one had any men in the room.) Behind the couch stood a tiny corner cupboard in which my heavy coat took up all the room. Everything else stayed in my American-made bags shipped from Skåne.

My landlords were Mr. and Mrs. Rock. They were clothing wholesalers from Vienna. Mrs. Rock had a daughter from her first marriage, Herta Fischer, who was a well-known pianist. Every morning Frau Rock came with tea in a silver pot. At home in Skåne I never drank tea, as it was served with milk or cream and looked repulsively watery. But as she served me in this elegant way I became a dyed-in-the-wool tea drinker. I bought bread and butter and that was my complete breakfast. When I tasted herb bread for the first time I thought I'd never tasted anything so wonderful. Before I knew what it was called I'd eaten the whole loaf. But my passion for herb bread did not last long.

The day for my first lesson with my new voice teacher, Joseph Hislop, was coming up. He was from Scotland and had been a famous tenor with, among other opera houses, the Met, which he named on his business card. His first marriage was to a daughter of a wealthy Göteborg baker. He was a good-looking man and at this time was between fifty-five and sixty. It had been years since he had performed. Two pianists accompanied in his studio. One was a German, Anita von Hillern-Dunbar, a lovely older lady with melancholy brown eyes and thick graying hair worn in a bun on her neck. The other was a considerably younger woman, Wivan Wennberg from Stockholm. She always had cold hands (it was wartime and one had to be economical with fuel), and as often as possible she warmed her hands in the arms of her pullover. Both were versatile and could sight-read anything. Hislop apparently thought that I knew what a good audition I had sung and he thought it necessary to put me in my place. The chastisement was completely superfluous, as I was alone in the big city and very meek.

He began by asking whether I knew of the violinist, Fritz Kreisler. Yes, by chance, I knew of him. "If you took his violin and handed it to a café fiddler, do you think it would sound as beautiful as when Kreisler plays it?" he asked me arrogantly. No, I didn't think it would. "No! What I am telling you is that it means nothing to have the most beautiful voice in the world if you have nothing here," he said, pointing to his toupee.

After this he wanted to know if I had finished high school and whether I was fluent in any foreign languages. My answers did not reveal anything particularly positive in either field and I felt myself becoming smaller and smaller.

"What does your father do?"

I murmured that my father was a landowner and farmer.

"Oh, my, the dumb farmer . . ." he chuckled scornfully, and then followed with, "Birgit should be aware that it is not really possible for a farm girl to become a singer." I was deeply hurt by this remark, in spite of its being said by a former scribbler and typographer without a professional diploma.

I no longer remember just how I found my way out of that torture chamber, but I do remember going back home and sobbing bitterly.

The next lesson was, if possible, worse than the first. I was asked to repeat all he had told me about the basics of singing. Unfortunately I was unable to recall anything other than how deeply he had offended me. Of course, I could not bring that up. My silence caused him to yell at me saying he had no desire to preach to deaf ears but would make this one exception. Then began the too, too slow repetition of the groundwork that was as illogical as it was incoherent. As soon as I was out the door I wrote down every word he had said and could make no sense from this torrent of words. I then learned this stupidity by heart, hoping he would be able to explain what it all meant. But these pearls of wisdom about which he reproached me were never referred to again.

I possessed a powerful voice that carried well and bordered on being a mezzo. Considering the little training I had enjoyed up to now, it was a wonder that the voice was continuing to grow.

Mr. Hislop maintained that I "hooted" like a ship and at some tone or another he would wander in the direction of Nybrokajen and call out "anchors away." Perhaps there was some pedagogical purpose behind this, as it had the effect of leaving the hooting in. But what could I do instead of this? Good question! Hislop was continually comparing the human voice to the sound of the violin, which has a thin, even, intense but soft, carrying tone. Naturally that is ideal and all singers aspire to this goal. But neither Hislop nor I knew how to achieve this. Instead of a lighter attack of the tone forward in the resonance (in singers' terminology called "the mask" because it lies behind the forehead around the eyes and nose) where it could intensify, he directed all the work right to the vocal cords. This approach caused a great deal of tension in the throat. True, the tone created this way was intense but it sat in the wrong place and was completely without overtones.

Why did he teach in this way? First, he himself sang with pneumatic pressure on the vocal cords, which certainly contributed to shortening his singing career. Second, he knew nothing of the basics of deep breathing and where the tone should gently rest on the air column. With this knowledge the tone is correctly placed and the vocal cords are protected from bearing too great a burden.

I knew nothing then of these rather simple and self-evident basics but that was after all what I had come to Stockholm to learn. That Hislop could not teach these things is certainly deplorable. He was simply one of all too many voice teachers who have not mastered the fundamentals of their craft. In this respect, voice students are still today much sinned against. I did not understand then that my way of singing was wrong; I simply sang and fought my way through the difficulties, and Hislop, who had meanwhile realized that I was not so dumb, praised me for my progress. My fellow students, cleverer than I, often canceled their lessons and I was happy to take over the free lesson time. He let me know what a great honor was bestowed upon me.

One of the first "pieces" he assigned me was "Casta Diva" from Bellini's opera *Norma,* one of the most difficult of all arias, and one that only the most technically advanced singer should attempt.

Naturally this method of pressing on the throat was very wearing and by the end of the winter semester I was vocally exhausted. I was unable to vocalize the "ee" vowel without the voice trembling and I was often going flat. Deep breathing and support was not within my ken. This is comparable to removing the foundation of a house. When the foundation is removed the house begins to wobble and will collapse.

For one and a half years I worked on Hislop's method without questioning it, only blaming myself for not understanding his teachings. And Hislop was now so friendly and warmhearted, taking such pleasure in my progress that I was taken in and all too ready to believe him. We singers have it especially difficult in that we carry our instrument inside ourselves and cannot judge our instrument in the same way as a listener. Before we learn how to feel and to hear our own voice, we are totally dependent upon the teacher, and if this teacher is a charlatan it can mean catastrophe for the development of the voice.

In the music academy we received instruction in many subjects: Italian, German, French, makeup, harmony, speech and declamation, solfège, fencing, piano, and much more. Had I, as some recommended, given up the music academy and Mr. Hislop and studied all these courses privately, it would have been costly enough to ruin my parents. Scholarships were not available at that time, and who could borrow money with vocal cords as collateral? As it was, I managed the first year to come out all right with the three thousand kronor from Stina. Later I received a Christine Nilsson Scholarship amounting to some 1,500 to 3,000 kronor and made out all right with additional work in churches and small engagements.

For my first big engagement I have to thank Bertil Lindquist's good friends. The newspaper *Ord och Bild* (Words and pictures) was to celebrate an anniversary in the stock exchange and I was invited to sing. It was the bitter cold winter of 1942. A skillful dressmaker made for me a white dress with gold sequins at the waist and on the shoulders. It cost 150 kronor, which was about three times as much as my fee. The crown prince, Gustav Adolf VI, was there with the crown princess and they seemed to be quite impressed with my Danish diction in some of the songs on my program. My friendly landlady lent me a beautiful gold necklace with matching bracelet and I felt very elegant. I had moved from Strandvägen to the Riddargaten, as I could not afford to keep the room over the Christmas holidays.

Gunnar Mascoll Silfverstolpe wrote a poem about the celebration that appeared the next day in the *Stockholms-Tidningen* and in which I was mentioned:

> Then Birgit Nilsson appeared with accompaniment.
> Sang for us like a priest of Apollo in white raiment.
> Sang with a tone like a tempting Siren.
> Songs of Stenhammer, Petersen-Berger, Sjögren, and Alfvén

The evening was brought to an end with dinner and dancing in the mirrored banquet hall of the Grand Hotel. Among others I danced with the famous painter, Isaac Grünewald who declared I had a diamond in my throat that still needed to be cut to be perfect. I still remember his perverse sense of humor when he complained to me that he was married to a "disgusting, ugly old witch. There she is." He pointed out a fantastically beautiful blonde. I wondered what would have happened if I had answered, "But she isn't so ugly." Grünewald was recently married to this young painting student. His first wife, the great artist, Sigrid Hjertén, had been institutionalized.

The day after the celebration I had to give a detailed account to Mrs. Blomquist of all the wonderful things I had experienced. Since I had borrowed her jewelry she felt she had almost been a part of the celebration.

It was, as I said, an unusually cold winter and as the temperature in my room never got above sixty degrees Fahrenheit, I suffered constantly from colds. I bought an electric kettle so I could boil water for tea but I was not allowed to use it in my room. It was feared that the steam would harm the furniture. Instead I was permitted to use the electrical outlet in the kitchen as long as I did not use too much electricity. To be sure that making tea would not be forbidden, I heated the water to near boiling in my own room and then went into the kitchen and plugged the kettle in for the brief time needed to reach the boiling point. And lo! My landlady, observing, chirped delightedly, "Did you ever see the likes! This can't be using much electricity if it boils so quickly!" (I enjoyed my tea.)

By now I had finished the first year of the academy and the holidays were facing me. As Hislop was so satisfied with me and had praised me so, I assumed I would receive some recognition from the academy that would carry with it a financial reward of 100 to 125 kronor. With this I would have enough to get home without having to ask my parents for money. Wonderful!

However, there was neither recognition nor money, which made me sad and angry at the same time. I knew there were fellow students who had received acknowledgment who were nowhere near as studious as I was. My anger gave me the courage to call Hislop. He declared my parents were sufficiently well-off that I had no need of such a grant. I did not believe him for one minute. In the end, it was not about the scholarship, merely the recognition. After making this clear to him, I hung up feeling desperate.

After I paid for my fare back home I had one krona left. The bus from Båstad to Svenstad cost either ninety öre or 1 krona 10, I couldn't remember exactly. The nine-hour trip seemed longer and my stomach was growling from hunger. As I arrived at the Båstad station and went to buy my bus ticket I broke out in a cold sweat. But luck was with me! The fare was ninety öre and I arrived proudly back home with ten öre in my pocket.

After I had eaten my fill, it was time for me to help with the milking. The farmhand and the girl helper were both pulling turnips. I soon learned I had nearly lost the fine art of milking. Before I had left for Stockholm in the autumn of 1941, I could milk ten cows in no time. Nine months later my arm muscles were seemingly paralyzed. It was not an able milkmaid who returned to Nils and Stina, but in a few weeks I had regained my old strength.

I was "flooded" with a couple of offers for engagements. One day when I was busy in the vegetable garden a car drove up and the owner of the Pershög (a restaurant with a dance floor) got out. He sought me out and made the following offer: I would sing in the restaurant for an hour then help them for an hour pulling weeds. I call that a talent for deal-making! It was terribly embarrassing for me to be found working on all fours in the vegetable garden, and it definitely put me at a disadvantage in the negotiations. But he was nice and offered a fair fee of 150 kronor.

Another dance hall where I sang was the Südsee (South Sea), in Västra Karup. There the walls and pillars had paintings of palm trees, which justified the exotic name. I often went dancing there and admired the artists on the stage. Now I took my place among them, standing there in the same white dress I wore for the stock exchange celebration, singing for the young people of Bjäre. Maybe some aesthetes turned up their noses at my singing in a dance hall, but that mattered not to me. Many classical singers earned their keep in the beginning by singing lighter music, and that money is no more foul than any other.

The owner of the Südsee was named Schuster-Elof and he was a clever businessman. After my first performance he wrote saying he wanted to send me on tour through southern Sweden. He said we would be "swimming in money." But nothing ever came of this great project. I did sometimes sing in other than "disreputable" places (even though I earned the best money there). Twice a week I was engaged by Albert Runbäck to sing in the evening Gregorian Chant services in Bästad. The precise and strict church music was new to me and proved to be a great learning experience. I earned the magnificent sum of three kronor each evening, and I gladly cycled the six kilometers there and back.

I also gave a concert before a full house in Ragnar Blennow's church in Björnekulla. We had not agreed upon a fee. After the concert, which had been successful even beyond our expectations, Blennow, slightly nervous, asked what I expected to be paid. "Well, I am very expensive," I said, and after a pause went on, "I will ask exactly what you ask for a voice lesson: five kronor." Tears welled up even in Blennow's glass eye.

Erland Skagerberg was a leader of church music in Förslöv. He was a small, thin man with tremendous energy and he had a plan that would test this energy: he wanted to put on Handel's *Messiah* with full chorus, orchestra, and soloists. Presenting such a work in a rural area was a gigantic undertaking and not without risks. But he wagered and won. The first year he began carefully. I, for example, learned both the soprano and alto solos and lent support to the sopranos of the chorus. It was a great success and the following year he was able to engage well-known professional soloists. The opera singer, Folke Jonsson, from Ängelholm, was the bass; Madeleine Uggla (mother of Magnus Uggla) was the alto. The performance of the *Messiah* became a tradition that continued for many years and was given in the concert house in Helsingborg. The public showed great enthusiasm and tickets were sold out half a year before the performance.

The academy's winter semester was already beginning and I went back with a rested throat and renewed strength. A family acquainted with the Lindquists had a daughter who was marrying in the Jacobs church and I had the honor to sing at her wedding. Waldemar Åhlén was the organist there and Johannes Norrby, the director of the concert house, was soloist in the church. I sang Beethoven's "Lobgesang" and something else that has slipped my mind. After the ceremony the jovial and friendly Johannes Norrby spoke to me, indicating that he was very impressed with my singing and offered me an audition for an eventual engagement. I was so taken off guard by his offer, I assumed he meant engagement in the chorus. When I told Hislop about it, he exclaimed, "You will not sing in the chorus. In a few years you will be the soloist there!" Undaunted by my not following up on the offer of an audition, Norrby continued to show interest. Whenever I sang in any school concert, there he was, sitting smilingly in the fourth row.

About a year later Norrby organized in Stockholm's downtown business center a concert he called "Familiar Music" and I had the opportunity to perform a number of songs of Stenhammar, Sjögren, and Erland von Koch. The next day William Seymor, in *Nya Dagligt Allehanda* (New general daily), wrote: "She has a voice and her name will certainly be written in big letters."

Not that I was always a success; at my audition at Swedish Radio Nathanael Broman rejected me, saying I sang flat. He was undoubtedly right. My pressured vocal technique tired my voice and now and then would cause me to sing flat.

Meanwhile, Professor Tor Mann, who taught conducting had had his "ear" on me, so to speak, ever since hearing me sing Beethoven's "Ah, Perfido" and Elisabeth's "Dich, teure Halle" from *Tannhäuser* in a school concert. One of the students who would later make a name for himself, Siegfried Naumann (who was also from Skåne), conducted the orchestra of the music academy on that evening.

A month after I had been rejected by Nathanael Broman I was invited to sing on Swedish Radio in a student recital under the baton of Tor Mann. What sweet revenge! Mann was a wonderful conductor and to work with him was refreshing and inspiring. We repeated this concert in Jönköping and in Göteborg where in the paper we read: "Tor Nilsson, conductor, and Birgit Mann, soloist"! The crazy name mix-up in no way diminished our success. The composer Gösta Nyström, who was also a major critic, called me a "Wunderkind" of singing.

Six months later in Stockholm we were equally successful, in spite of my nerves causing me to drop a quarter note in "Dich, teure Halle" Yngve Flykt closed his hymn of praise in the *Expressen* with "whoever has her development in his hands has an enormous responsibility." In the review I was called the "Baby of the Academy."

Something rang true in this comment as I noticed the heightened interest in my development on the part of Einar Rolf, director of the academy. Through the grapevine I heard he had summoned Hislop to his office and reprimanded him. Director Rolf believed I had sounded better when I sang for my entrance exam than I did now. This, after two years of lessons. I was completely unaware of this conversation between Rolf and Hislop. Naturally, I was taken aback when, during my next lesson Hislop, obviously irritated, asked me how long I intended to aim at one target and shoot at another. "Don't blame me," he snarled. "It isn't my fault that you always shoot where you are not aiming."

Now I was totally at a loss; up to now, he had alwways professed himself satisfied with me. I answered sincerely that I did not hold him accountable for any vocal setback, that it was unquestionably my fault. When I later learned of Rolf's meeting with Hislop, I was for the first time really confused and began to question Hislop's teaching method. At the same time I knew some of his students had taken other teachers on the side.

As soon as I returned to Skåne for the holidays I sought out my old voice teacher Ragnar Blennow. He was convinced that I would resolve my difficulties. Even today I am not sure if he realized in what danger the bad singing technique had put my voice. When I was totally rested my voice sounded very good and those who heard me were impressed with the young, beautiful quality. No one suspected then how wasteful I was with my capital.

I almost always received good critiques and the offers for engagements increased. Everything was looking up. However, I was becoming more and more critical of the vocal training that I was receiving and asked myself many questions that I had never raised before. In any case, I was in no position to take the initiative and change teachers.

There was an easy camaraderie among the music academy students. Aside from Uno Ebrelius (who began at the same time as I) there was among Hislop's male students a favorite, the charming Per Grundén, who always wore a white beret. Then there was Ulla Sallert. She quit after a year and became a great prima donna at the Oscars Theater. The talented Ingebjorg Kjellgren, received an engagement at the opera and Ingrid Eksell also became a member of the opera. However, she soon got the female lead in *Brigadoon* and joined the roster at Oscars. The director of the opera, Harald André issued an ultimatum: either the opera or Oscars. Eksell decided in favor of the musical, which I think was probably a mistake.

Together with the so-called auditors who occasionally took part in the lessons, we students were twelve to fourteen in number. The period of study to become a soloist encompassed three years, and there were many good teachers. Signora Silvia Tomba, the Italian teacher, tortured us mercilessly with grammar. Fräulein Rut Bergström, with the eternal flower-decorated straw hat, worked untiringly to get the speaking voice to sound in the resonances of the head, thereby protecting the vocal cords. As I sang in my throat, I spoke in the same way. With her "M-exercises," such as "Månne mamma minns mina himmelsblå förjätmigejer som blommade i mitten av maj," which strengthened the head resonances, she taught me to speak as long as I wished without ever tiring the voice. With singing, however, it was another question. Whenever I tried to use the "M Method," Hislop would bellow his usual "Anchors away! The ship is leaving!"

I realize that I have an unusual speaking voice that most people recognize and often imitate. My speaking voice has become my identification. As soon as I get into a taxi in Stockholm and give the address to the driver, without his even turning around I hear, "Aha, Birgit Nilsson is in town."

Fräulein Fredga's rhythm lessons were intimidating. When she showed off her enviable private students—who could do five beats with one arm while doing four with the other, nodding the head twice, and taking three steps all at the same time—then I cowered and thought again of the vegetable garden as a welcome alternative to all this.

The charming Bernard Lilja made it easy for me. With my perfect pitch I had no trouble making a particular pitch or sight-reading.

Gustav "Zur See" Nordquist, the distinguished composer, taught harmony. He was a real gentleman, who generously dedicated all his lovely songs to me. Really, I had not much talent for this course, which, since I had no desire to compose, I didn't take too seriously. Nevertheless, I completed my compulsory exercise but without a great deal of imagination. Once, when I had very little time, I dashed off at the last minute something in C major of which I felt almost ashamed. As Nordquist played it on the keyboard he said I had copied the last movement of Beethoven's Ninth Symphony, "Freude schöner Götterfunken, Tochter aus Elysium." I didn't know the Ninth then and was completely blameless, but I'm not certain that Nordquist believed me. It was more than a little annoying that Beethoven discovered his main theme so long before I did.

My piano teacher, Gottfried Boon, was one of the finest Sweden had to offer. He was one of many of our famous concert pianists who had gone into teaching. I functioned as guinea pig and my lessons were attended by a great many future piano teachers. This was not exactly an inspiring situation. In fact, I felt myself almost degraded. I got difficult pieces on which I had to spend hours practicing just to play them reasonably well. I did not aspire to being a pianist so I actually practiced more wrong than right; nevertheless, the day before the performance, I pounded the keys like a madwoman. After a sleepless night I appeared for my lesson, a nervous wreck with a guilty conscience. Boon "sang" the melody the whole time with his dentist drill tone, all the while trying to loosen up my tense shoulders and get my sweaty hands to flit over the keys. It was really more torture than piano lesson and the memory still returns in my nightmares.

The very successful choir director, David Åhlén, who was Eric Ericson's teacher, conducted the chorus of the academy once a week. It was unbelievable what nuances and expressiveness he could bring out of us: heavenly sounds, and the pianissimo was like the softest whisper. Most chorus sopranos, at least in Sweden, sing in falsetto with lots of air in the tone. My voice was certainly not meant for choral singing. This boy-soprano tone tired my voice and it lost its proper placement. No matter how I tried I would come in with too much volume, which Åhlén instantly quashed. I only had to draw a deep breath and he stopped me even before I had sung a tone. I eventually solved this problem by moving my mouth silently.

With the end of the spring semester in 1944 I had completed the solo-singing study and was entered into the opera school without having to audition, which was quite unusual.

My finances were as short as the summer was long. Paying engagements were nowhere in sight. Then I got the idea of asking at the employment office for artists if there were any openings for me. After I explained that I didn't want to perform in the amusement park, they offered me the job of appearing with a small orchestra in a restaurant, the Lindgården out in Djurgården. I had two appearances every evening; on Sundays, I sang in the afternoon and evening. My salary was 1,280 kronor a month, which was fantastic, and I accepted the position immediately. Naturally I had to improve my wardrobe considerably. I had a couple of long gowns and now it was necessary to get another. It was of light summer material, with red poppies on a light yellow background. Actually, it was curtain material but it was quite lovely. For the Sunday afternoon appearance I wore a short dress of blue-gray crepe. To go with this I bought a pair of gray shoes of genuine leather with high cork heels and ankle straps (my legs looked especially good with ankle straps) and to top it off, a matching handbag. The crowning glory for this outfit I found in a secondhand shop in Gamla Stan for ten kronor: a white ostrich feather. I had it dyed to match the dress and made from it a very becoming hat. Ah, was I ever elegant that summer!

Life was easy and beautiful and I had the entire day free. In the evening I took the ferry from Skeppsbron over to Djurgården (then I lived in the old city) and the little boat ride was wonderful each time. The repertoire I sang in the Lindgården was a mixture of popular songs but I sang everything from *Carmen* arias to "Violets for Mother."

When the engagement ended I returned home happily, with money in my pocket. There I received an offer to sing in a more upscale restaurant, the Torslund in Ängelholm and in the Hotel Skälderviken.

I was most happy to sing for Gustav V in the church in Båstad. Every year for the tennis week he came to Båstad and on Sunday went to church. I was to sing an aria from Bach's *Pfingstkantate* (Pentecost cantata). Albert Runbäck had an austere taste in church music. Bach, Händel, and Runbäck were performed; no one else need apply. I was tense and nervous because of singing for the king himself and had prepared myself carefully. It was going quite well until suddenly there were alarms sounding and people running in the church. I didn't know whether to stop in the midst of my aria, but I knew something dramatic had happened. Afterward I learned that the king had an acute attack of "summer sickness." There was no toilet in the church, however, and the king refused to accept some makeshift solution. I heard that one of the church caretakers came running with a collection basket. The only thing I know for sure is that there was one very disappointed and sad girl who came there to sing for the king.

In the opera school one could choose to study with a private teacher—footing the bill yourself, of course. I looked for a new teacher right away, which got Hislop's nose out of joint. My choice was Arne Sunnegård, a coach in the opera school and voice teacher for those who were studying to become voice teachers and church singers. He had a wide repertoire and was a musician of the old school. In addition he took a few private students.

We worked on getting my head voice back, to which end we almost exaggeratedly darkened all the vowels. Sunnegård was not exactly careful in his treatment of the voice; if you wanted to be heard above his unnecessarily loud piano accompaniment then you had to forget any nuances below a good, solid forte. Because my voice was at that time darker, almost like a mezzo's, he wanted to build my high voice. For this reason I was constantly given exercises that went to high C and I sang them until I was hoarse and could hardly speak. I remember how shocked my future husband was when I came home in this condition from a voice lesson. In addition, Sunnegård wanted the low tones to be taken with raw chest with no mixture with head tones. I was clever enough to avoid this.

Sunnegård nevertheless had unusual musical knowledge and could work on many different kinds of music. I sang for about four years with him, two years of which he spent out of the country. During this time I was my own voice teacher, which was quite all right with me. I learned at the opera a whole string of new roles such as Sieglinde in *Die Walküre* and Brünnhilde in *Siegfried,* Lisa in *Pique Dame,* and still more. When Sunnegård came back he was impressed with my progress, and I had a hard time convincing him that I had learned all this by myself. But the stage itself was invaluable help and proved to be my best voice teacher.

It was clear to me that there were new fields to conquer, mainly in interpretation and vocal nuances. I wanted my voice to be beautiful as well as powerful. One day I wanted to speak with Sunnegård about a small detail (I had already begun to question his method). He maintained that I had to produce the consonant D with the tongue on the lower teeth and not on the upper teeth as I was doing it. When I wanted to discuss this with him, he flared up and yelled like a banshee, demanding to know if I had doubts about his teaching. He, who had worked in Germany as well as the United States, had to know better than I.

"And if this doesn't suit you. . . ," he called out with a dismissing arm gesture, ". . . then it's best we call it a day," said I, completing his sentence with no gesture. With that I left the room and disappeared forever from his army of students.

Another voice teacher, who for some time had wished to work with me, approached me again. I figured that if I didn't like it, I would only have wasted a half-hour. So I went for a lesson. But so simple it was not.

He began the lesson by gripping my larynx and pressing it down. For two weeks my larynx was so sore I could hardly speak. After recovering from this laryngeal torture, I sought out the great Wagnerian Nanny Larsén-Todsen. In the expensive forty-five-minute lesson she spent at least thirty minutes unreservedly praising her own incredible career. She informed me that she was known in Germany as the "Queen of Bayreuth." After three so-called lessons with her, I hadn't learned any more about singing, but I could pass any exam in Todsen 101. From this time on, I decided I was now and forever finished with voice teachers. Amen!

In the Opera School we were taught not only music and acting but, as I mentioned earlier, also languages, gestures, declamation, and fencing. For the last art form, I unfortunately had no talent. Perhaps it would have elevated the excitement for the audience if Tosca, instead of stabbing Scarpia with a fruit knife, had challenged him to a duel!

Now and then the soubrette voices received chances to do small roles such as pages, but my more dramatic voice did not suit such roles. The same applied to Siw Ericsdotter, who was singing evenings in the chorus at the Oscars Theater. Lilly Furlin, also a future Wagnerian, traveled sometimes to the school at Sigtuna and jumped in as cook when she needed to earn some money.

My sole music lesson was usually with Kurt Bendix on Friday at nine in the morning. I have never been a morning person, and it was near torture for me to have to begin the day with the act 3 aria of the Countess in Mozart's *Marriage of Figaro.* Bendix later often described how I burst in at the last moment hot and breathless, threw my coat on the bench, took a breath, and began to sing.

Kurt Bendix was born in Berlin and was engaged at the Stockholm Opera at the age of twenty-three. He was thought of as a "Wunderkind" and remained at the opera well beyond the age of retirement. He was a knowledgeable and very skilled musician, and he liked to let us young people share his rich experience. He also had a great sense of humor, from which we all benefited in our struggle with Mozart and other operatic giants.

The work with Ragnar Hyltén-Cavallius was not so beneficial. At home I had worked with an amateur theater group—rather successfully, I might add. I loved being onstage and burying myself in a role that was often dramatically different from my true personality. Cavallius robbed me of all my joy in acting. He often made fun of us and imitated our errors with outrageous exaggeration. About me he always said that I looked "like a hopping rabbit." In spite of his zealous demonstrations I never could understand what I was doing wrong. He forced us repeatedly to do set gestures without motivation; he called these gestures "classic." I finally found myself so affected and ridiculous that I was reluctant to go onstage and make the simplest gesture. But Cavallius was really in his element when he could show us how one played a romantic scene. His hazel eyes sparkled, his cheeks glowed under the rouge when he tried to seduce one of the students with erotic hip swaying. There was more than a little truth in the comment the opera director, John Forsell, made during rehearsal: "My dear Cavallius, in you the world has lost a real femme fatale!"

Twice a year we had performances.

The main performance was in spring, and we were singing then with orchestra on the main stage of the opera. Especially good were the scenes from *Don Giovanni* (in which I sang Donna Anna), *Fidelio, Macbeth,* and the final trio from *Der Rosenkavalier* with three fresh young voices—Eva Prytz, Ingrid Eksell, and me—making this a musical sensation long remembered in the city.

After two years the academic courses in the opera school were finished. But not all the students were considered qualified for engagement in the "holy hall" in Gustaf Adolfs Torg (square). I had the good fortune to be accepted into the opera automatically, without auditioning.

And thus began the road, strewn with roses and thorns, to the tempting artistic horizon.

Excerpts from two letters written to my first teacher and discoverer, Ragnar Blennow, follow:

Stockholm, April 4, 1944

. . . now I have found the solution, and you can believe me there is a noticeable difference, as now everything sounds full and round. Probably you ask yourself who helped put me on the path. Well, I have thought through everything, got everything in order, as often in the end you are thrown upon your own resources. One morning I woke up and began thinking over what I could do. I could hear your words ringing in my ears, telling me to "open the entire airway." I jumped out of bed and made the pharynx totally loose and simply let the air flow through. What a difference! I hardly trusted my ears. Before, I held the throat tense and clamped down on the breath, making the tone edgy and strained sounding. I feared I would lose the image of my new way of singing, but I was successful in retaining it. The difference

was immediately noticeable and Hislop as well as my fellow students were astonished. Hislop said he was happy that I now had such beautiful high notes. Well, he may be happy, but he certainly didn't help me to get them . . .

Stockholm, May 14, 1945

I am extremely distrustful of anyone who calls himself a voice teacher. When you audition, you are told you are doing everything wrong. It is amazing that there is no pedagogue who can accept the method of any other. I know exactly what I can do and what I have still to learn, but you only get confused when you're always told you have to start all over again. . . . I have to rid myself of pressing on the throat. May I sing for you this summer? You have to promise to be very strict with me; only then can I make something of myself . . .

THE STOCKHOLM OPERA

ACT 1

The evening of October 9, 1946, was windy and overcast. The young girl from Skåne who was coming from the old part of town and going in the direction of Österlånggatan was on her way to the Royal Opera for the first performance of her life as a professional opera singer. Five days earlier during a concert in Malmö she was informed that she was to jump in as Agathe in Weber's *Der Freischütz.* The singer who was to sing the role was on leave, and the director noticed too late that there was no one else who had sung the part. The choice to take over the role fell upon the young singer who up until now had had no assignment in the opera.

These were stressful days, not helped by the fact that the singer who was to jump in was already aggrieved. She did not totally please the director, who maintained that, among her other anatomical disadvantages, she had unattractive legs. The young girl from Skåne held quite a different view: next to her voice she thought her legs were her most attractive feature. In spite of her pique, however, she decided to take the chance. After the concert in Malmö she caught the night train to Stockholm. The sleeping car was too expensive; besides, she had to stay up all night to learn the role of Agathe. The first rehearsal would be the next morning with none other than the famous seventy-seven-year-old German conductor, Leo Blech, who had taken refuge in Sweden. It was no small assignment that lay before her but it was not impossible; the role was not difficult for her to learn and she had good visual recall and absolute pitch. Moreover, she could study a role without having to sing or play it at all. She heard the music in her head when she read the notes. She had already sung the big aria in concert but everything else was new territory for her. Naturally, she had seen performances of *Der Freischütz* but that was not quite the same as performing it herself.

On the way from her little apartment in Gamla Stan to the opera house she had to cross a big bridge. There she stopped, gazed into the depths of the dark, cold water as if hypnotized, and was overtaken by dark thoughts. If it was so terrible to be an opera singer, a swift leap into the water would be a deliverance.

She stood there by the cold iron railing and thought of what had happened. The piano rehearsal went miserably. A number of small mistakes had slipped in, making the conductor's bad mood even worse. His bellowing that she was untalented and unmusical undermined her confidence, so that she actually made many musical errors. She sang, cried, and sobbed her way through the whole rehearsal. The stage director, Anders Henriksson, was not to be seen. The good old character tenor, Simon Edvardsen showed her the stage direction and he gave her his handkerchiefs, which soon became soaking wet from her tears.

As a "special honor" Leo Blech arranged an orchestra rehearsal that his assistant, Bertil Bokstedt, would conduct. Bokstedt was friendly and understanding and the rehearsal went well—which, strangely enough, intensified her sense of impending doom. How would it go when that evening she had to sing with the frightful maestro?

"No, never," she thought as she stared, confusedly over the bridge's railing. But then she thought of her parents in Skåne. How sad they would be! Their only child, who against their will went to Stockholm to seek her fortune and ended by drowning herself in the river!

She shook off all the miserable thoughts, dried her tears, and hurried on to the stage entrance of the opera. There she went up countless steps to the tiny dressing room given to beginners. Someone came with a blond wig parted down the middle with "Gretchen" braids that felt like an iron band around her head. Then she put on the costume of the other singer and rushed down the stairs to take her first look at the stage and the sets before the curtain rose.

In her first scene, Agathe sits demurely in a chair sewing her trousseau, an immense sheet, while she sings a duet with her young relative, the lively and cheerful Ännchen. Nervous and tense, her gaze never leaving the conductor, our singer did not put her foot firmly on the floor; her leg began to tremble and with it the entire sheet. No one in the auditorium could miss the "shaking aspen leaves." And what made the attack of nerves especially unfortunate was that the singer's discoverer and teacher, Ragnar Blennow, had come all the way from Skåne to hear the performance. Now he belonged, so to speak, to the mourners. Poor Ragnar!

But everything went better than the debutante feared. She certainly had a voice and she could sing, but there was the raging animal trainer before her and that was almost more than her nerves could stand. And then it happened: in the big aria, which she had already sung in concert, she robbed him of a quarter note. Maestro Blech sprang up like a jack-in-the-box, brandished his fist, made horrible grimaces, and looked like his own death mask. But all at once our girl from Skåne was totally with it and corrected the mistake before the old man could even remember it. The remainder of the performance was uneventful.

In the intermission, Maestro Blech made it known he expected her to ask forgiveness for the sloppy mistake. Our singer had already heard that in such cases it was in the interest of the singer to shed a few crocodile tears and appear totally remorseful. This might help or even work to one's advantage.

But the young girl from Skåne found that she was sufficiently humbled and she did not have it in her to ask for forgiveness. Forgiveness, for what? Had she not, through her undaunted jumping in, rescued the opera from a cancelation? Otherwise the conductor would have sacrificed his fee for the evening. He, the wrathful old man, should be thanking her. Never would she ask his forgiveness! And so the head of the opera, Harald André, was told that she was unmusical, untalented, and above all, rebellious.

Certainly these words fell on fertile soil.

When I awoke the next morning I thought at first I had had a nightmare. Had it really happened? Had I really sung in the opera yesterday? Was Leo Blech actually so shameless? I pulled the blanket up over my head and pretended I didn't hear the telephone ringing insistently. I felt I couldn't bear another cold shower and did not wish to be reminded that I was called unmusical and untalented. "Untalented and unmusical, unmusical and untalented," rang unceasingly in my head.

But the telephone would not stop ringing, and after a long battle with myself I got out of bed and answered it. A female voice was on the other end and declared she was from the *Dagens Nyheter* (Daily news). She had heard of my glorious debut and wanted to come with a photographer and interview me. Not for one moment did I believe that the *Dagens Ny-*

heter was calling. I was sure that a friend or a colleague was playing a joke on me. At this moment I was not in the mood for a joke and I answered bluntly that she should make better use of her time than making fun of me; if she thought she could do better than I had she was welcome to try.

It really was the newspaper reporter on the telephone and, though pleased, I was rather embarrassed. "Glorious debut," she said. I jumped into my clothes, ran into town, and bought all the newspapers I could carry (which was a lot). Mamma mia! It was simply unbelievable. *All* the reviews were overwhelming. Ingmar Bengtsson, for example, wrote in the *Svenska Dagbladet* (Swedish daily) under the headline "Successful Agathe Debut":

It was a wise move to allow the young singer, Birgit Nilsson from Skåne to make her debut as Agathe on Wednesday. . . . Birgit Nilsson distinguished herself through her assurance and well-balanced artistry to a degree not expected of a beginner. Her voice has a fresh, Nordic quality, a clear top, and well-carrying mezzo timbre in the low voice, indicating a dramatic soprano. It is not often that a beautiful voice is combined with such intelligence, but such depth of expression and musical flexibility as Birgit Nilsson revealed has to be inborn; these qualities cannot be learned. The public gave her a well-deserved ovation and would certainly welcome hearing her in another role. Perhaps a new Elisabeth?

In *Dagens Nyheter,* under the byline "H.L." the longtime critic Falke Hähnel wrote:

. . . in the year 1918 a singer by the name of Nanny Larsén debuted at the opera as Agathe in *Freischütz.* One is reminded of that when one writes about the debut of Birgit Nilsson in the same role. . . . The young lady possesses an unusually beautiful soprano that will probably develop into a dramatic soprano. In vain one looks for any words of caution or admonition to give her. The evenness of the registers is astonishing for a beginner; the voice is well-placed with no ambient noise. . . . I have already mentioned the bravura with which Birgit Nilsson mastered the second-act aria and the "Prayer" in act 3. She gave a warmth of tone and spirituality to her expression. . . . The singer is statuesque, has an expressive face, and moves with dignity. Perhaps her apparent aversion to sitting still has to do with a dramatic temperament with which we have yet to become acquainted.

I was absolutely convinced that Harald André would be swayed by these great reviews but he remained untouched. Leo Blech's words carried more weight and it was "thumbs down" for Nilsson.

. . .

Naturally the question remains: Why was I accepted for an opera scholarship when the head of the opera was so unfavorably disposed toward me?

I believe I have my teachers at the opera school to thank, as they also had positions at the opera: the stage director, Ragnar Hyltén-Cavallius and the conductor Kurt Bendix. They had recommended me so highly that André could not in good conscience overlook me.

I did not suffer financially. At the opera I earned four hundred kronor a month and Tor Mann had given me the opportunity to accept various concert engagements with the greatest orchestras in the country. In addition I sang with the choruses of the Marien, Johannes, and Adolf-Fredriks churches for funerals in both the northern and southern parts of the city. This brought in five to ten kronor per burial.

I was permitted to sing Agathe two more times before the scheduled singer, Anna-Greta Söderholm, returned from Göteborg. During all three performances I felt equally terrible. It was like appearing before the judge. My career as an opera singer would not last long, I had already decided. The contract covered two years and I could hold out that long, but after that I would establish myself as a concert singer.

A few performances followed: a scene from Andreas Hallén's *Harald the Viking,* celebrating the one hundredth birthday of the composer; three appearances in *Gyllby, the Daughter of the Court;* and a speaking part in *The People from Värmland.* Perhaps this last role, that of the haughty Britta, was typecasting: my best line was "I don't have to toe the line before you men." Apart from these few roles, I had nothing to do at the opera the rest of the year. Contacting Johannes Norrby, the obliging head of the concert house, was my next goal. He engaged me for a number of concerts.

In one of the first concerts I sang the soprano part, Från Havsbandet, in Hugo Alfvén's Fourth Symphony (From the cliffs). Presumably the celebration of his seventy-fifth birthday prompted the composer himself to conduct. The Fourth Symphony had its beginning in a summer some thirty years before. At that time Alfvén was pursuing an intense affair with a married woman who lived on a neighboring island in Schärengürtel. When her husband was away, which apparently happened frequently, she put a light in the window. That was the signal that the "coast was clear"; the lovesick master of tone would throw himself into the water and, defying death, swim to his sweetheart. He said in his memoirs that the Fourth Symphony was composed in his mind during these exciting swimming expeditions.

Two soloists, a tenor and a soprano, took part in this symphony. Two people, lovestruck, who in the darkness of night are consumed by longing. There is no text. The soloists sing on the sound "Ah." At the beginning it seems the two are far from each other; one hears only a despairing call in the night. Soon they are nearer one another, the duet becomes more passionate, until finally the music explodes in a climax (a specialty of Alfvén). After the concert I received the following letter from Alfvén:

Birgit Nilsson, you wondrous artist! Permit me to extend to you my warmest thanks and deep admiration for your glorious singing in my Fourth Symphony, which I heard in a radio broadcast on Sunday. How beautiful and warm your sound and how charged with passions your wonderful voice glowed in the big climaxes! Your singing made the evening an unforgettable event for me. With high admiration,

Yours gratefully,
Hugo Alfvén

I answered his letter, expressing my happiness that my performance had pleased him, and asked if it would be too presumptuous to ask for an autographed photo. By the next post I received his letter saying he would gladly give me his photo: "but," he continued, "I counter with the unashamed wish to have your autographed photo." Shortly thereafter I received a large studio photograph of the great maestro with a dedication, "Great Artist! Here the photo. Do not forget the hard terms that I made. Your very devoted, Hugo Alfvén."

I didn't know what to do, as I could not believe he really had an interest in receiving my photo; surely this was nothing more than a bit of flattery from an innate gentleman and well-known ladies' man. Before I had made a decision, Hugo Alfvén reminded me again of my promise. The next day I went to the royal photographer Uggla and sent him what I thought was a representative picture. A week later I received another letter:

"Miss Birgit Nilsson! On returning from a journey I found your portrait awaiting me, for which I cannot thank you enough. I look at it every day—much too often as it is dangerously lovely and resembles you perfectly. It is simply one of the most beautiful portraits I have ever seen. And out of your

intense, passionate gaze the entire Fourth Symphony sounds again, especially the part where your voice resonates over the orchestra. I would like to say still more about your fascinating picture, but I am clever enough to know when to stop.

Yours devotedly,
Hugo Alfvén

Apparently Hugo Alfvén was also a master in orchestrating letters to ladies.

In the spring of 1948 there was talk of producing Verdi's *Macbeth* in October. Sigurd Björling and Hugo Hasslo were to alternate in singing Macbeth. The famous Fritz Busch was to be the guest conductor and his son, Hans Busch, was to be stage director. The youngest and brightest star of the opera, Inga Sundström, was chosen for the role of Lady Macbeth.

She was a very gifted singer, musical, and she possessed an interesting personality. Actually she had been a jazz singer, but she had since abandoned that genre and given herself over to the power of operatic singing. She was engaged in the Kungliga (Royal) Theater in Stockholm, where, in a short time, she was showered with various roles all of which had one thing in common: they were absolute voice killers for a debutante. What else can one call such roles as Berwald's *Estrella di Soria, Turandot,* or Elsa from *Lohengrin?* It was not certain that Inga Sundström would be able to sing Lady Macbeth, as she was afflicted with allergies. Fritz Busch, who was in Holland at the time, became doubtful and requested a substitute be engaged. The only singer Harald André found was a lyric soprano who was quite attractive but sang mostly operetta. But Ingeborg Berling, a voice teacher in Stockholm, remembered a young singer by the name of Birgit Nilsson whom she had heard perform the Sleepwalking Scene of Lady Macbeth at the opera school.

Berling gave my name to Hans Busch, who happened to be in Stockholm then, and late one evening, when I had just listened to Klemperer conduct Beethoven's Ninth, I made my way to the home of the Berlings and auditioned for Hans Busch. He was impressed and promised to see that I received coaching on the role. I got two hours with Bertil Bokstedt out of this, but as soon as Hans Busch had departed my coaching sessions were "forgotten."

Summer vacation had begun and I went to my parents in Skåne. Meanwhile I was sorry there were no further discussions with the head of the opera, who apparently forgot his glib promises more quickly than he could close the door in your face.

The summer in Skåne was wonderful, not least because I had recently become engaged to be married. I was happily oblivious to the Stockholm Opera, which was closed for two months. When the season began I had absolutely no desire to return to Stockholm. What would have been the point? I requested an extra week's leave and the request was granted without quibble. The week passed all too quickly; eventually I had to go. The moment I let myself into my apartment in Gamla Stan the telephone rang. It was the opera telling me that at ten the next morning I was scheduled for stage rehearsal with Hans Busch. Inge Sundström was ill and had canceled her engagement for Lady Macbeth. I broke out in a cold sweat at the very thought of meeting Hans Busch and the other cast members on the next morning. As I didn't even know which scene was to be rehearsed I had to learn the entire opera from memory! The whole night long I slaved away and regretted not studying the part during vacation instead of waiting for the opera to give a sign of life. Mercifully I was saved by a temporary reprieve: the next day I was told that the stage director could only begin rehearsals two days later. Hurrah! Now I could prepare myself better.

As I arrived, Sigurd Björling, known as punctuality personified, was already there. I knew him from *Freischütz* in which he had sung Kaspar. He looked at me with undisguised skepticism and asked, "How is this going to go?" That was all I needed for my adrenaline to rise. He had evidently forgotten how he had felt as a beginner, singing the small part of Zuniga in *Carmen* when the Carmen (the prima donna Gertrud Pålsson-Wettergren, a butcher's daughter from Eslöv) called out to him, "Mr. Björling, you have lost your place!"

With my adrenaline in full supply, I began the first aria, which is quite dramatic. I brought the full feeling out in my acting, causing not only Hans Busch but Sigurd Björling to be speechless—and the latter was unaccustomed to being speechless. It was not long before Björling's opinion circulated through the city: his colleagues called him the "Björling Newsletter" as he always had the most recent tidbits to send through the grapevine. His latest "newsletter" reported that in the opera house there was a young singer with the low voice of Gertrude Pålsson-Wettergren, the middle voice of the dramatic soprano Britta Herzberg, and the top voice of the coloratura soprano Hjördis Schymberg. How very practical to have the best vocal qualities of three prima donnas combined in one person! With this advance praise I felt I had good wind in my sails.

Thus my fear gradually abated, and the rehearsal period turned out to be wonderful and deeply satisfying. When one day ended, I looked forward to the next day. Fritz Busch was really a happy surprise: a completely different kind of conductor! In those days, there were great opera conductors who were also great human beings. He appeared calm and confident, capable of exercising authority over the orchestra, chorus, and soloists without impudence or volcanic outbursts. Indeed, on the international scene he was known as "Father Busch."

His son, Hans Busch, was also equally agreeable. As he had until now directed mostly Mozart operas, perhaps he had taken too much to heart from the Marionette Theater. Almost every accent in the music was represented by a gesture. Later in my career I learned that excessive gestures did not underscore the demonic and satanic evil of Lady Macbeth. As usual, my work with Hans Busch, my first stage director, was very exciting. He never allowed me to slack off: I had to run up and down steps like a wretched ghost, and more than once I found myself out of the breath I so urgently needed for this strenuous role.

In the beginning it was difficult to coordinate everything that one has to do simultaneously onstage: sing beautifully, recall the text and notes, act convincingly, blend in duets or large ensembles with the other singers and—above all—stay in contact with the conductor. If one made a note or a rest longer or shorter than the baton of the conductor indicated, there could be a catastrophe. I was incapable of relying on the prompter; I found it disturbing to be hounded by someone who was like an echo in advance.

Actors have it easier in this regard. If they want to vary the rhythm by declaiming somewhat more slowly or taking a shorter time between sentences, nothing terrible ensues. On the other hand, they have to create the desired atmosphere on stage by themselves, while the singer has the advantage of the wonderful music into which the composer has poured his whole soul.

An older colleague and a true gentleman, Einar Larsson, stood in the wings and noticed how I was perspiring, struggling with the vocal and histrionic interpretation. He took me aside and gave me some words to live by: "Young lady, if you continue like this, you'll be finished in half a year. You rush around like a crazed rat, forcing your voice until it hurts. Think of this: the public should be shaken, not you. This is theater, my dear child. You cannot act so realistically that you harm your voice. Here it is theater, theater, theater!"

Thank you, dear Einar, those were the right words at the right time. I have never forgotten them even though it took me a while until I learned to incorporate your wise advice.

The premiere went splendidly. Only the staging was said by the critics to be incoherent. Sigurd Björling sang Macbeth with vocal and dramatic vigor. Arne Hendriksen was Macduff, and Conny Söderström sang the small role of Malcolm. But soaring above us all was Sven Nilsson, who sang Banquo. What a personality and what an artist! He had had to flee Dresden in the middle of the war without taking anything from his home. He had been the principal bass in the Dresden Opera. The Kungliga (Royal) Theater in Stockholm welcomed him with open arms and he did not have to fall back on his original profession as chemical engineer. I am proud to be distantly related (daughter of a cousin twice removed) to Sven. He was not only a fine artist but also a fine and noble person, an inspiration to us all.

I myself was delighted to be unanimously acclaimed in the next day's newspapers; the only negative thing written was that I had too beautiful a voice for Verdi's idea of Lady Macbeth. Obviously the critics knew of a certain letter that supported this point of view. After the performance of *Macbeth* in Florence in 1847, with Barbieri-Nini as Lady Macbeth, the opera was given a year later in Naples with a certain Madame Tadolini as Lady. The opera director received a letter from Verdi, saying, "Madame Tadolini has a wonderful voice, clear and gentle but full. The voice of Lady Macbeth should be hard and hoarse. The voice of Madame is like an angel. Lady Macbeth should have the voice of a devil."

But the origin of Verdi's protest lies elsewhere. It was said that the amorous Verdi was having an intimate relationship with another singer to whom he promised the role of Lady Macbeth. In his effort to keep his promise he was cunning enough to make the role unappealing to a woman with a voice such as Tadolini's. What lovely-voiced singer with any self-respect would take on a role in which her voice should sound as hard and hoarse as a devil's? Certainly, Verdi's request for such a voice in his Lady Macbeth is rarely honored. Had Verdi for one moment truly desired the singer to have a character voice, without cultivation, he would surely have written different music for her. In fact, the role is one of the most diva-demanding in all of Italian opera. It requires a beautiful voice with vocal refinement, one that cannot devolve into a raw devil's voice.

My success is summarized in an interview with the *Svenska Dagbladet:*

> . . . to awaken one day and be famous is a fortune given to very few. . . . the young singer can, without exaggeration, include herself in this select group as the Friday newspapers have simply showered her with praise on her debut as Lady Macbeth.

In all, there were ten performances of *Macbeth* within the relatively short time of twenty-one days, and I looked forward to every one as a child looks forward to Christmas. Yes, it was really wonderful to be an opera singer! Suddenly doors that had been hermetically sealed were opened. I received offers from everywhere. A very impressive engagement in the Konsertföreningen was *Den judiska sången* (The Jewish song) by Moses Pergament, a huge choral symphony set to a text by Ragnar Josephson. The work was a protest against the inhuman cruelty being inflicted upon the Jews by the Third Reich. Pergament feverishly composed the work in six weeks in 1940. It was a gripping, shocking work in which I had the demanding soprano part. Even today, fifty years later, I can relive the convulsive lamentation of the introductory funeral march and the bright, luminous comfort of the choral music.

Leo Blech had obviously changed his mind about me, as I was to sing Venus in *Tannhäuser*, a new production conducted by him and directed by Hans Busch. I had always dreamed of singing Elisabeth in this opera and the director of the opera, Harald André had frequently promised me the role. However, the Elisabeth had long been assigned to Anna-Greta Söderholm (the singer originally intended for Agathe) who was then Leo Blech's favorite singer, and she did have an unusually beautiful voice. Set Svanholm sang Tannhäuser; this the first of our many, many collaborations.

The director elected to have Venus in a black wig. An astonishing choice: the sensual magnetism of the sinful goddess, Venus, is more often emphasized by a vivid red, seductive headdress. The reviews were very positive even though some thought I should have sung the Elisabeth (of course, I agreed completely). The competent (but unpredictable) critic, Teddy Nyblom wrote in the *Aftonbladet:*

> Among the debuts, Birgit Nilsson stole the show. It was wonderful to hear her, but she looked like a country Gretchen or a picture from an old-fashioned French postcard.

Two days after the premiere I received a penny postcard with the short but comforting lines: "Bravo, Bravo! Greetings, Leo Blech." Hurrah! I was rehabilitated!

ACT 2

After a long absence from the opera house, the consummately brilliant opera *Der Rosenkavalier* by Richard Strauss, was to be restored to the repertoire. The premiere was scheduled for February 27, 1948. I was not at all enthusiastic about being cast as the Marschallin; I felt I did not have enough experience of life to bring what was expected to the role. At that time, however, you did not have a say in the casting. You just had to do whatever you could with whatever parts were given you.

Nils Grevillius was the conductor of *Rosenkavalier* and the work was perfect for him. What a wonderful conductor and what elegant baton technique! When it came to those special "Strauss moments," he rose to his full height and let the orchestra pour out glorious waves of tone. Ragnar Hyltén-Cavallius was the stage director, and it turned out to be a great success for him. He handled the comic, busy crowd scenes extremely well.

The title role, the Rosenkavalier—or Octavian, as he was called—is a so-called pants role which means the character is sung by a female portraying a young man. Our singer, Benna Lemon-Brundin, was absolutely brilliant and the first singer I ever heard in the role. I have since heard others sing the part more beautifully but in portraying the role, she has never been equaled. Benna generated a special aura about the young lover, particularly his adoration of the older woman. And what a noble bearing she gave the young aristocrat in his attraction to the young maiden! Eva Prytz was, with her light, floating tones, a charming Sophie. Sven Nilsson gave an exceptional interpretation of Ochs; despite the crudeness of his text, he never allowed any vulgarity to creep in.

Especially strong, in my memory, is the character of the little black boy who comes in at the very end of the opera looking for Sophie's handkerchief. The young girl who played this part was extremely graceful and her movements fit completely with the music. The young girl was Ann Margret Pettersson, who today is an internationally recognized stage director.

I remember nothing of act 1 except being terribly nervous, having a terribly unflattering wig on my head and having to wear the fur-trimmed morning dress that Nanny Larsén-Todsen had worn in the 1920s. The moths had feasted on the collar and I was inhaling a nose- and mouthful of fur with every breath, which was driving me mad. As the act ended I had not the slightest idea of whether I had finished singing or had more to sing. The day after the premiere I wrote in my diary: "Splendid notices! I am astounded!"

In the third act there was one embarrassing moment. Karl-Gustaf Lindström, an excellent tenor from Malmö, sang the role of the Innkeeper who announces the Marschallin's arrival at the inn. There Baron Ochs was discovered in flagrante as he flirts with Octavian who is dressed as a young girl (it can be confusing here with the genders!) Lindström should have sung: "Ihre hochfürstliche Gnaden, die Frau Fürstin Werdenberg!" but he missed his cue. One of the "Haushofmeistern" was sung by Sture Ingebretzen, a good tenor from the chorus. He noticed the omission, saw a chance for a solo, jumped in the very last moment and sang in full voice Lindström's line "Ihre hochfürstliche Gnaden, die Frau Fürstin (*slight pause*) Venusberg!"

A warning was given to Lindström who had excused himself because of an urgent call of nature. Heartless colleagues immediately bestowed upon this elegant entrance of the Princess the sobriquet of "Lindström's Piddle Motiv."

In the spring, Beethoven's *Missa Solemnis* was performed, a work that had not been given since the 1930s. Erich Kleiber was guest conductor and the soloists besides myself were Lisa Tunell, mezzo-soprano; Gösta Bäckelin, tenor; and Sigurd Björling, bass.

It is generally accepted that Beethoven did not make things easy for singers. Perhaps the problems can be attributed to his deafness; in any case the *Missa* was somewhat uncomfortable for my voice. Erich Kleiber, in contrast to his rather tall son Carlos, was quite short. He conducted with short, small gestures, and one had the impression that he wanted to compensate for his small build with the strict, whiplike gestures of an animal trainer. Nevertheless, it was tremendously interesting and informative to sing under his direction. The orchestra and chorus sounded simply wonderful!

When I had no performance at the opera I was singing with the important orchestras of the nearby countries. Over in Copenhagen, especially in the Tivoli, the interest shown in me culminated in a yearly concert under the baton of Nils Jörgen Kaiser. For many years I maintained a real love affair with my Danish public. A favorite memory of mine is that of my very first concert in Copenhagen, the Christmas concert in Tivoli in 1947 in the Oddfellow Palace shared with the wonderful Italian soprano Maria Jolanda di Petri. In the same year, when completely unknown in Sweden, she had given an unforgettable "Liederabend" that captivated the Stockholm music lovers. The Copenhagen concert is engraved in my memory. Max Hansen and the film actress, Lilian Harvey, as well as many others took part and Christian Felumb conducted.

In the coming season I was to sing the role of Senta in *Der Fliegende Holländer* of Richard Wagner. The premiere was to take place on November 4, 1948, with Leo Blech conducting.

With all that was happening professionally that year, I also got married. On September 10, I attained the elevated status of becoming Mrs.

Bertil Niklasson. The wedding trip was postponed because of Leo Blech's rehearsal schedule, but we managed to go to Paris in the spring of 1949 for our honeymoon.

Leo Blech was convinced that everything was in order so far as my musicality was concerned. He seemed, in fact, quite satisfied with me and as a sign of his approval, he presented me with a sticky licorice throat lozenge, a supply of which he carried in his pocket (the manufacturer supplied him with these gratis). This fuzzy little lozenge lay like cotton around the heart.

My mother Stina freed herself from all the daily duties on the farm in order to come to the opening. It was the first (and, sadly, the last) time she was in Stockholm. My husband and I had bought a home near Lidingö and there was plenty of room for her with us. Stina felt like a fish in water and in fact stayed beyond threshing time, when she normally would be feeding, well, not the biblical five thousand, but easily fifteen extra men in Svenstad. Now, with her away, the able household staff was left to cope. Stina was very pleased with the performance, although at the same time worried that the profession of opera singer would prove to be too strenuous for me. She was reminded of the tendency to tuberculosis that ran in her family. In my new life, she would not be able to fend off the hard blows for me, and that worried her.

Senta, in *Der Fliegende Holländer,* was never one of my favorite roles. It has always been difficult for me to portray a fanatical daydreamer; I prefer to be very active onstage. Also, the role was not without its vocal challenges. The ghostly chant: "Johohoe! Johohoe! Johohoe!" is followed by a dramatic increase in intensity interrupted by a sudden "piu lento" and a highly lyrical phrase that Verdi would have called "con un fil di voce" (with a thin thread of voice). The sequence of notes is tricky, stretching over thirds and fourths that cover both register changes in the voice; that is, in the lower voice from D, F, and B, and in the upper voice D, F, and G. If one gives a little too much on the low tones as the phrase goes higher, the high tones will be unsteady and lack overtone. If one takes the low tones too lightly, then the high tones lack support.

In the duet with Erik, Senta sings at one point, "I am just a child and know not what I'm singing." I don't know how other Sentas have interpreted this strange sentence, but it was difficult for me to sing these words with a clear conscience. Sometimes I was tempted to sing "how" instead of "what." The duet with the Dutchman does not lie comfortably. The writing here puts demands on the voice between the two registers and grinds away on the fourthspace E, F, and F sharp. If one does not sing lightly and with support, by the end of the duet, the tongue and larynx have exchanged places. And just in this moment one soars up to not one but *two* long-sustained and brilliant high Bs!

With hindsight I can understand my mother's fear that I could over-extend myself. Nonetheless, when I think of what happened later, I am glad that she heard me at least once in an opera.

In my diary from this time there is often written "have a cold" or "have a terrible cold." The day of the *Holländer* premiere bears the entry "have a terrible cold!" A few days later I received a penny postcard with the words "Dear Miss Senta Daland. When one sings as you did yesterday then one doesn't need to be concerned about being hoarse. It was very beautiful. Bravo! Best greetings, Leo Blech."

Erich Kleiber was again in Stockholm for a performance of Beethoven's Ninth at the Concert House and to conduct a performance of *Holländer,* and on both of these occasions, I had the pleasure of singing with him again.

In the spring of 1949, Mozart's *Don Giovanni* was scheduled for a new production. There were five of us classmates, about the same age, from the opera school who were cast in the five major roles. Åke Collet, a tall, elegant, young man who had put opera ahead of his education in business, was to be the Giovanni. Eva Prytz, who had already established herself as a lyric soprano without peer, was cast as Zerlina. Lilly Furlin, a promising future Wagnerian in the spinto classification, though not entirely right for Mozart, was Elvira. Paul Höglund, a talented bass was Masetto. In addition, Gösta Björling sang Don Ottavio; Sven-Erik Jacobsson was Leporello; and "the most beautiful bass voice in the world," Leon Björker, was the father of Donna Anna. I was cast as Donna Anna. Herbert Sandberg (Leo Blech's son-in-law) was conductor, and Ragnar Hyltén-Cavallius, the stage director.

There was a superabundance of unusually beautiful voices in the opera. In the lyric classification there were no less than five young singers: Anna-Greta Söderholm, Inga Sundström (unable to perform because of illness), Lily Furlin, Siw Ericsdotter, and myself. Inge Sundström unfortunately never returned to the opera. My voice was not especially cut out for Mozart but I sensed how important this music was for my voice and battled bravely with the difficulties. Lilly Furlin had a rich, warm voice and enjoyed great success as Genoveva in Natanael Berg's opera of the same name. The head of the opera, however, was of the opinion that she could not fulfill the demands of the role of Elvira. Instead of being given the chance to develop her voice in less strenuous parts, she was brutally dismissed. Today, when I hear anyone complaining that the opera houses have no consideration for voices, I say to myself: "you should have been in the opera house in my day." In little more than a year I studied seven very different roles and performed them. All the roles were a bit too demanding (to put it mildly) for an inexperienced singer like me: Senta (*Holländer*), Sieglinde (*Walküre*), Brünnhilde (*Siegfried*), Donna Anna (*Don Giovanni*), Strauss's *Ariadne* (in a radio broadcast), Lisa (*Pique Dame*), and Ursula (*Mathias der Maler*).

Many have asked me how I lived through such a heavy workload. I usually answer: "Either you die or you survive. What doesn't kill you makes you stronger." I became very strong and in fact grew through the unconscionable demands. Although I am predisposed to frequent colds, I don't remember in my first ten years, ever canceling a performance.

Suddenly Stina was gone. A little less than a month before the *Don Giovanni* premiere, my mother was killed in a traffic accident. She was standing with a few neighbors at a bus stop waiting for the bus to Båstad when a drunk driver careening at high speed ran them down. She was thrown seventy-five feet down the street. Nils saw the accident from a distant window and leaped onto his bicycle to make certain it was not Stina who was hurt. But it was she. He held her in his arms as she breathed her last breath. The driver was shaken and confused and the police authorities never conducted an investigation, out of pity for the desperate driver. On March 12, at nine in the morning, just as I was on my way to the opera, my father, completely beside himself, called and tried to tell me what had happened. It was as though the floor had collapsed under me. I could do no more than scream insanely for minutes on end. Then a surreal kind of calmness and strength came over me. I had to get to Skåne quickly; it was there I was needed, not only to stand by my father, but also to help with all the practical things that had to be done. I stuffed a few necessities in a bag, took a taxi to the city, and stopped long enough to purchase mourning clothes at Metz on the Kungsgatan (King Street). Two hours after the horrible news of her death I was sitting in the train to Hässleholm where Bertil, who had veterinarian work in Skåne, awaited me.

The burial was conducted throughout with solemnity. All the mourners gathered at the home of the deceased, where they partook of food and drink. Then began the long procession to the church. First, an automobile with two flags, then a hearse pulled by two horses, then a car with the next of kin, and after that the long line of mourners. Every house along the three-mile way to the cemetery was decorated with juniper branches. The villagers wanted, with this lovely custom, to show their respect and affection for the deceased.

I could not see how I could go back to Stockholm and leave my father alone. Because of this I asked the conductor, Herbert Sondberg, to release me from taking part in the premiere of *Don Giovanni.* He was most friendly and understanding but said they had no one else and it would be impossible to find someone who could learn the role in three weeks.

The rehearsal period was difficult for me, even though it helped get my mind off my troubles. My mental state on the evening of the premiere was hardly that of a rondo, and my acting was burdened by a tense and un-Mozart-like rigidity, which was mentioned by the critics. For my singing, however, I received only praise. The moody and feared Teddy Nyblom was at the premiere in a generous frame of mind and gave everyone a good review. About me he wrote: "Above all, Birgit Nilsson with gold in the throat and a dependable and brilliant top, which she uses to create the most distinguished Anna since the days of Jenny Lind."

Two days later, as Carl-Axel Hallgren took over the Don Giovanni, the critics were again at the performance, and I received wonderful praise from all of them—except Teddy Nyblom who apparently had sobered up: "Birgit Nilsson should guard against unsupported screams in the high tones." This review I have memorized. It hit me hard.

Before the spring season of 1949 was over, I received a new assignment: Lisa in Tchaikovsky's *Pique Dame!* The premiere was to be in October. Conductor and stage director were one and the same: the Russian-born Issai Dobrowen. He came to Sweden as a refugee and, after a short time of earning his living as a grade school music teacher, was grabbed by the Stockholm Opera. Soon there was a downright "Dobrowen mania" sweeping the country. He presented to the Swedish public some of the greatest Russian operas, which had never been heard in Sweden—most notably, an unforgettable performance of Mussorgsky's *Khovanshchina* with Leon Björker.

In that fall, the much-admired singer Joel Berglund became the director of the opera. I, personally, was very happy with the new boss. Berglund was a friendly and sympathetic man who brought with him great understanding of singers' problems. His word was his bond and we delighted in the new sense of security. With working conditions improved, the pleasure of performing was heightened.

As usual, the *Ring of the Nibelungen* was planned for the fall. This cycle was presented at least once a year and was always cast with members of the Stockholm Opera roster. Brünnhilde had to be newly cast, as the wonderful Irma Björck had retired. I shall never forget her farewell performance in *Walküre* only six months before. I wept during the entire performance. How could a singer voluntarily give a farewell performance? This is almost like being a mourner at one's own funeral. I swore then that I would never give a farewell performance—a vow I had to take back some thirty-three years later.

Britta Herzberg wished to crown her career with the role of Brünnhilde and it should have been so. She was to sing the Brünnhilde in *Die Walküre* and *Die Götterdämmerung,* while the Brünnhilde in *Siegfried,* which lay a bit too high for Madame Herzberg, was entrusted to Inez Köhler, a confident and good singer of the older generation who had not been employed much in recent years. Herzberg's star role, Sieglinde, was not yet cast, and she could obviously not sing Brünnhilde and Sieglinde in the same opera. The choice was Lilly Furlin, who was made for the role. I was champing at the bit with my Lisa in *Pique Dame* and did not come into the question for the *Ring*—or so I thought.

Dobrowen was an interesting man: fiery and temperamental, he demanded total commitment from those onstage—not only the soloists but from the chorus. He fired up the orchestra and the singers to unheard-of intensity. He demanded all that was in one—and sometimes more than one had to give. Isa Quensel portrayed the Countess in *Pique Dame.* What she created with her subdued voice and expressive gestures was no less than masterful. The performance received high praise.

For the entire fall I was overtired and depressed. The shock of my mother's sudden death, which I had repressed, came to the fore and tortured me day and night. And the many strenuous performances didn't help matters.

The straw that broke the camel's back was the surprising news that I was to take over the Sieglinde as well as the *Siegfried* Brünnhilde *three weeks before the premiere.* I have never found out why the two singers cast for these roles dropped out (or were dropped). Now I had to get these two roles drummed into me by my righthand man, Pol Kurt Bendix. Because there was so little time, we left all the musical interludes out, just working on the actual vocal lines. William von Wymetal, an Austrian, who had put down roots in the United States, was the guest stage director.

The first stage rehearsals were terrible. In the first act of *Walküre* there are many interludes that demand Sieglinde's histrionic interpretation—and in our haste, forced upon us by my need to memorize the vocal parts of the role, we had left out these interludes. After the first rehearsal, I spent the night at the piano learning this music, which I had to know by the next day.

It took me some time to fall asleep because of the stress. After another fourteen days of lying in bed and staring at the ceiling in a kind of hallucination, repeating these roles over and over, I began to fear for my sanity. It happened that I had a concert in Helsingbord with the excellent and inspiring conductor, Håken von Eichwald. I was able to spend two nights at home in Svenstad where I could calm my spirit and get back to my normal sleeping routine.

Britta Herzberg was not only a gifted artist; she was also an elegant lady. She made no secret of the fact that she could best portray a role when she was in love and the object of her affection was subject to change. Wymetal, who was a true gentleman, was in his sixties, and the admiration of Herzberg was tremendously flattering to him. She received his unreserved attention through the many long rehearsals. I had to fight through on my own as well as I could, and suffered greatly from a feeling of inferiority.

Shortly before the beginning of act 1 of *Walküre,* Herzberg came rushing into my dressing room with her brown wig in hand. Completely beside herself, she declared she would be unable to sing if she did not have a blond wig. In short, she wanted me to exchange wigs with her. I still recall this scene with crystal clarity. The prima donna assoluta appealed to me with her big blue eyes; in an instant she had the hairpiece. Then with a quick gesture, she handed me her bird's nest, which was two sizes smaller than my blond wig, wished me luck and fled from the room. I would be lying if I said I was happy about this exchange.

The prima donna's coming into my dressing room had a tragicomic aspect. She was covered in some indescribable rag that, upon close examination, and with much goodwill, could be called a dressing gown. It had been so frequently mended and patched that it was impossible to discern what it had originally looked like. How was such a thing possible with a prima donna of the Royal Opera?

The dresser explained to me that Herzberg was very superstitious and she would not risk using another dressing gown other than this one, which she had used in her debut in 1924. It was now so worn out that it had to be mended after every performance to keep it from falling completely apart. And me? After only three years in the opera I was on my second dressing gown!

The sound of the miraculous music made me forget the disagreeable mess. I gave myself totally to the singing and acting and was fascinated with the role of Sieglinde. It is such a grateful part; indeed, I think it would be difficult for anyone to fail with this role. Set Svanholm was a wonderful partner as Siegmund; Sigurd Björling, an imposing Wotan; Leon Björker, a threatening Hunding—and as Fricka, Margareta Bergström was majestic. Britta Herzberg had put some of Sieglinde's qualities into her portrayal of Brünnhilde and was a warmhearted, earthy woman. Nils Grevillius conducted with even more than his usual elegance.

Yngve Flykt in the *Express* wrote: "Birgit Nilsson must have dreamed of portraying Sieglinde, the role of a lifetime (*Author's note:* If he only knew!) Here we experienced a definitive breakthrough in the development of a great singer, a portrayal in which every tone was filled with beauty and vitality, an interpretation that proved a total success."

A week later, *Siegfried* was on the program. I thought I had received the absolute minimum in direction in the stage rehearsals for Sieglinde, but what I received as Brünnhilde made the work in *Walküre* seem a model of detail. The stage director had simply not come up with any suggestions for me. There were so many other singers to look after; besides, in a few days Herzberg would be singing the Brünnhilde in *Götterdämmerung,* which is longer and more difficult than the Brünnhilde in *Siegfried.*

The so-called dress rehearsal for *Siegfried* still lives in my memory. Brünnhilde is lying on a rock, deep in her long sleep and will be awakened from her unconsciousness through Siegfried's kiss. At this moment, Siegfried (alias Set Svanholm) prompted me in one ear, "Now you must awaken, after a while you will slowly rise up. When I give you a sign you will greet the sun, the light, and the day."

The awakening went quite well, but when the orchestra played the magnificent Greeting Motif of Brünnhilde, I thought my heart would spring out of my chest. There shimmered the most beautiful sounds I had ever heard. I was literally stunned. Herbert Sandberg, who was conducting *Siegfried* for the first time tried to help me but I was as though turned to stone. The few times I tried to open my mouth it was either too early or too late. In deep despair, I covered my face with my hands, fled from the stage to my dressing room, and put on my coat. Before anyone could react to this I was in my little Fiat 500, driving home to Lidingö. There I threw myself on my bed and sobbed bitterly over the collapse of my opera career. It didn't take long for the director himself, Joel Berglund, to take charge. Until today I do not know if he was being honest or just making excuses to restore my confidence. He said he was sorry the conductor had caused such difficulty for me! Sandberg was indeed a novice at conducting *Siegfried* and the director begged me to have patience with him. I answered that even though he might not have complete mastery over the score, I had only myself to blame for my actions. But if he really wanted to give me another chance, I was more than willing to try again.

Once again there was a premiere and once again the critics were effusive. Gustav Hillerström wrote: "Birgit Nilsson is no longer on the way to being a world-class Wagnerian; she is already there!" Ingmar Bengtsson of the *Svenska Dagbladet* declared the Brünnhilde to be one of my best portrayals. But what pleased me the most was the enthusiasm our greatest star, Hjördis Schymberg, had for my singing.

Was the shock of the first meeting with Brünnhilde still in my bones? Or was it the problem of bringing out this many-sided character in the short, but intense, time she has to sing? The demands of the *Siegfried* Brünnhilde are tremendous; at the same time the physical freedom is restricted by the music itself. The *Siegfried* Brünnhilde always cost me more in nerves and stress than the other two Brünnhildes put together.

A few days later, *Götterdämmerung* was on the stage and it was time for me—just as in *Rheingold*—to dive into the Rhein and become the Rhein maiden Woglinde.

In March, Joel Berglund wanted to present the first Swedish performance of Paul Hindemith's *Mathas der Maler*, based on the life of the sixteenth-century painter Mathias Grünewald (alias Mathias Nithardt).

In Germany the Nazis had forbidden this opera. First, because the Catholics' burning of heretical writings was too reminiscent of Nazi book burnings. Second, the work is imbued with a strong, humanistic spirit. Mathias fought for the right to life and freedom for mankind. He turns away from the lovely Ursula and does not allow himself to be drawn into religious confrontation. A revelation inspired his life's work: the Isenheimer Altar. Soon after its completion he departed this world. The opera was given outside Germany during Hindemith's exile. Hindemith himself wrote the libretto, which blends very well with the music in which old German folk tunes and Gregorian chant are linked together. For our production we obtained the head of the Munich Opera, Georg

Hartmann as stage director, and the costumes and sets were borrowed from the Munich production.

Sigurd Björling, as Mathis, brought new colors to his histrionic palette and was vocally wonderful. The young Elisabeth Söderström drew an endearing picture of the fourteen-year-old Regina, daughter of the leader of the peasants, Schwalb (sung by Conny Söderström). Arne Ohlsson was cast as the young Cardinal. I received the dramatic role of Ursula, the woman whom Mathis loves and who loves him. Herbert Sandberg had not only translated the German text, he coached the singers thoroughly and conducted. The work with Dr. Hartmann proved to be most informative and extremely interesting.

The performance was, justifiably so, very successful even though the response of the public could have been better. Sten Broman of the *Sydsvenska Dagbladet* ended his review:

> [It] was a superb performance that one will never forget. This is, however, a completely different matter for the standard operagoing public of Stockholm, which loves simple romance and honeyed tones and is hardly sensitive enough to the far-reaching development of opera after Wagner and Puccini to really understand the significance of this inspired work.

To what extent the critic, Broman, was speaking for himself, I cannot rightly judge.

ACT 3

Exactly one year after the *Ring* of 1949, Hans Knappertsbusch, the redoubtable Wagner conductor, came to Stockholm.

He was to conduct the *Ring* and *Rosenkavalier,* and so great was the excitement and anticipation, we all ran around like chickens with their heads cut off, asking when rehearsals would begin. Days passed and no rehearsals were held. We saw Knappertsbusch only through the window of the opera house bar where he sat with his favorite drink, Swedish punch. There was another Swedish specialty that he liked: the "Pocket" calendar. It was said that he had purchased two dozen of these little books to give to his German friends. Because "Tasche" in Swedish is "ficka," the word "Fickkalendar" was displayed on every page. Friendly colleagues well acquainted with the German language explained to me that this word had a rather different, risqué meaning in German.

I don't believe that Knappertsbusch had any rehearsal with the orchestra. He was known for not liking to rehearse, but when he stood on the podium—over six feet of genius in suspenders—the musicians were in heaven.

An orchestra member said after a performance of *Götterdämmerung:* "You sit here all year long, battling the impossible phrases, cursing Wagner, who can't write anything playable for one's instrument. In the end, you're resigned to playing only what is absolutely necessary. And then comes a sorcerer and handles it all just by breathing easier. Nothing special—but suddenly every note can be played."

Ten years later, after a premiere of *Götterdämmerung* with Karajan in Vienna, I met the famous concertmaster of the Vienna Philharmonic, Willi Boskosky. He said it really *was* impossible to play all the notes that Wagner had set down. Silently I asked myself whether the sorcerer Knappertsbusch could have cut the Gordian Knot in Vienna.

It was a brilliant move by Joel Berglund to get Knappertsbusch to Stockholm, as he brought the *Ring* performances up to an international level. The public responded with an enthusiasm for Wagner that had never before been tapped, and the orchestra worshipped the master who brought about such a metamorphosis. Knappertsbusch wanted to engage Sigurd Björling as Wotan and me as Sieglinde for the reopening of the Bayreuth Festival in the summer of 1951. Sigurd accepted the offer but I felt I was not experienced enough to tread the boards of the greatest Wagner stage in the world.

After my first engagement outside Sweden (in Berlin), there was a new challenge awaiting me in Stockholm: the dream role of all spintos, Puccini's Tosca. It was not a new production and I feared the rehearsal time for the demanding role would be insufficient. I shared this anxiety with the director, who promised that I could work with the experienced Gertrud Pålsson-Wettergren. She was already retired but worked occasionally in the newly established opera studio, brought into being by Issai Dobrowen. It was generally felt (that is, noised abroad) that Gertrud Pålsson-Wettergren was a dyed-in-the-wool diva. Nothing could have been further from the truth! It was more than wonderful to work with her. She was understanding, inspiring, and blessed with an intuitive "feel" for the theatrical that I have seldom found in another singer. Physically, she was a rather heavy woman, with a kind of lumbering gait. Onstage, however, she was transformed, her movements light as a feather.

The first thing I had to learn was how to manage a gown with a train. Traditional costumes for Tosca often include a train, the longer the better. In Vienna I wore an evening cape with a train that almost equaled the width of the stage. The train can be moved only with the foot; under no circumstance can you grab it with your hand and toss it about. Besides, it should lie in a lovely half-circle when you are seated.

The studio had a closet used by the cleaning staff, and there we found the requisite props in the form of a very long smock and a broom. The arms of the smock were tied around my waist, serving as the train. The long-handled broom made a fine walking stick for Tosca in act 1, as it was the custom for ladies of that period to deck themselves out with the six-foot-long staff. I did a lot of striding around and twisting about before the train ceased to wind itself like a long snake around my feet. Karl Gustaf Lindström (who later took over the role of Cavaradossi) assisted in all this.

I was overjoyed to work with the "girl," as I jokingly called her. Everything was suddenly so easy and at the same time felt so right. One could think, feel, and react; in other words, your acting grew out of motivation. That seems self-evident and quite simple but after the teachers I had had, who forced me into the set gestures and standard poses they had used from Year One, the work with this lady came as a true liberation. Gertrud Wettergren and I became friends for life.

Arne Hendriksen was a fiery and inspiring Cavaradossi and Scarpia was definitely one of Sigurd Björling's best roles. After Tosca has stabbed Scarpia with a knife, she takes the passport from his hand, a pass he has handwritten, allowing Tosca and Cavaradossi to flee Rome. Sigurd made it a habit to write something personal. Once he wrote: "Today you are, if that is possible, better than ever. Your Scarpia." Reading such words on the supposed passport made it rather difficult to express the loathing that Tosca, according to the libretto, felt for the dead Scarpia.

I believe *Tosca* was an opera that lay close to the heart of Nils Grevillius. It was moving and exciting to see the maestro, after a beautifully sung aria, take his handkerchief and wipe away a few tears.

Performances of *Tosca* were hardly over before it was time to learn another extraordinary role, that of Verdi's Aida. This was to be a new production. The opera had succeeded in bringing the Russian-born stage designer, Nicola Benois, from Italy. The former head of the opera, Harald André, was stage director, and Fritz Busch was the guest conductor—all of which created a feeling of confidence.

We had no tenor on our roster who sang the demanding role of Radames. Some suggested by Busch were declined and some (Einar Andersson, for example) refused the part. One of the tenors enthusiastically recommended by Busch was Erik Sjöberg from Copenhagen, a former shoemaker from Bornholm. As it turned out, Sjöberg had a marvelous voice. Of all the tenors with whom I have sung throughout my long career, there were three whose singing went directly to my heart: Benjamino Gigli, Giuseppi di Stefano, and Erik Sjöberg. Unfortunately, his career did not unfold as one had hoped. His nerves were not made for the stressful and grueling profession, and he had only a short career.

Britta Herzberg was cast as Amneris but an illness prior to the premiere demanded that Margarita Bergström take over. Herzberg recovered quickly and sang in later performances. Sigurd Björling and Erik Sundquist alternated as Amonasro. Sven Nilsson was Ramfis and Folke Jonsson, a sympathetic colleague from Ängelholm in Skåne and a wonderful bass, sang the King. Harald André was masterly in his handling of crowd scenes and these were filled with life and energy. There were many "supers" hired for the Triumphal March. Individual direction was, however, not André's strong suit. In action scenes he depended on one of his three pat movements: both hands on the chest and upper body swaying from side to side as though you held in your arms a baby with colic.

Aside from a few exceptions the bombastic mounting of *Aida* was a tremendous success. I personally thought that my Aida put all of my past performances in the shade. I profited enormously from the work with Maestro Busch. The role emphasizes more soft and lyric singing than had my previous roles, and I was given the chance to bring in more nuance and to develop piano and pianissimo dynamics. The critics were as one in declaring I was ready for an international career.

As for myself, at this time I had not the slightest desire to leave the Stockholm Opera. First, I thought it expedient to become a first-class singer in Sweden rather than an average one internationally. Second, I commanded no foreign languages. The guest conductors, however, did not share my opinion. With Leo Blech, I had already had a lovely success in Berlin; Knappertsbusch had plans to engage me in Bayreuth; Issai Dobrowen and La Scala offered me the role of Jaroslavna in *Prince Igor.* And now Fritz Busch came with an offer to sing Elettra in Mozart's *Idomeneo* in Glyndebourne in the summer of 1951. I hesitated as long as I could but finally "Father" Busch's persuasiveness won out and I accepted the engagement.

The spring brought me much work. Along with eleven *Aida* performances, I sang Venus in *Tannhäuser* and Donna Anna in *Don Giovanni.*

For a little variety in the midst of all the opera, I had three performances as soloist in Beethoven's *Missa Solemnis,* with Fritz Busch conducting.

The day before my departure for Glyndebourne I gave a guest performance as Tosca in Helsingfors. The Finns are such unbelievably good hosts. After every performance there is a festive dinner with vast amounts of food and even more to drink. As I had to leave for England the next day I tried to break away early. No Finnish host, however, takes such an attempt seriously. "But Madame Nilsson," opined my dinner partner, "you are a true Viking, aren't you? When Kirsten Flagstad was here for fourteen days as guest she didn't ever want to go home and rest or sleep. We ate and drank until six in the morning. She took the morning flight to London and sang a recital that evening. You see, that is a real Viking."

After a two-month-long stay in Glyndebourne, which was very interesting and successful, my fall season began with an important concert in Göteborg conducted by Tor Mann. The concert was climaxed by my passing a kidney stone during the night, a horribly painful experience that ended with my being hospitalized for nearly a week.

In Stockholm *Aida* was again in the repertoire, and this time Set Svanholm was going to be Radames. He was a thoroughly musical and intelligent singer who, in one week, sang the entire *Ring* (Loge, Siegmund, and both Siegfrieds) in the original German at the Metropolitan. The following week he sang the same roles in Stockholm—this time in Swedish!

There was a slight mishap in the *Aida,* or rather a slip of the tongue. Svanholm sang, as we all did, in Swedish; in act 3, however, he accidentally slipped into Italian and consequently continued in that language. This brought him some harsh words from the critics, who often used him as scapegoat. There were many in Sweden who shared my opinion that Svanholm was not so celebrated in Sweden as he should have been. In Vienna, for example, he was tremendously popular; later in my career, I was witness to the "Svanholm mania" that broke out every time he appeared in Vienna. Nevertheless, he was always happy when he returned to Stockholm Opera and to the Jakobs-Kirche where he had been the choir director.

After the usual *Ring* performances in the fall I was plunged in over my head learning Elsa in *Lohengrin.* Once again I had to call on Kurt Bendix, the artists' one-man rescue squad, to learn a new role in no time at all. The role is longer and more difficult than, say, Elisabeth in *Tannhäuser* (which I, in spite of all the promises, had not been allowed to sing).

The performance was for me a great disappointment as the conductor was, to put it bluntly, drunk! New in the part and not yet certain of its huge demands, I needed all the help I could get. But when I needed a clear entrance cue in a musically difficult place, I received a grin and a hand kiss. Talk about a nightmare! Strangely enough, no one seemed to notice the condition of the conductor. A few critics noted that he whipped the orchestra to an unusual momentum—quite possible, as they were playing out of sheer terror. I came off with the usual praise of my singing, though some critics sensed a certain insecurity in the histrionic portrayal.

On a few occasions I had the pleasure of singing with the fantastic Nicolai Gedda, who sang Don Ottavio, my betrothed, in *Don Giovanni.* Aside from the recording of *Der Freischütz* on which Nicolai sang Max and I, Agathe, we never sang together again, which I very much regret. I have the feeling that Gedda thought our voices did not blend well. In any case, that does not alter my opinion that we had in him one of the best, most musical, versatile tenors in the world.

Leon Björker sang the Commendatore, Donna Anna's father, in all the performances. He was a constant prankster, playing jokes on his colleagues offstage and on. And what pranks! When I was in great shock over Giovanni's murder of my father, and was collapsed over his dead body, it was his habit always to tickle my knee. I tried to get him to stop by pulling on a few of his chest hairs when I opened his shirt to look for the death-dealing wound. One evening when he was particularly fervent about tickling my knee, I thought, "Just wait till I open your shirt. You'll find out what real pain is." At that I gave a hard pull on his chest hair and Oh, my God! I had a toupee in my hand! Never was I so near to interrupting a performance. I was shaking from laughter but hoped I could make it appear to be crying. The conductor, Herbert Sandberg, on top of things, helped me to get back on the right track.

But that was not all: Donna Anna falls in a faint as servants put her father on a stretcher to carry him out. One night, as this was taking place, the "Corpse" unnoticeably took the hem of my nightdress and pulled it up over my head as they passed by with him, leaving me literally undressed. Probably no Donna Anna ever regained consciousness more quickly than I did on that evening.

At the same time *Don Giovanni* was playing in Stockholm I was invited early in 1952 for two guest performances of Donna Anna in Florence and Padua. The performances were in Italian, of course, and the conductor was the famous Tullio Serafin.

The trip to Florence was very exciting and I had many lovely experiences. My husband Bertil and I were able to spend Christmas as well as New Year's Day there. You can spend Christmas in far worse places than Florence, even though the rehearsal lasted until nine P.M. on Christmas Eve. Tullio Serafin was a wonderful conductor, very secure, calm, and good-humored. He reminded me of "Father" Busch. The ensemble was of the highest caliber, with the Russian-Italian Nicola Rossi-Lemeni, the son-in-law of the conductor, singing the elegant Don Giovanni. Giuseppe Taddei was the Leporello, the best I have ever experienced, an unbelievable singer and artist—and an excellent colleague.

In February the Stockholm Opera was pleased to have a guest performance of the celebrated and honored tenor Benjamino Gigli as Cavaradossi in *Tosca.* As I was for the great singer an unknown quantity, he was sent a tape of my voice. I was found worthy by the maestro and was accepted as his Tosca. Gigli arrived in an elegant fur coat with matching hat, ready to do battle with the cold winds and the icebergs.

He was also reassured, as well as a little disappointed not to find any polar bears or wolves (at least not four-legged ones) frolicking about on the streets of Stockholm. In addition to his son-in-law he brought an entire entourage: a secretary, coach, dresser, manager, and physician. Not one of these gave the impression of being younger than the sixty-two-year-old Gigli; we frequently couldn't help wondering who was taking care of whom. A full hour before the beginning of the performance Gigli wandered around the stage, made-up and in costume, reviewing his staging. One could see he was nervous and tense before his entrance. The jovial and avuncular Gigli made no effort to portray a young, fiery lover. But he sang! And how! I have never in my life been so deeply impressed by a singer. His voice was like a stream of molten gold. He could do anything he wanted with his voice: crescendo, diminuendo, and again crescendo, without noticeable register changes and always maintaining the same seductive sound. He was no actor, but it was not necessary for him; his voice told us everything. Indeed, it seemed almost more natural for him to sing than to speak. Afterward in the Operakällaren, the elegant restaurant under the opera house, he continued to sing. Until three in the morning he sang Italian songs and serenades beautifully. His salary he donated to the Soloists' Club of the opera, a return kindness for having been honored by King Gustav V with the Medal of Arts and Letters. At his departure on the night train to Rome, all the opera's soloists and the director assembled at the train to see him off, all of one voice in calling out our good wishes to this unique artist and man who had completely won our hearts.

As Gigli noticed that my husband had come along to bid him farewell, he pretended to be the jealous lover, calling out, "Ah, il mio rivale," and pretending to aim a pistol at Bertil. As the train began to move away, Gigli still stood at his open window, shooting away with his hate-filled "Pow, Pow, Pow." Naturally, I did not then have any idea that I would later be invited to spend a few nights in his bed—but more about that later.

After my second guest appearance in Genoa (Italy was a country I immediately fell in love with) I had to travel directly to Göteborg for a concert with the French conductor Albert Wolff. Along with arias from *Aida* and *Ballo,* it was thought that some orchestrated songs by Gunnar de Frumerie would go well in the contemporary part of the program. I had never performed any of this composer's works and I had no piano at my disposal in Genoa. So, necessity being the mother of invention, I studied the notes "dry." When I got to Göteborg I was of course curious about how the music with the orchestra would sound. The experience was a total joy; the songs of Gunnar de Frumerie sounded just as wonderful as they did in my silent study of them.

Albert Wolff wanted to engage me for Tosca, in a guest performance for the Paris Opera, but when I found out I would have to learn the role in French it was not particularly difficult for me to decline the offer. The review of our concert in Göteborg is proof of our resounding success. As Torsten Alberg wrote: "it was a tidal wave of all imagined or dreamed-of musical wonder. One was plunged into a kind of mental ecstasy and desired to hear nothing more when the sound of her voice had ceased. . . . In our memories remains the great talent with which Birgit Nilsson honors us. It belongs to the unforgettable."

In April and May 1952 in Copenhagen, the Swedish Week included guest appearances of the Royal Theater of Drama and the Royal Theater of Stockholm.

Along with some orchestra concerts in the Radio Hall and in Tivoli we were to give two performances of *Walküre* at the Royal Opera. Except for the internationally renowned tenor Torsten Ralf who sang Siegmund, the cast was that from the Stockholm Opera roster. I have never heard a singer with such fantastic head resonance as Torsten Ralf. All his tones lay like a string of pearls, forward in the "mask." I became absolutely addicted to this "cathedral" sound. This is how I wanted to sound! Ralf had an unusually large head, which most certainly contributed to making this phenomenal sound.

. . .

King Fredrik of Denmark was a great admirer of Wagner's music and a passionate conductor. He requested that Grevillius conduct the performance in Copenhagen. There was a rumor that the king had studied conducting under Grevilius; at any rate, the two knew one another well.

The king attended the orchestra rehearsals and at the premiere had his orchestra score on his lap. He was accompanied by Queen Ingrid and the queen mother, Alexandrine. *Die Walküre* had not been performed in Copenhagen for some time and the public received us with great enthusiasm. It was a wonderful success for the Stockholm Opera and its members. We were showered with flowers and crowned with praise. Banquets, reception by the crowned heads in the palace, evening invitations—all contributed to our relaxation and comfort. We Stockholmers were quite overcome by the hospitality and warmheartedness of the Danes. It was a happy, celebrated, and falling-over-tired ensemble that was returning to the—in every respect—cooler Stockholm.

The Danish reviews were effusive. In Stockholm I was often referred to as the successor to Britta Herzberg. Britta and her husband, Einar Beyron, also a famous singer, were beloved and unbelievably popular; they were known as the "lovebirds" of the opera. They often sang together in *Tannhäuser, Tristan, Lohengrin,* and so on. The very elegant couple was engaged by the advertising agencies to make exclusive products even more exclusive. Reading the newspaper, you might suddenly come upon: *The lovebirds of the opera always use Coryfin.* Perhaps there was still someone who didn't know Coryfin was a throat lozenge!

While in Stockholm I was compared with Britta Herzberg, in Copenhagen, I was said to be the top Wagnerian soprano, the successor to Kirsten Flagstad. Naturally, I was overwhelmed by being mentioned in the same breath as this shining star in the heaven of vocal artists.

After the guest performance in Copenhagen, a Danish writer who signed himself "H.V." wrote:

> But the greatest thing taking place on the stage was Birgit Nilsson, who sang Sieglinde. When one hears her fantastically large and golden soprano, there is simply no question about who will be the successor to Kirsten Flagstad as the world's leading Wagnerian soprano.

From Copenhagen I went directly to Helsingfors to appear as soloist in an orchestra concert. But it cost me great effort. I was suddenly extremely exhausted and breathing shallowly with pain in my right side.

Back at home I went to the hospital for X-rays but nothing disturbing was found. In the meantime, the pain became worse; at times I could move only by dragging myself over the floor. With the next X-ray the trouble was discovered. I had pleurisy and there was a spot on the lungs. Tuberculosis! Just when it seemed a fine career lay before me! Half of the right lung was grown together with the pleura.

Summer vacation had just begun and, as I did not want to stay in the sanatorium, I went home to Skåne. There I rested, took things easy, went for walks, and took disgusting medicine. At the beginning of the fall season I went back to Stockholm and put myself into the hands of a famous lung specialist, Torsten Bruce. The spot was smaller and I slowly began to do some rehearsing. Every inhalation was terribly painful. A singer with only one and a half lungs is extremely handicapped. I shall never forget the day on which I, tired but happy, succeeded in singing the whole role of Tosca. In spite of my handicap I did not cancel a single performance in the season.

A few years later Torsten Bruce published a book on tuberculosis in which he included an X-ray of my lungs with the following words: "This is the way healthy lungs should look." This was certainly a review with which I could be satisfied and for which I was very thankful.

In the spring of 1953 there was the Swedish premiere, in concert form, of Béla Bartók's opera *Bluebeard's Castle,* which would be broadcast over Stockholm's radio. The young Ferenc Fricsay, Hungarian-born and newly appointed head of RIAS Berlin, was the guest conductor. He had made a name for himself in a very short time as one of the most praised conductors in Europe. Bernhard Sönnerstedt, with his beautiful and well-trained baritone voice, sang Bluebeard and I sang Judith, his fourth wife. *Bluebeard's Castle* is actually a psychodrama. There is no action onstage; the dialogue between the two is sung quasi-recitative before a background of orchestral illustration. The increasing excitement in the music creates more and more tension until at last, the secrets that lie behind the seven doors are revealed. The seventh door opens into a mausoleum with all the earlier wives of the Duke. Judith does not share their fate. Bartok composed the opera in 1911, but the Hungarians considered the work to be unplayable. The first performance did not occur until 1918 at the Budapest Opera.

Ferenc Fricsay reminded one more of a Prussian than a charming Hungarian, and his instructions were often given with military sharpness. At one such time a French horn player felt it necessary to go against the wishes of the guest conductor. Fricsay immediately stopped the dress rehearsal and demanded that the player remove himself. The rest of the orchestra made it known to the conductor that in such an event they would all leave the podium. Fricsay put down his baton, said thank you, and left.

There was a moment of awkward silence until someone noticed the conductor, Kurt Bendix, sitting in the auditorium. Without hesitation he came up to the podium in his muffler and galoshes, and continued the rehearsal as though nothing had happened. He commanded a huge knowledge of the repertoire and there was a fair chance that the next day he would lead the first Swedish performance of this opera. However, the next day both Fricsay and the horn player were in their places.

A month later the same work was given a radio broadcast in Copenhagen with Lavard Friisholm, a Dane, as conductor. At the dinner after the concert the head of the radio station, Kai Aage Bruun, gave a speech in which he paid me one of the greatest compliments I've ever had: "Sweden can keep Skåne, Halland, and Blekinge (Swedish provinces that before 1658 belonged to Denmark), but we want Birgit Nilsson back."

Finally, after so many years of longing and expectation, I was going to sing Elisabeth in *Tannhäuser*. From my first year at the music academy it had been my dream to sing this role, and now the dream was to become reality. The opera was to be given a new production, which meant there would be sufficient and thorough rehearsal. Emil Pretorius, who during the period of National Socialism had done most of the stage settings for Bayreuth, was to be responsible for the scenery for *Tannhäuser*. Georg Hartmann from Munich was again invited for the stage direction and Sixten Ehrling would conduct. Conny Söderström was an inspiring Tannhäuser; Siw Ericsdotter, a colleague from the opera school, was a splendid Venus; Erik Sundquist, a noble Wolfram; and Elisabeth Söderström sang captivatingly the role of the shepherd.

I don't know whether it was from my own and others' high expectations or from the trouble in breathing that my impaired lung still gave me, but I was not at all satisfied with my performance. It was a stereotypical interpretation of the role and I had the feeling I was watching myself and smirking as I sang. Moses Pergament hit the nail on the head when he wrote in his review:

Birgit Nilsson shows an enormous development of her splendid voice but neither her acting nor her psychological identification with the role is enough for a believable characterization. This sometimes made itself felt in the singing.

It was not until several years later, when I sang the seductive Venus and the pure Elisabeth in the same performance, that I succeeded in capturing the innermost meaning of Elisabeth.

Somewhat later in the season Aase Nordmo-Løvberg debuted as Elisabeth and the critic Teddy Nyblom wrote the headline: A GREAT SINGER IS BORN. That this was no exaggeration can be attested to by anyone who had the joy of hearing her sing at the Stockholm Opera.

I spent the greater part of the summer of 1953 in Germany, singing the soprano part in Beethoven's Ninth Symphony in Bayreuth and six performances of *Fidelio* in the festival at Bad Hersfelder. The opera was given in the ruins of a medieval church. What an atmosphere for Beethoven's music! The church had been inadvertently burned by Napoleon's soldiers, who were using the sanctuary for their camp. The many intervening years had given the place a noble patina.

In the fall season there was a new role awaiting me: Isolde in Wagner's *Tristan und Isolde.* The premiere had taken place the past spring, with Britta Herzberg shouldering the mantle of Isolde for the last time. She had become the incarnation of Isolde, and it was undoubtedly difficult for her audience to see someone else in the role.

The first of September was the day of my first Isolde. In the spring I had studied the part for an entire month with Herbert Sandberg, the conductor. He was a knowledgeable and experienced coach; thanks to his help, I felt very confident with the role of the Irish Princess. Georg Hartmann, who did the stage direction, returned to rehearse with me. *This* time, thank God, I was well prepared for the part, the longest role in operatic literature. I was looking forward to the premiere with great joy. I felt as a racehorse must feel at the starting gate: ready for victory. A marvelous experience!

Set Svanholm was singing his sixty-seventh Tristan, and it was wonderful to go through this ordeal by fire with such an experienced partner. Margareta Bergström was Brangäne, Sigurd Björling was Kurwenal, and Sven Nilsson was King Marke, my betrayed husband. My instrument behaved well in all parts of the voice, and it was a marvelous feeling to sing. I believe in such moments the singer experiences the thrill of singing even more intensely than the audience.

One says the moving force behind Wagner's masterwork was his unfulfilled love for Mathilde Wesendonck. She was the one who furnished the inspiration for this magnificent love poem of Wagner's, a longing that goes through the work like a brilliant red thread, connecting the beginning to the end. In a letter to Mathilde Wesendonck, long after the passion had spent itself, he writes: "That I composed *Tristan* I give eternal thanks to you from the depths of my soul." Wagner was the eternal seeker after the perfect love, which he—fortunately—never found. Otherwise *Tristan* might never have been composed! I am deeply grateful to Wagner's unfulfilled search for perfect love.

My success as Isolde was complete and I can risk stating that I succeeded in every way to the utmost of my capability. Two great Isoldes, Nanny Larsén-Todsen and Britta Herzberg (as well as the great Brünnhilde, Irma Björck) were in the audience. A few days later, Hovsångerska Herzberg called me and congratulated me. She found it wonderful that I had not made a single mistake. The amazing thing about this artist was that she did not read music; therefore she was always impressed when someone commanded a role without any musical mistakes. Two more *Tristan* performances followed.

ACT 4

The twenty-sixth of September 1953 was a great day: I was to sing *Tosca* for the first time with Jussi Björling. I admired him endlessly and was afraid I would not be able to please him. God knows, one had heard of all the peculiarities of great singers, and I was certain Jussi would have many of his own. My fears proved to be unfounded. He was the most considerate and uncomplicated partner one could wish for, with a voice that mirrored the Swedish spring with fresh birch groves, blue sky, and dew-fresh grass. And beneath this smoldered an Italian fever like the lava of Vesuvius.

His voice serves as a model for singers all over the world. There are many tenors who try to emulate him by listening to his recordings. But what is the imitation worth? There was only one Jussi. He was tremendously generous toward his colleagues and saw to it, for example, that everyone got as many curtain calls as he did. When he felt he was being unfairly treated, however, it was advisable to stay out of his way.

As a very young man Jussi once sang in the choir of the Jakobs-Kirche where the choir director, the opera singer Set Svanholm, was keeping everything musically together, correcting the young tenor at one point. He made the suggestion that Jussi should sing in the correct tempo—a suggestion probably best left unsaid. Jussi, who was financially in the black that day, turned on his heels and went to the exit. In the door, he paused and with the impudence of a country bumpkin: "Get yourself a better tenor (*pause*) if you can find one!"

The *Tosca* performance went splendidly. When one sings as inspirationally, beautifully, and musically as Jussi, it carries over automatically to his partner and I believe I sang better than usual. It was quite clear that the audience had come mainly to hear Jussi. I therefore wanted to show that there was also someone else on stage who could sing. My father, Nils, came to Stockholm to hear Jussi in person. He was a great admirer of Jussi and had named one of his dogs after him. As the public responded to my aria with long, deafening applause, Nils turned to his neighbor and said with humor but not without pride, "You don't have to applaud, that's only my daughter up there."

In the spring of 1954 the opera *Salome* by Richard Strauss was to be given in a new production. It had not been performed in Stockholm since 1932. Sixten Ehrling was the conductor and Gören Gentele, who gave up the spoken theater in favor of the opera, was the stage director. The sets were by Stellan Mörner. It was planned that I would sing the Salome, but I was not at all happy about that and fought against it tooth and nail. Until then I had sung exclusively noble characters with epic breadth and seriousness. Here I would have to portray a fourteen-year-old animal disguised as human—with, however, by Strauss's own indications, the voice of an Isolde! Besides, I couldn't perform the twelve-minute-long Dance of the Seven Veils; my impaired lung could not bear that strain. I brought up all of the problems, but Gentele had a solution ready for each of my objections. I held fast to my decision not to sing Salome, but he was well known for his ability to wear one down. Every morning for two weeks he called at eight in the morning, using his considerable charm and even more considerable art of persuasion until I finally gave in.

To begin with, the vocal technique required a great adjustment. In order to sound like a young, innocent maiden, I had to sing Strauss's vocal line with a much slenderer tone than I was accustomed to. As to the musical interpretation, it was in those days a matter of using your own intuition and imagination. Today, with the tremendous number of recordings available, you can listen and decide which suits you best to imitate. This is a reliable method but one that nips in the bud any personal or artistic development.

The stage rehearsals with Gentele were unusual. He broke down all foregone conclusions we had—in my case, that I was not the right type for the role. He worked wonders! I practically lived at the opera house with the rehearsals lasting sometimes until midnight. Every step, every gesture was set. This precision was especially true in the two mimed scenes, which Gentele created like no stage director before him. In the one where Salome bends over the corpse of Narraboth, she smells blood; in that moment, a bloodthirsty desire is awakened in her and she knows then she wants the head of Jochanaan. The other scene takes place at the cistern to which Jochanaan has been returned after resisting all of Salome's seductive wiles. In a towering, hysterical frenzy that ends in erotic lust and gratification, Salome throws herself onto the cistern. We called this scene the "Brunnenszene," but my colleagues renamed it the "Brunstszene," or, Salome in heat.

The rehearsals with Ehrling and Gentele proved to be one of the most inspiring and worthwhile times of my career. We took almost two months for stage rehearsals and musical preparation and not one moment was superfluous or boring. A great contrast with the directors who have nothing artistic to offer; after a week of rehearsal, you've had enough. We had three stage rehearsals in costume and makeup, which is most unusual. This extra time gave us great confidence, which made it possible to give our utmost for the premiere.

Herodes was played by the best singing actor in the opera, Arne Hendriksen. Siw Ericsdotter portrayed the ungrateful role of Herodias, Sigurd Björling was, as Jochanaan, a steadfast proclaimer of the Word; Kerstin Meyer sang the Page; and Einar Andersson sang Narraboth.

After the curtain fell there was at first a long and almost uncomfortable silence. But then the applause broke forth and seemed never to end. The audience was clearly moved and left the hall shattered. Some fainted, some felt ill, and the wife of the minister of finance suffered a miscarriage that night. The perverse and depraved Salome got the blame for it all.

Birgit Cullberg choreographed the twelve-minute-long Dance of the Seven Veils. This is really an undertaking bordering on the impossible for a nondancer. When you think that a solo number for a professional dancer is seldom longer than three or four minutes, it was comforting to be relieved now and then by a trained dancer or a few ballerinas. Actually, it was rather embarrassing to be carried in on an enormous platter, sitting cross-legged, like a 150 lb. Buddha. As soon as I was recovered from my respiratory indisposition, I was able to perform the dance myself which I later did at La Scala, the Metropolitan, and the Teatro Colón in Buenos Aires.

One says that after Strauss and a good friend had attended Oscar Wilde's play *Salomé*, he was unusually quiet on the way home. The friend asked him eagerly, if he thought the play would make a good opera libretto. "Quiet," answered Strauss, "I'm already composing it." When one thinks what a stupendous gift Strauss had and how easily he expressed himself in music, you can imagine it did not take long for the completion of the 1905 opera.

Anna Oscár was the first Swedish Salome in 1908, when the opera was given in Stockholm. Following her was Signe Rappe, the daughter of the strict, religious minister of defense, general Rappe. In those days it was deemed highly inappropriate for a daughter of a good family to devote herself to the theater but the disillusioned father comforted himself with the thought: "If Signe must be an opera singer, then I'm glad she is at least making her debut in a religious opera." What the general said after attending her performance has not been handed down to us.

I certainly don't want to tire my readers with more lovely reviews, but I cannot resist quoting the last lines of the long review by Lennart Swahn for the paper *Arbetet:*

> [In] the midst of all this dramatic brew one is almost driven to call "STOP!" One wants to draw back and get a deep breath in order to be able to enjoy and absorb more. Spiritual involvement has its limits even when it comes out of the most musically beautiful sinner—Salome!

"Salome mania" was rampant in Stockholm. At the opera the rarely seen "Sold Out" light was switched on for every performance. Myrstedts Carpet Corner christened a new rug "Salome," which sold like hotcakes. Offers dropped like hail and the fans crowded together. King Gustav Adolf VI attended three performances. At first he came alone; the second time Queen Louise accompanied him; and the third time he brought with him Queen Ingrid of Denmark and Princess Sibylla. As the severed head of Jochanaan was delivered up out of the cistern on a silver platter I saw Queen Louise draw back in her seat and cover her eyes with her hands. It was exciting and gratifying to see so many members of Swedish royalty spontaneously and without obligation coming to the opera performances.

In this year I was awarded the title of Hovsångerska. Another joy of this *Salome* was an enormous flower arrangement sent to me from my first opera director and antagonist, Harald André. This lovely gesture he continued from then on at each of my Stockholm premieres until his death. Another milestone in this year of honors was performing with my first teacher and discoverer, Ragnar Blennow, in Hyland's *Carousel* in a radio broadcast.

"Salome mania" was just receding when the telephone-terrorist, Gentele, renewed his attacks. This time it was about *Carmen*, which was to come in the fall of 1954. Again at eight every morning for three weeks he talked about how fantastic I would be as Carmen under his direction. It was almost irresistibly flattering that he believed so completely in my talent. But this time I remained firm with my "Sorry, no." In the first place the role lies too low for my voice; if I endeavored to sing a part that sat mainly a minor-third lower than any other part in my repertoire, I risked losing the ease I had in my high voice. Moreover, I had so many engagements outside Sweden that I really could not accept this role. It was not easy, however, to decline the offer from the charming Gören Gentele.

The spring of 1954 was filled with engagements. In between the *Salome* performances I had guest appearances over all of Europe. Often I had four, sometimes five, big performances in one week. From the role of Salome I learned a great deal. The soft and mobile nature of the role caused my body to be freer and more relaxed, which resulted in my finding a deeper anchoring in the support musculature.

Between *Salome* performances I had two appearances in Brussels as soprano soloist in Verdi's *Requiem*. Upon my arrival I contracted a vicious cold and feared I would have to cancel. In my desperation I locked myself in a practice room and worked, thinking things through and observing my sensations. It was most important to protect the vocal cords, to use the head resonance to the maximum, to reduce tension in the neck and jaw (always a hangover from my student days), and to establish a connection between the deep support muscles and the breath. There must always be an air column that carries the tone into the mask, like a Ping-Pong ball bouncing on top of a fountain.

Fortunately I managed to get through both concerts with no problems. The change that my method of practicing wrought was probably not noticeable to most of the audience. Only an expert would have noticed that I sang more with my natural voice. All at once it was clear to me what to do! I had a new way of controlling the voice. Never again did any, and I mean *any*, teacher speak to me about support and breathing technique!

The Queen Mother Elisabeth was at the first concert in Brussels and I had the honor of visiting her in the royal box. Shortly before my departure, I spent almost my entire fee on a gorgeous, beautiful diamond ring for myself (I bought a nice tie for my husband). I thought I deserved this bit of validation after all the years of drudgery. Unfortunately the validation did not last long; the ring was stolen from my luggage during a flight from Munich.

After an engagement in Bayreuth as Elsa in *Lohengrin,* I went directly to Basel for a new production of *Tristan* with Günther Treptow, the famous German tenor, as Tristan. I sang three performances of Isolde, the first of many in the German language.

Back in Stockholm, interesting projects awaited me. Next were three performances as Isolde and three appearances in Beethoven's Ninth with Josef Keilberth conducting. Keilberth was not new to Stockholm; he had conducted the *Ring* and *Aida* the year before, in the fall of 1953. Moreover, I had just sung under his baton in Bayreuth. Keilberth was a singer's conductor; everyone loved to sing with him. He liked the modern concept of Wagner, which harmonized with the new Wagner-style in Bayreuth: more flowing tempi and a constant effort to let the singers come into their own.

There were three wonderful *Tristan* evenings. Set Svanholm was in splendid form, and to sing with Keilberth was to be in seventh heaven. He let the orchestra carry the singers instead of drowning them. Later I would often have the pleasure of singing in Munich with him.

Britta Herzberg had retired and I was assigned to take over the *Götterdämmerung* Brünnhilde. This is the longest and most difficult as well as the most wonderful of the three Brünnhildes in the *Ring.* December 13, 1954, was the premiere. Kurt Bendix conducted excellently. As with so many other operas, I had studied *Götterdämmerung* with him. The role demands not only a well-carrying top but a solid low and middle voice as well. Wisely, I avoided making the low tones louder with chest voice (very tempting, especially in the scene with Waltraute). But in this way my voice was just as fresh at the opera's end as at its beginning. In my diary I wrote: "I felt I could have sung the part again. Wonderful!"

Harald André was the stage director for the *Ring,* but I cannot for the life of me remember if I received any direction from him, and if so, what. What does remain in my memory is the final scene with my horse, Grane. In the dress rehearsal I stuffed the horse with sugar cubes so that he remained calm, but I forgot the sugar for the premiere. When the horse and I made our entrance and Grane realized I had no sugar cubes for him, he began to bite me. I held him fast by the halter, whereupon he

When Mother and Father were young.

I liked Karin from Gothenburg very much—she was supposed to be a one-time summer nanny, but she stayed many years on our farm until she married. Since I had no siblings, she became like an older sister to me.

My father, Nils, was once asked why he acquired all sorts of animals for the farm. "Because the little gal likes them," he said (a modified truth).

I grew up here, on the farm in Svenstad, in West Karup parish on the Bjär peninsula. It has been in our family since Skåne became Swedish territory, and I am the seventh generation descendant of its founder, Wahlberg, a cavalryman of Karl XII.

Long before I became a court singer I was a "Court" actress in a small amateur theater company in the neighboring parish of Hov (court). My most vivid memory is that there was a cat named Petrus, and that the man with the basket was my spurned suitor.

Even more vivid is my memory of Ragnar Blennov, my first voice teacher and "discoverer." Gradually he drew out my voice and self-confidence and got me to finally dare to apply to Stockholm's Music Academy.

Legendary Concert House director Johannes Norrby, a passionate spirit, guided me early by giving me career-enhancing concerts.

"Class photo" of the Opera Academy's 1946 performance. In addition to kapellmeister Kurt Bendix and director Ragnar Hyltén-Cavallius, there were many promising names in that class: Ingrid Eksell, Eva Prytz, Eva Gustavsson, Lilly Furlin, Ingeborg Kjellgren, Olle Sivall, Åke Collet, Gunnar Sandvold, Ebba Ragnarsson, and Karl-Olof Johansson—all became successful soloists.

An aspiring debutante in 1946, as Agatha in *Der Freischutz.* My own prologue was just as dramatic as Weber's opera, and the path to a triumphant premiere and media accolades was truly strewn with thorns. All the same, the Opera's directorship thought me "unmusical and untalented," and decided I would have to mature on the sidelines.

Here I am between two Opera directors, Set Svanholm (*left*) and, from Munich, Georg Hartmann (*right*), who was guest dramatic director in Stockholm. The man in the middle is just as interesting: my relative Sven Nilsson, who was a star in Dresden but came home during the war to continue a career at the opera that would last beyond his seventy-fifth birthday.

My first "important" concert took place at the Concert Association with director Tor Mann. He discovered me at a student recital when I sang Beethoven's *Ah Perfido* and Elizabeth's opening aria from *Tannhaüser.*

Elsa in *Lohengrin* was my debut role in Bayreuth in 1954. Wolfgang Windgassen sang the part of Lohengrin, and Ludwig Weber played the king. We would later meet many times on the legendary Wagnerian stage.

Astrid Varnay sang the role of Ortrud. This brilliant artist debuted at the Met astoundingly early at age twenty-two as Brünnhilde in *The Valkyrie.* At that age I was still pulling up turnips at home in Svenstad.

The charismatic Wieland Wagner, one of the Master's two grandsons who were rival directors in Bayreuth and made the festivals a pilgrimage site. Here he directs Brünnhilde in 1965's *Siegfried.*

Tristan and Isolde, Bayreuth, 1957, under Wolfgang Wagner's direction, with Wolfgang Windgassen as an unforgettable Tristan.

After Wieland's death, Wolfgang took over the responsibility for his brother's staging. Here Wolfgang thanks me and Martti Talvela after *Götterdämmerung* in Bayreuth, 1967.

The Met's 1959 *Tristan and Isolde* was honored as "The Best Show on Broadway," but the performance became legendary for another reason. Without warning, all three Tristan tenors fell ill, but Met director Rudolf Bing solved the problem: Ramon Vinay, Karl Liebl, and Alberto da Costa each sang an act—no Isolde has ever consumed so many Tristans in one night!

The handsome American Jess Thomas is one of my favorite Tristans. In the fall of 1971, we sang together at the Met in the most beautiful staging of *Tristan* I've ever experienced.

Aase Nordmo-Lovberg was a fine colleague and brilliant singer during the years we sang in Bayreuth together. Here she is as Sieglinde in 1960's *The Ring*, in which I played Brünnhilde. Thus we formed a Scandinavian colony.

Tosca in Zurich in the 1960s with Jussi as Cavaradossi. Here we both gave encores of our arias.

Beniamino Gigli also had a divine voice—it was absolutely phenomenal how a song flowed out of this sixty-year-old. The photo was taken at a guest performance at the Opera in 1952!

Richard Strauss' *Die Frau ohne Schatten* introduced me (as the Dyer's Wife) to the legendary Dietrich Fischer-Dieskau (as Barak) in a performance at the Deutsche Oper in Berlin. In addition to his celebrated book on Wagner and Nietzsche, he must hold some kind of record in album recordings.

An opera could be written about Met director Rudolf Bing. I worked with him for many years, and perhaps he enjoyed our sharpened verbal repartee and witty letters as much as I did. Signing a contract with Bing was an event to immortalize in a photo.

Music always sang inside the soul of director Karl Böhm. Not only was he an unparalleled Mozart and Strauss interpreter, but he was also a devoted Wagner conductor. Böhm was my favorite *Tristan* conductor. Here I share him with Leonie Rysanek in one of his rare moments of good humor.

Salome at the Met in 1965 with Karl Liebl as Herod. I first did the role in 1954 at the Stockholm Opera, after much hesitation. I was afraid of the arduous Dance of the Seven Veils. Through the years, Salome became a successful role—and the veils went like clockwork!

Beethoven's only opera, *Fidelio*, at a 1966 staging at the Met with the inspiring Jon Vickers as my husband, Florestan. Here I've just freed him from imprisonment in chains.

Tosca in 1968 at the Met, which became more and more my American "home." But I made my U.S. debut in 1956—in Hollywood! An impresario had heard my Salome on the radio and immediately invited me to sing in the enormous Hollywood Bowl concert arena, which seats 25,000—I had "only" 19,000 people in the audience at my American debut concert.

tried with his rear end to push me toward the orchestra pit. My husband, Bertil, who is a veterinarian, was sitting in the first row and his expert knowledge of animals told him what could happen. His face went white from fear. To distract Grane from his fixation about the sugar, I jumped around the stage with him during which antics I was singing the most difficult passages in the scene. Breathing a sigh of relief, I was able to steer my "colleague" to the wings where we were later to be swallowed up by the consuming flames of Valhalla. But I was not yet free of the horse; Grane was to come before the curtain to receive his well-earned applause. But then he was quiet. Someone had hung a sack of oats around his neck.

I shall never forget the final "Bravos" as I took my last call before the fire curtain. A large number of the audience in the parquet had departed. In the middle of the auditorium stood an elegant young man, who waved a white scarf at me and threw me hand kisses. After getting out of my costume and makeup and into my street clothes, I left by the stage exit. There he was, waiting for me. "Oh, Madame Nilsson," he swooned, "you were simply fantastic! Wonderful!"

"Thank you very much," I answered, flattered, "I'm glad my Brünnhilde pleased you so much."

"Yes, naturally," he hurried to answer, "but I have never seen a woman master a horse as brilliantly as you."

Before the rehearsals for Rolf Liebermann's *Penelope* were to begin in February 1955, I sang two guest performances out of the country: Donna Anna in Naples with Karl Böhm and the Vienna Staatsoper ensemble, and Elisabeth in *Tannhäuser* in Basel.

The first performance of *Penelope* was in summer 1954 in Salzburg, and within a few months the opera was performed on six other stages. March 17 was the date of the Stockholm premiere. The work is a so-called semi-seria-opera, which takes place in two ages: Antiquity and Modern Times. The protagonist, Penelope, appears in two forms. She is the Penelope of Homer's saga who faithfully awaits the return of Odysseus *and* she is the contemporary Penelope whose husband is declared lost in battle and assumed dead. Penelope has remarried but one day receives the news that her husband was a prisoner of war and is on his way home. The present husband persuades her to go to the marketplace to greet her first husband, but there she receives the news that he has died on the way home. Overwhelmed with guilt she returns to her second husband, who meanwhile has committed suicide. Desperate, Penelope sinks to the floor where she sings a very difficult and demanding aria.

In the part taking place in Antiquity, Odysseus returns but is only a phantom. He died on his journey and his return is the product of human imagination. Art can explain and release, soothe and heal. The creator of this gently worded, rather confusing libretto was Heinrich Strobel. The composer, Rolf Liebermann, was strongly influenced by twelve-tone music, although not pedantically so. He makes great demands on the voice and his vocal writing almost approaches the unsingable. More than once I saw black before my eyes at the big dramatic outbursts. In the study of this awkward role of Penelope, which in performance does not sound so difficult as it is, my perfect pitch stood me in good stead—plus my well-developed feel for mathematics.

Sixten Ehrling was competent and always well prepared, as was Birger Bergling, who designed the sets and costumes. Bengt Peterson could finally prove his ability as a clever, thoughtful, and exciting stage director.

Liebermann and his wife came to the premiere. After the performance all the participants gathered at our home in Lindingö, where we celebrated until early in the morning. Later, whenever I met Liebermann anywhere, he always referred to how lovely it was for him and his wife in Stockholm. He was head of the Hamburg Opera and later worked in Paris. I sang often under his aegis, particularly in Hamburg.

The next new role, the *Walküre* Brünnhilde, was also in the spring of 1955 and I accepted it reluctantly. This meant I would never again sing Sieglinde, a role I truly loved. I actually shed a few tears when I had to say farewell to Sieglinde in favor of Brünnhilde. Sixten Ehrling was the conductor and everyone who was new to his role received an orchestra rehearsal for his or her scenes. Exactly eight minutes before the end, the players put their instruments down, as the scheduled time for the rehearsal had come to an end. Ehrling thought, rightly so, that it would be better to stay on for eight minutes instead of calling another rehearsal the morning of Easter Saturday. Not one of the musicians was in favor of remaining. Maybe they thought the extra rehearsal of eight minutes was an empty threat. But it wasn't. On the Saturday before Easter, a regular rehearsal was held, a slap on the wrist for the orchestra.

It was a fresh, new quartet taking on this *Walküre:* the conductor Sixten Ehrling, Aase Nordmo-Løvberg as Sieglinde, Bette Björling as Fricka, and I as Brünnhilde. This production was said to be the best that Stockholm had heard in a long time.

I soon learned to love Brünnhilde as much as I had loved Sieglinde and I sensed that the three Brünnhildes in the *Ring* were right for my voice and temperament. But I did have two more opportunities to sing Sieglinde: in 1957 at Bayreuth, and in 1974 at the Metropolitan Opera.

. . .

One day there was a knock on the door of the opera director, Berglund. There stood an Italian who said he was a tenor and would like to audition. He had no special references other than that he had studied voice and was working for the ASEA. After his audition, Berglund asked him what role he wanted to sing. "Cavaradossi in *Tosca* with Birgit Nilsson and then die," he answered in broken Swedish. There really were a number of *Tosca* performances in which I sang with this tenor, Luigi Carrara, and when *Turandot* was put back into the repertoire he proved to be the only tenor who could negotiate the role of Calaf.

In the beginning Carrara was well received by the critics and the public. Naturally he had to fight with the pronunciation of Swedish and, of course, he had not learned to act at the ASEA. But he was wonderfully endowed vocally and had a splendid top. In addition, Carrara was a singer you could count on, as opposed to all the "civil servant" singers whose principal work was collecting a paycheck. Carrara had difficulty in meeting the high standards of the opera so, instead of helping him over a few stumbling blocks, a few know-it-alls began to use him as a scapegoat. Unable to ignore the abuse and to overcome his problems, he actually became the kind of singer the harsh critics and indifferent musical staff had claimed him to be all along. That is just *one* example of many hopeful singers who, because of a lack of direction and support, lose their self-confidence and whose development comes to a standstill. But what opera house interests itself in the development of singers? The trial-and-error method is so much easier.

In a *Tosca* performance in December 1955, when Luigi Carrara was still thought to be of international star quality, we had a guest Scarpia, an African American baritone by the name of Lawrence Winters, who the public (especially the ladies) and the critics said was a knockout. After his first guest appearance as Rigoletto, every performance was sold out. What a singer! What an actor! His voice was mellow as well as intense; he did not lose vocal quality in the nuances he brought to his singing; and his stately appearance was as arresting as his voice. Like a wild panther, he was ready at any moment to pounce upon his victim, Tosca. In the midst of the seduction scene (I feared every second that he would break my ribs) I could not avoid noticing the strong smell of alcohol on his breath. I learned later why. A Swedish impresario had invited Winters to dinner before the performance. Without knowing the alcohol content of the Swedish potato brandy, he washed down the typical Swedish "Smörgåsbord" with quite a few glasses of this noble drink.

He was also impressive as Amonasro in *Aida*. Unfortunately a terrible thing happened to me here. As the winter was extremely cold I had put on heavy long underwear, which I intended later to exchange for something of lighter weight that I had in my dressing room—I thought. But there was no lighter-weight underwear to be found. The heavy underwear was much too thick to be worn with my tight-fitting Aida costume. So! Without underwear! The role of Aida requires, of course, that one is made up dark-skinned. As the costume was ankle-length I thought it unnecessary to make up my feet and legs as one only saw my feet. Besides, I did put on a pair of dark brown stockings (*Author's note:* the practical pantyhose had not yet come on the market). Naturally, I had not reckoned with Winters's vehemence. At one point he threw me across the stage with such force that my dress flew over my head. There I lay with my brown-stockinged legs and naked white posterior! In the intermission Winters came to me and begged my pardon. He was in despair and said that if he'd only known that I was without panties he would have kept his enthusiasm to a minimum. But how could he have known?

That was the first and last time I went onstage without underwear.

In the spring of 1956 Set Svanholm, Sigurd Björling, and I had a great success in Hamburg with a Wagner concert. The public went crazy and we had to repeat almost every number. On the way back Svanholm asked me about my schedule and complained that I sang too seldom in Stockholm.

"Have no fear, if you were the opera director, I would stay at home with you," I joked.

"You would swear to that?" he asked.

"Indeed, but there is no Bible on the plane so we will have to wait," I answered. The next day my eyes almost fell out of their sockets from astonishment. In the paper was the news that Set Svanholm had been made director of the Stockholm Opera.

The end of April that year, Set Svanholm and I were invited to sing at the dedication of the new opera house in Düsseldorf. Beethoven's *Fidelio* was chosen for the opening performance. The role of Fidelio was, at that time, only the second part I had not sung first in Stockholm.

A month later the Stockholm Opera presented a guest performance of *Walküre* in Wiesbaden's May Festival. New to the ensemble was Sven Nilsson as Hunding and Kerstin Meyer as Fricka. Even though the critics thought the sets and costumes a bit worn, they had only superlatives for the singers and orchestra. When Set Svanholm became director of the opera, he wanted to present me in a new role and asked me what I would like to sing. I thought about it a few days. Of course there were a lot of interesting roles to consider but the problem was that I could not see when I would have time for doing a new production. Then Sandburg came to the rescue with the idea of the title role in Puccini's *Turandot.* The role is vocally demanding but short. Turandot has nothing to sing in act 1.

"That will do very well," I said, innocently, "it seems just right for me and I can even rest a little." I did not know then that Turandot is known as a real voice-killer in the opera repertoire.

I took the piano score to Rome and between *Fidelio* performances I studied *Turandot* in Swedish with an Italian coach. He tore his hair in desperation over the Swedish, which he said totally destroyed the beautiful line of Puccini's music. (Later in my career I sang *Turandot* not only in Swedish but in Italian and German. The latter sounds even worse than the Swedish.)

Four days before the dress rehearsal I got back home. The Princess Turandot is a rather static role. The entire second act she stands majestically on the top of the long stairs (in Stockholm these were narrow and wobbly as a henhouse ladder) and tosses out throat-wrenching high tones. Much of the opera could be rehearsed without my presence.

The production was old and worn-out. The staging was taken over by Bengt Petersson, with Herbert Sandberg conducting. The dress rehearsal went off uneventfully and it felt good to ring out all those high notes in a big hall. After the second act, Svanholm came onstage. He looked happy and satisfied. Then suddenly a member of the chorus, a tenor, called out, "We want another Turandot!" Svanholm was embarrassed and went to the chorus to see what their complaint was.

"We are all going to come down with colds," said the tenor. "The way Birgit sings, we're all going to freeze!"

From the acting point of view *Turandot* does not present a colorful spectrum but works better as a fresco in black and white. The libretto is taken from an old Chinese story about a cruel princess who, after putting to death many suitors, finds herself at last with her coldness melting, in the heat of fiery passion. The cold and unfeeling character of Turandot is mirrored in the second act in the vocal part, which requires tones like sharpened steel but which, after the kiss of Prince Calaf, changes in color to the warm vulnerable sounds of love and pity.

Luigi Carrara sang the role of Calaf beautifully and the gratifying role of Liu was shared by Eva Prytz and Elisabeth Söderström, both ideal for this part. The blind Timur was song by Folke Jonsson with power and warmth. The premiere was a rousing success, and the "Sold Out" lights blazed again. The king and queen were in their loge, which incidentally is one of the worst places in the house, from the standpoint of acoustics and visibility. The critics painted us in the most glittering colors. I had no idea then that I would be responsible, at least in part, for giving a rebirth to Puccini's last opera in both Europe and America.

ACT 5 (FIRST FINALE)

It became more and more difficult to do all that Set Svanholm expected of the singers under contract. Offers streamed in from all parts of Europe and now there was interest from America. In 1956, I appeared at the Hollywood Bowl (an open-air stage with twenty thousand seats) and at the San Francisco and Chicago operas. In addition, I managed a few months for a guest engagement in Buenos Aires. The Stockholm Opera began to see that it was going to be difficult to keep this bird in its cage. Therefore they suggested that I take a guest contract instead of a full engagement. Even this compromise did not appeal to me; I wanted to be totally free.

Many of the artists at the opera, before and after me, asked to be given leave for either a shorter or longer time. When one weighed the advantages and disadvantages, the future for a "freelancer" did not appear too rosy. It was always comforting to come back "home," where there was a nice pension awaiting one in what might be the not too distant future. Naturally I had not completely given up this somewhat mercenary way of thinking.

The competent and experienced finance manager at the opera thought it was obvious that I would have a pension no matter what my decision. This news made me very happy. I thanked him and bowed and left thankful for the benevolence showed me: the assurance of a pension and singing for a mini-fee.

After singing sixteen years as guest, and having reached the required age for a pension in Sweden, I heard nothing about a pension from the opera. I made contact with the pension office, which by then had other people in charge. In fact, the former opera director, as well as the finance officer, had died. Gören Gentele, who was the present director, stood like a living question mark as I asked for the promised pension. Gentele left the matter in the hands of the current finance officer, Gunnar Sträng, who, gawking over his glasses, muttered, "There can be a question whether Birgit Nilssen should receive a pension? Such nonsense I have never heard."

Today I feel happy that in all the many years as guest I was the big draw for the opera, with sold-out performances and elevated prices the norm. One may assume, then, that I did not put too great a burden on the opera's skimpy budget.

RUDOLF BING

Of all the opera directors with whom I have worked during my career, Rudolf Bing was the most effective. He was exact and he was strict, especially during my first years at the Metropolitan. He had no patience with prima donna antics but held fast to his rules and regulations. Everything was planned down to the last detail in advance. Probably a reminder to send Christmas greetings was written in his calendar in May.

For example, one knew in April when rehearsals were going to be scheduled for the following February! This is unheard-of even in the opera world, where planning well in advance is routine. Bing did not have the common touch; he could be spiteful and arrogant, and as he never revealed his private life he was not a favorite with the press. If there was dirty linen to be washed, it would not be in public.

Every morning he took the subway from Central Park South to West 39th and Broadway. He wore an elegant, perfectly tailored suit and the obligatory bowler on his head, his briefcase under his arm. He looked exactly like a British banker who had given the Rolls-Royce and the chauffeur the day off. He had won his battle with Oxford English and there remained not a trace of an Austrian accent. He moved with purposeful strides, looking neither left nor right. Anyone thinking they could stop him long enough to make small talk saw their chances fade as he strode by. (Whenever a wall of autograph seekers was looming before me, I tried Bing's method. It worked every time.)

To tell the truth, Rudolf Bing was not so hard and inhuman as he wanted to appear. He enjoyed saying, "Under my forbidding appearance beats a heart of stone." I doubted this appearance of hardness, however; if he were so cold, why did he blush so easily? And he did blush on occasion. He was a good-looking man, aristocratic, slim, fine-limbed, with a noble profile and a beautifully shaped head. He had a sharp mind and a good sense of humor—two characteristics not typical of unfeeling people.

Rudolf Bing was born in 1902 in Vienna. The Viennese claim his father was a coal dealer. Bing said he was the son of a business manager of a steel factory, and we can assume he knew best. His schooling was often interrupted and he tried to develop his various artistic talents, which extended to painting as well as to singing. This avenue did not lead where he had hoped, and for a time he ended up working in a bookstore to support himself. In this bookstore there was also a theater agent. After a short and unlucky stop in the film world (as assistant to none other than Max Reinhardt), he became business manager for the famous actor, stage director, and opera director Carl Ebert at the Städtische Oper in Berlin. That went very well until the day in 1933 that both Bing and Ebert were ordered by the Nazis to give up their positions. At first, Bing foolishly tried to collect what was due him contractually. But once he saw the SA troops on the streets, openly taking Jews prisoner and dragging them away, he quickly returned to Vienna. There his family cared for him and his young wife, the Russian ballerina Nina Schelemskaya-Schelesnaya.

One day Bing received a letter from Fritz Busch, the famous conductor who had been in Berlin as guest conductor during Bing's time Ebert's business manager. Busch had received a letter from a wealthy Englishman by the name of John Christie. This gentleman owned a large estate about sixty miles south of London called Glyndebourne. There he had built a small opera house for his talented wife, the young Canadian singer, Audrey Mildmay. And now within a few months, Mr. Christie wanted to arrange a Mozart festival. Christie had succeeded in getting Carl Ebert to do the staging and once Bing had considered the situation carefully, the two of them plunged into their work with great enthusiasm.

During Hitler's regime in Germany, it was not difficult to persuade singers to come to Glyndebourne. In the first year Bing had no special title, but functioned as jack-of-all-trades. He did everything from picking up singers from the train station to throwing himself into the Dragon's costume for *Magic Flute* performances. Soon, however, he became not only director of the Glyndebourne Festival; he also founded and was artistic director of the Edinburgh Festival. In 1949 he was named general manager of the Metropolitan Opera in New York. Bing's career shot up as straight as his own posture.

Even before my debut at the Metropolitan, Bing had secured my services for the 1960–61 season. I was contracted to sing Turandot, Fidelio,

Brünnhilde and one performance of Senta in *The Flying Dutchman*. Unlike myself (honestly) he predicted my future success and wanted to be sure he had me under contract. But that my success would be as great as it proved to be, not even the self-confident Bing had anticipated.

Three days after the *Tristan* premiere in 1959, Bing asked to meet me as soon as possible in my hotel. It concerned an important additional clause in my contract. My hotel was besieged by reporters and photographers, but naturally the general manager had precedence. He took out his copy of my contract and asked me to sign the additional clause. I read it and broke out in laughter. I read that so long as I was under contract at the Met I was forbidden to sing in any nightclubs or other obscure places. Also, I could not accept any film offers without the approval of the Metropolitan Opera. Mr. Bing had already seen several of his singers, eager for greater fame and fortune, take engagements in Las Vegas and similar places. Recent defectors included among others the Wagnerians Lauritz Melchior and Helen Traubel. As I recovered from my surprise, I explained with somewhat exaggerated hilarity that even though the idea of singing in striptease joints or nightclubs did not interest me, I would not consider *signing away* my right to do so. I suggested that he should not doubt my character and my sound judgment.

The press had called the new production of *Tristan und Isolde* "The Best Show on Broadway," and the storm of ticket-seekers confirmed their view. Tickets were sold on the black market and the lines at the box office reached all the way around the opera house. On the day of the third performance Mr. Bing called me, awakening me from my vocal beauty sleep. "Mr. Vinay is ill," he said. Naturally I was disappointed but pointed out we were fortunate to have Mr. Liebl, who had rescued the premiere.

"Yes, but he is also ill," Bing answered.

"And so we are not having a performance?" I asked, seeing immediately the possibility of a free evening and more time to rest the voice after all the excitement and stress the premiere had occasioned.

"No, there will be a performance in any case," Bing assured me. He seemed actually to be in a good mood on the telephone as he explained to me that the boys were not so sick that they could not sing one act each: "Vinay will sing the first act, Liebl the second and the stoutest I have saved for the last, so that Miss Nilsson will have a soft body to sink onto after the Liebestod: da Costa sings act 3."

The last idea was actually a necessity, as da Costa only knew act 3! I was certainly curious about the outcome of this arrangement—three different lovers in one evening—and I hoped the newspapers would not get wind of it. How naïve a simple girl from Skåne can be! Naturally Bing had informed every reporter and photographer in New York and the outlying counties. They all had to have a picture of Isolde extending the Love Potion to three Tristans. The three tenors were embarrassed and hesitant about posing together (and no wonder!) but there was no way out. As Tristan wears the same costume in the first two acts, Mr. Liebl appeared in the photo wearing a cape with stand-up collar. Each of the tenors made a point of informing the press that *he* was the one really indisposed. Mr. Bing wrote in his memoirs:

> In *Tristan,* Birgit Nilsson celebrated one of the greatest triumphs in Metropolitan's history. . . ."
>
> When the house lights went down, before the music began, I came onto the stage and was greeted by a great moan from all corners of the house—the General Manager appears only to make the most important announcements, and everyone thought he knew that this announcement had to be: Miss Nilsson has canceled.
>
> So I began by saying, "Ladies and Gentlemen, Miss Nilsson is very well," which brought a sigh of relief from almost 4,000 people. Then I went on: "However, we are less fortunate with our Tristan. The Metropolitan has three distinguished Tristans available, but all three are sick. In order not to disappoint you, these gallant gentlemen, against their doctors' orders, have agreed to do one act each. Fortunately the work has only three acts." And there was a roar of laughter. Never has *Tristan und Isolde* started so hilariously.

The premiere of *Tristan* had already occasioned so much publicity in the principal newspapers of the world that the Three-Tristan performance could not possibly compete. Still, one headline announced: "Swedish Soprano Uses One Tristan per Act or One Isolde = Three Tristans."

After the New Year's celebration with good friends in Palm Beach, it was time to return to New York for the next *Tristan* on January 9th, a Saturday matinee. This was one of the beloved radio broadcasts from the Metropolitan, which reached between 75 and 100 million listeners. In the intermissions the sponsor of the broadcasts, Texaco, presented programs that were interesting as well as educational. There were interviews with various artists, discussions about music and opera, the Opera Quiz, and much more. These Saturday broadcasts were greatly sought after by the singers. Such a broadcast reached a tremendous public, larger than you could reach in a whole career of only stage performances. Therefore it was most important to get at least one broadcast in the season. I had the good fortune, without putting any pressure on the management, to sing in no fewer than three broadcasts.

On Friday, the day before the matinee, Mr. Bing asked Bertil and me to come to his office. He had something important to discuss with me. In the spring, when the Met's regular season ended, they went on tour to many of the big cities in the United States and Canada. These tours reached from Dallas and Atlanta in the South to Chicago and Toronto in the North. Sets, props, technical personnel, secretaries, coaches, directors, orchestra, chorus, and ballet traveled by train to the various cities. In some cases the stars were permitted to take a plane. For many of the company members this was a time they looked forward to, almost like a vacation. One learned about other cities and other customs. One was welcomed everywhere, and every city took great pains to see that everyone was comfortable. In addition, the salaries were considerably higher than those for New York performances.

A new production of *Turandot* was scheduled for me in the following season and all the tour cities expressed a desire to have Franco Corelli and me perform in that opera in the 1961 tour. This suggestion did not appeal to me at all, as it meant I would not be in Europe until the end of May. By then the spring in Sweden is past and there is nothing in the world to compare with a Swedish spring. No, I absolutely did not want to go on the tour. Bing took his art of persuasion to a new level; when that did not work, he offered me the staggering sum (compared to the Met's fees then) of $3,000 per evening. The highest fee the Met paid at that time was $1,000 dollars per evening, and only a handful of singers commanded that fee. Most of the artists were on a weekly salary that varied greatly but never went over $1,000 dollars a week.

Maria Callas, for example, received more than $1,000 per performance. They agreed on $1,001 in cash and Bing gave instructions to pay in one-dollar bills. Callas's husband, Mr. Meneghini, had demanded this extra dollar and Bing thought it served him right to get it all in one-dollar bills.

With his offer of $3,000, Bing assumed he had won me over. But I put my cards on the table and explained to him that the money in this instance played no part in my decision. If that were the case I would have accepted the offer for a concert tour that paid $4,000 dollars per evening with a minimum of twenty concerts. Mamma Mia! *That* I should never have mentioned. There followed an explosion of such unbelievable proportions, I feared Bing would have a heart attack. His face became purple and he fought for breath. He forgot his lovely Oxford English and roared,

"So eine Schweinerei!" (What a dirty trick!) in genuine Viennese dialect. He threatened to make a scandal in all the papers, declaring that I was blackmailing the Metropolitan!! I got up and left his office without a word, deciding to take the next convenient flight back to Sweden and leave Bing and his performances to fate. I was furious and offended; I certainly had not blackmailed anyone and it seemed utterly impossible to continue any relationship with Mr. Bing.

I asked Bertil to book us on the next flight to Stockholm. But men!! First they hem and haw about whether it is worthwhile to be angry before they pound their fist on the table. In the most businesslike tone he asked what I hoped to gain by keeping to my resolve to leave. He pointed out that I certainly did not wish to have a reputation at this point in my career as a scandal-provoking prima donna. There were enough of those around. In short: I stayed on to sing my Isolde the following day. But I laid a few more coals on the fire when it came to the "Curse" in act 1 and I sang: "Vengeance! Vengeance! Death to us both!" It seems Mr. Bing took this tempest rather personally. The next day I received a bottle of champagne with a card quoting a line from *Tristan:* "Now let us drink to peace."

I wrote in my diary after our clashing: ". . . had a fight with Bing about the tour. Was depressed and had a terrible headache."

On the day following the *Tristan* I wrote: "I did not feel in form vocally but had great intensity." You can say that again!

So Bing got his way. I went on the tour and I felt very comfortable in the easy camaraderie of my fellow artists. We were all more or less dependant upon one another. Even Bing retreated from his usual standoffishness and I got to know him more personally. At premieres and official dinners he often escorted a pretty ballerina from the ensemble. His wife, Nina, was rarely present and never accompanied him on the tour.

In Dallas it was unbearably hot. Most singers would not risk going into the pool for fear of vocal indisposition but I, from the sun-starved North, took no heed and threw myself into the cool water at every opportunity.

One afternoon when the thermometer hit 102 degrees Fahrenheit, one of the loveliest of the prima donnas came to the pool. Obviously she was aware that Mr. Bing was present, as she wore a superelegant ensemble in the latest fashion: large-brimmed hat, huge earrings, matching handbag and shoes with yard-high heels, and *gloves!* In addition she was in theater makeup, including false eyelashes. I have the injudicious habit of speaking before thinking and called out, "Anna, take off those gloves and jump in!" Bing almost fell into the pool himself from laughing.

Franco Corelli sang Calaf. He was, if such were possible, more anxious about his voice than any other tenor I have known. For example, he refused to sing in an air-conditioned opera house. It disturbed me to hear this, because it was possible that to appease Corelli they might shut off the air-conditioning. I reminded Bing that my costume weighed about thirty pounds and that I was risking my life to sing this voice-killer role in the heavy costume in the intense heat. He calmed me down, saying as soon as Corelli began to sing, the air-conditioning would be turned on. And he assured Corelli that the climate control would be shut off. I have no idea whom he fooled, Corelli or me, but I do know that I perspired dreadfully on that evening.

In Philadelphia, Corelli discovered that my dressing room had a piano and his did not. Bing, who had made it his life's goal to satisfy all of Corelli's wishes, came to me and hesitatingly asked if I would allow the piano to be moved to Corelli's dressing room. "Gladly," I said, "but I have absolutely no time to give him piano lessons."

Another time, in Memphis I believe, Bing asked me to be especially friendly and considerate toward Corelli as his dog had become very sick the previous night and Bing was forced to call the veterinarian at three in the morning. "Mr. Bing," I answered, "I'm beginning to ask myself if it wouldn't be preferable to be a dog in your opera company instead of a singer."

Once in Cleveland, Corelli, was feeling indisposed on the day of an *Aida* performance and feared he would have to cancel. Bing was nervous as he was not exactly overstaffed with cover tenors. And who could jump in for the world's best tenor? Besides, the public would be greatly disappointed. On the morning of the performance Bing decided that he and his assistant, Robert Herman, would appear in pajamas with lighted candles in their hands; awakening Corelli, they would fall on their knees before his open door. They took the elevator to the eighth floor, rang the bell, and fell on their knees, the lighted candles in their hands. Suddenly the door opened, revealing an angry old lady with curlers in her hair. As she saw these two little angels, she lost it, clutched at her heart, and called alternately for God and the police. It took some time to quiet the old lady, after which the opera directors went down to the seventh floor where they repeated the procedure. In their haste they had gone one floor too high on their first try.

In Chicago there was a critic by the name of Claudia Cassidy. She was known for her idiosyncratic musical taste and could be nasty when the spirit moved her. The only singers who found her ear sympathetic were Italian tenors. At *their* sound, she melted like a snowball in hell. The

Metropolitan gave a guest performance in Chicago and Mme. Cassidy tore the Met to pieces, especially the general manager, Rudolf Bing. On the day after the massacre the two met by accident on the street. Bing assumed a surprised expression and purred most charmingly, "Oh, Madame Cassidy, how nice to see you. . . . I was not aware that you were in town."

President Johnson wanted his wife, Lady Bird, to attend a performance of the Metropolitan Opera. She was invited to join Mr. Bing in his box (an honor that we singers seldom, if ever, enjoyed). She had just taken her seat when the entire audience rose and greeted her with thunderous applause. Lady Bird rose and gracefully accepted the acknowledgment of the public. At this moment Bing saw that Lady Bird had a very uncomfortable chair and used the opportunity to exchange the chair for a better one. He quickly took the chair away but she sat down before he could get the new chair in place, and she disappeared from the eyes of the public! It was said that Lady Bird took the unfortunate incident in stride but the Secret Service was not so gracious.

Shortly thereafter Bing wanted to speak with me about a contract renewal for the coming year. As usual he wanted me for many more performances than I was able to give him.

"The public will get tired of me if I sing so often," I said in my defense.

"As long as you sit with me, you need not worry about that," he answered.

I remembered suddenly the incident with Lady Bird and reminded him that sitting on the chair *he* offered was not necessarily the safest place to be. Bing blushed and laughed heartily, pleased by my barb.

Over time we became good friends. Bing knew that I was (like most Swedish singers) very disciplined and did my work with no unnecessary waves. He was once asked if it was difficult to work with me. His reply: "Not at all, one has to simply put in enough money and out comes wonderful music."

Rudolf Bing did not always have it easy. One of his great prima donnas, the wonderful Renata Tebaldi, made the demand that he stage Cilea's *Adrianna Lecouvreur* for her when she returned to the Met. Bing was reluctant but gave in to the demand. A few weeks before the premiere, Tebaldi canceled and remained in Italy. This was a real blow for Bing and we all sympathized with him. At that time I was in Paris. We had bought a home there and, as usual in France, there were various legal difficulties. I sent a telegram to Bing, saying I would arrive one day later than expected because matters concerning the house purchase needed to be cleared up. I received an answer from Bing that he expected me on the scheduled day—period. I knew that the rehearsal was not of great importance. It was a piano rehearsal for Elisabeth and Venus in *Tannhäuser*. I knew my roles and no other singer was involved; therefore I remained in Paris. When I arrived, as I had said, one day late, there was no bouquet from Bing for me and he did not let me hear from him. After four days came the bouquet of roses with a card: "Sorry the flowers are so late, but are we not all tardy sometimes?"

Remembering the Tebaldi incident, I sent a thank-you note: "Thank you very much for the wonderful roses. Do not waste time regretting that they were late. Better late than never."

Many of us hoped that the old Met would still stand as a theater and not be torn down to make way for a new skyscraper. We signed petitions and contributed money to rescue the Met. In fact, Bing was quite critical of all our activity. He did everything he could to further the destruction of the old Met, perhaps fearing there could be competition between the new Met at Lincoln Center and another opera company in the old building. He got his wish. The old Met is no more.

I believe it was a shock for him when they moved the Met into the new house at Lincoln Center. Everything seemed so terribly large and spacious, so strange and cold. In the old Met, everything and everyone was within arm's reach, so to speak. In the new house it took an eternity to get from one department to another. Some months after moving in, there were two rooms discovered without doors, completely walled up. Good thing no one was inside!

When he moved into the new house Bing was sixty-four, and it was probably the last time he would make such a gigantic change. More than once in my dressing room he wept in regret that he had not said farewell when the old Met disappeared.

I will not say that Bing became less good as general manager. On the contrary, he became different, more human. He realized he could not hold the reins so tightly as he once had done. He gave his coworkers more responsibility, which made them less dependent upon him. But he always accepted full responsibility for the mistakes made by others. Rudolf Bing was a genuine director, from head to toe.

Karajan had not been invited to conduct at the Met because of his Nazi past. Meanwhile he had directed and conducted his own *Ring* production in Salzburg, and he entertained the hope of conquering the New

World by doing a similar *Ring* production at the Met. Bing was interested and invited me to portray the Brünnhilde in this *Ring* but I wanted nothing to do with it. I had had more than enough of Karajan in Vienna with his eternal lighting rehearsals. As they said in Vienna, time, money and people were wasted to satisfy Karajan's hobby. My relationship with him was clouded, anyway, by my having had the unbelievable insolence to decline some of his offers—among others, the *Elektra* in Salzburg. When Bing stipulated that I would be cast as Brünnhilde, Karajan telegraphed, "O.K., assuming that she still has a voice."

I was then forty-eight years old and at the peak of my career. Sometimes circumstances make it difficult to sing, but when one feels unwelcome, it is insufferable. In an interview I was asked why I didn't wish to sing in Karajan's *Ring*. I answered, "Only happy birds sing and in Karajan's *Ring* this bird would not be happy." Bertil too thought I should not allow myself to be persuaded. He had vivid memories of how unhappy I was during all the meaningless rehearsals in Vienna.

There followed a fervent exchange of letters and telegrams between Bing and me concerning the Karajan *Ring*. A large part of this correspondence Bing has covered in his memoirs. Among other things he wrote me that he hoped I knew that he, of course, preferred me to Karajan—to which I cordially replied that I, rest assured, preferred Bing to Karajan.

At my next guest performance Bing came to my dressing room with Karajan's contract in his hand. "In a word," he asked, "yes or no? If you say no, I'm tearing up Karajan's contract." At that I was plagued with feelings of guilt. The Metropolitan had not mounted a new *Ring* for an eternity. Should I be the one to deprive them of? Bing won out, as usual.

When Karajan came he succeeded in creating the greatest possible confusion in the rehearsal schedule. In one blow he threw out the time-honored system that had been strictly adhered to. One had to sit around all day now, waiting to find out whether a particular scene would be rehearsed. At this time I had some *Tosca* performances to sing, which the Met rehearsal department took into consideration in their planning of *Walküre* rehearsals. But not Karajan! The most strenuous orchestra rehearsals were often scheduled on a day when I had a *Tosca* performance, or on the day before. This meant simply that I missed the rehearsal.

The stage could not be dark enough to suit Karajan (most of the time this was called a lighting rehearsal). Bing sat in the auditorium often, attempting to make sense out of it all. Finally he would leave, shaking his head and saying, "I can make it that dark in a second with the main switch."

On the evening of the premiere I found on my dressing table a large package. It contained an actual miner's helmet with a red light at the front and reflectors on the sides and two tightly mounted little wings, as on a *Walküre* helmet. The sender wished to remain unknown, but the interest in the helmet on the side of the general manager's office seemed very great. Karajan had apparently heard of the miner's lamp, as he asked in the intermission from whom I had received it. I answered honestly that I did not know but had the strong suspicion someone in the manager's office dreamed it up. He muttered something and left.

In his last years Bing, to express his gallantry, got into the habit of falling to his knees whenever we first met up again in New York. In 1970 he was given British citizenship as a reward for his cultural work in England and was knighted by Queen Elizabeth. The next time we met after that, I complimented him that his genuflection had become much more beautiful since his practicing it for the queen.

After he retired as general manger of the Metropolitan, Sir Rudolf received many offers from universities and theaters. One he accepted was a professorship at Brooklyn College. The students were delighted and thought he was the best thing that had happened to them since the Beatles. Now, that is high praise! He also joined Columbia Artists as a consultant.

At the New York City Opera they were performing Henze's *The Young Lord* and Sir Rudolf was offered the title role. He was to play a distinguished, elegant, and arrogant gentleman. He was onstage the whole time without a single word to speak or sing, having to make his effect through his personality. No easy assignment. In his memoirs he writes that he did a very acceptable job. However, he did not get a follow-up offer for *Hamlet* at the end of the run. I was in San Antonio on the day of the premiere and I remember sending him a telegram:

> Even if your role is speechless, I am sure you will have the last word. Love, Birgit
>
> Don't forget many great artists have made their way from the City Opera to the Met!

One has to consider that the New York City Opera, even though a small rival, was definite competition for the Metropolitan, and Sir Rudolf was never too happy that it existed. On the other hand, the Metropolitan had incomparable means and resources so that a genuine rivalry never came into question.

It was definitely Sir Rudolf's last year at the Metropolitan. He was seventy years old and had managed the Met for twenty-three years. To everyone's surprise and great joy, Gören Gentele from Stockholm was chosen as his successor. Sir Rudolf was becoming more and more depressed as his retirement drew near. He had certainly made himself comfortable in the new house and gradually given over a large portion of the workload to his staff. Down deep, he probably hoped that the board would plead with him to stay on for a few years.

When a singer comes to the years when there is difficulty with the voice and still hesitates to retire, it is often said: Isn't it better when the public says in disbelief, "He is no longer singing?" instead of "Is he *still* singing?"

It can be difficult to follow this stern advice, but on April 22, 1972, the huge gala was given for Sir Rudolf's farewell. On the stage of the Met were chorus, ballet, and orchestra, plus forty-one singers. And not just any singers: Joan Sutherland, Leontyne Price, Monserrat Caballé, Leonie Rysanek, Plácido Domingo, Franco Corelli, Jon Vickers, and Luciano Pavarotti, to name but a few.

Sir Rudolf wished for me to close the gala concert with the end scene of *Salome,* with Karl Böhm on the podium. "And," said he, "as added excitement you can bring my head in on the silver platter."

As Sir Rudolf was one who could take a joke as well as make one, I answered that it wouldn't be necessary; I had enough imagination. But imagine my astonishment when, on the evening of the gala, I came into my dressing room and found, sitting on the piano, a lovely sculpture of Sir Rudolf's fine head on a silver platter! Among opera fanatics, friends, and fans, rumor spreads very quickly. Someone had heard Sir Rudolf's candid offer and took up a collection for this work of art. After the gala, which began at 8:00 P.M. and ended long after midnight, Sir Rudolf and Gören Gentele came into my dressing room to admire the wonderful gift. Then Sir Rudolf turned to Gentele and said, "Now you see how easy it is here at the Metropolitan for the head of the general manager to roll."

CITY OF MY DREAMS

1 (*DREAMILY*)

Vienna is the city of my dreams. There is something very special about the Viennese. Even on my first visit my heart started beating in three-quarter time. In spite of its nearly two million inhabitants, Vienna is a charming, comfortable little town. One does not experience the stress, coldness, and dissension that one feels in other large cities with fewer people than Austria's capital. Vienna is blessed by the free and easy lifestyle of its inhabitants, who refuse to be drawn into the dog-eat-dog way of life of a big city.

The Viennese have been bequeathed a treasure of culture to watch over, about which they are, rightly, very proud. I don't believe I exaggerate when I say that the apple of their eye is the Staatsoper. The great opera house stands in the middle of the city, literally and figuratively the heart of Vienna. The Staatsoper, built in 1869, was almost completely destroyed during the last week of the war in March 1945. But on November 5, 1955, the opera had been rebuilt and was ready for rededication. A month before, the Burgtheater, also damaged and restored, had reopened. Austria's rebuilding of two important theaters, when so much of the country remained in ruins, showed clearly its love for theater and opera. And it explains much about the character of the Viennese.

In spring 1954, I was to make my first guest appearance in Vienna. The effervescent Vienna of the Hapsburgs and Kaiser Franz Josef had transmogrified into something dark and oppressive. The Russians and the other Allied powers still occupied all the important buildings and hotels. Travelers had to stay with friends or seek out small inns for their lodgings. In the underheated Pension Schneider, I often slept in muffler and sweater, with my fur coat as additional blanket.

During the ten years that the Staatsoper was not operational, operas were performed in the Theater an der Wien. This is a smaller theater but one with a great past: built in 1801 and still standing, it was, in 1805 (during Napoleon's occupation of the city), the scene of the first performance of Beethoven's *Fidelio.* The house resounded as well with countless performances of Strauss and Lehar operettas, and those vibrations still linger in the air.

In this theater I came to guest in four different roles within the space of nine days. And that was not the worst: I was singing each role for the first time in its original language. In German, I was performing Elsa in *Lohengrin,* Leonore in *Fidelio,* and Sieglinde in *Walküre;* in Italian, *Aida.* I was granted a musical run-through with piano with the various conductors, but the staging rehearsals were conspicuous by their absence. This may seem unusual and a bit penny-pinching but was looked upon as totally normal. Shortly before the performance an assistant stage director would come by and explain when and where I would make my entrances and exits. The assistant, Josef Witt, a charming gentleman and former opera singer, closed his "tour" with a gracious "and otherwise we play the opera totally within the intentions of the composer."

This information was without doubt important. The first time I saw my colleagues was during the performance, with the exception of Max Lorenz, the stylish and famous Wagnerian, who actually came to my dressing room and introduced himself. He sang Lohengrin as well as Siegmund in my performances, an unusual singer and actor whose first words to me were: "Kyss mig i arslet!" (Kiss my ass!) This greeting did not quite meet the romantic expectations of a young singer. When to my shy "What did you say?" the same sentence was repeated in more sonorous Swedish, I realized I had heard him correctly. There was an explanation: Max Lorenz had appeared in Stockholm in 1936 in the *Ring,* and was taught this rather uncouth phrase as a form of greeting. He was proud of knowing this bit of Swedish. I put on a good face and pretended to be flattered by the invitation.

Rudolf Moralt, on the podium for both the *Lohengrin* and *Walküre,* was a secure and responsible conductor. Two days before the *Fidelio* performance I was informed that *Fidelio* could not be given and *Tannhäuser* would be performed instead. Could I sing the Elisabeth? Inside I shook like a leaf but accepted as if this were the simplest change in the world. After a moment it occurred to me that I only knew the part in Swedish! There followed two days and nights of intensive cramming. The conductor, Felix Prohaska, who clearly noticed my German-Swedish gibberish, gave me a thorough piano rehearsal. Hypernervous is a mild description for my condition before the performance; paralyzed would be the more accurate word. I, who had never needed a prompter, was glued to the prompter's box. In the intermission Bertil came backstage, white as chalk and shaking. When he saw I was about to have an attack of hysteria, he decided to keep quiet and disappeared as quickly as he'd come. But everything has an end, even the worst nightmare.

Even in the throes of my language misery I was able to appreciate Wolfgang Windgassen's Tannhäuser. Shortly thereafter I was pleased to sing again with him at Bayreuth.

The musical direction for *Aida* was given to an empathetic and delightful young conductor, Berislav Klobučar. Truly a singer's conductor! Of my four performances, only *Lohengrin* and *Tannhäuser* were reviewed. I received somewhat overgenerous reviews. It seemed no one took umbrage at my struggle with the German text. I even received applause after the "Dich, teure Halle" (unusual for this opera). I was offered a half-year's engagement for the following season but could not accept as I had a three-year contract with Stockholm.

My next guest performance in Vienna was completely unexpected and took place a month after my first appearances. This time I had the pleasure of singing with Sigurd Björling, which was always comforting. Sigurd was at this time more accustomed to "guesting" than I. Besides, he was a fine colleague who was never without something new and funny to relate.

On the flight to Vienna, his seat next to me became suddenly unoccupied. Had he disembarked? The explanation: In those days there was a great deal of smoking in airplanes, which did not please the Hovsångar at all. He immediately betook himself to the only smoke-free place in the plane: the restroom. He would undoubtedly appreciate the smoke-free cabins in airplanes today.

Our guest performances were *Der Fliegender Holländer* and once again *Die Walküre.* Sigurd was an excellent Wotan as well as a very good Holländer. In the intermission before act 2, when Senta makes her first entrance, the conductor, Rudolf Kempe, came to me, introduced himself and asked if I had been given the cuts they used. No, I knew nothing of any cuts. Now I not only had to follow a conductor with whom I had never sung, I had to remember the newly learned German text *and* learn what cuts were made. Notwithstanding, everything went without catastrophe onstage. It would not be honest to say, however, that I gave a first-class performance. I think under such circumstances I can only give about 70 percent. Obviously it was enough, as I was invited back for more appearances in Vienna.

In that year, 1954, I was there around Christmas as Isolde. The Tristan was Rudolf Lustig, who had a rather baritonal quality in his voice. Brangäne was the famous German mezzo Margarete Klose. One could hear she was perhaps nearing the end of her career but her portrayal of Brangäne was marvelous. Heinrich Hollreiser was a wonderful *Tristan* conductor who had much to do with the tremendous ovation we received. In the audience was the newly appointed director of the opera, Karl Böhm. According to his assistant, Egon Seefehlner (who would later be the director), Böhm supposedly said, "But she is a soubrette!"

His opinion was probably based on the "Wagner sound," which often came from pushed-up mezzo-sopranos who had a dark, heavy, "fat" sound. My vocal technique made for a slenderer sound than my predecessor, not so dark and heavy in the low range, and, therefore, a more carrying, powerful top. One of the critics wrote the headline: "WAGNER THAT SOUNDS LIKE MOZART! BIRGIT NILSSON, A FABULOUS SINGER!"

Wonderful! The Vienna critics were delighted that it sounded so easy and natural when I sang, no matter how difficult the role. That was my calling card, so to speak, that I could bring forth, with ease, the clarion-like high tones. I have heard Wagnerian sopranos who began to yell when going into the high register; to quote Elisabeth Söderström, "It sounds as if they're working out some personal frustration."

On the day after the *Tristan* performance Dr. Böhm wanted to speak with me. He astonished me with his openheartedness; as soon as I returned to the Pension Schneider, I jotted down as well as I could recall, in my not-too-full datebook, the content of our conversation:

> Well, that was quite an Isolde. Every tone produced without strain from beginning to end. Your voice reminds me of Flagstad's. I have never heard such a healthy-sounding voice. When Mme. *X* expressed a desire to sing Isolde with me, I told her, "All right if you promise to sing all the notes, *really* sing all the notes. I cannot give *Tristan* in a provincial version merely because you want to sing Isolde."

Those were not exactly kind words coming from the director of the Staatsoper, especially when speaking to one of Vienna's most beloved singers. And, surely, it was even more ungracious of him to repeat the conversation to me. The point of this meeting was to engage me for the role of Donna Anna in *Don Giovanni,* which Böhm and the Vienna Ensemble were to perform in Naples in two months. It was going to be another five years until his "soubrette" would sing her first Isolde with him—at the Metropolitan Opera in New York.

The old sets at the Theater an der Wien were very shabby and poorly maintained. There was no thought of new productions as the Staatsoper would reopen in all its splendor in a very short time. Indeed, the restored house opened on November 5 with Beethoven's *Fidelio.* The director of the opera conducted, as he did most of the premieres in the first week.

To be honest, I had hoped to be included in the reopening but it was not to be. I sat as Elisabeth in *Tannhäuser* in my dressing room in Strassburg, and during the intermission listened on a small radio (not without a few pangs of regret) while Martha Mödl sang *Fidelio.*

Vienna had such wonderful singers who had performed there even before the war. I think of such singers as Hilde Konetzni, Maria Reining, Elisabeth Schwarzkopf, Leonie Rysanek, Christel Goltz, Hilde Güden, Sena Jurinac, Irmgard Seefried, Wilma Lipp, Max Lorenz, Julius Patzak, Anton Dermota, Paul Schöffler, Ludwig Weber, Erich Kunz, Walter Berry, and Otto Edelmann. At that time there were no Wagner operas on the program that were in my repertoire. Thus I secretly gave up hope of singing at the Staatsoper.

But on the twenty-sixth of January 1956, I had my first performance in the new Staatsoper singing Donna Anna in Mozart's *Don Giovanni.* The new auditorium with its twenty-three hundred seats offered a worthy frame for the fantastic stage settings and elegant costumes. George London, an American, was a unique Don Giovanni and unbelievably beloved in Vienna. Julius Patzak was Donna Anna's betrothed, Don Ottavio. In spite of his advanced age he still possessed a wonderful high lyric tenor.

Two days later I sang Donna Anna in Munich, which meant keeping my tongue under control; I had just sung the opera in Vienna in the original language and had to switch to German for the Munich production.

In the early 1960s many of the great conductors such as Busch, Furtwängler, Erich Kleiber, and Clemens Krauss passed on. This explained to some degree why Böhm's term as Director of the Staatsoper did not last very long. He was in too great demand the world over as guest conductor.

One lovely day as Böhm returned to Vienna after a particularly long period away on guest performances there were a large number of reporters waiting for him, all with the same question: When does the director think he will carry out his duties at the Staatsoper?

The sixty-two-year-old Böhm was angry at such a question and answered in exasperation: "If you think that I will sacrifice my career for the Staatsoper, you'd better think again." The next day all the newspapers were full of outrage at Böhm's undiplomatic remark.

On this evening *Fidelio* was performed with Böhm conducting. I was on a rehearsal stage in the opera house, which had a loudspeaker connected to the stage. We heard the stage manager call the conductor and ask the singers to take their places for the beginning of the opera. Suddenly there broke out a horrible, seemingly endless noise with whistling and catcalls for Böhm. This lasted eight minutes. Only then could the performance begin!

The day after that, Böhm asked to be released from his directorship of the opera. There was wild speculation as to the new director. . . . they chose Herbert von Karajan. He wanted to produce the *Ring* with himself doing the stage direction as well as the conducting.

Everyone, including myself, thought Astrid Varnay would sing Brünnhilde. She was, all things considered, the predestined Brünnhilde in Bayreuth where she had already sung under Karajan. But it did not turn out that way: she was on his "blacklist" because at some time she had raised a few objections to his method of rehearsing.

It seemed without doubt that Leonie Rysanek, born in Austria, and the declared favorite of the Viennese, would be Sieglinde. But oh my, how one can be fooled! Leonie, who had a large repertoire of roles in Italian as well as German had, quite justifiably asked for a salary increase that would put her on the same level as other sopranos (for example, Birgit Nilsson). Instead of meeting her demands, Karajan put her aside just to show her that the Staatsoper could get along without her and engaged Aase Nordmo-Løvberg as Sieglinde—one of Leonie's best roles.

From our days at the Stockholm Opera, Aase and I were good friends. We were very comfortable together and lived in the same hotel.

Expectations were spiraling about Karajan's doing the staging as well as the conducting. In Vienna I had already sung at least ten of my roles in productions where I had little or no rehearsal. But with Karajan it did not go as I thought it would. Musical rehearsals were rare and the staging was taxing, with the performers groping through the sparse stage lighting that flickered directly above. In order to have the light on your face while singing, you had to go about like a revivalist preacher, face turned heavenward. As soon as the aria ended you were again engulfed in darkness. Thus the days passed in these wonderful circumstances. Karajan would not hear of our having a coach at the rehearsals. In order to save our voices he played a recording—surprisingly, not his own!

There was a reason for this: he had not yet recorded the *Ring* but possessed only a recording with Knappertsbusch, whose tempi were half as fast as Karajan's. Ironically, Astrid Varnay was the Brünnhilde. It was not only exhausting but psychologically difficult, not to say torture to have to adapt constantly to someone else's interpretation without losing your own sense of self.

On the day between the dress rehearsal and the premiere, Aase and I were as usual dining together. She seemed unusually restless and unhappy, complaining about every little thing. I did not take it seriously as she looked well. I thought she was just nervous about the premiere, which was haunting her. The next day, as I opened up the paper I saw the reason for her unhappiness. The journalists in Vienna had uncovered a scandal: Karajan forces Aase Nordmo-Løvberg to announce she is ill. Leonie Rysanek will sing in her place.

Under pressure from the newspapers, Aase confirmed that she had been forced to claim illness and cancel. I cannot to this day understand why Aase with her wonderful voice was so brutally tossed aside. The whole thing must have come out of some misunderstanding. I must believe that anyway, until I find some better reason.

Karajan was not a one-on-one instructor, and he never discussed the interpretation of a role. It was enough for him if you found the spotlight and reined in your acting. Privately, Karajan was a dignified man, with elegant bearing. But when he came onstage to demonstrate movements, his own became very strange. He strutted about like a cock in a henhouse, his rear end stuck out and his head in the air. I grant, this rustic description does not fit into the Karajan myth but it was *exactly* so.

Aase, having no great experience with how various stage directors worked and how they gave directions, took Karajan's movements too literally. Perhaps when he saw them imitated, he thought he was being ridiculed. That could be why he removed her from the production.

But how do you explain to the public the 180-degree turnaround at the last moment? Cancelation because of illness is always a good excuse—providing the singer goes along with the farce.

As I was recovering from the shock of the newspaper article, I called Aase, who was miserable. I tried to cheer her up and said she should appear at the premiere and let everyone see that she was well and in good spirits. She thought that was a great idea and took my complimentary ticket, which placed her in the third row directly behind the conductor.

It was a lovely ensemble that Karajan had assembled. Siegmund and Sieglinde were sung by Ludwig Suthaus and Leonie Rysanek. Karajan had Rysanek, who was singing in Stuttgart, picked up in his Rolls-Royce on the day of the performance. She was a wonderful and warmhearted Sieglinde, and Gottlob Frick, a demonic Hunding. Hans Hotter, a head taller than everyone else, was both histrionically and vocally an imposing Wotan. Fricka was sung by Jean Madeira, a versatile American artist who unfortunately died far too young. The eight Walküres were cast with stars: Christa Ludwig, Ljuba Welitsch, Margareta Sjösted, and Lotte Rysanek (Leonie's sister), to name but a few. The stage sets were designed by Emil Pretorius in a half-realistic, half neo-Bayreuth style.

March 23, 1957, was a great evening. The auditorium was filled with Vienna's most prominent citizens and we singers were attempting to outdo ourselves. Karajan created a crystal-clear reading of the score and his quick tempi were filled with drama and excitement. As I sat in my dressing room and prepared for my entrance in act 2, I listened to act 1 over the loudspeaker. How magnificently the orchestra created the feeling of the terrible storm sweeping over Hunding's hut! The musicians whipped up such a squall that, in spite of the warmth of the dressing room, I shivered from the cold.

To begin act 2, I had to stand exactly in the right square yard; otherwise I would have to call out my "Hojotoho" in utter darkness. The singer had to find the light, not the reverse. In truth, *we* were the lighting technicians. Again and again the concertmaster would hand over a telephone to Karajan during the performance so he could be in contact with the electrician, and all the while Karajan was waving his baton accurately and untiringly. It was hardly inspiring to see this telephoning going on. The orchestra pit in Vienna is rather high, so his double duty was obvious to the public. But maybe that was the whole point. What do I know?

At any rate, the premiere was a great success, and the reviews were very good. Someone wrote that the conductor must have geared the volume of the orchestra to my voice, as the other voices were from time to time drowned out.

The *Walküre* was performed three days later and again at the festival in June.

As I had devoted most of the fall season to South and North America, I gave December to the Staatsoper.

Siegfried was to be in the program. Because the role of Brünnhilde is relatively short, during the rehearsal period I was able to perform some other roles in my repertoire.

With Rudolf Moralt as conductor, I sang Isolde, with Elisabeth Höngen, a wonderful personality, singing Brangäne. Ludwig Suthaus was Tristan. Even though he was approaching the end of his career, he was still an imposing singer. After Isolde's "Liebestod," I must sink lifeless over the dead body of Tristan. I had fallen carelessly over his arm and Tristan must have suffered from some phobia or other; he whispered to me to shift my position or he would suffocate.

"I am dead and cannot change my position," I whispered. He became more and more hysterical and began to hyperventilate. It was terrible. At length he fiddled around with his free hand and opened his shirt while I meanwhile had risen up so much that I was almost no longer touching him. These were taxing minutes until we finally got into a position that seemed right.

In addition to this *Tristan* I also sang *Fidelio* with Karajan as well as my first *Turandot* in Vienna—an old production and sung in a German translation that nevertheless put the public into a premiere frame of mind.

I was very happy to have as Siegfried, Wolfgang Windgassen, a very musical singer, steeped in the Wagnerian style. This time Karajan had provided for many rehearsals on the so-called rehearsal stage. I remember especially the rehearsals for the final duet. Instead of rushing toward one another and timing it so that we fell splendidly into each other's arms on the C Major chord, Karajan asked that in the foregoing measures we move slowly toward one another. With the first touching of the fingertips, we should react as though an electric shock went through us. No matter how often we rehearsed it, he never felt we were "electric" enough.

"Give me room," said Karajan impatiently to Windgassen, "*I* will be Siegfried . . ."

As Karajan touched me with his fingertips, he asked, confident what the answer would be: "Do you feel something now? Do you feel something?" I was between a rock and a hard place. Had I said, "Oh, yes!" I would have negated Windgassen's erotic magnetism. Of course, saying yes would have made me a lifetime favorite of Karajan's. I decided to stick with the truth and shook my head regretfully. Karajan, whose belief in his erotic magnetism was absolute, blamed it all on the coldbloodedness of the Swedes. I suggested then that he take *my* place and play the scene with Windgassen, but this alternative did not appeal to him. He did not fall into this trap.

Karajan had still another idea. As Brünnhilde is awakened after many years of sleep by Siegfried's kiss, her stirring should happen very slowly and by degrees. I was supposed to rise, half-asleep and still stiff. I thought it a good idea and played it as he wished. We rehearsed the scene on the stage with Karajan sitting in the auditorium. After the rehearsal he came into my dressing room and asked in amazement, "How do you do that?" I stood there questioningly, not knowing what he meant. "How do you rise from a lying position with your feet not leaving the floor and not using your hands?"

The well-trained, athletic maestro got onto the floor and tried the "trick" but he couldn't do it. I "forgot" to tell him it was not difficult to manage when the stage was raked and the floor was slanted in the right direction!

The premiere on December 23 was a brilliant Christmas present for all of Vienna's Wagnerians. Herbert Schneider in the *Neuem Kurier* (New courier) wrote in part:

> Vocally and visually Birgit Nilsson was everything one could wish for as Brünnhilde. A dramatic soprano with complete vocal power, who will have most people raving "Once there was a . . . ," and to all appearances one will want to engage her the next time *Siegfried* is filmed. Her majestic stage presence and the depth of her expressiveness secure her place as a triumph of the best music theater. . . .
>
> Five hours of this festive atmosphere lead finally to a storm of applause for the singers and the creator and spirit behind the event, Herbert von Karajan.

For the second time we celebrated Christmas in Vienna. December 26 and 27, *Walküre* and *Siegfried* were on the program. I had already won a large number of friends and fans who, in an effort to create the proper Christmas spirit, had provided me with not one, but two Christmas trees.

From a jeweler and his family, who were opera enthusiasts, I received an antique silver pitcher on which there was engraved the likeness of Jenny Lind. The story goes that after her debut in Vienna a real Jenny Lind mania broke out. In days gone by, silver pitchers and other things of value bore the image of the admired one—today, it's T-shirts.

In April 1958 the Vienna Staatsopera—singers, conductor, and orchestra—performed *Walküre* at La Scala in Milan. I was singing for the first time on the stage of La Scala and it awakened a desire for more. Eight months later I was there opening the season as Turandot.

In Vienna in September 1958 a new production of Verdi's *Ballo in Maschera* was planned and I was to sing the role of Amelia, a part I had not yet sung. With the exception of *Fidelio,* Elettra in *Idomeneo* and now *Ballo,* I had sung all my roles in Stockholm first, which gave me a feeling of security. Now it was time to test in unknown waters, namely, an Italian role with the most famous Italian tenor, Giuseppi di Stefano. It was tremendously exciting. Josef Gielen (father of the conductor Michael Gielen) was stage director and Ita Maximowna was responsible for the beautiful, glorious stage settings.

I was primarily interested in how the work with Giuseppi di Stefano would go. During the rehearsal period for *Ballo* we were scheduled to appear together in *Aida* and *Tosca.* In the previous week I had heard him sing with another soprano as Tosca and witnessed something I would have thought impossible. In the love scene he clearly avoided engaging in any physical contact with his beloved Tosca. I boiled over in outrage at his behavior. On the way home after the performance I thought over what my deportment would be when I sang *Tosca* with him two days later. It would be love at a distance! But how I was fooled! A more fiery and amorous Cavaradossi could not be wished for by any Tosca. He gave so many kisses and embraces that it was almost impossible to get a tone out now and then. And they say prima donnas are temperamental!

A few days later, "Pippo" (as di Stefano was called) and I were to appear in *Aida.* This caused me a sleepless night, not because of Pippo, but rather the conductor—Karajan. As none of us had sung *Aida* with him, there was a short musical rehearsal with the maestro at the piano. As I began my first solo in the tempo indicated in the score, he interrupted me immediately, "Much too fast! Take it half as quickly." These slow tempi he stayed with during the whole rehearsal. I spent the whole night worrying how I was going to manage Aida in these extremely slow tempi.

The evening of the performance I was tense and nervous. At my entrance I actually felt my knees shaking, something that had not happened since my debut as Agathe. Before my first cue I took such a deep breath that I felt it in my toes and hoped to get through the long phrase. But before I had sung the first word, Karajan was two bars ahead of me! I had never before nor have I since sung Aida in such fast tempi.

Karajan was often inconsistent. During a performance he often handled things completely differently than he had in the rehearsals. He frequently claimed the singers were too loud. "*Piano, pianissimo!* With me you need not sing loudly, I will accompany you." Had the singers taken him at his word they would not have been heard; during the performance Karajan was very loud indeed. He even gained followers with his "loud playing" and many conductors gravitated to this method—without giving thought to the fact that big voices were becoming rarer and, especially in Wagner, roles were being cast with lighter voices.

Once we had a discussion about shadings and nuances. Actually it was more of a monologue than a discussion as no one was brave enough to question any of Karajan's ideas. Near the end I risked asking one question but can't remember exactly how I put it. I do remember Karajan's crushing answer: "*You*, at any rate, are not able to sing *piano*."

"Oh, I can, but only if the *orchestra* can play *piano*," I heard myself saying. Quickly, some of my colleagues tried to relieve the tension by laughing.

Karajan was a classic hypochondriac. He was convinced he was going to die any day, and had his doctor present at every performance he conducted. During a performance of *Götterdämmerung* I came down with a gallbladder attack. Karajan was most understanding and sent his doctor to me. I received an injection, enabling me to finish the performance. I had an appointment with the doctor the next day and I arrived punctually. He did not examine me; instead, we mostly talked about my career. He asked what I took before a performance to be really in form. I said I took nothing; I was of the opinion that one took medicine only when ill. The doctor then recommended something that would quiet the nerves and sharpen concentration. In other words, I could be mentally crystal-clear. He wrote me a prescription for this wonder drug. The prescription was not heavy and took little room in my handbag but it burned like fire. As soon as I was outside, I threw it in the first wastebasket I saw.

I wonder how many others in my situation would have rejected the offer of the doctor to find a singers' paradise on earth: no nervousness, head crystal-clear, and 100 percent artistic concentration! And I would rather not think about what would have become of me had I fallen for this magic medicine. Fortunately, my instinct and level-headedness protected me from a greedy doctor without a conscience.

The rehearsals for *Ballo* went uneventfully. Every day I felt more secure in my new role. The opera was given in the American version; that is, without the homosexual Gustav III, who was more attracted to Oscar than to Amelia. It was a real pleasure to be among singers of such brilliance as the *Ballo* cast.

Giulietta Simionato, who sang Ulrica, was for a long time the most distinguished Italian mezzo-soprano. She was rather short, which she compensated for with heels like stilts. Her almost static demeanor was enhanced by her charismatic personality, and her voice was like a fireworks display with no sparing of the chest tones.

Ettore Bastianini had one of the most beautiful baritone voices I ever heard. He used about two stock gestures and was not a convincing actor—but he could sing! Unfortunately, he died far too young.

Erika Köth was from Germany, a very sweet, uncomplicated person with a great sense of humor. She was extremely musical and had a splendid lyric-coloratura voice.

Giuseppe di Stefano possessed an especially beautiful voice. It was impossible not to be moved; he truly had the sound of tears in his voice, without being oversentimental. His wonderful *piano*—and his stirring voice—moved his audience amost beyond endurance. Pippo was a big kid with a lot of charm. He didn't take the profession too seriously and he certainly didn't carry discipline very far. He was a passionate gambler and spent most of his free time in the casino. In the fall we had a few performances together, not only in Vienna, but in Chicago and La Scala. The casinos did a lot of business.

Finally, we had a conductor who could set the Italian musical line aglow, the Greek-born maestro Dimitri Mitropoulos. He was an uncomplicated and shy man, but what a phenomenal conductor! I never saw him use the orchestra score, not even in rehearsals, where even those who conduct from memory use the score. He knew every number, yes, every, note of the score. His *Tosca* with George London as Scarpia, Giuseppi di Stefano as Cavaradossi, and me as Tosca was a performance that as they say, the Viennese would not quickly forget.

And the premiere of *Ballo!* What vocal writing, what music! The performance with Mitropoulos and the wonderful Italian singers will always remain in my memory. All the reviews were glowing, and I was particularly happy about the special praise I received for my *piano* singing, a nuance the Viennese love above all else. They claimed that my singing would one day be legendary and that I was the successor to the greatest opera star of all time, Maria Jeritza. The future looked rosy and it was wonderful to be alive!

II (*WITH ELAN BUT WITHOUT RUSHING*)

September is an ideal month for a visit to Vienna. The weather is agreeable, not too warm, not too cold, and theaters and concert halls beckon with new programs. Here I could admire my fellow Swede Zarah Leander as Mother Courage. She invited me to a delightful dinner party at the Drei Husaren restaurant to celebrate the end of her performances.

I loved to meander around Vienna, where reminders of the culture are imprinted on every old house. One sees very frequently a brass plaque, reading, "Here lived Ludwig van Beethoven." He must have been a restless soul—or was it perhaps some difficulty in paying the rent?

It is balm for stressed nerves, spend some free time in the Stadtpark near the statue of the Waltz King, Johann Strauss, captured for eternity playing his violin, or to listen to the Wienerkappelle play while watching peacocks strut about in full display. Then an outing to Schönbrunn or Grinzing (weather permitting, and it often does)—no wonder Vienna is forever the city of my dreams!

I recall most happily an evening at a Heurige to which I was invited by Bundeskanzler Bruno Kreisky and his wife, Vera. We were five persons completely alone, without security officers or bodyguards. No one came up to us or disturbed us in any way. The Viennese granted the nice couple their privacy and their lovely, relaxing evening.

A Swedish singer, Per Grundén, a friend from high school days in Stockholm, was appearing at the Volksoper, and there was a long line of admirers attending his performances. He not only sang beautifully, he was beautiful to look at: blond, blue-eyed, and the possessor of perfect "Colgate-white" teeth between which lovely tones emerged. In spite of the feverish adulation he enjoyed, he remained a true friend and colleague. I spent many wonderful times with Per Grundén and his wife.

Another friend and colleague from my student days in Stockholm was Ulla Sallert. For a long time, she had been the prima donna at Oscars in Stockholm. Before her guest performances in New York, where we met again, she had added to her credits a long run of *Annie Get Your Gun* at the Volksoper. I have the utmost admiration for Ulla as an artist.

A place I visited often in Vienna was the Dorotheum. It is probably best if I lay my cards on the table and admit I am a dyed-in-the-wool auction hound. At least twice a week I could be found at this fascinating emporium. Every weekday, auctions were held in the various departments of the auction house. Antiques, jewelry, art, furniture, curiosities—all were going under the hammer. One had only to throw on one's oldest rags and put on dark sunglasses and hope not to be recognized.

Carlo Maria Giulini was almost as crazy an auction hound as I, but he only went to the furniture department; therefore, we had never to fight over an object of mutual interest.

Going to auctions is an exciting and educational hobby. I sometimes took friends along to the Dorotheum and they became as addicted as I was. Once I had great good luck, as I obtained a beautiful brooch on the first offer I made. The moment the hammer fell, a man rushed over to me. He was desperate because he had missed the bidding and offered me double what I had paid for the brooch, but I declined his offer. Then he began to ask me if I were married and, if so, what my husband would say to my purchasing such an expensive piece. I said I would take the risk of a severe tongue-lashing in exchange for such a treasure.

In connection with the Wiener Festspiel, the centennial jubilee of the first performance of *Tristan und Isolde* was to be observed with a new production, opening on June 25, 1959. The stage director and conductor was to be the head of the opera himself, Herbert von Karajan. Wolfgang Windgassen was Tristan; Hilde Rössl-Majden, Brangäne; Otto Wiener, Kurwenal; and Gottlob Frick, King Marke. The stage settings were designed by Emil Pretorius. They were a compromise between new Bayreuth and the Viennese style. The first and last acts were depicted realistically, while the second act was conceived as an Impressionist painting in various tones of blue—an echo of Wieland Wagner's 1953 *Tristan* in Bayreuth, which had obviously fascinated Karajan when he conducted the opera there in that year.

Karajan's conception of Wagner's most beautiful opera was symphonic; and the singer was included in the package of something seen as more-or-less *a concert version*. In the quieter moments one could come through quite clearly but in the big crescendos singers were ruthlessly swept off the stage. I was perhaps the only one who could sometimes be heard through the loudest orchestral volume, though even for me it was an uneven battle. The *Arbeiterzeitung* wrote at the end of its review: "Isolde's Love Death became a melodic duel between the singer and the orchestra from which the conductor, with the advantage of his long baton, emerged the victor."

Rudolf Bing from the Metropolitan in New York was present at the premiere. A few days later he offered me a guest appearance as Isolde at the Met, so I guess that some of my singing got through!

It is a kind of status symbol for conductors to conduct without a score. It is said that Toscanini started this fad, but the reason he conducted without score is that his vision was so poor he had to conduct from memory. A concert conducted without a score is admirable but after all, the musicians have their notes right in front of them. In the worst case the conductor can always, as someone put it, follow the orchestra. But when the conductor of an opera has the soloists, chorus (and, in Karajan's case, telephone and lighting) to control, it is totally irresponsible to conduct from memory. Just being aware that the conductor has no score before him makes the singers nervous and insecure. Singers have a lot to memorize and a Wagner opera is generally four to five hours long. I have lived through several totally unnecessary catastrophes with these "scoreless" exhibitionists. It is extremely difficult artistically to be subjected to this.

Just such an incident happened in a *Tristan* performance with Karajan. After singing in act 1 continually for seventy-eight minutes, and with the intermission not providing sufficient rest, I found myself completely disoriented in act 2. Indeed, I drew a blank and lost any sense of where I was in the music. Karajan noticed my situation immediately, but as he was conducting from memory he was of no help to me. He turned to the first violins and pretended to be very busy with them. The half-asleep prompter was not to be brought around and it seemed to me an eternity until I was back on track, at which point Karajan resumed his normal stance and his usual transcendental air.

When the renowned conductor Knappertsbusch was asked why he did not conduct from memory, he answered, "Because I can read music."

Karajan had for years a private secretary by the name of André von Mattoni, a most efficient person, and a man of the world from head to toe. Formerly he had been an actor. As Karajan was very aware of expenses, especially when they came out of his own pocket, he arranged for Mattoni's salary to be paid by the Vienna Opera. Mattoni was very proud of his advancement: now he could put his acting talent to good use, in his dealings with all the superstars of the opera. His main function consisted in keeping the maestro in a good mood and seeing that anything disagreeable was swept under the rug.

I liked André very much; he was cheerful and knew how to use his charm. In addition he was very hospitable. Not only were my husband and I invited to his lovely home in Vienna, but during our recording sessions in Rome, we were guests at his summer residence. André von Mattoni was loyal to the point of self-sacrifice and identified 100 percent with the needs of his boss. When he spoke of Karajan, he always used the editorial "we." One day before a performance he appeared in my dressing room and without casting an approving glance at himself in my large mirror (as he usually did), he burst out radiantly, "Birgit, we have just got married and have today returned from our honeymoon."

What did this mean? Karajan had just married for the third time. This new wife was a French model by the name of Eliette and they had just returned from the wedding trip. *All three!*

The *Walküre* and *Tristan* rehearsals were time-consuming and often meaningless but they were nothing compared to the *Götterdämmerung* rehearsals. For about two weeks all cast members with principal roles were scheduled from 10 A.M. for rehearsals with Karajan. Very often after waiting for thirty to forty-five minutes, a secretary would arrive with the information that Karajan was held up. Karajan expected, however, that we would all return at seven in the evening, when he would in all probability have time to rehearse.

After a few of these incidents I suggested that after twenty minutes of waiting for Karajan we just return to our homes. We could not let ourselves be treated like children. No one risked taking me up on my suggestion. I thought to myself that no one there would have put up with this foolishness if it had been any other conductor's rehearsal.

One fine day I had had enough and after twenty minutes went back home. Karajan was furious but I really didn't care. I had enough of his idiosyncrasies that were not accomplishing anything professionally. Only too gladly would I have given up the Brünnhilde.

Besides all this, Karajan was constantly calling for lighting rehearsals, which were done with the recorded music (this time Furtwängler and Kirsten Flagstad were on the program). The singers were later freed from this and stand-ins replaced us. But the technical personnel were at the end of their patience. These people decided in their own charming, Viennese way to teach him a lesson in giving him a laurel wreath to celebrate the seventy-fifth lighting rehearsal. Karajan put on a good face, crowned himself with the laurel wreath, and went on playing around with his lighting arrangements. In fact, there were over eighty lighting rehearsals!

This slave-driving created a crisis, as the technical personnel had to be given substantial overtime pay. *That* put an end to Karajan's finger exercises on the lighting board of the Staatsoper. The Philharmonic, which seldom complains about too little rehearsal, also was dissatisfied. They had had only two rehearsals—which reveals the great confidence he had in the orchestra; remember those eighty lighting rehearsals!

The *Ring* had not been given in its entirety in Vienna since the early 1940s. Since then, there had been hired many new musicians who had never played the *Ring. Götterdämmerung* is not only very long but very difficult but there were no further orchestra rehearsals: over this department Karajan had great control, and he allowed the music to be sacrificed for the sake of the lighting (which was not in his sphere of expertise).

Notwithstanding, I think I can safely say the *Götterdämmerung* was the most distinguished of the *Ring* performances. The abstract and the realistic melded together rather well, if not perfectly. The scene with the Rheinmaidens—who sang from the wings while their mock-ups, like dead fish, floated over the stage, each on its own cable—could have been done less provincially and would have been dramatically more convincing.

All the parts were cast with first-class singers. Thanks to the Philharmonic and Karajan's expertise as conductor, the *Götterdämmerung* was musically a deluxe performance.

Margareta Sjöstedt, a Swede, was a member of the Vienna Opera Company. She was often cast in character roles and in the *Ring* she sang a Rheinmaiden. But she had also been heard as Cherubino, Octavian in *Rosenkavalier,* and other principal roles. She had time for us all, and the Swedish singers sought out Margareta and her delightful companionship. She cheered me up on many a lonely evening in Vienna. She later married Dr. Heinz Krause and they made a charming couple, adding their own bit of color to Vienna's cultural life.

While I was appearing at the Staatsoper, Set Svanholm had some concerts in Vienna, and Jussi Björling recorded Verdi's *Requiem* (one had no idea that it would be his own requiem). Set had brought along my beautiful "Litteris et Artibus" medal, which I had been awarded but was unable to accept personally in Stockholm. This had to be celebrated. I invited all the Swedes to dinner in that lovely restaurant, Die Drei Husaren. I tried to get as Swedish a meal as possible but I do not remember the main course. I do recall that the dessert was crepes with marmalade. Jussi gave a toast to the "little cake crumb," as he called me, and then we sang until the walls shook. The other guests enjoyed the free concert while they dined on their Wienerschnitzel.

For the festival of 1961 a new production of *Turandot* was planned. This was never a favorite opera of the Viennese, but this time it was unconditional surrender. Leontyne Price was beloved in Vienna and she was simply wonderful as Liù with her creamy soprano and her finespun *piani.* Giuseppi di Stefano was the Calaf and he was THE tenor of the moment. Nicola Zaccaria sang Timur. The famed stage designer Nicola Benois came from Italy, as did the stage director, Margarethe Wallman, a former dancer and choreographer. The sets were identical with those from La Scala of 1958 (although better executed). Francesco Molinari-Pradelli, an Italian, conducted.

My ten-yard long, dark blue velvet train, lined with blood-red silk, was a heavy burden to "schlep" up the many steps—*and* I had to sing the big aria from the back of the deep stage. They said it was as though I were singing from the Hotel Sacher, across the street from the rear of the Staatsoper. I was standing so high on the top of the steps, the audience in the balcony could see only my shoes. But they still claimed to have heard me. The distance to the conductor was overwhelming; I saw him as through the reverse end of opera glasses.

The sets and costumes were executed in the greatest detail and no cost was spared (which gave the critics something to complain about). I personally feel that this ancient Chinese fairy story should be a feast for the eyes as well as the ears. In Germany, the sets for *Turandot* are often dark and shabby, which in my view is simply not right for this opera. But, as one critic wrote, "where do you find voices such as Nilsson, Price, and di Stefano, who can compete and overpower such optical splendor?"

It was again a great evening and the public, which had had to pay double the usual price, applauded as though they had received double value for their money.

After the occupation forces had left Vienna, the city recovered quickly from the general exhaustion. The newly renovated hotels stood ready again to receive guests. I was actually the fifth guest to be welcomed by the Hotel Imperial, where formerly kings, royalty of all descriptions, and even Richard Wagner had stayed. In the beginning I was quite spoiled, as the staff outnumbered the guests. But no good thing lasts forever. In a moment of inexcusable carelessness I scorched the desktop with my travel iron. I overgenerously compensated the hotel for the desk, but I still received a scolding letter from the hotel's director (as though I were not already sufficiently embarrassed!).

And so I shook the dust of the Imperial off my heels (if there was any such thing as dust in the nearly unoccupied hotel) and moved into the Hotel Sacher. Unfortunately, there was something about the filling in the pillows that greatly disturbed my sleep. I then switched over to the Hotel Europa until the day the corner room I always had (large enough for all the flowers I received) was given to an American family.

Meanwhile enough time had passed since the scorched desktop incident, and I was received again at the Imperial with open arms. But it was still more convenient to live at the Sacher, from which one had only to cross the street to be at the stage door. And the marvelous Tafelspitz (filet of beef)! The pillows with the disagreeable filler had been replaced with down, and so for me it was finally the Sacher. But over the years I had quite an interesting tour of the Viennese hotels.

The dissatisfaction of the singers under permanent contract to the Staatsoper was becoming more noticeable. Karajan was against a permanently employed ensemble and wanted to implement the "staggione system" of guest artists, the way La Scala operated. Therefore he made an agreement with La Scala by which Vienna was supplied with Italian opera stars. These singers were paid about four times the fee that those under permanent contract received. It happened often that even for small roles Italian singers were brought in for sky-high fees. This caused Leonie Rysanek, under permanent contract, to complain bitterly that the Emilia in *Otello* (who sings only a few bars) drew a higher fee than she who sang the principal female role of Desdemona.

I myself had no complaint, as my fee, like those of Leontyne Price and Elisabeth Schwarzkopf, was paid through Milan. It was said that Karajan was the biggest winner in this transaction—which doesn't surprise me. He was always a good businessman when it came to his own finances.

All this talk of finances reminds me of an incident. During an orchestra rehearsal, Karajan stopped suddenly and pointed to me, saying, "Let's do that again but this time with more heart. That's the place where you have your purse."

"Oh, Maestro," I purred with thinly veiled sarcasm, "I'm so pleased to find we have something in common."

I think my answer, strangely enough, amused him: later, when we were on better speaking terms, he enjoyed telling this story to my friend and colleague Theo Adam.

There were many splendid and extravagant premieres of Italian operas with artists such as Renata Tebaldi, Mirella Freni, Leontyne Price, Mario del Monaco, Franco Corelli, Giuseppe di Stefano, and many others.

These exclusive guest performances could take place, however, only in the weeks of May–June or September–October, when La Scala was closed and the artists were free from obligations there. During these months Karajan was himself in Vienna, but during the months he was not there and the Italian singers were busy at La Scala, the level of the Staatsoper performances sank noticeably. But that did not seem to disturb Karajan. When *he* was in Vienna there were gala performances, after which all the financial resources were used up and famine prevailed.

Where was Karajan when not in Vienna? An oft-told joke about the maestro gives one answer: One day when his Rolls-Royce was being overhauled and one of his associates had flown to London on the private jet, Karajan was forced into the unusual position of taking a taxi. He got in, sat down, and gave no destination. The driver finally asked, "Where to, mister?"

"Oh, it doesn't matter. I'm expected everywhere."

Some of his other important positions were: principal conductor for life of the Berlin Philharmonic, artistic director of the Salzburg Festival, conductor at La Scala, director of concerts at the Wiener Gesellschaft der Musikfreunde, conductor of the London Philharmonic Orchestra and, added to these assignments, an immense number of featured guest appearances.

In 1963 a new production of *La Bohème* was planned. For this the Italian singers needed an Italian prompter. Prompters are generally trained conductors who can not only give every word and musical cue but also can sing the cue, when necessary. The prompter is indispensable for anyone who is not in total control of his or her role—or for a conductor who conducts from memory. Karajan engaged a well-known Italian prompter for a very high fee. The union protested, but Karajan ignored their objections. As the premiere was to begin and the Italian prompter took his place, a strike broke out. There was a riot in the auditorium and the audience had no choice but to return home. A few days later the *Bohème* opening occurred—but without the Italian prompter.

When Karajan took over the Staatsoper he did not want the title of director, but rather artistic director, with an administrative director at his side. This office was held by quite a few distinguished people—all of whom, for various reasons, eventually resigned. On someone's recommendation Karajan offered the post to a lawyer, Dr. Egon Hilbert. Dr. Hilbert had been chief of police during the Dollfuss regime in the 1930s. Upon Hitler's annexation of Austria, Hilbert was taken to a concentration camp. At the beginning of the 1950s he was head of the Bundestheater administration in Vienna and later head of the Austrian Kulturinstitutes in Rome.

One of my guest performances in Rome was a *Walküre* being performed by the Vienna Staatsoper in which Sigurd Björling was also taking part. The Austrian Kulturinstitut invited us to a big party and arranged for a private audience with Pope Pius XII. This was an unforgettable ceremony. From his time as apostolic nuncio to Berlin, the pope was a great lover of Wagner's operas. He wanted to know what roles each of us sang and expressed his regret at no longer hearing Wagner in the opera house.

At the beginning of the 1960s Dr. Hilbert was director of the festival of the Theater an der Wien. In 1963 he accepted, with a shout of joy, Karajan's offer to become administrative director. Hilbert bordered on being a real opera fanatic; he would have sold his mother if it would have helped the Vienna Staatsoper. As a strict Catholic, he gave a better ambience to the opera. When he spoke with his hectic high-pitched voice of "our opera," he turned his gaze upward to heaven. He worked twenty-five hours a day and looked upon the opera as his personal empire.

Karajan and Hilbert were an odd pair, and many questioned whether this "marriage" would last for long. Hilbert talked a lot, wrote a lot, and loved long-winded discussions. He was always stressed out—or, at any rate, he created that impression. He cared about the singers; sometimes he thanked a singer for a wonderful performance before the singer had even gone onstage. Karajan, on the other hand, spoke very little and gave brief and disjointed answers. He was forward-looking whereas Hilbert was conventional and traditional in his tastes.

During the time in which Hilbert was director of the Theater an der Wien festival he had a very prominent guest conductor who frequented Vienna's houses of prostitution in his free time. The pious Hilbert was outraged and decided to reprimand him, begining with "My opera house is not a brothel!" In his agitation it came out as "My brothel is no opera house!"

"You are absolutely right," answered the conductor. "And I am one of the few in your opera house who is qualified to judge."

It happened, as the prophets of doom predicted, that the Karajan-Hilbert "marriage" was not long-lived. More and more misunderstandings piled up. In May 1964 Karajan felt it advisable that he step aside as artistic director of the opera. But he left the door open a little: he said he would leave it in the hands of the next director whether to invite him to remain as conductor and stage director. Yes, indeed, the new director. Karajan believed the Karajan-Hilbert dual directorship to be inviolate, and he was convinced that his departure would automatically bring about Hilbert's resignation—as had been orally agreed upon. But the lawyer Hilbert was looking ahead. In the contract it was worded so that in the eventuality of Karajan's leaving, Dr. Hilbert *could* also leave his post. The little word *must* he had taken care to change to *could.* Hilbert continued on, following his motto "The fort must be held until it falls." And he stayed as director of the Opera until *he* fell; he died on the way home from work.

Karajan's returning as guest conductor and stage director under Hilbert, the watchdog before the golden door, was of course unthinkable.

After Karajan had thrown in the towel, his supporters tried to make life difficult for the steadfast Hilbert. The performances were often interrupted by derisive calls from the claque. When, for example, Florestan in *Fidelio* asks the prison warden, Rocco, who the governor of the prison is, some Karajan fan yelled out, "Egon Hilbert."

The untiring Hilbert fought on even more fanatically, if that were possible. Soon the Italian stars were back, but now with straightforward and "legal" contracts with the Staatsoper. He engaged Wieland Wagner as guest stage director and appointed the young, talented Otto Schenk as chief stage director. The greatest coup was engaging Leonard Bernstein, Karajan's most distinguished competitor, to conduct *Der Rosenkavalier, Falstaff,* and *Fidelio.*

In a short time Bernstein became the idol of the Viennese. He was charming, warmhearted, and generous, and he knew how to treat his public. He soon had them eating out of his hand. His press agent let it be known that Bernstein *adored* red roses. *Voila* there appeared for every performance a huge bouquet of the most beautiful long-stemmed red roses. Soon a new bouquet was arriving before every act. Granted, it was rumored that the same roses were being reused. Even the arrangements for improving Bernstein's mood had their practical side.

Bernstein perspired, embraced, kissed, and jumped like a tiger when he conducted. The leaps got higher and higher as the performance progressed, and when TV cameras were present, he would go wild. Once he landed (unintentionally, I presume) on the lap of the concertmaster. (Compared to the unapproachable, Garbo-like Karajan,) Bernstein was a shot in the arm. Lenny embraced the whole world and had a fire burning in his soul; what a pity he burned his candle at both ends.

Why did Karajan have such an aversion to Bernstein? One felt something there but could never put one's finger on it. Perhaps some truth can be found in what Bernstein secretly revealed to me. One lovely day, after a performance, I took a plane from Munich to Vienna. As it happened, Lenny Bernstein was also on board. On the seat next to him was his briefcase with the largest nameplate I've ever seen on an attaché case. It was even too large for the White House. The silver letters were at least three and a half inches high and created a prominent decoration all across the case. Bernstein acted as though he were going to drop dead on the spot because the stewardess did not know who I was, and the embarrassed young lady had to hear what a famous passenger she had on board.

I looked meaningfully at his nameplate but held back any comment. There was an unspoken harmony between us and we were soon on the subject of Karajan—a theme close to his heart. When I asked why the two of them could not abide one another, he began without further ado to tell about their first meeting many years ago. Karajan was conducting *Carmen* at La Scala and Lenny Bernstein was in the auditorium. Lenny found, however, that Karajan's conducting was beneath criticism and did not want to go backstage after the performance to congratulate him. (Here I have to say that I never heard Bernstein say anything positive about anyone's conducting; only his sarcasm was effusive.) Anyway, instead of going backstage he went directly to the Biffi-Scala, a nice place within easy reach of the opera house where one could get a meal late at night. After a while Karajan came in with his right hand man, von Mattoni. Karajan went directly over to Bernstein whom he had discovered, so to speak, "in flagrante," and introduced himself. Bernstein thanked him dutifully for the evening's performance and encouraged him to join him at his table.

To avoid speaking about the miserable *Carmen*, Bernstein asked Karajan how he spent his free time in Milan. Well, he said, he went skiing in the Alps and could recommend it highly. Bernstein showed no interest and said he could not go skiing as he had no equipment with him.

At three in the morning there was a knock on Bernstein's door at the Hotel Duomo where both he and Karajan were domiciled. There stood Karajan with his arms full of ski gear, which he offered to lend Bernstein. Lenny was touched at the friendly offer and put aside his ingrained Jewish hatred for the Nazis. The two sat together and talked all night as though old friends.

Bernstein asked why Karajan had not conducted in the United States and Karajan answered quite frankly that because of his political past he was not sought after in the States. Bernstein said that Karajan had many admirers in the States and that as the war had ended so long ago it was possible it was all forgotten. They agreed that Bernstein would look into any possibilities and try to make the right contacts for Karajan.

There came out of this a concert in Carnegie Hall in New York City. The concert was sold out, but ended with frenzied booing against Karajan. Bernstein hurried immediately to Karajan's dressing room to give him some consolation. There was already a throng of autograph seekers and Bernstein waited politely in the group until his "turn" came to speak with Karajan. Just as he reached the door, von Mattoni coldly slammed the door, with the explanation that the maestro was too exhausted to receive any more admirers.

Bernstein later tried to get in touch with Karajan in Salzburg and Vienna but to no avail. Karajan either looked straight through him or simply turned away. Bernstein was convinced that Karajan believed he (Bernstein) was responsible for the demonstration against him in New York. He regretted that he was powerless to rectify this great misunderstanding.

As I was in such charming and fascinating company, my flight seemed very short. At the airport there were hoards of people: photographers, journalists, opera and concert mangers, as well as recording company representatives and a secretary with an armful of Bernstein's favorite red roses. As we came from the plane's gangway and Bernstein came into view of this army awaiting him, he put his arm around my shoulder and called out in a hoarse voice: "Just married!" There was general amusement in the crowd but the excited secretary rushed to me (with a photographer) and stammered, blushing and paling alternately: "Congratulations, Mrs. Bernstein!"

The newspapers apparently latched onto the overwhelming news and one read the next day: "the newly married Leonard Bernstein arrived in Vienna yesterday with his wife." Accompanying this was a large picture of the "young pair." I am convinced that Bernstein's lovely wife, Felicia, a Chilean actress, had to develop an elephant hide to deal with her husband's practical jokes.

Bernstein was a born gentleman; he insisted I take his red roses. Unfortunately I never sang any opera with Bernstein but we did some concerts together in Europe as well as America.

In Rome he conducted his first *Fidelio* in a concert version that was telecast. I don't think he ever learned that singers were vocally limited in the length of time they could rehearse. He was always irritated that we couldn't go on for eight to ten hours singing with full voice.

"You are such a prima donna," he would say, looking at me. "*I* sing day in and day out with full voice"—the reprimand given in his scratchy, nicotine-ridden, whisky voice.

The singer who was doing the Marzelline never hesitated to show her enormous adoration for persons in power—particularly conductors. Without a thought she turned her gaze heavenward and blurted out, "No, one doesn't notice any difference at all!"

Bernstein claimed to have been the career-maker of various singers, among them Maria Callas and Christa Ludwig. He asked me once whether I had heard Christa's Marschallin in *Rosenkavalier.* Naturally, I had heard her and she was wonderful, but I thought she was better as Octavian. Hearing her sing "Mein schöner Schatz" alone made it worth going to the opera. Then Bernstein asked if he had conducted the performance I heard.

"No, it was Karl Böhm," I answered.

"Ah, yes, Böhm. He has destroyed everything I taught Christa. You should have heard her with me. *That* was unforgettable," he gushed.

Bernstein wanted to be both friend and patron of the singers. During a *Fidelio* rehearsal he stopped and said, "You are absolutely fantastic, Birgit, now that you are doing the high notes as I suggested."

I didn't think he was serious, and I answered drolly that it was indeed wonderful and fortunate that in my old age I had developed this beautiful top—and so suddenly. "One can't expect to be engaged forever just on one's good looks," I added.

Afterward, I was sorry about my light answer. He was dead earnest about what belonged to the vocal sound of the "Bernstein Show." I think he wanted more to convince himself when he assured others that he could bring about all manner of wonders. One thing he said facing a full-length mirror at the entrance to the stage of the concert hall in Stockholm, is a classic. Bernstein was standing reverentially before the mirror and rearranging an unruly lock of hair when he noticed he was being observed. He pulled himself up to his full height and said to his mirrored image, "Lenny, this is not mere narcissism, this is true love!"

In the autumn of 1965 I was engaged to sing Elektra in a new production with Karl Böhm conducting and Wieland Wagner as stage director. Leonie Rysanek was to be the Chrysothemis and Regina Resnik the Klytämnestra, Eberhard Wächter was Orest. (He was later made director of the Staatsoper but died suddenly a short time before taking office.)

I was looking forward to working with these outstanding artists. I was especially anxious to see how it would be to work with Wieland Wagner outside his domain, Bayreuth. I had recently sung Elektra in the spring of 1965, in a beautiful production in Stockholm. Now I was ready to set sail upon unknown waters. The year before, Karajan had invited me to sing Elektra with him in Salzburg but, to his great displeasure, I declined. I wanted to have the role "in my blood" before I risked working together with Karajan.

Wieland Wagner had directed a *Salome* production in Vienna just a few months earlier. Unfortunately, I have to say from the point of view of one of the audience I was somewhat disappointed. The scene was set in a backyard of the palace into which all the sewers emptied—a rather strange place for King Herod and his guests to take their ease. Salome was poured into a plain, long, and tight-fitting sheath, in which for most of the evening she had to worm her way forward on her stomach. After ten minutes of this there was no doubt that Herod's stepdaughter, his adored one, was a mermaid. Poor man!

Also I had reservations about some elements of Wieland's conception of *Elektra.* He wanted everything completely static, without any display of emotion. Only Elektra, with her raven-black hair and stark white face, could express the threatening revenge and rage that the role demands. Had this been a film in which the camera can get under the skin of the actor, I could have made sense of Wieland's intentions, but in an opera house seating twenty-three hundred people who don't have the advantage of Bayreuth's phenomenal lighting, I felt it was not enough, even meaningless. When I heard Strauss's powerful and gripping music, my intuitive reaction was to take part in the explosiveness of the music with more active interpretation. Admittedly, Wieland's lighting of the Dance of Death was masterly. While I whirled about with hands reaching to the sky, only the upper body was lit. It appeared as though I was floating toward heaven. Was this perhaps a memory of his Isolde? As *Elektra* later became a repertoire opera and the lighting was put into the hands of an assistant stage director, Wieland's ingenious effect soon disappeared.

No one could wish for a better Chrysothemis than Leonie Rysanek or a better Klytämnestra than Regina Resnik. There were many mezzo-sopranos who sang and played the part of Klytämnestra excellently but Regina *was* the murderous queen. It was highly inspiring to sing with Leonie Rysanek. We knew each other through and through and she was a phenomenal Chrysothemis. There were some who thought Leonie's acting was exaggerated, but I don't agree. When one feels a role as intensely as Leonie, does there is no possibility of overacting.

Karl Böhm was not in the best of moods during the rehearsals and his behavior toward the Philharmonic did not earn their support (to put it mildly). They knew him from way back and did not take offense at his moodiness, but the atmosphere was not congenial and I found it difficult to feel comfortable in my work. Also, Böhm had the unfortunate habit of singling out someone performing a smaller role to be the "whipping boy" on whom he could vent all his irritation. I think Böhm was the last of his generation of conductors allowed this freedom.

Karajan was clever enough to handle his musicians differently. I never heard him say anything malicious or denigrating to the orchestra musicians. With singers who dared to contradict him, he used a very calculated method: he simply mowed them down. He would drown them out with the orchestra, he would bring the orchestra in before the singer had quite finished the phrase, he would rush the tempo of the most grateful vocal phrases—and so on and so on.

Listening over the loudspeaker in my dressing room I could tell immediately which singer had fallen into the bad graces of the maestro. Later, it was often myself and then it was like spitting into the wind. As petty and grudge-holding as Karajan was, he could be as wonderful and inspiring when one was on good terms with him. Then he was without equal. One sang as though transported on a cloud and he followed (almost) like a shadow, no matter what liberties one took.

A conductor with whom I often performed in Vienna and elsewhere was Berislav Klobučar. He was a wonderful conductor for singers, with an enormous repertoire and well-grounded knowledge. I had the feeling that he was underestimated in Vienna. When I asked one of the opera directors why Klobučar never received a new production in Vienna, he shrugged his shoulders and said, "He never comes into my office."

I don't know if it was a first-come-first-served basis behind this policy, or whether there were other games being played behind the scenes. I was very pleased that Klobučar, on my recommendation, conducted my first *Elektra* in Stockholm. That was thirty years ago but every time he has a guest performance in Stockholm, Klobučar mania runs high on the stage as well as in the orchestra and auditorium.

A new production of *Tristan und Isolde* was scheduled for December 1967. It was the third production in which I had participated in Vienna, and without question the most beautiful. Back to realistic interpretation! Günther Schneider-Siemssen designed the wonderful sets that, along with the stage direction, brought out the meaning of the music ideally.

The stage direction was in the hands of August Everding, later head of the Hamburg and Munich operas. *La Traviata* was the only opera he had directed up to this time, and he admitted later that he had never been so nervous as at the first *Tristan* rehearsal.

I had by then sung Isolde about 150 times and I feared I was immune to any new ideas. Everding said later in an interview how disagreeable it was for him to have to give me sixty new stage directions and that he was speechless when the next day I carried out fifty-seven of them. Professor Everding was stimulating; the work with him always made sense and achieved good results. He was always searching, as he was new to the world of stage direction. But it is exciting and instructive to look at a situation from various angles when a better characterization is the goal. And very important: One is never too old to learn something new, particularly in this profession.

A new Tristan appeared: Jess Thomas, from California. He had already made a name for himself in Europe—in Bayreuth and elsewhere—and we had already sung together at the Metropolitan in *Aida, Turandot,* and *Fidelio.* But we had never sung *Tristan* together.

Thomas had studied psychology and had built a most thorough interpretation of his role. In addition to performing, he enjoyed designing his own costumes. The tall, slim, and good-looking Thomas had little by little moved from the Italian roles into Strauss and Wagner. The big, noble quality of his voice carried well over the waves of orchestral sound. He never marked, and the long strenuous Wagner roles presented no problem for his vocal resources.

At the premiere Jess presented me with a shining gold cup—though without a love potion. He was a loyal colleague and good friend. Ruth Hesse sang and acted Brangäne very movingly. We worked well together and had a way of laughing over the same things. But as the premiere neared, her nerves began to play tricks on her and she imagined everyone was against her. Once the first performance was behind her, she was again herself.

Otto Wiener, an Austrian veterinarian, was an excellent Kurwenal. His Hans Sachs in Bayreuth was highly esteemed and I often sang Brünnhilde to his Wotan. The impressive Finnish bass Martti Talvela was an imposing King Marke, vocally superb. What a marvelous singer! And last but not least, my favorite *Tristan* conductor, Karl Böhm, who fortunately was in a very good frame of mind. The Philharmonic and Böhm knew one another inside and out, and he knew how to draw out unbelievable *Tristan* colors from this orchestra. The papers wrote that there had not been more satisfying music-making since Furtwängler's day. They were also amazed at my Isolde, with which everyone thought they were long familiar. I was glad to read:

> . . .it was a spiritual, subtle, and consummate interpretation, which she, when demanded, vocally enhanced with a soft, soulful *piano.* The ideal sound from the orchestra and Nilsson's voice in perfect form and clarity—a dreamed-of performance one hopes to relive.

Thank you, Wieland.

A wonderful conductor and a superb coach who took time to attend piano rehearsals (who does that today?) was Josef Krips. Because he primarily conducted Mozart, I did not often have the pleasure of singing with him. I recall, above all, Handel's *Samson*, in a concert version given in Vienna's Musikverein and a solo concert with orchestra. *Fidelio* in London and Vienna belong also to the highpoints of my brief time with Krips. He loved voices; now and then he could be pedantic, but he took sufficient time to rehearse until everything met his requirements. And what one could learn from this wonderful musician! Those were happy times I love to reflect on.

In Vienna there was a change of directors. After Dr. Hilbert, who died in 1968 on the way home from a day's work at his opera, came his assistant director, Dr. Heinrich Reif-Gintl, who was appointed director in 1969. He was a congenial and quiet man who disliked any unnecessary confusion around him. Reif-Gintl had been employed by the opera since 1923 and had worked under eight opera directors. What he must have known about the Staatsoper!

After Reif-Gintl came Rudolf Gamsjäger, who formerly had been head of the Konzerthaus. He was a tall, elegant man and had been married to the famous soprano, Wilma Lipp.

Because I was working more and more often in the United States, my guest performances in Vienna became less frequent. Besides, my salary at the Staatsoper had not kept up with my fees elsewhere. But my love of the Staatsoper, the public, and Vienna was reciprocated and that is what's most important.

In 1968 I became engaged—literally—to the standees of the Vienna Staatsoper! They took up a collection for a fantastic gift: a gold ring in which Isolde's image is engraved. It is one of the most beautiful gifts I have ever received.

It was the custom after each performance for a large number of the standees, from the 500-person capacity of the standing room, to accompany me to my hotel. The procession took up the entire Kärtnerstrasse. As I lived farther away, in the Hotel Europa, it could be quite a while until traffic was back to normal (this was before Kärtnerstrasse became a pedestrian zone). Sometimes the guests in the hotel looked out their windows anxiously when they heard the hoard of people outside, thinking a fire had broken out. But the doorman quieted their fear, explaining it was only Frau Kammersängerin Nilsson, coming home from her performance as usual. In that year, 1968, I was named Kammersängerin (a title conferred upon singers of long-standing excellence, literally, Court Singer) as well as Ehrenmitglied (honorary member) of the Vienna Staatsoper. That is an honor on as high a level as being accompanied to my hotel by the standees.

I believe the new director, Rudolf Gamsjäger, was astonished that I did not ask for an increase in my fee. Perhaps he feared I would leave him in the lurch; one day he said to me, "I presume you have so much money that you don't need any more. But how would it be if each season in which you appear you receive a gold plate?"

I thanked him and made a polite bow. And in fact, when the fall season began I received my first gold plate. In the following year the next one came faithfully—even though Gamsjäger complained that gold had become much more expensive.

In the third season, as agreed, I received another gold plate. While I sat there awaiting my entrance I took the lovely plate out of the carton to admire. Auction-hound that I am, I always carry a pocket lens in my handbag. Automatically I perused the stamp on the back with the magnifying glass and learned that this plate was not gold but merely gold-plated silver. My letter to Gamsjäger, in which I thanked him for the gold-plated gift, read thus: "It doesn't matter that you could not afford a gold plate. I only hope that I still have enough gold in my throat that I will not have to resort to silver."

Before the next performance Gamsjäger came to me with lowered gaze, red with embarrassment. After a moment's hesitation he asked if I were an expert in recognizing precious metal.

"I am no expert, but I can tell silver from gold. And I hope as director you can too," I answered.

In the doorway he turned and promised to frame my letter.

During the twenty-eight years I sang in Vienna I sang my entire repertoire many times over, with the exception of one role: the Feldmarschallin in *Der Rosenkavalier.* Why? I was simply too cowardly to put myself in competition with the genuine articles of "Wiener-Gemütlichkeit." I actually saw ten different Marschallins at the Staatsoper and they were all admirable, each in her own way. I was most moved by Hilde Konetzni. She was the mature, experienced Marschallin with her heart in the right place. The others, most of them, wanted to portray the Marschallin as too young and outgoing. One must not forget that a woman of thirty-five in the Rococo period would be more like a woman of fifty today.

I will never forget Konetzni's performance, with Heinrich Hollreiser conducting wonderfully. When she was next cast as the Marschallin I attended and anticipated a wonderful evening.

But this time Böhm was conducting, and one could tell instantly that the chemistry between Böhm and Konetzni was not right. All her emotions seemed shut down; everything that had moved me so deeply before had disappeared. This was a real example of how tremendously important a conductor is to a singer. I use this example whenever anyone says a conductor is there only to wave his stick and beat time, while the orchestra musicians ignore him and stare at the notes. The truth is, singers and instrumentalists see everything in the blink of an eye—and I do mean *everything.*

It is perhaps known that the tuning in Vienna is much higher than in many other houses, almost a half-tone higher. Most singers, especially the tenors, dread the high tones. I never gave much thought to this higher tuning until I came directly from New York where I had sung several *Elektra* performances. Now I was to sing the same role in Vienna. I battled the entire evening like a madwoman. The tuning of the Metropolitan orchestra was, so to speak, still in my throat and it was tremendously difficult to "crank up" to the pitch of the Vienna Philharmonic. I had throughout the evening the feeling that I was singing too low (and, believe me, that is not a good feeling).

Another time I was scheduled to sing, after Christa Ludwig, three performances of Lady Macbeth in an already rehearsed and finished production. It was wonderfully staged by Otto Schenk. Klobučar, with his wonderful command, had taken over the baton from Karl Böhm. I was never so nervous about a high tone as I was about the D-flat, to be sung in the softest *piano,* at the end of the Sleepwalking scene. It felt like a D and it was not exactly *pianissimo:* rather, using my last strength made it more of a *forte.*

The Philharmonic refused to change their pitch as it gave a more brilliant sound to their already brilliant higher tones. They also wanted to be seen and the orchestra pit was not as deep as in most other houses. Thus, the orchestra in Vienna is not only unusually brilliant but unusually loud. But this is the price the singer must pay to sing with the fantastic Vienna Philharmonic.

My personal record on curtain calls occurred after an *Elektra* performance in Vienna. On that evening in 1975, as I remember, we had seventy-two curtain calls. I remember the musicians of the Vienna Philharmonic at the end of the performance put aside their instruments and went to dinner. When they returned to get their instruments, the audience was still there applauding. The curtain calls that evening lasted longer, I believe, than the performance of *Elektra* itself, which is only one act. Plácido

Domingo is in the Guinness Book of Records with seventy curtain calls, but that is not quite in accord with the facts!

Ultimately I decided to add another role to my repertoire: the Dyer's Wife in *Die Frau ohne Schatten.* Before, when considering this opera, I could not decide which of the roles to choose, the Dyer's Wife or the Kaiserin. Both were within my range. At first I thought it would be the Kaiserin, a glamorous role with many high tones. And so I declined the Met's offer in 1966 to sing the Dyer's Wife at their celebration of the opening of the new house in Lincoln Center.

Leonie Rysanek, for twenty-five years the Kaiserin without equal, tried to talk me into singing the Dyer's Wife. When I was a guest in her lovely home in Munich she gave me, before I retired to bed, her piano score of *Die Frau ohne Schatten* as night reading. The next morning I had decided. Although the part was difficult as well as long, requiring a compass of more than two and a half octaves. I decided it had to be the Dyer's Wife. In December 1975 I sang the role for the first time with Klobučar conducting in Stockholm. In 1976 I sang it with Sawallisch in Munich and in 1977 came Vienna, where the production was old and not nearly so beautiful as the one in Stockholm (indeed, the most beautiful of any I had seen).

All the roles in Vienna were cast with ideal singers. Karl Böhm had assured us that any cuts he made in the Strauss operas were with the agreement of the composer. I risk stating that Strauss would have had a heart attack if he had experienced Böhm's slaughter of *Die Frau ohne Schatten.* Among other great scenes the most spectacular scene of the Dyer's Wife was cut. Admittedly the scene is demanding, but either you master a role or you don't touch it. This is an artistic decision that everyone has to make.

What would one think if Tosca's aria "Vissi d'Arte" in act 2 were cut? It would create an unheard-of scandal. But *Die Frau* is not so well known and therefore Böhm took the liberty of cutting the roles to fit the singer. Naturally he did not anticipate that I would want to sing this big scene, the highpoint of the opera, uncut. Which is what I did.

Leonie sang the Kaiserin. I believe it was her greatest role. Every evening when I had a moment free I stood in the wings and thrilled to her fantastic interpretation and wonderful high voice. Ruth Hesse mastered completely the unbelievably difficult and long role of the Amme. And everyone's favorite colleague, James King, sang a wonderful Kaiser. Walter Berry was my husband, Barak, the Dyer, so-called because he tanned animal skins.

Walter Berry is a wonderful colleague with the most marvelous sense of humor in the world. You are never bored in his company. Besides that, he is a splendid singer and actor. The Dyer is one of his best roles; he often sang it with his former wife, Christa Ludwig, as the Dyer's Wife.

One had to be very cautious playing the Dyer's Wife opposite Berry; even Strauss saw her as a battle-ax! (Perhaps his wife, Pauline, whom he loved above everything, was the prototype for this termagant. She was the model for the female role in *Intermezzo.*) As Berry made his Barak the most pitiable, love-hungry and henpecked husband you could imagine, it was not necessary to make the wife so coldhearted. In my opinion, Barak is not so pitiful. I see him more as a pasha who wants nothing more from his wife than the satisfaction of his lust whenever he is in the mood. He has absolutely no understanding for his wife's dreams of romance and a better life. She has a roof over her head and food—what more does she need? Day in and day out she is slave to his three lazy brothers who are constantly underfoot in their shabby hut; Barak, unmoved, looks the other way while they try to grope his wife. In her desperation and loneliness she sends out signals meant to make Barak jealous. And he becomes jealous, which is actually an expression of his bruised ego. The Dyer's Wife loves her husband and down deep she longs for the fulfillment of their love as much as he. But in the dreariness of everyday life, they cannot find a way to one another. All this must be kept in mind when Berry is performing Barak. Otherwise, there is the danger of the wife coming off as a real shrew.

The Dyer's Wife was a wonderful role. Compared with the goddesses, Valkyries, ice-cold princesses, or other bloodthirsty characters that I often portrayed, she was one of the few women of flesh and blood. After the first performance in Vienna, Leonie, who was, so to speak, the godmother of my Dyer's Wife, said admiringly, "I was sure you would be fantastic as the Dyer's Wife but I had no idea you would be *this* fantastic." Greater praise I could hardly wish for. It was strange how long her words echoed in me.

My opera career, which I had intended to close earlier, was prolonged by the success of my Dyer's Wife. Frankfurt, Hamburg, Berlin, Buenos Aires, San Francisco, New York—all offered me guest appearances as the Dyer's Wife, and I did really love the role. So it wasn't until June 1982 that I finally ended my opera career.

III (*WITH SENTIMENT*)

It is difficult to find the right time to withdraw from the scene. When is the right moment? Is it when the voice is at its absolute high point, even though you may remain undeveloped as an artist? Or should one accept that the compass of the voice decreases, yet continue to give all that one has learned from life? Another option is to change "Fach" (voice classification) and compete with the mezzo-sopranos. Such "retirement" roles allow you to coast on your past popularity.

I knew for some time that I would not like living on my past successes. If there is one thing I cannot bear thinking of, it is to be pitied by the public. But one is so horribly alone in this decision! You cannot burden your friends with the question and expect them to treat the delicate problem with total honesty. Why should they? And your closest friends, who probably would understand that it is time to think of retirement, will try to dissuade you. The final notes in the *ritardando* of a career carry their own drama.

Deep down one knows why singing is no longer so easy, why the nights before a performance are becoming more wakeful, why the whole day before a performance becomes an inferno of self-doubt and pressure. But then, after the performance, one is showered with flowers and greeted with bravas as enthusiastic as ever. One is happy and thankful and says to oneself, "See how well it went! All that worry for nothing!" But at the same time a small voice is whispering in your ear, "Don't you understand? All the cheering *now* is for what you *were.*"

Everyone knew that my last performances in Vienna were planned as part of the festival on June 9 and 30, 1982. Both performances were of the Dyer's Wife. It was easy to figure out that my so-called farewell performance was on June 30, and word reached my ear that a worthy farewell was planned. I feared that after twenty-eight years of such a close friendship with my wonderful Viennese public, I would never be able to keep the sound of tears out of my voice. I had wept with many friends after their farewell performances but then, at least, I did not have to sing. Now it was a matter of my farewell performance—no, no, I just couldn't!

Therefore, I canceled my final performance on June 30th and wrote a letter to the director, Egon Seefehlner in which I stated my reasons.

Instead of June 30, my last opera appearance was in Frankfurt on June 16, where I was engaged to sing Elektra. It was a great performance and I felt I was in my best form, as though it was the high point of my career.

At the end of that *Elektra* I said to my colleagues: "This was my final performance."

And I was at peace with this decision.

IN A WORD — BAYREUTH

Bayreuth is truly a special chapter in my life. But before I go into all that, I would like to give a short historical overview of this remarkable city, which was put on the map by one man: Richard Wagner.

It is said that Richard Wagner, as a twenty-two-year-old conductor from Magdeburg, led a concert in Bayreuth and fell in love with the city and its surroundings. He became obsessed with one dream: an opera house would be built here in which only *his* works would be performed!

Before his dream would become reality, however, he had to endure years of mental, artistic, and financial difficulties that would severely test his otherwise unshakable faith in himself. His heavy burdens would eventually be lifted through the support of King Ludwig II of Bavaria, whose generosity brought the ambitious project to completion. On August 13, 1876, Richard Wagner's Festspielhaus was dedicated with a performance of the *Ring of the Nibelungs* with Wagner as both stage director and conductor.

Two years earlier, in April 1874, Wagner, with his wife, Cosima, and five children, moved into their newly built villa. Cosima was the daughter of Franz Liszt and the two oldest of the children were from her first marriage to the conductor Hans von Bülow. In a letter to King Ludwig, Wagner wrote: "Thanks to the help of Your Majesty, my new house stands finished here. I have thought long about a suitable name. The following rhyme will reveal what I have chosen: Hier, wo mein Wähnen Frieden fand / Wahnfried sei dieses Haus von mir benannt." (Here, where my longing found peace / I shall call this house Wahnfried.)

Richard Wagner died in 1883 at the age of seventy. He rests in the garden of the Villa Wahnfried with his wife Cosima (who died forty-seven years later).

Cosima made it her life's work to surrender everything to her husband's desires, philosophy, and ideas. Everything must serve to develop and perfect the artistic goals of Wagner. When she assumed the directorship of the Festspielhaus after his death, she looked upon it more as a mausoleum than a forum for living art. Nothing could be changed, everything must continue as it was in Wagner's lifetime. On this point she perhaps misunderstood the constantly searching Richard Wagner who, in spite of his contradictory nature (he was born under the sign of the Twins) lived by the motto "Children, make something new!"

The only son of Cosima and Richard Wagner, Siegfried, was the sole heir to Bayreuth. He grew up in the shadow of four sisters and a strong-willed mother; it was very difficult for him to "cut the cord." He hung onto Cosima's apron strings until he took over Bayreuth at the age of thirty-nine.

A student of Engelbert Humperdinck, Siegfried Wagner composed a number of operas. In the 1930s his works were performed in Germany with various degrees of success. In addition, he was active as a conductor and, in particular, the *Ring,* in Bayreuth. His major strength was in stage direction; unfortunately, however, he was given little opportunity to develop this talent. Cosima permitted no changes, no new style. The eye of the master held it to be thus; thus shall it be forevermore.

In 1915 the forty-six-year-old Siegfried married an eighteen-year-old English girl, Winifred Klindworth. She gave birth, in rather quick succession, to four children: Wieland, born in 1917; Friedelind, 1918; Wolfgang, 1919; and Verena, 1920. Winifred was only thirty-three years old when Siegfried died of a heart attack on August 4, 1930. Four months earlier, Cosima had died at the age of ninety-two. Now Winifred was the sole heir and manager of the Festspielhaus. She was a resolute, well-spoken, and energetic lady. Perhaps she was sometimes *too* resolute.

Adolf Hitler, an Austrian politician and amateur painter, was making a name for himself in the 1920s. Eva Chamberlain (Siegfried Wagner's sister) and her husband invited him to visit the Villa Wahnfried. Winifred was immediately drawn to this interesting guest and made no secret of her fascination. This meeting laid the foundation for a long-lasting friendship that had far-reaching consequences. In 1926 she became a member of the National Socialist Party. Her husband, Siegfried, preferred to remain nonpolitical. Hitler was a great Wagner enthusiast and regularly attended the Festspiel in Bayreuth. After the death of her husband, Winifred, as director of the Festspiel, offered this spectacular guest lodging in her home. He was seen, more or less, as a family member: the children said "du" to him, and they, like Winifred were allowed to call him "Wolf."

After Hitler came to power, he, of course, had control over the Festspielhaus. He shared control with Winifred, in all probability, as she was still the queen of Bayreuth, but it was Hitler himself who decided what was performed, and with which conductors, singers, and stage directors. Suddenly there arose a problem with the Italian maestro, Arturo Toscanini. He refused to conduct in the Nazified Bayreuth which Hitler, since his takeover of Germany in 1933, had made his own personal culture center. In Hitler's opinion, Toscanini's son-in-law, the Jewish pianist, Vladimir Horowitz, was a great embarrassment. In spite of this, he sent a personal letter to Toscanini, begging him to stay. In vain! Wilhelm Furtwängler was talked into taking Toscanini's place. (In an earlier power struggle between the two, Toscanini had been the victor.) Furtwängler returned in 1936 to conduct, among other operas, *Lohengrin* with Maria Müller and Franz Völker—a splendid performance, available on CD today. The soloists that decade included Frida Leider, Kirsten Flagstad, Nanny Larsén-Todsen, Friedrich Schorr, Lauritz Melchior, Max Lorenz, and many others. In the 1930s many Jewish artists were on Bayreuth's roster. Among the soloists there was no race discrimination; there, different rules applied.

Hitler evidently thought his powerful spirit was somewhat cramped in Bayreuth. Shortly before the outbreak of the Second World War, Hans Reissinger, Winifred's architect in Bayreuth, presented her with drawings and a model for an "Adolf-Hitler-Festspielhaus" that was to be built in Theta, a short distance from Bayreuth. One can only speculate how this plan sat with Winifred Wagner. As the war went on into the mid-1940s, when the world already saw Hitler as the loser, his followers planned a festival in Bayreuth. It was to be a manifestation of the victory of the German nation and was to take place in 1947. By that time, however, Bayreuth, like most of Germany, lay in ruins, and Hitler had committed suicide.

After the war Wieland Wagner and his sister Verena found refuge with their families in Nussdorf on the Bodensee. Friedelind had distanced herself from the family since 1939 and had made her way to America by way of Switzerland and England.

Wolfgang Wagner's family and Winifred settled in Oberwarmensteinach in the Fichtelgebirge, not far from Bayreuth. The Villa Wahnfried was almost completely destroyed during the bombing attacks, while the Festspielhaus, miraculously, was spared.

The postwar period was difficult for the Wagner clan. Winifred Wagner withdrew not only from her leadership of the Festspiel but from all public events. Sixty percent of her assets had been confiscated, she was not permitted to vote, and she had to give up any rights to a pension. For many years, she lived in a kind of self-imposed exile in the Fichtelgebirge. In 1956 she returned to the Villa Wahnfried and lived in an extension of the Siegfried-Wagner-Haus. Wieland and his family moved back into the main house, the actual Villa Wahnfried. To make plain the rift between mother and son, Wieland had a wall erected between the two houses.

Shortly after the war's end Winifred had a visit from Klaus Mann, the son of Thomas Mann, who had left Germany in 1933 and was one of the most important anti-Nazis. Before the interview, Winifred said to Klaus Mann (at this time an American press agent), "One question you need not ask: no, I did *not* sleep with Adolf Hitler!"

I remember Winifred Wagner rattling around in her little Volkswagen, a cigarette dangling from the corner of her mouth. She was an elegant, rather tall woman who wore her graying hair in a large bun at the nape of her neck. She had an opinion on everything and was fearless about expressing it. Once she invited a few "selected" singers to afternoon tea where she—probably to the surprise of some—was an amusing and charming hostess. There was a documentary about Winifred Wagner on film in which she talks about her—to put it mildly—eventful life. One of the last questions she answered was how she would react if Adolf Hitler suddenly came to the door: " 'Welcome. How nice to see you.' I would say. Why not? He was, after all, my friend." She would die at the age of eighty-two and to the very end appalled those around her by never recognizing any fault in her most outrageous deeds and ideas.

In 1951, after seven years of silence, the doors of the Festspielhaus opened once again. After the war, Germany was an impoverished country, lying in ashes. Many cities had been razed to the ground. Everywhere there were buildings, once imposing, but now only evidence of the anguished German Reich. Living conditions were unbelievably horrible. Yet even then, in spite of all deprivation, there was a hunger for culture.

Hardly had the piles of rubble stopped burning before the Germans, under the most makeshift conditions imaginable, began to give concerts and to open their theaters and opera houses. The rebuilding of the destroyed or bombed theaters began.

Fortunately, the Festspielhaus had escaped destruction. Nonetheless it had to undergo a complete renovation. During the Occupation, the opera house served not only as a storehouse but as a brothel for the American soldiers. At least the debauchery occurred in an atmosphere of culture.

Winifred Wagner, because of her exclusion from the Festspielhaus, was forced to sign an agreement in which her sons, Wieland and Wolfgang, took over the direction of the Festspiel.

On a lovely, cold winter day in the 1950–51 season, I received a letter from Bayreuth offering me the role of Sieglinde in *Die Walküre* for the opening of the Festspiel in July. I was as surprised as I was flattered at the great honor: so early in my career, to be invited to this Mecca of Music! To tell the truth, however, I was a bit relieved that I had to refuse the invitation. I was already engaged to sing Elettra in Mozart's *Idomeneo* with Fritz Busch in Glyndebourne, an engagement I thought less prestigious. The young Austrian soprano Leonie Rysanek received the offer and sang Sieglinde in my place at the opening of Bayreuth.

Soon after the correspondence with Bayreuth, I was taking part in a concert at the Titania Palace in Berlin, my first engagement outside Scandinavia. The conductor was the legendary Leo Blech, who had personally requested that I sing Sieglinde in act 1 of *Die Walküre.* Hans Beirer sang Siegmund and Gottlob Frick was Hunding. Wolfgang Wagner, on his own volition, came from Bayreuth to hear the concert. I was most impressed to meet in person Richard Wagner's grandson, who said he hoped to see me soon in Bayreuth.

It didn't take long for another letter from Bayreuth to reach me. Wieland requested that I come for an audition, on the main stage of the Festspielhaus, for a possible engagement in the 1952 season. I didn't agree to this right away: I pointed out that I had been offered an engagement for the 1951 season *without* auditioning and was sure I could be invited again under the same conditions.

Another year passed until the invitation came. This time I was to sing the soprano part in Beethoven's Ninth Symphony. The Festspiel was to open with this work under the baton of Furtwängler. I accepted the engagement even though this part is not exactly a favorite of mine (I'm sure many other sopranos feel the same way). The part is short, difficult, and ungrateful. Perhaps Beethoven was getting back at some soprano for something.

And so I finally got to Bayreuth. I was almost in shock as I neared the Festspielhaus on the Green Hill. My heart beat faster when I realized that I would be performing in Wagner's Temple! Had I not had the opportunity to attend the dress rehearsals of both *Lohengrin* and *Tristan* before it came time for me to sing my comparatively small part in the Beethoven, I'm not sure I could have gotten through it.

The singers were, on the whole, excellent—but I had assumed that everyone who sang in Bayreuth was superhuman. Instead they had faults and flaws like everyone else. I imagined the Festspielhaus to be a huge, imposing edifice. It actually looked more like a well-tended wooden hut. And the inside furnishings? Surely they would be of crystal, velvet, and silk—all the things for which Richard Wagner had a weakness. But no, the auditorium was extremely spartan, furnished with bare wooden seats that, frankly, were very uncomfortable.

In one aspect, no expense had been spared; everything was sacrificed on the altar of acoustics. Wagner, who was quite short, must have worked out the distance between rows himself; for it was only bearable for people under five feet tall.

During the indisposition of Furtwängler, Paul Hindemith took over the baton. He was a better composer than he was conductor. The other soloists in the Beethoven were Ira Malaniuk (from Ukraine), the bass Ludwig Weber, and the tenor Anton Dermota (both from Austria). I believe I fulfilled my obligations to the satisfaction of those concerned. I certainly received very good notices.

As I had finally found myself in Bayreuth I could find no reason to deprive the Wagner brothers of the pleasure of auditioning for them. Auditioning is the worst thing I can imagine. One has to be in top form, both in appearance and in voice. It reminds me of a country horse market—the only difference is they can't examine your teeth to see if you've lied about your age. After I had sung arias from *Die Walküre, Lohengrin,* and *Tannhäuser,* Wieland invited me to come to his office. Now imagine this: there he actually fell on his knees before me! Highly confused, almost hallucinatory, I was thinking: "Here kneels the grandson of Richard Wagner before you. Never tell this to a soul because no one will believe you." In my hallucinatory state, I heard him say, "Frau Nilsson, what do you want to sing? Express your wish and the role is yours."

Then he said I was a new Maria Müller, "She was a wonderful, lyric soprano exactly like you. Promise me you will never sing Isolde or Brünnhilde as these parts are too dramatic for you." As I explained that in two months I was going to sing Isolde in Stockholm, he frowned darkly. But the sun broke through immediately: Wieland promised I would hear from him as soon as he had decided which role would be best for presenting me to the world audience of Bayreuth. I left the office on cloud nine, delirious with having delivered Wieland Wagner a knockout blow.

If anyone had told me then that it would be ten years before I would actually work with Wieland, I would have laughed. But so it was. I heard nothing more from him. In the meantime it had become apparent that he had fallen on more than his knees before another singer, and like other gods before him, had lost the battle with Cupid's arrow. This singer was given the role that would have gone to me. I admit she was very good. She was also a good colleague and quite charismatic on stage. Strangely enough, a few years later she disappeared from the stage of Bayreuth. Meanwhile I had established myself in the "stable" of brother Wolfgang. In addition to the unending administrative details he attended to, he had begun to do stage direction and for the 1954 season I was engaged for the role of Elsa in *Lohengrin* with Wolfgang as director.

In the beginning of my time in Bayreuth I found it difficult to tell the brothers apart. They were as alike as two peas in a pod, but when I got to know them better the similarity disappeared. I couldn't believe I had once been unable to tell them apart. Wolfgang was two years younger than Wieland, middle height, a little shorter than his brother, with wavy hair that curled at the neck (just as his grandfather's did). He was also, it appeared, unaware of his charm. In his youth he studied music but his hand and lower arm were severely wounded in the war and he was forced to give up his dream of being a conductor.

Wolfgang spoke of the great Richard as "my grandfather," whereas Wieland called him "Richard Wagner." Wolfgang knew almost everything about his grandfather. He had a practical side as well as an artist's temperament, and he heard and saw everything and was everywhere present. One day an unabashed driver had for the third time, parked his car in Wolfgang's reserved parking place. He solved the problem by simply letting the air out of the tires. Probably no one ever parked in this space again—especially not the original guilty party!

Wolfgang was very close to his mother, maybe closer than the other three siblings were. Probably that was because he had been sickly as a child and the love between him and his mother became very strong. He supported her and took her in during the difficult time after the war, and he was always ready to defend her.

In June 1954, I came to Bayreuth to begin my rehearsals. Bertil drove me in my superspeedy auto, a Kaiser, a real hot number in mother-of-pearl rose. My colleagues called the car, with envy in their voice, "The Ship" and I was very proud of this equipage. Unfortunately, it looked a lot better than it ran. It was quite unreliable and didn't even last the time in Bayreuth.

I had taken lodgings in a villa in the Rheingoldstrasse, where I had two rooms and a piano. The rent was unbelievably high, at least in comparison to my salary. Wagner had created a luxury locale and the townspeople wanted to make whatever profit could be made. If you sang in the Wagner Festspiel they presumed you were wealthy or would be so when the season was over. Friday was the bath day for the family from whom I rented my two rooms, and for this event there was warm water. This meant *be there* if you wanted to free yourself from the accumulation of the week's stage dust.

The two months in Bayreuth seemed never to end. It was an unusually wet and chilly summer and I froze in my little apartment as well as at the Festspielhaus. Bertil was not able to stay the whole time because of his work. I missed him as much as I missed the bright summer evenings in Sweden. Here it was already dark by nine in the evening and in the middle of summer! My nine performances were scheduled so that there wasn't enough time to go home in-between. The trip from Sweden to Bayreuth, with layovers in Copenhagen, Frankfurt and Nuremberg took longer than a flight to New York! Bayreuth was a godforsaken little nest in my opinion. Every attempt at improvement came to a standstill and was blamed on the war. For the first time in my life I saw how the farmers worked their land with cows and oxen. The women who were over fifty wore black dresses with checkered aprons, and headscarves tied under their chins. I liked that in Bayreuth people greeted each other with "Grüss Gott," as is the custom among Catholics. No matter how I tried I couldn't keep my tongue from coming out with the Swedish "Ryggskott!" which means lumbago; a little protest from a Protestant among Catholics. I tried to look as friendly as possible with my "Ryggskott" so they would not take it the wrong way if they noticed a difference.

I had the opportunity to work with a fantastic coach: Herman Weigert, a thoroughgoing musician of Jewish heritage. Jews were once again welcome in Bayreuth! He was engaged at the Metropolitan Opera in New York and was married to the phenomenal singer, Astrid Varnay. Astrid, of Hungarian descent, had been born in Stockholm. Her father was for a short time a member of the Court Orchestra before they emigrated to the United States. Astrid and her husband had been engaged for the reopening of the Festspiel in 1951 and in their own ways, they had both been instrumental in the success of the festival.

Astrid and I are within a month of being the same age—though some thought we belonged to different generations as her career began conspicuously early. At the age of twenty-two she jumped in at the Met for Helen Traubel as Brünnhilde in *Die Walküre* and a week before substituted for an indisposed Lotte Lehmann as Sieglinde in the same opera. When I was twenty-two, I was still pulling up carrots in the vegetable garden.

Learning the role of Elsa was an especially rewarding musical experience. Rhythmically, the role is totally unpredictable. It teems with eighth notes and sixteenths that in one bar are dotted and in the next, for no apparent reason, even. I learned the part in Stockholm very quickly and the coach there did not take the trouble to point out my musical sloppiness. It is a tremendous lot of work to study a major role, but to correct learned mistakes that have become subconscious reflexes is indescribable drudgery. In any case, I learned a lesson for the future: right from the beginning one has to be exact, even pedantic, about the correct note value.

Herman Weigert was the most phenomenal musician and coach that I had ever met. I would not have thought it possible to include every facet of the role in the work: phrasing, nuances, expression—everything. He gave me some excellent, general advice. For example: never just jump into a phrase unprepared: rather, think through the way you want to feel the phrase and build it musically. At certain dramatic moments when volume was called for and I would begin wasting my vocal energy by letting all the floodgates open, he would look at me over his glasses and advise me to hold my fire: "Here the orchestra is so loud that it is useless to try to be heard." At other places he would suggest, "Give here a little more voice; here the orchestra is so transparent that it subordinates itself to accompanying the singer. With such stones, Frau Nilsson, one builds cathedrals."

I received many rehearsals onstage with our stage director, Wolfgang Wagner. His most important work with me was to restrain my often violent, unmotivated gestures—or at least help me to control them. All the roles in his *Lohengrin* were stylized, and the stage was—exactly as in Wieland's production—almost lacking in any stage decoration. It demanded a great personality to make herself noticed or to bring the role to life. The Wagner brothers were pioneers in the modern art of producing opera. It was a great challenge; one had the feeling of standing totally naked on stage. The role had to come to life through one's own personality and interpretation of the words. All other guides to interpretation were to be found in Wagner's music. The rehearsals were not made easier by the fact that Wolfgang Wagner spoke Oberfränkisch. I, who had enough trouble with any kind of high German, stood there like a human question mark after his stream of incomprehensible words. It made no sense to question him about anything, as this simply brought on a fifteen- to twenty-minute lecture that undoubtedly would have been quite beneficial had I only been able to understand him. He gave people instructions spoken into a tape recorder and then let someone who understood Oberfränkish translate.

My dear coach, Herman Weigert noticed my problem and asked me whether I understood what Wolfgang was saying.

"Not much," I answered frankly.

"It's not all that important," he answered, comfortingly.

I understood Weigert to mean that once one masters a role musically and understands the entire scope of the musical expression, the stage direction is not of great importance. As always, I came through somehow in spite of the Oberfränkisch. I think Wolfgang was quite satisfied with me.

The cold, rainy summer had made itself felt in the throats of the singers. We all came down with colds at one time or another. Astrid Varnay, the prima donna assoluta, went around with a placard on which was printed, "I am not allowed to speak!" As the new kid on the block, I didn't risk complaining that I had a sore throat. I just rehearsed and sang with full voice. In addition to singing seven Elsas in *Lohengrin,* I was scheduled to sing Ortlinde in two performances, a so-called small role in *Die Walküre.* In Bayreuth, however, there are no small roles; every part you sing there is major.

Kirsten Flagstad sang Ortlinde and other smaller roles such as Third Norn and Gutrune in *Götterdämmerung* in her first year in Bayreuth. Only in the following year was Sieglinde entrusted to her.

One Sunday morning I awakened with no voice, I couldn't even speak. Panic-stricken, I hurried to the piano and tried to sing a few tones. Nothing. The middle voice didn't work at all. The tones broke as in yodeling or there was no sound at all. This had never happened to me before and it never happened again. The doctor in Bayreuth thought I had strained my voice by singing with a bad cold. He had no remedy to get me through the dress rehearsal scheduled for three days later.

Despair and depression do not come near describing the way I felt. I hesitated to confide to Wolfgang what misfortune had befallen me and saw myself as a pariah who would be cast out of Bayreuth. In the midst of all this fear and misfortune came a little ray of hope.

For the first time in a month I had three days in a row free, no rehearsals. These days I decided to spend in two ways. First, *no* talking. Second, very, *very* carefully, vibrating the head voice by humming on "m" and then trying with a soft tone to bring the voice down on the sounds "my," "mi," and "miei" to the middle voice. I could detect a little improvement each time, even though I still couldn't imagine singing the entire role in the coming dress rehearsal. If I were unable to sing the dress rehearsal, I would not be allowed to sing the premiere—at least, that's what I thought. I just couldn't bring myself to inform Wolfgang. Somewhere in my soul I had belief in a miracle.

The dress rehearsal began at eleven in the morning as usual. The auditorium was full. At best I hoped to get through the first aria, "Elsa's Dream," right at the beginning of the opera. I didn't dare think any further than that.

I took a deep breath, brought forth a light, almost Mozartian tone and let it vibrate in the forehead (or in the "mask," as singers say). This avoided unnecessary pressure on the vocal cords. One tone followed another under secure control (this called for keeping a cool head). It went much better than expected. When the aria ended, I felt better and thought I was in condition to go a little further, even though the opera has three long acts. The role of Elsa itself is long, and in the scene with *Lohengrin* in act 3, dramatic. Of course one can always hope for a miracle! I got through the entire role and after four hours did not feel at all tired. I *sang* my voice back to health!

After the dress rehearsal I again had a few free days before the premiere. Now I was no longer worried about my voice, as I had learned to trust my new technique.

Every performance, especially a premiere, is fraught with nerves. I always felt especially anxious in Bayreuth, face-to-face, as it were, with the Wagner Tradition. Most of those in the audience really know their Wagner. As the environs of Bayreuth have not much to offer, audience members had a great deal of time to prepare for each performance. The Wagnerites attended lectures, studied the libretto, debated endlessly, and so on and so forth! Wagner, and Wagner alone, was on their minds—and their obsession extended to the Wagner brothers, whose modern and thought-provoking productions often unleashed heated discussions.

The artists who had the honor of delivering Wagner's music were under the most intense scrutiny of the public. The listeners sit during the performance rapt. *Nothing* escapes them. If someone needs to cough, he would be well advised to consider choking to death rather than die by the sharp elbow and murderous glare of his neighbor. I knew a group of Franciscan monks from the United States who went to a performance in Bayreuth. A fly sat on the nose of one of them. He tried, as discreetly as possible, to shoo it away but every time his arm moved he received the sharp blow of an elbow in his side. After a third attempt he gave up and the fly sat pertly there for the rest of the act.

I shall never forget the premiere of *Lohengrin.* I entered, as stipulated by the stage direction, in a trancelike state, looked down at the conductor, Eugen Jochum, for my cue—and almost fell over. There he stood on the podium, in a plaid summer shirt with short sleeves and open collar! An unbelievable affront to the audience, who were in evening dress. As I had the conductor in my line of vision almost all the time, I found his appearance highly distracting. It wasn't until the intermission that I realized that because of the partially covered orchestra pit the conductor was invisible to the public. Only the orchestra and the singers had to accustom themselves to this disrespectful manner of dress. Thomas Schippers, an American, actually conducted *Meistersinger* in Bayreuth in shorts. At his next performance he found a tennis racquet placed on the conductor's stand by the musicians. He got the message and abandoned all such eccentricity for future performances.

The *Lohengrin* was superbly cast. The title role was sung by Wolfgang Windgassen. His voice was basically a lyric tenor, not big but beautiful and well-focused. I preferred him to the older, so-called Wagner singers who had a tremolo of a minor third, making it difficult to tell exactly which tone they were trying to sing. Windgassen was a singer with great style and control. He never had to force. When he thought that a conductor was taking no heed of the voice and encouraging the orchestra to extreme loudness, he brought his voice down to half-volume until the conductor realized he had better hold the orchestra down. He learned this trick from his father, Fritz Windgassen, a famous Wagner tenor as well.

Ortrud was sung by Astrid Varnay, who was phenomenal. She had the ability to express in both her voice and acting every emotion from the fawning submission to the raging fury of Ortrud. In my opinion, her interpretation has not been equaled by anyone else. Hermann Uhde, a German, was ideal as Ortrud's husband, Telramund, a weak and willing tool in Ortrud's intrigues. As Herald we had none other than Dietrich Fischer-Dieskau. Three splendid basses played King Heinrich. Ludwig Weber, from Vienna, was a veteran singer and incomparable artist. Josef Greindl was truly superb with his darker-colored bass. The young Theo Adam, was vocally of lighter weight than the others, but very quickly made the part his own. Only a few years later we would hear him as an unforgettable Hans Sachs and Wotan.

Eugen Jochum was a very able conductor. At this time he did not have the recognition he was later to receive, although he was already fifty-two. Joseph Keilberth conducted the last two performances of *Lohengrin.* He was beloved by all the singers. Calm and very accurate, Keilberth was a genuine singer's conductor and it was always wonderful to sing with him. Sadly, he died far too young, while conducting the prelude to *Tristan* in a Munich performance.

I also sang Ortlinde in *Die Walküre.* The *Ring* was given every year and did not, for that reason, need any comprehensive rehearsal. Wieland was the stage director of the *Ring* but his wife Gertrud, a choreographer, was doing the brushup staging. I was very sorry not to be able to work with Wieland himself. We were eight highly restricted Valkyries, all striking the same pose with hands on hips. We stood there like so many Greek vases, though probably not so fragile.

I have the feeling that I irritated Frau Wagner, but I cannot remember at this point in time just why. Granted, it was always difficult for me to hide my impatience when I felt that a rehearsal had accomplished nothing. Maybe that was the reason for her irritation.

Elsa was a great success for me in Bayreuth, and I had taken my place in the top flight of Wagner singers. I had the feeling, however, that Wieland was trying to avoid me. Even though the two brothers were agreed upon the goal of renewing and developing Bayreuth, one could not help noticing a certain adversity, particularly from Wieland's side. It was as if he could not grant any success to Wolfgang. More than once he threw a wrench in the works.

The next year would see a new production of *Der Fliegender Holländer.* Knappertsbusch was to conduct, with Wolfgang doing the stage direction. Wolfgang offered me the part of Senta, which made me very happy. Shortly before the end of the Festspiel, he told me that Wieland had decided that I would share the six performances with Astrid Varnay, inasmuch as she had no new assignment for the next season. I understood this point of view and agreed to it, as Astrid was unquestionably one of the mainstays of Bayreuth. Nonetheless, I agreed to the sharing of the performances *only* with the stipulation that I would sing the premiere. But, no, it was decided that Astrid would sing the first performance. Given this news, I decided to put a considerable distance between Bayreuth and myself. Wolfgang tried hard to talk me out of my decision but I was unswayed. Nothing, however, prevented my feeling greatly disappointed.

I shall never forget the final performance of *Lohengrin.* I was convinced it was the last time I would stand upon the stage of Bayreuth and fought back my tears. As we came to the end of act 3, where Lohengrin takes his farewell of Elsa and gives her his horn, shield, and ring, the dam broke! My tears were contagious and my Lohengrin wept with me; together our tears flowed to the opera's end.

After two months' sojourn, a most unhappy singer left Bayreuth to return to Skåne. Still, I could look forward to the next summer in Sweden, doing what I wished, enjoying the long bright summer nights so pleasing to me.

Just as I was beginning to lick my wounds, there came a telegram for me from Munich. Professor Knappertsbusch wished to have me for the following summer, 1955, for all the Brünnhildes in the Munich Festival. What a victory! At that time, there existed a certain rivalry between Munich and Bayreuth to see who could produce the best performances in their festivals. This suited me right down to the ground! I did not have all the Brünnhildes in my repertoire at that moment, but there was time. I interpreted Knappertsbusch's offer as revenge against the Wagner brothers' decision not to give me the premiere of *Der Fliegender Höllander* in the coming season.

Bavarian Radio carried the entire *Ring* and in the spring of 1995 a CD of one of my performances of Brünnhilde in *Götterdämmerung* was brought out. This was the first time I had sung the role in German.

September 1956 found me in Buenos Aires, where I was singing the roles of the Feldmarschallin in Strauss's *Der Rosenkavalier* and Donna Anna in Mozart's *Don Giovanni.* On the first day of the Argentinian spring, September 21, I received a telegram from Wolfgang Wagner, asking if I would like to sing Isolde in the coming year, 1957.

And *how* I would like to! Isolde in Bayreuth! Pure bliss!

But in the next moment I remembered that I should still be offended. So I telegraphed him back that I was not interested. There followed another telegram, very tempting, with names of the conductor and other singers. They were all fantastic and I began to weaken. I conferred with Bertil as to how I should handle this. He said I should not forget that at this time the world-renowned opera houses were beginning to offer me very attractive contracts and it was more important for Bayreuth to engage me than it was for me to be engaged in Bayreuth. After some deliberation I accepted but only with the stipulation that my fee should be increased 50 percent. Justice must be served!

The fees in Bayreuth were shamefully low. One sang there for the honor of being in Bayreuth. My request for a 50 percent raise was immediately granted but my punishment of Bayreuth went further than I expected. The directors felt forced to raise the fees of *all* the singers. When I returned to Bayreuth in 1957, many of the colleagues thanked me for helping them receive a salary increase.

The *Tristan* rehearsals began with great momentum. I felt more at home now in Bayreuth. For one thing, I had made progress in the German language; I even understood some Oberfränkish. And besides, I knew most of my colleagues.

Wolfgang Windgassen was, to my great joy, my Tristan. Grace Hoffman, born in America but living in Stuttgart, sang a wonderful Brangäne. She was a good colleague, direct and never fearful of expressing her opinion. No one could sing Brangäne's Warning more perfectly than she, and it was one of the high points of the evening to hear the beautiful sound of her voice penetrating the darkness of night, while I was enfolded in Tristan's arms. As the years passed we sang together many times in various operas in Europe and North America. Her friendship and good humor meant much to me and we had a lot of fun together, which helped make some of the more boring rehearsals enjoyable.

Hans Hotter and Gustav Neidlinger alternated in the role of Kurwenal, completely different in their interpretations but equally authoritative.

And finally, the thirty-five-year-old Sawallisch conducted. What a talent! What a gift! Nature was almost profligate when it came to him. In addition to his musicianship he was good-looking and had a wonderful tenor voice with perfect pitch. It was a pleasure to work with him and he spared no effort to get what he wanted. He gave everything, formed every word with his lips, and interpreted every role with his body language. He was spoken of as the new Toscanini and the expectations as to his future career were great.

Sawallisch was a master at rescuing precarious situations. Even today I remember the "Love Duet" in act 2 of the premiere. Tristan and Isolde were in complete ecstasy, repeating each other's name again and again, with "Ewig, Ewig" interspersed. The orchestra plays here an ever-returning motif on which the singer cannot depend. Tristan and Isolde must simply listen to each other and make all their replies to each other. Suddenly, the totally unexpected happened. Windgassen, always so secure, oh my, got lost! I was immediately confused and completely lost the thread. For a long time (well, to *me* it seemed an eternity) no one sang—and compounding the horror, it was a radio broadcast. I knew that soon I had a high B to sing and stared down at the conductor spellbound. He raised his hand and gave me the exact entrance, I came in with the high B on "Ewig," and the evening was saved.

The same thing supposedly happened in Bayreuth between Nanny Larsén-Todsen and Lauritz Melchior, with Toscanini conducting. They got lost in the same devilish duet. Todsen rushed forward with outstretched arms to get help from the conductor but Toscanini tore his hair and cried from confusion. Because he conducted from memory, he was unable to rescue the singers. The duet, as the story goes, ended in musical chaos.

Along with six evenings as Isolde, I sang the Third Norn in both performances of *Götterdämmerung* as well as two Sieglindes in *Walküre.* The long, drawn-out tempi taken by Knappertsbusch, who conducted the *Ring,* were not only in accord with Wagner's indications but musically deeply expressive.

Ramon Vinay, a Chilean tenor, was an inspiring Siegmund. He was very much in demand as dramatic tenor and two years later would be my Tristan at the Metropolitan in New York. He was very popular, and on the days when he was not singing in Bayreuth he took off to Salzburg where he assumed the role of Otello. Once, during a performance of *Tannhäuser,* his nerves as well as his voice failed him: during the intermission between acts 1 and 2, he fled head over heels through his dressing room window. The festival management searched everywhere for him but he was not to be found. Instead of finding Vinay, they ran into Windgassen, who thought he was taking a quiet evening stroll. Instead he found himself shoved into a car and driven in unseemly haste to the opera house. The second act could begin as soon as he was in costume and make-up. And so it did, as though nothing had happened. Windgassen was a professional from head to toe and fortunately had the necessary nerve for such an adventure.

I remember very well the rest of the cast in *Die Walküre.* Hans Hotter with his 6 feet 4 inches height, was an imposing Wotan. Wieland Wagner had looked with a loving eye on Greek mythology in his version of the *Ring,* and Hotter looked the perfect Greek god with his blond wig and Hellenic-inspired costume. His interpretation of the role was thought out down to the minutest detail, to every raising of his eyebrows and every shrug of his shoulders. The effect was as though everything was computerized. But he was not a computer; he was a great personality. Rarely did he look at his favorite daughter, Brünnhilde; in his opinion, it would have diminished his divine image. The public was deeply moved and brought to tears, although his colleagues were somewhat less than enraptured. But it is the audience that pays, and we artists are engaged to pluck the heartstrings of the public.

Astrid Varnay was a superior Brünnhilde. Georgine von Milinkovic, a Yugoslavian, was a very personable Fricka, and Josef Greindl, an unbelievable Hunding. His talent for matching the word and tone quality to the situation was phenomenal. In act 1, when Hunding sends his wife, Sieglinde, out of the room as he notices her intense interest in their guest, Siegmund, he sings, "Fort aus dem Saal, säume hier nicht! Den Nachtrunk rüste mir drin und harre mein *zur Ruh.*" (Leave the room, don't linger here! Prepare my night drink and wait until I come to rest.) Greindl delivered those last two words with such lustful insinuation that everyone knew his meaning was quite the opposite of rest.

As Sieglinde, I received stage direction from Gertrud as well as Wieland Wagner. Although this was not a new production, it was not easy for Wieland in only five days to work with every individual involved in the *Ring.* The little I got to know of Wieland whetted my appetite for more. Nonetheless, I did not appreciate his trying to create competition between Varnay and me. As usual, I again had a great success, confirmed by both the press and the audience. To my great pleasure and surprise, I received a huge bouquet of dark red roses from Wieland after the premiere.

There was another fantastic Brünnhilde in Bayreuth who alternated with Astrid Varnay, Martha Mödl, a German who was a great artist and great personality. (Is there such a thing as a great artist who is not a great personality?) Wieland Wagner had talked her into abandoning her natural voice classification of mezzo-soprano, and pushing the voice up a few tones into dramatic soprano territory. She had a beautiful velvety quality and was a wonderful Kundry, Brünnhilde, and Isolde. Occasionally Wagnerian dramatic sopranos were originally mezzo-sopranos, for example: Olive Fremstad (Swedish-Norwegian), Anny Konetzni (Austrian), Helen Traubel (American), and many others. These voices had by nature a fuller-sounding middle range than the natural dramatic soprano. In Wagner's operas there are many scenes that lie more advantageously for a mezzo than for a soprano, for example: a large part of Sieglinde's "Der Männer Sippe," Brünnhilde's "Todesverkündigung" in *Die Walküre,* and Brünnhilde's scene with Waltraute in act 1 of *Götterdämmerung.*

But when the tessitura lies higher, in the comfortable range for the soprano (in *Siegfried,* for instance), the darker voices can be in trouble. The role of Brünnhilde in *Siegfried* can easily be a nightmare for the heavier voices. In those cases the high C at the end was often taken an octave down. The "Hojotoho" in *Die Walküre* is another exposed bit of singing.

Helen Traubel had it transposed, while others fight a losing battle trying to get to the high Bs and Cs.

My good friend Grace Hoffman toyed with the idea of singing Brünnhilde in *Die Walküre.* She had a high mezzo and I can well understand the temptation that existed there. But I don't believe she ever seriously followed through. I got a rise out of her by saying if she really wanted to sing Brünnhilde, I would stand in the wings and sing high notes for her. Actually, she did sing the Brünnhilde without telling me, but it was a one-time event. After some successful years as a soprano, Martha Mödl returned to Bayreuth to the mezzo-soprano role of Waltraute (in which performance I sang Brünnhilde). She was a very fascinating artist, who always sang from the heart.

Astrid Varnay was a quite different kind of singer. Her interpretations stemmed more from the intellect. Musically, she was head and shoulders above her colleagues. Her middle voice, in its firm and dark timbre, reminded one more of a mezzo. She had through technical dexterity acquired high tones, although they did not always match the sound of her natural timbre. So far as I know, she always sang soprano roles—except for Amneris in Verdi's *Aida.* Her debut in that part took place in Chicago at the Lyric Opera. When her friends and colleagues asked why she was singing Amneris instead of her usual role of Aida, she said, "For a thousand dollars I would sing Wotan."

In private life I was often taken for Astrid Varnay. The doorman at the Festspielhaus had real difficulty telling us apart. But one day he proudly proclaimed he could see the difference: Varnay had blue-green eyes and mine were brownish-green. The next day, with my sunglasses on, I received Varnay's mail from him. Later on, he had another trick to recognize us: the voice. The next day, faced with both sunglasses and no greeting, he was lost again.

I was invited to a banquet given by the Wagner clan. Across from me sat a man who suffered from compulsive chattering. He wore me out and I was simply unable to get across to him that I was not the person he thought I was: Astrid Varnay. He covered me with compliments and spoke of how marvelous I was (that is, *she* was). I thanked him with a crooked smile and hoped the theme was therewith closed. But no, he then continued with how surprised he was that this newcomer, Nilsson, was praised to the skies while I (Varnay) was so much better. I called on my crooked smile again, thanked him, and began to speak with my neighbor. In this moment a lady from a neighboring table came over to me and twittered with a well-carrying voice, "Frau Nilsson, I have to thank you for your fantastic Isolde, etc. etc." This brought the compulsive talker to a stunned silence. The man alternated between red and pale. I felt a little sorry for him but I was very happy that something finally shut him up.

Many years before, I had received a letter from the former head of Covent Garden in London, Sir David Webster. He was very excited and was enclosing a copy of a contract for a future guest performance. He recalled how stunned he was, when we met in Vienna, that I had no contract with Covent Garden. But I was absolutely not in Vienna during the time in question. My doppelgänger, Varnay, was haunting me again.

In later years, Astrid moved into mezzo roles. Whereas formerly she sang the title role of Elektra, she later essayed Klytämnestra, Elektra's mother. When I sang her daughter Elektra, I kidded her by calling her "Mutti." She also sang the Amme in Strauss's *Die Frau ohne Schatten,* and I often sang the Dyer's Wife in the same opera, which gave us many years of working together even after Bayreuth.

Wolfgang Wagner's staging of *Tristan* was given twice more, in 1958 and 1959, with approximately the same cast. A young, gifted tenor, Fritz Uhl, sang Melot all three years. He soon wore the mantle of Tristan; indeed, by 1960, we were the lovers in the Decca recording of *Tristan,* with Georg Solti conducting (or, rather, Sir Georg, by that time).

Musically, Wolfgang's *Tristan* performances were first-class, and in their austerity they were scenically appealing. The provocative stage directors had not yet, thank God, begun their devastating interventions.

Usually I lived in the Hotel Reichsadler, but when the Festspiel began I had to seek other living quarters because the festival guests, of course, had to have the best accommodations. In an emergency one could get a room (that is, closet) without bath that looked out on the back street. There you were subject to disturbances from two sides: traffic noise and the constant deliveries to the hotel, day and night. That meant you simply tried to tune the noise out when you ran out of earplugs.

The food in the hotel was quite good, though after a while the menu became monotonous. One day, however, the chef was apparently overtaken by a burst of energy. There was a new dish on the menu: Omelet à la Varnay. Astrid was tremendously popular in Bayreuth and certainly deserved this honor. I was informed that this was a French omelet with fresh raspberries and, naturally, I wanted to try this heavenly concoction. With great dignity the waiter set the porcelain plate down before me. Suddenly something very strange occurred. The whole plate seemed to move. I looked closely and discovered the plate was almost completely covered with tiny insects! The omelet had been made with *wild* raspberries, and when the little insects felt the heat of the omelet they fled for their lives to the safety of the cool edge of the plate. I called the waiter and with ill-concealed gloating burst out, "Aha, deswegen also!" (So, is *this* how you get the bugs out of the raspberries?)

The next day they had Rumpsteak à la Nilsson.

Once each summer all those taking part in the festival were invited with their spouses to the Villa Wahnfried. There was all manner of food and drink. No one was to be unhappy. There was considerable horsing around, and singing of a kind strictly taboo in the opera house, with dancing until the early hours of the morning. Sometimes things got so out of hand that one wondered if Richard (or at least Cosima) was turning in the grave out there in Wahnfried's Park.

In 1960 there was to be a new *Ring* presented in Bayreuth. This would be the second since the reopening of the theater in 1951. This time Wolfgang Wagner was to have the responsibility for the production and stage direction. For the first time in the history of *Ring* productions, Wolfgang had constructed a thick, heavy, concave disc, which was suspended over the stage floor. This light-colored disc was somewhat slanted and was to symbolize the friendly world. In opposition to this concave side, the convex underside was a dark, gloomy color, and representing the world of evil that created the ring and the curse on the gold. The disc could be broken down into three segments and two sectors, and these five parts could be moved in any direction. With very artistic lighting one could mount the entire *Ring* using these parts of the disc as the various sets.

Only twice during the four performances was the disc complete and intact: at the beginning, before the power of gold had brought evil into the world; and at the end, after Valhalla had gone up in flames and the ring had been returned to the Rheinmaidens. Only then were we given hope for a new and better world. This ingenious idea of the *Ring* disc would be taken over not only by Wieland, but throughout the opera world, at least by those houses that wanted to connect with Bayreuth's new art form. Producers took a long look at Bayreuth and copied the productions, just as the gowns of the top fashion designers are copied by dress factories.

The results were quite varied. No one equaled the Bayreuth original; they lacked the lighting possibilities—and above all, the superb lighting designers—that the Wagner brothers had.

Still, Wolfgang did have difficulties with his *Ring* disc. A dangerously short time before the premiere it was found that the mechanism that moved the disc, made by a steel construction company in Bayreuth, was much too weak. One morning it gave way under the enormous weight. This was no misfortune but a real catastrophe. Rumors of what had happened spread like wildfire in the city. No one could see how any sort of performance could come out of this, and Wolfgang had everyone's sympathy. The only one unshaken by it all was Wieland. One day Wolfgang got a useful tip from a gas station owner in the city. This man knew a merry-go-round builder in Coburg who worked with hydraulic systems. Wolfgang got in touch with this man, who succeeded in constructing, in record time, a special hydraulic system that put the whole construction on firm footing.

Naturally, much time was lost because of this incident. Wieland refused to help by giving up any of his planned rehearsal time (he did not have a new production this year). And so we had to work into the night to make up for the lost time.

Wolfgang's cast looked quite different from Wieland's two productions. The American bass Jerome Hines, over six feet tall, sang Wotan for the first time. I shall never forget the premiere of *Die Walküre.* Just seconds before the curtain went up on Wotan's most important act (and Brünnhilde's to some extent), Wolfgang rushed onto the stage and almost tore off Wotan's finger, on which was shining a ring almost as large as the Niebelungen ring. Wotan was about to tell how he obtained the ring and used it to pay for the construction of Valhalla, and how he had later thrown the ring into the Rhein. This fact seemed to have escaped the notice of the new Wotan and he protested loudly, swearing he would not sing without his talisman. But Wolfgang ended the argument as victor and disappeared in the last moment with the fetish.

Wolfgang Windgassen sang Siegmund but was replaced in the following year by Fritz Uhl. Siegmund was not one of Windgassen's best roles, as it lies too low for a real lyric tenor. Gottlob Frick, the darkest bass sound in the world, sang Hunding as well as Hagen.

Two of my best friends and colleagues were the Norwegians Ingrid Bjoner and Aase Nordmo-Løvberg. Ingrid sang Freia in *Rheingold,* Helmwige in *Walküre,* and Gutrune in *Götterdämmerung.* Later in her career she had great success as Turandot, Isolde, Elektra, and other big dramatic roles.

Aase sang Sieglinde in *Walküre* and the Third Norn in *Götterdämmerung.* She was the acknowledged favorite not only in Norway, but in Stockholm as well. In parts of her voice she reminded one of the young

Kirsten Flagstad. Grace Hoffman sang the Siegrune in *Walküre*, Waltraute in *Götterdämmerung;* in the previous year she had been Fricka in *Walküre.*

Hans Hopf sang the title role in *Siegfried* and Siegfried in *Götterdämmerung.* He was singing both roles for the first time and naturally had put in yeoman's work to have readied these mammoth roles for performances on the level demanded by the Bayreuth Festival. Formerly he had sung primarily the Italian repertoire, but was now beginning to concentrate on Wagner roles, which suited his robust voice very well. Hopf was an incomparable raconteur, and one was never bored in his company. I remember a New Year's Eve in Bertil's and my New York apartment, which we spent in the company of Hans Hopf and Gottlob Frick. We laughed our way out of the old year and into a good part of the New Year. Hopf and Frick, both from Munich, were good friends. In Bayreuth they shared an apartment during the rehearsal period. (As they were both prototypes of masculinity, they risked no innuendo.)

The dress rehearsal of *Siegfried* went off without any major mishaps, even though when Siegfried awakened the sleeping Brünnhilde with a kiss, he sang, "Brünnhilde bin ich, die dich erweckt" (Brünnhilde am I, that awakens you). Amazing things can happen in a dress rehearsal. Wolfgang likes to tell of Lauritz Melchior's working through the dress rehearsal of *Siegfried* with the piano score in his hand. Notwithstanding, he came later to be regarded in the United States as the greatest Wagner tenor in the world.

The excellent Rudolf Kempe was the conductor of this *Ring.* I had sung these operas with him in London in 1957, and I remember how delighted I was to hear he would be in Bayreuth. But here he was unrecognizable. In Bayreuth he appeared awkward and complained that he could not hear the singers. The acoustics in Bayreuth are especially good. In the auditorium the balance between singer and orchestra is perfect, but for the conductor, who is standing in the middle of the thundering sound and with the pit partially covered, it is not easy to hear the singers. Kempe was not the first to complain of this problem. If memory serves, Georg Solti was said to have been bothered by this. On the other hand, Karl Böhm and Sawallisch never complained about not hearing the singers. I personally believe there are two kinds of opera conductors: those who sing the vocal lines along in their heads and those who listen for the singers. The latter kind will always have difficulty in Bayreuth. I recall that Eugen Jochum explained how he "rescued" himself in Bayreuth when he was conducting *Meistersinger.* The chorus, which was far upstage, was inaudible but he watched a tall bass who had impeccable articulation and followed the movements of his mouth. This was his way of rising above the problem.

In almost all the productions of the Wagner brothers, the stage was built so that it sloped toward the audience, the so-called raked stage. But in their *Ring*, the stage was excessively raked. For the public this is very effective, but for the singers, it's a tremendous strain on the back and feet. I sometimes wished I had one leg shorter than the other. At least the movements across the stage would have been easier.

We often hear how easy it is to sing in Bayreuth and how fantastically the voices carry. The latter I am ready to concede; however, I do not find it all that easy to sing there. I realize that one is heard well, but when a stage puts the enormous orchestra sound right in your ears, you are easily tempted to give more than necessary. The covered orchestra pit was to blame for this. In 1960, when I was singing Brünnhilde, the four operas were given with one free day between *Walküre* and *Siegfried.* I managed this without a problem, but I found in general it was not good for singers to work under this pressure. Therefore, I demanded another free day between *Siegfried* and *Götterdämmerung.* I ran up against resistance from the Wagners, who felt the public would not put up with the extra free day because their stay in Bayreuth would be too long and too expensive. I asked if this exacting audience would not find it more important to hear rested, fresh voices than to save a few marks on a hotel room. Apart from that, Wouldn't it be a good idea to give another opera on the day the *Ring* cast performers had free? I won my case; eventually, the four *Ring* operas were performed with two days between each performance.

The performances in Bayreuth began as early as 4 P.M. This timing was difficult; it meant that right after lunch one had to go to the Festspielhaus. I was always in my dressing room two hours before the beginning of every performance. After act 1 there was, as I recall, a long intermission, lasting one and a half-hours. In this interval the audience could partake of their German "Abendbrot" (supper; literally, evening bread). The other intermissions were shorter, lasting fifty minutes or so.

It was not easy to keep concentration on a high level during these long breaks, and I often had the feeling the voice would just shut down. The voice had to be kept warmed-up by all manner of exercises. There were many in the audience who did not have supper in the first interval, probably because of the high cost of meals there. A few had the disagreeable habit, particularly when it rained, of visiting the singers in their dressing rooms. This passed the time (for *them*), and later they could brag about what news this or that artist had to tell them. But it was a very disturbing custom, nonetheless. It was impossible for me to sit there and chat away about nothing, and in the next moment throw my entire being into the interpretation of one of opera's most demanding roles. I often locked the door and refused to answer the repeated knocks. There were those who simply would not give up but returned every ten minutes. I sat there like a bird in a cage. On Astrid Varnay's dressing room door was often a sign just like the doctors use: "Keine Sprechstunde" (No visiting hours).

After a good meal it could happen that the Festspiel guests were satiated and tired. The wife of the Aga Khan, the (Princess) Begum, very beautiful and elegant in her chiffon creation was returning to her seat in a row where a gentleman had made himself comfortable by opening a part of his tuxedo. As she passed, the gentleman rose and remembered to close his zipper. But a second too late: the delicate chiffon of the Begum's gown was caught. No matter how they pushed and pulled, the dress was held fast. They heard the second act bound together; whether in the intermission the ladies' or men's restroom was used for the freeing of the chiffon from the zipper, nobody knows. Later, the Begum had great fun relating this story—without, however, revealing that it was she herself who was caught in the zipper.

When the first *Ring* was over, I was able to go back to Sweden for fourteen days and enjoy the Swedish summer, swimming, letting myself go, and singing a few concerts in Copenhagen's Tivoli and in Gröna Lund in Sweden.

As the second *Ring* got under way, I caught a horrible cold and had to cancel. Astrid Varnay jumped in for me. On the next performance, I managed to get through the *Siegfried* Brünnhilde. After that my fever shot up and I felt really ill. Wolfgang Wagner's charming wife, Ellen, visited me in the morning. She had a fantastic gift for me: Richard Wagner's handkerchief! She and Wolfgang hoped the gift would make me feel better! It was a very large silk handkerchief with a Persian design that Wagner used to stuff in his right trouser pocket, from which it hung down to his shin. He was a zealous nose-blower and always kept such silk handkerchiefs at hand. It was clearly well used, as there were many small, fine darning stitches in the weave of the silk. I was greatly touched by Ellen Wagner's lovely gesture, but, unfortunately, it offered no magical cure. I had to cancel the *Götterdämmerung* and return home to recover from my flu.

. . .

Isolde is surely the dream of every dramatic soprano (and perhaps other sopranos). When I learned that Wieland was planning a new production of *Tristan und Isolde* in 1962, I thought, "It's now or never. This will be my only chance to work on a role from the ground up with Wieland."

I heard rumors, however, that he was toying with the idea of a young Isolde, one, in fact, who had never sung the role previously. Wieland had approached two mezzo-sopranos about the role but almost at the same time decided to give the role to this soprano. It was said that he must be very much in love to find her voice beautiful. I guess, love is not only blind but deaf.

I found no explanation for Wieland's not offering me the Isolde immediately. Perhaps, in spite of his falling to his knees before me ten years ago, I was not his type. Or had I had *too* great a success in Wolfgang's production? Possibly he thought that, as I had sung eighty-seven Isoldes, I would not be open to new ideas. Or, perhaps, because I had just had a triumph as Isolde at the Metropolitan Opera. I really can't say. Had Karl Böhm been conducting *Tristan,* perhaps he would have requested me. In any case, just as I had given up all hope, I received the offer. I swallowed my pride and answered after a half-second's reflection: Yes.

One could ask why I was so keen on spending the whole summer in Bayreuth and giving up the thought of any vacation, which I really needed. It was certainly not the money that tempted me! The rehearsal period was not paid and the fee was a tenth of what I was demanding in my other German engagements. But I had an unshakable feeling that working with Wieland would help me further my artistic development, which I needed. I thought there was no other director who could accomplish this.

It was a quite reserved Wieland Wagner who greeted me at our first one-on-one rehearsal. I, of course, knew him at that time, but it was almost as though we were meeting for the first time. He was at the ready.

He was dressed sportily, his hair was sprinkled with gray, and he had watery-blue eyes that were totally expressionless when he looked at you. But you felt that behind this was a great intensity. His hands were expressive and beautifully formed with slender fingers and bitten nails. He had a soft, sensitive mouth and lovely teeth. He laughed occasionally, either from nerves, malice, or embarrassment. His sense of humor was evident more in his shoulders, which he moved up and down, rather than in his eyes. His temperament could be likened to that of a volcano, with the eruption signaled by a soft whistling, like a teakettle beginning to boil over. His mother, Winifred Wagner, could confirm that over the years, many bacon and egg breakfasts had landed on the wallpaper. "Herr Wagner," I heard myself saying. "I have sung Isolde eighty-seven times and . . ."

"You don't need to tell me that," he interrupted, "I know that all too well."

"Let me continue," I said raising my voice, "I have, as I said, sung Isolde eighty-seven times. But I have the intention of forgetting all the interpretations up to now and working with you as though from the beginning."

"Very good," he answered—but I could tell that he didn't quite believe me.

We began the rehearsals. After an hour Wieland began to see that I had meant what I had said. His expression had brightened noticeably, and I noticed our working together afforded him as much pleasure as it did for me. Everything seemed to fit together nicely.

As a young man, Wieland had studied painting and sculpture; he was, in fact, a very good painter. This ability, together with his almost frightening talent for sharp observation, made it possible for him to bring out the individuality of his actors. He made the role fit the personality of the performer much as a tailor fits a dress to the individual's form.

Most other stage directors with whom I have worked had the interpretation of the role laid out long before they had set eyes on the particular artist who would play the part. In other words, the dress was already finished and the artist had no choice but to squeeze into it no matter how uncomfortable it was or how ill-fitting the style.

What heaven! Wieland could bring out the most varied characterizations through the mere suggestion of a gesture. The complicated psychological problems he explained through contemporary, irreverent comparisons, which kept us all in a good mood.

The three-hour rehearsal went by in no time. Wieland himself was more than satisfied and I looked forward to each day's rehearsal. After six days, I had the concept of the role clearly in my mind, and it was, in many ways, a new Isolde that saw the light of day.

I have always loved the first act. It has so much depth and there are many possibilities for expression. My first stage director was the former director of the Munich Opera, Rudolf Hartmann, who staged this opera in Stockholm. He emphasized again and again that the first act was pure hate and it had left its scars. I, however, had the feeling that Isolde had more colors on her palette than black and white, but I was unable to find expression for the various shadings.

When one is engaged for a guest performance in strange countries and is on unfamiliar stages, it is not often that one gets to work personally with a stage director. This could be because they are always short of time. For my part, I think it has its roots in the unspoken rule: "Do not meddle with the prima donna." What a pity!

Before, I always played Isolde in the first act as filled with hate and seeking revenge. But now the role received a new dimension. Except for an almost animal wildness in the tumultuous moments, Isolde's longing was brought out in her voice, her body language, and her facial expression. Especially in the dialogue with Tristan, full of double-meaning exchanges, this is true. Her lips speak of humiliation and revenge but her heart speaks only of love. Over Isolde's entire persona must be written, "I love you! I love you!" This work brought about a far-reaching change: at some point, there was talk of Nilsson's "new" Isolde. Wieland Wagner himself described his three Bayreuth Isoldes as follows: "Martha Mödl was the tragic Isolde, cursed by fate; Astrid Varnay was the revenge-seeking Isolde; and Birgit Nilsson was the loving Isolde."

Now is the time for a short summary of the story of *Tristan und Isolde.* Isolde, a young Irish princess, discovers one day a canoe floating near the coast. In the canoe is a wounded knight with his sword by his side. She brings him on land and tends his wounds with the magical healing art she has learned from her mother.

Suddenly, Isolde recognizes the wounded knight as Tristan, who had killed her betrothed, Moralt, in battle. She is crazed with anger and seizes his sword, intending to kill him. At this moment he opens his eyes and looks upon Isolde. She is stricken with the wonder of love, as though struck with lightening, and lets the sword fall. She continues to care for the murderer of her betrothed until he is able to return to his homeland and relative, the old King Marke of Cornwall.

The king has heard of the lovely Isolde, the heir to the crown of Ireland. He commands Tristan to return to Ireland and bring Isolde back to Cornwall to be the future bride of King Marke. This is the prehistory.

As the curtain rises on act 1, Isolde is seen onboard a ship that is bringing her to Marke's castle. She comes out of her deep shock and wants to know where the ship is taking her. When told, she spews invective against Tristan: "Fluch der Verräter! Fluch deinem Haupt! Rache!

Tod! Tod uns beiden!" (Curse the traitor! Curses upon him! Revenge! Death! Death to us both!)

She then commands Brangäne to bring Tristan to her. There ensues a dialogue thick with double-meanings, in which both attempt to cover up their love—Isolde, from pride, and Tristan, because of his duty to King Marke. In the hopelessness and confusion, Isolde orders Brangäne to prepare a potion, a drink of reconciliation, she tells Tristan. But before Tristan's visit she has apprised Brangäne of her plan: she is ordered to prepare a poisonous drink. Tristan must die. Tristan, in their strange dialogue, lets Isolde know that he realizes what is awaiting him but takes the drink from the cup. Before he has finished the poisoned drink, Isolde tears the cup from his hand and downs the rest of the drink. She falls into Tristan's arms, thinking they will die together.

Brangäne, knowing the depth of the love Isolde has for Tristan, cannot find it in herself to do Isolde's bidding. She wants Isolde's feelings to be returned; instead of a poisoned brew, she prepares a love potion.

As Tristan and Isolde awaken from what they believed to be a last embrace and realize they still live, they break into a jubilant love duet. Then comes the signal that they are approaching the coast of Cornwall where King Marke awaits them. Brangäne releases Isolde from Tristan's embrace and informs her that she gave them a love potion. Isolde sinks, half-fainting, in Brangäne's arms. Against her will, she is taken on land and led to her future husband, King Marke.

The second act consists for the most part of the passionate love scene with the long, wonderful duet between Tristan and Isolde (who is now the wife of King Marke). This duet is the high point of the act. The lovers wait impatiently every evening for the darkness to protect them in their love tryst. Brangäne warns Isolde that Melot (who also loves Isolde) is spying on the lovers. But Isolde does not take her seriously. She sets her maidservant straight by reminding her that Melot is Tristan's best friend and looks after her (Isolde's) well-being better than she (Brangäne)—until one evening Tristan and Isolde are discovered by a hunting party led by King Marke and Melot. After Marke's long monologue expressing his disillusionment, a fight breaks out. Full of guilt and remorse, Tristan purposely throws himself in the path of Melot's sword and is wounded.

The third act takes place in an isolated wilderness in the mountains of Brittany where the wounded Tristan has been brought. He is very weak and near death. In his feverish delirium, he dreams day and night of Isolde and imagines he sees her ship nearing the coast. His trusted servant, Kurwenal, keeps watch, looking toward the sea. At last he sees a ship on the horizon. Tristan summons his last bit of strength, goes to Isolde with unsteady steps, falls into her arms and dies.

Another ship arrives, with King Marke onboard. Kurwenal prepares himself for a battle. Before the king can explain that he has come in friendship, Kurwenal has killed Melot and is himself fatally wounded.

Brangäne has explained to the king about the exchange of the drink on board the ship and King Marke has sailed in haste to Tristan and Isolde to forgive them. But it is too late.

I have sung *Tristan* with many wonderful conductors, thirty-three, to be exact. But I have no hesitation in saying that no one could measure up to Karl Böhm's musical interpretation. It was from beginning to end a declaration of love.

Böhm, during this *Tristan* production, was himself going through a difficult time personally. His wife, Thea, always his greatest admirer, had to undergo a serious operation, the outcome of which was uncertain. One noticed that he often wiped away tears as he conducted and I felt certain that this *Tristan* was dedicated to her. To everyone's joy, Thea did recover and regained her health and was present for the following seven summers in which *Tristan* was given.

Wolfgang Windgassen was again a marvelous Tristan, with more depth than ever to his interpretation. Kerstin Meyer sang a wonderful Brangäne, a thoroughly believable self-sacrificing maidservant. One did not doubt for a moment that she, in the dark of night, would represent Isolde in the marriage bed, so that King Marke did not notice Isolde's absence when she and Tristan met. Wieland often said it was difficult to find an ideal Brangäne as she must be willing to subjugate herself to the role of a loyal servant. Most of them want to play first violin.

Josef Greindl sang and played the part of King Marke with nobility and honor. Eberhard Wächter made the role of Kurwenal his own. Nils Möller interpreted Melot with great intensity. Gerhard Stolze as the Shepherd and Georg Paskuda as the Seaman proved there is no such thing as a small role, and a young tenor, Hans Hanno Daum, did extremely well with the part of the Helmsman.

Wieland's genius for lighting made a set almost superfluous. With the exception of a very prominent phallic symbol, the stage was empty. Until then no one had displayed such talent in the use of projections, color, and lighting to create effect—indeed, to enhance the romantic drama of Wagner's music. I am very grateful and happy that I was a part of this *Tristan,* one of the most fantastic operatic experiences imaginable—and the one that Wieland said came as near as possible to his ideal.

The celebration after the *Tristan* premiere in the Neue Schloss began unusually late. The audience held us with their enthusiasm for a long time, until all the lights were turned off. Even then our exit was barricaded by autograph seekers with programs extended. Very tiring but also very satisfying.

I sat at the banquet table between Karl Böhm and the mayor, Hans Wild. We were still overcome from the tremendous thrill of the performance. Karl Böhm was in the best of moods (which, God knows, was not always the case) and in an attack of exaggerated praise, turned to me and said, "Birgit, when you stop singing, I will stop conducting."

This unheard-of compliment was hard for the mayor to trump. He was quiet for a while and then said to me, "Miss Nilsson, we would be honored to have you buried in Bayreuth!"

Wieland achieved his greatest artistic triumph with this *Tristan*, and engaged me for the Brünnhilde in the *Ring* he was going to direct in 1965.

With the exception of the year of the 1965 *Ring*, I sang Isolde every season until 1970. Wieland also staged an *Elektra* in Vienna in 1965 with Karl Böhm as conductor, Leonie Rysanek as Chrysothemis, and Regina Resnik as Klytemnestra. Both singers were unequaled in their roles, and the production proved a tremendous success for everyone involved. I remember Wieland was of the opinion that my Elektra had given a lot of competition to my Isolde. He also said in an interview: "Nilsson was famous before she was great." That was certainly true. But in this case, Wieland Wagner was to blame: after falling on his knees before me so long ago, he let too much time pass before we worked together.

But back to the *Ring* of 1965.

Wieland had again assembled an overwhelming ensemble. After his huge success with *Tristan*, Karl Böhm was chosen as the conductor. Böhm, who was known primarily throughout the world as a Strauss and Mozart interpreter, surprised many with his sure grasp of Wagner. It was no Knappertsbusch *Ring* with long, sustained phrasing and crescendos reaching bombastic fortissimos. Böhm's tempi were more flowing, and compared to Knappertsbusch, his orchestral sound was transparent in its brightness and clarity.

The *Tristan* as well as the *Ring* were recorded live. Leonie Rysanek and James King were perfect as the ill-fated Wälsungen pair. They were also real friends and good colleagues. The first act crackled with eroticism and the curtain fell not a moment too soon. We avoided witnessing Sieglinde's

Order ID: 002-5909893-4496268

Thank you for buying from Richard G. Lee on Amazon Marketplace.

Shipping Address: Barbara Garrison 48 KNOX CIR EVANSTON, IL 60201-1912		Order Date: Shipping Service: Buyer Name: Seller Name:	Dec 23, 2009 Standard barbara garrison Richard G. Lee

Quantity	Product Details
1	**La Nilsson: My Life in Opera [Hardcover] by Nilsson, Birgit; Popper, Doris...** **Merchant SKU:** Q0-LH6S-8WGF **ASIN:** 1555536700 **Listing ID:** 1025ERIAHV7 **Order-Item ID:** 27969515293674 **Condition:** New **Comments:** Private Collection; 2007, Estate of Birgit Nilsson, A personal memoir, a good read for the interested, though perhaps not the last word. No shelf wear, no wear and tear. Not Priced, Shipped from NYC

Thanks for buying on Amazon Marketplace. To provide feedback for the seller please visit www.amazon.com/feedback. To contact the seller, please visit Amazon.com and click on "Your Account" at the top of any page. In Your Account, go to the "Orders" section and click on the link "Leave seller feedback". Select the order or click on the "View Order" button. Click on the "seller profile" under the appropriate product. On the lower right side of the page under "Seller Help", click on "Contact this seller".

breaking of her marriage vow. In 1965, the stage directors still left something to the imagination of the audience.

Martti Tavela, a Finnish bass was a convincing Fasolt and a powerful Hunding. Ursula Böse sang Fricka. Josef Greindl's Hagen was hard to surpass. He replaced George London as the Wanderer in *Siegfried.* Kerstin Meyer sang Waltraute and a Rheinmaiden. Gustav Neidlinger was incomparable as the wrathful Alberich. Erwin Wohlfahrt was the absolute best Mime ever. Gutrune and Gunther were also cast with stars: Ludmila Dvořáková and Thomas Stewart. Theo Adam was an introspective Wotan without pathos.

Wieland brought out all of Adam's potential. His youthful appearance and jaunty carriage worked for this interpretation, and he was an intriguing and quite different Wotan than we have come to expect. Brünnhilde was in the beginning a young fresh warrior maiden. During her "Hojotoho" cry she frolicked about the stage gaily, declaring that upon the appearance of his distraught and offended wife, Fricka, she would abandon him.

Wieland wished to have me bring out the variety in the phases of Brünnhilde's life. At her awakening in *Siegfried,* she is still the daughter of a god, but when she sees Siegfried, the audacious young hero, her maternal feelings are awakened. She is so much wiser than he is, she wants to protect him: he is, after all, the son of Sieglinde and Siegmund, therefore her nephew. But soon other feelings develop; the affection between Brünnhilde and Siegfried becomes love. The opera ends with a soaring duet of unheard-of vocal demands, crowned by Brünnhilde's sustained high C in the most difficult of keys, C Major.

At the beginning of the first act of *Götterdämmerung,* she is the ever-faithful wife. At the act's end, as Siegfried goes off seeking new battles, he gives her his ring and she gives him her horse, Grane. Soon, however, Brünnhilde experiences the most shameful betrayal by her hero. Siegfried has been made to forget Brünnhilde through a magic drink prepared by Hagen. Siegfried's former life and Brünnhilde are erased from his memory. He takes another woman in marriage, Gutrune.

Betrayed, Brünnhilde turns into a vengeful woman, and she is drawn into a plot against Siegfried in which she reveals that he can be wounded only in one place on his back. Siegfried is stabbed there by Hagan's spear and the fallen Siegfried is brought to Brünnhilde's side. She orders a huge pyre to be built and Valhalla to be destroyed by fire. Once again, she has become the omniscient daughter of a god. After Brünnhilde has taken the ring from Siegfried's finger, his corpse is laid on the pyre that will engulf Valhalla in flames. With Grane, her loyal steed, Brünnhilde rides into the flames, joining her fallen hero in death. The way is herewith opened to a new and better world.

During a rehearsal for *Götterdämmerung,* Böhm shouted to Wieland and me onstage: "Such a Brünnhilde I have not heard in forty years!" I was audacious enough to ask whom he had heard back then. I suppose I offended him; he didn't answer.

It was impossible for Wieland to dedicate enough time to every singer, as he had to have all the *Ring* operas ready at the same time. "But," he said, "what we have not been able to do this year with individual instruction, we will have to refine next year."

The premiere was a great success, and the press predicted this would be a history-making *Ring.*

Wolfgang Windgassen sang his hundredth performance of *Siegfried* with a voice as fresh as it was for his first. After the premiere, I received a telegram from Wieland: "Dear Birgit, yesterday you surpassed yourself. I am grateful to you and sincerely admire you. Yours, Wieland Wagner"

Unfortunately there was no opportunity for Wieland Wagner to refine the *Ring* the following season. On the seventeenth of June, 1966, Wieland was taken to the hospital. No cause was found for the illness, and he himself made light of it. Peter Lehmann, today director of the Hannover Opera, had been an assistant stage director in Bayreuth since 1960. He was given the responsibility of reaching the same high standard of the previous season by following Wieland's directions. No easy task! In spite of his illness, Wieland did not release the reins. He was kept informed through Peter Lehmann and also through the others in charge. He was sent audiotapes of the rehearsals and he took part in all that was happening.

Peter Lehmann did an astonishingly good job in this difficult situation. Also, he was always calm and friendly and never let himself be put under pressure nor become part of any intrigue. A year later, I sang Brünnhilde in Chicago in a very successful production that he directed. He also directed the staging for a *Lohengrin* at the Metropolitan Opera for which Wieland Wagner had originally been engaged.

In Wieland's *Ring* there was, as usual, no scenery. The stage was a raked oval disc with a blue backdrop for the horizon. Everything else was effected through lighting, color, and projections. When a genius puts his stamp on a work, wonders happen. I remember very well his direction of *Rheingold* in the 1950s. As the curtain rose, the entire audience drew back in their seats. The stage looked to be full of water, as though in the next moment the powerful Rhein would overflow and drown the viewer. Fantastic!

Wieland Wagner loved leather. All the singers wore costumes made from leather, at least in his last stagings. As Isolde, I had three leather costumes, a black one in the first act, a rose-colored one in the second act, and a yellow in the third act. As Brünnhilde, I wore various leather costumes, from black to light gray to white. It could be unbearably hot in Bayreuth; during long, demanding acts, the sweat ran down one's back in streams. I tried to talk Wieland into using a lighter material—I was really suffering—but I was not successful. For the premiere of 1966, when he was in the hospital, I sent him a gift of a leather tie to remind him of our discomfort in the leather costumes. He got my point and thanked me, very amused.

The one time that I found 90°F as rather cool was when I returned from a guest performance from Verona in 1969. I had sung *Turandot* there and worn a costume made of white *plastic* with lace sewn over it. It was 104°F in the shade! I found the complaints and sighs of my Bayreuth colleagues totally exaggerated. Compared to the sauna I had come from in Italy, this was quite agreeable.

The devastation in Germany from the war had been tremendous, but the leveled cities and villages were unbelievably quickly rebuilt. Bayreuth had changed as well: it was easier to find lodging in hotels and even in private homes. Many of the middle-class landlords were looking for a way to get rich quick. One summer, I asked a real estate agent to look for a private lodging for me for my two-month stay in Bayreuth. I obtained a bungalow a little way out of town, near the woods where deer roamed about. As the end of the festival neared, I went to the owner, an elderly man, to settle up. He declared I had rented the house for three months instead of two, that is, until the twentieth of September. I pointed out that this was not possible: by then the festival was over. Moreover, I was engaged in Buenos Aires and had to be there by September 1. But he was not to be put off and insisted upon being paid for an extra month, which I naturally did not do. I contacted the real estate agent, made my complaint, and asked them to prove that I had agreed to take the house for two months, not three. But they were apparently of the opinion that singers come and go, whereas the bungalow was permanently available for rental. They also pretended to be unable to find the verification of the rental period. It ended by my having to engage an attorney who found the advertisement proving that I was in the right. By that time, however, the old man had died and my attorney had also departed this world. Finally the heirs and I divided the court costs.

It was on October 17, 1966, in New York, that I was informed of the tragic death of Wieland Wagner.

The music world had suffered a great loss and everything at once seemed empty and meaningless. In his forty-nine years, he had only begun to explore his creative potential. I personally believe that if Wieland had lived longer, he would have moved more and more away from the abstract and found an interesting romantic style. There was much in his stage direction that, in my opinion, pointed to this.

Many of the productions he directed were performed long after his death, the *Tristan* until 1970 and *Parsifal* until 1973.

In the spring of 1967, Bayreuth made a guest appearance in Osaka with Wieland's staging of *Walküre* and *Tristan*. Pierre Boulez had conducted a noteworthy *Parsifal* in Bayreuth and Wieland, before his death, had indicated his desire to have him conduct the *Tristan* in Osaka. Unfortunately, Boulez came to Osaka obviously unprepared. Perhaps it was Wieland's death that made it difficult for him to probe the depth of this opera. I cannot say for sure. Boulez is primarily known as a conductor and composer of contemporary music, and the step from that music to the incarnation of romantic opera is unquestionably a big one. If one remembers, however, that Wagner composed *Tristan* in 1857, then the music is forward-looking and modern. We had a piano rehearsal with Boulez, and it was fortunate that Windgassen and I were there to give him the tempi, the transitions, and so on. It seemed almost as though this French conductor had never opened the orchestra score. To make matters worse, he was conducting a Japanese orchestra that was playing *Tristan* for the first time. One hardly dared hope for a miracle. And, indeed, there was none. The first act, normally seventy-eight or seventy-nine minutes long, he whipped through in sixty-seven minutes. Act 2 went even faster, as the music is more romantic, and for modern composers and conductors, romantic music is almost unbearable. It was the only time I was happy that Wieland was not present.

In his last months, Wieland had worries about Bayreuth and these pessimistic feelings surely made his illness worse. One of his assistant stage directors, Nikolaus Lehnhoff (he was stage director for the phenomenal *Frau ohne Schatten* in Stockholm), permitted me to read a letter in which

Wieland expressed his worries about the future of Bayreuth. Among other things, he wrote: "when Nilsson and Windgassen no longer sing, we can close up shop."

Fortunately, no one is irreplaceable, not even Wieland Wagner. His brother, Wolfgang, has been now for about thirty years the artistic director as well as the business manager of the festival. Bayreuth is almost unrecognizable today and he has spared no effort to carry out Richard Wagner's motto: "Kinder, schafft Neues!" (Children, make something new!). Only time will tell whether he will be like Fafner, jealously guarding his gold; like Alberich, who seeks power at the expense of love; or like the aging Wotan, guiding the festival toward a secure place in history.

Wolfgang often says it is not necessary to engage the most famous artists. He prefers to bring in young artists who will, through their appearance at Bayreuth, become big names. Therefore, the Festspielhaus of Bayreuth has slipped into the background. Except for the appearance of the internationally known Plácido Domingo for a few summers, Wolfgang practices what he preaches. Perhaps he has not always been successful in his artistic efforts; there are definitely many Wagnerians who, in spite of their loyalty, wish that old Richard had added two words to his motto: "Kinder, schafft Neues—und Besseres!" (Children, create new things—and better ones.)

I believe the standard in my day was high in every sector. Stage directors, soloists, chorus, ballet, and conductors were the very best. If I had to select one group as superior, it would, without hesitation, be the chorus. At the recommendation of Karajan in 1951, Wilhelm Pitz was named chorus director. He came from Aachen, where Karajan had been conductor. For the chorus members, Pitz and his wife traveled all over, listening to more than nine hundred singers. From these he selected the hundred best to make up the Bayreuth chorus. Pitz's method of getting the chorus into shape was phenomenal. It is difficult to describe what he did; he was simply a magician. He created a precision and a dynamic range that was most impressive. Not only every syllable but every consonant was clearly spoken at the same time in a precision one would not think possible. Word of Pitz's genius spread rapidly. Opera houses, concert managers, and recording companies showered him with tempting offers. Wilhelm Pitz was also a sympathetic and modest man who had an inexhaustible reservoir of anecdotes, mainly concerning famous conductors. Pitz and his wife, Erna, were like rays of sunshine in Bayreuth. Pitz stayed with Bayreuth until his death in 1973.

The German Dance and Chorus Union struck a medal in memory

of Wilhelm Pitz, and I was honored to receive this medal in the summer of 1991 during a ceremony in Bayreuth. The celebration was centered around singing, music and oration, and attended by, among others, Peter Lehmann, who served as moderator. He gave a wonderful speech on the theme "The Natural Wonder from Skåne." Wolfgang spoke in his High German to celebrate the day and was not stingy with superlatives, which was usually not the case. He declared me an example, a role model if you will, for the youth of Bayreuth. As I was thanking him for the decoration and honor, I was asked to give a spontaneous account of some of my memories of sixteen years of events and adventures in Bayreuth. The ceremony included the "Wach'auf" from *Die Meistersinger* performed by the chorus and orchestra of the festival. At the close, Kammersänger Manfred Schenk (my last Wotan) sang "Mein Herr und Gott" from *Lohengrin,* conducted by Norbert Balatsch, Pitz's successor.

The year 1970 was definitely the last for Wieland's *Tristan*—and the last Bayreuth year for my fantastic colleague and friend, Wolfgang Windgassen, with whom I had sung more than ninety *Tristan* performances.

He had sung at Bayreuth for nineteen years and felt he had done his part in the development of the festival. Now he was the director of the opera in his birthplace, Stuttgart. He needed his summers for planning the future seasons and for vacation. I found it to be a good time for me as well to make my farewell to Bayreuth. For sixteen summers I had appeared there in Wieland's productions, as well as Wolfgang's, and had sung all the Wagner roles closest to my heart.

Windgassen made his taking leave of Bayreuth public, while I decided to keep my decision to myself. Windgassen deserved to be feted personally, without having to share honors with anyone. Besides, I have never understood how anyone can give a farewell performance. It is sad enough, for the one leaving, without making everyone else sad too. I look in astonishment at colleagues who, from year to year, go about giving farewell appearances, the "last," the "very last," and then an "extra" of course "at the wish of the public," and so on into infinity. Naturally, it is difficult to stop but isn't it more difficult to swallow the bitter medicine drop by drop than to take the full dose all at once? No, it was tragic enough to say farewell to Bayreuth without letting it be known.

The last performance of *Tristan* came to be an evening to remember. Everyone outdid himself. Windgassen was celebrated with unbelievable enthusiasm, and I also received my share of the applause. In spite of the many curtain calls there was an atmosphere of sadness and regret hanging over this performance. As the last chord died away, there was a great stillness that seemed to last forever until the audience could bring itself to applaud. It was one of the most deeply felt moments for me in all the years at Bayreuth.

Perhaps most stirring of all: directly after the end of the first act, in front of the Festspielhaus, the stage sets from act 1 were set afire. After act 2, those sets were added to the fire. Thus, an hour after the end, all traces of the *Tristan* were gone, forever erased from memory.

On the day after, I met Wolfgang Wagner. I had not informed him of my decision to leave Bayreuth, and he had assumed that I would return the next summer to sing Brünnhilde in his new staging. As I shared my decision with him, his great disappointment made me feel guilty. So I promised him that I would be ready to help him should he find himself in an emergency. A few years later his daughter, Eva (who still worked at Bayreuth before being shunted aside), told me they had actually tried to locate me. I had gone to Switzerland without making my address known but he had found another Brünnhilde to save the performance.

What also almost broke my heart was that on the same day I met Wolfgang, his son Gottfried sought me out and tried to talk me into staying. He gave so many heartfelt reasons that I was almost swayed. Oh, he was a charming rascal. I loved this youngster. He was seven years old when I came to Bayreuth, a sweet child with blue eyes, appealing as a cherub, and with charm enough to make one melt. Now he was twenty-three, with the same blue eyes and curly hair and irresistible charm.

Just as I was going to board the plane in Nuremberg, Peter Lehmann, the assistant stage director appeared. He had driven from Bayreuth to give me the casket that he had rescued from the flames after the *Tristan.* In this casket all of Isolde's magic herbs were preserved. Here was hidden the secret of the love potion given to Tristan. And if there had been a few drops of something to give eternal youth . . . ?

Then I would simply have begun all over again.

BUENOS AIRES

"Buenos Aires" means "good air," and I can hardly imagine anything more appealing to a singer. But anyone who thinks that the city in the pampas is healthful for the windpipe will be damned disappointed.

Buenos Aires was in my day a city where you breathed exhaust fumes instead of air, and I doubt if it has changed since then. All the buses have the exhaust pipe on the side. The diesel fuel was of very poor quality and clouds of exhaust were constantly wafted over the pedestrians, who staggered about nearly unconscious. As soon as one had recovered slightly, the next bus came by with its poisonous puff. In the mid-1950s there were no traffic lights, and even after lights were installed it was years before anyone took them seriously.

It was September 1955 when Bertil and I, after a 48-hour(!) flight in a DC4 of KLM landed in Argentina's capital city.

Buenos Aires was a most elegant city, but oh, so terribly rundown! The walkways were full of deep holes, so that walking along one had to pay full attention or take the risk of breaking an arm or leg. The Teatro Colón, built in 1908, reveals a former affluence and an old, beautiful culture. All the great singers from years ago have performed here. The auditorium makes a magnificent impression and looks as though it seats five thousand (in reality it seats "only" thirty-five hundred). The hall is so generously laid out that one can sit in the parquet seats with legs outstretched. There, no one has to rise when someone wishes to come through the row. The "green room" in the Stockholm Concert Hall and the auditorium in Alice Tully Hall in Lincoln Center, New York, are similarly laid out, presumably at the request of the donor, Alice Tully.

The Teatro Colón engaged me for four Isoldes with the prominent tenor Günther Treptow as Tristan, the Yugoslavian Georgine von Milinkovic as Brangäne, the Hungarian Dezsö Ernster as King Marke and Fritz Rieger from Munich as conductor.

It was an unruly time, and in the province where the Peronistas had already given up, revolution had broken out. The capital, however, was still calm. Pictures of President Juan Perón and his late wife, Evita, were hanging in every other window, and statues of them were to be seen in every important place.

We had rehearsals every day on the huge stage. One could easily have used roller skates to land in Tristan's arms at the prescribed moment. The acoustics were wonderful and I was truly happy to be singing in this opera house. Admittedly, things could have been different in some ways. When one went from the dressing rooms past the men's restroom, the smell was so awful that it brought tears to one's eyes. But the theatrical culture and tradition were ever present.

The premiere went splendidly. *Tristan* had not been given for some years and the large colony of German immigrants was very happy to be again charmed by Wagner's hypnotic sounds. It was my eleventh Isolde. Shortly after our second performance, the threat of a revolution in Buenos Aires became serious. The last hope of the people rested in the rains coming, which they hoped would continue to fall from the heavens, since no Argentinean had any desire to run around the streets shooting off guns when it was raining. The ideal revolution in Argentina takes place indoors. And that has been known to happen: a small group of military forces simply marches into the office of the sitting president and forces him at gunpoint to name a successor.

The situation was serious. There was talk of evacuation but nothing happened. We singers stayed at the Claridge Hotel, which was not far from the harbor. Suddenly the rain stopped, and there was an immediate order forbidding anyone to leave the city. The hotel had no staff and we had only canned food for provisions. One was forbidden to fill the bathtub with water.

Then it happened! At two in the morning, shellfire and a hail of bullets broke out. We jumped out of bed and I grabbed two large bags and started packing my clothing. Bertil's trousers landed in one suitcase, so that he had to flee in his pajamas. The elevator was not running and we resided on the fourteenth floor. I battled bravely with the two suitcases while Bertil, apparently having adopted the Argentinean objection to getting wet, managed to locate an umbrella. When we got downstairs in hope of getting to safety—so to speak—we found there was no real air-raid shelter, only a cellar. In my entire life I have never been so afraid. I promised myself, in the event that I survived this, never to come here again. My German colleagues seemed to be cool and composed. In the recent past, similar occurrences had been for them a daily routine. In the early morning hours we finally heard on the radio broadcast from Montevideo that Perón had given up and was making his way to Uruguay. The headquarters of the Peronistas, which was across the street from our hotel, was blasted with shellfire and then burned to the ground. A few hundred followers of Perón perished in the fire, while about a hundred had capitulated and were led away with their rifles held high over their heads. It was horrible the next morning to look at the huge yawning hole that held the ashes of so many incinerated human beings.

After the inauguration of the new president, everything went on as though nothing had ever happened. No, not quite: the photos of president and Evita Perón had disappeared from the windows. Their statues were hanging by nooses from high branches of the trees, an easily grasped symbol.

After a few days our performances could again take place. Of course, we had lost time because of the revolution. Moreover, there was such a tremendous demand for tickets that the director of the opera decided upon an additional performance. We had a marathon, with three *Tristan* performances in four days—a feat I would not recommend to anyone, except perhaps in the time of a revolution. We later learned Perón's followers had used the Teatro Colón as an arsenal. How lovely that we did not know this at the time. It might have clouded the joy of singing!

Because of the political situation the bank would not give me a good exchange for my pesos (I was not foresighted enough to request payment in U.S. dollars). What should I do? Gold was inexpensive here in comparison to Sweden, and the Argentinean goldsmiths were far more creative than Swedish jewelers, with their boring Bismarck necklaces. Along with a nutria fur and some dirt-cheap shoes and handbags of crocodile leather, I acquired a substantial amount of gold jewelry. Bertil was not particularly fond of jewelry for men, but he had to lower himself to wearing several gold chains under his shirt on the trip home. He tinkled like a glockenspiel, albeit a tiny one. With a small part of my salary, we purchased stock. It was the time of the Cold War, and Bertil thought it was good, in case of having to flee, that we would be able to pay our hotel bill in the new country.

The stocks remained active and their value changed steadily with the currency, which was always unreliable. But just when I was many times over a millionaire in pesos, the zeros were erased and the currency had another name. You can't win!

On the flight to Munich, where I was recording *A Masked Ball,* we booked a so-called "sleeper." The beds were made up over the seats close to the ceiling of the plane. As usual, on routes I had never flown, I was anxious about falling asleep in case of an emergency (as though I could have done anything!) Therefore, I didn't close my eyes the entire night, while Bertil slept like a stone. At the Munich airport there were a few gentlemen from the radio in Bavaria, shuffling their feet nervously. "Are you ever late!" was their warm welcome.

They drove me directly to the studio after my 48-hour flight. To demonstrate how really happy they were to have me there, they began immediately with one of my most demanding scenes: Amelia's big aria in act 2. Albert Erede was the conductor.

In spite of my promises never to return to Buenos Aires, the following year found me there once again. This time I was appearing as the Marschallin in *Der Rosenkavalier* and as Donna Anna in *Don Giovanni.* Erich Kleiber, who was originally to have conducted *Der Rosenkavalier,* had died. Ferdinand Leitner, at that time general music director in Stuttgart, who was to conduct *Don Giovanni,* took over *Der Rosenkavalier* as well, with a practiced hand. This *Don Giovanni* had a dream cast. In particular, the pairing of George London as Giovanni and Lisa della Casa as Elvira was unbeatable.

The public at the Teatro Colón liked me. I made many friends and they were all hospitable and generous. There were invitations to dinner, which seldom began before 10 P.M. What I enjoyed most, however, were the invitations to a *quinta* (a farmhouse) outside the city, which anyone who was anyone possessed. There, the largest and most delicious cuts of meat I had ever eaten were grilled to perfection. The Argentineans eat enormous amounts of meat and it costs there only a fraction of what one would have to pay in other countries. In my circle of acquaintances there were some who owned estates of twenty thousand acres and fifteen thousand head of cattle. They lived in Buenos Aires and flew in now and then, on their private planes, to oversee their property. The wonderful ballads about Argentina by the Swedish poet Evart Taube were brought closer to me as I saw the land of his inspiration.

Left to ourselves, we loved to go to a simple restaurant, called El Palacio de las Papas Fritas. Along with the excellent meat, they had the best apple and banana crepe in the world. This crepe, which was not too thin, was covered with a thick caramel sauce and flamed with rum. It could not have been improved on by any gourmet. As a crowning touch, a spoonful of vanilla ice cream was placed on top of the warm crepe. This restaurant was a real find for any epicure. Writing about it, I feel an almost irresistible urge to get onto the next flight for Buenos Aires.

There was another restaurant that was almost as good as El Palacio de las Papas Fritas. I was allowed once to go into the kitchen to observe how they prepared their potato soufflés. They take thin slices of potato, which, deep-fried through three different temperatures of oil, become airy pillows. A delicacy that whets the appetite but much too complicated to make at home.

In Buenos Aires I had the pleasure of making the acquaintance of Carina Ari and of becoming friends with her. She was a wonderful woman and the whole world embraced her. A poor girl from the workers' quarter of Stockholm, she had rhythm and dance in her legs and succeeded in getting through the rigorous training in Paris to become a prima ballerina and choreographer. Her second husband was the Dutch "Liqua-King," Jan Henrik Molzer, one of the heads of Bols.

Carina and I had a mutual interest outside of music: attending auctions. Carina directed me to the best auctions. In addition to jewelry, she had bought at auction most of the furs belonging to Evita Perón! They were very chic styles but the white mink had taken on a yellowish tinge. The chinchilla cape also had a slightly jaundiced look.

Carina was unbelievably generous to others; with herself, however, she was thrifty if not miserly. Every year she traveled to Stockholm with her cat, Puss-Puss, whom she called her fiancé. She carried him in her handbag. The purpose of this trip was to eat crayfish *three times a day.* (Crayfish were only available in Sweden in August.) As she got older she devoted herself to painting and sculpture. During one of my guest performances in Buenos Aires I sat for her in her villa, La Monona Modell, for a bust that today is exhibited at the Stockholm Opera.

One time she gave me a tour of the villa. Next to her bed stood a packing case about 2½ ft. by 1½ ft. that was full of jewelry. The case stood open! Typical Carina. She fished out a gold ring with a large sphere in which a few diamonds were scattered. Carina saw the sphere as the earth and the small diamonds symbolized the great opera houses of the world.

Talk about bloody opera—here I'm washing my bloody hands during Lady Macbeth's sleepwalking scene in Verdi's *Macbeth* at La Scala in 1964.

Turandot is another horror show in which heads roll. This photo was taken during my second season opener as Turandot at La Scala in 1966. The role is small but demanding and is generally seen as a voice killer.

A final fine-tuning before my entré as Aida at the Met with director Georg Solti. He is a master even at the piano, and he has a unique way of accompanying with a keen ear to the singer. We had a very inspirational collaboration for many years.

Begum Aga Khan was an enchanting lady and a devoted opera aficionado. This photo was taken during a banquet after a performance in Bayreuth.

A scene from Act 2 of *The Valkyrie* at La Scala in 1958, where I played Brünnhilde to Hans Hotter's Wotan. With his imposing stature, Hotter suggested a figure lifted out of some Greek myth.

Sometimes during recordings and rehearsals there are long waiting periods, which can be spent in many ways, one of which is playing "skat." It's a game in which even beginners can win, which I apparently did in London, together with colleagues Thomas Stewart, Wolfgang Windgassen, Gottlob Frick, and Hans Hotter.

I am actually the only woman who has received the Illis Quorum size 18, a gold medal and chain, which is an immense honor conferred by the government. This photo shows the presentation by then culture minister Jan-Erik Wikström at Stockholm's Concert House in 1981.

Ben Heppner was awarded the Birgit Nilsson prize after the New Sweden gala in New York, 1988. He is now acclaimed as one of the foremost tenors in the world. Part of the prize included a guest performance in Stockholm, where he sang Lohengrin. The Birgit Nilsson Prize was instituted by the New Sweden Committee and is conferred every three years on an American singer.

The Swedish National Opera had guest performances in Edinburgh in 1974, where I sang Electra twice. The music festival has made that city a hub for world celebrities and lauded guests. In the "Swedish camp" were Ingrid Bergman and Lars Schmidt.

Franco Corelli was another magnificent Italian tenor; our *Turandot* performances at the Met became more or less legendary. The audiences sat up straight in anticipation of how the evening's choral duels would turn out. He held his high Cs so long that you'd think he would lose consciousness.

The Masquerade Ball, Vienna 1958, in the American version in which Gustav III is called Riccardo and is an English governor in Boston, where he is murdered by his secretary, Renato. I played his wife Amelia, and the governor's role was sung magnificently by the Italian charmer, tenor Giuseppe di Stefano.

Placido Domingo is one of the matador tenors of our time, but of course, he *is* a Spaniard. This megastar modestly claims that he can't hit high Cs—and then he goes and sings them with effortless elegance. Placido is humble, amiable, and loved by the whole world.

Dr. Antonio Ghiringhelli was the director of La Scala in the 60s, but no one knew whether that was due to his colossal fortune or whether a genuine interest in opera lay underneath. Here I am being thanked by the wonderful conductor Berislav Klobucar after a *Salome* performance.

A happy party at an unusual prize ceremony at the Swedish General Consulate in New York. Good friend and TV producer Lasse Holmqvist was there to hand over Malmö FF's (a soccer team) medals of honor to Skåne's native son and daughter, Sixten Ehrling and B. Nilsson. The event was witnessed by Ragnar Ulfung, Viveka Lindfors, and Anders Thunborg, among others.

Mingling after the 1988 New Sweden Concert were our king and queen, Håkan Hagegård, Eva Marton, Aprile Millo, Shirley Verett, and Elisabeth Söderström. Such concerts often turn into late but well-sung affairs.

I've been invited to the White House twice, first by Lyndon and Lady Bird Johnson, and then by Richard and Pat Nixon. I had to decline the first invitation because of concert commitments in Europe. The second time I came to the concert but not to the dinner since my pianist, John Wustman (*left*) wasn't invited. Nixon introduced me with an ostensibly improvised but very "studied" speech. As usual, the remarks were recorded on tape, a copy of which was sent to me along with the president's personally dedicated memoirs.

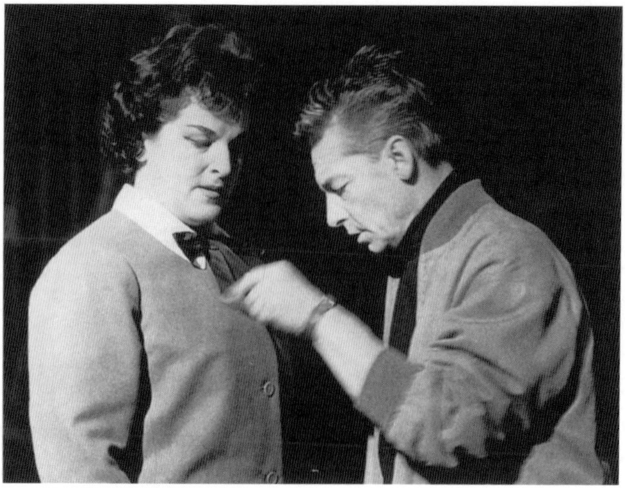

My "brother-in-discord," Herbert von Karajan, who says that "your heart, Mrs. Nilsson, is found where you keep your cashbox." I couldn't come up with a better retort to his quip than "Well, then we have something in common, Mr. Von Karajan."

There was a very skilled silversmith, jeweler, and opera lover in Stockholm by the name of Kristian Nilsson. He united his passions in some unique silver and mountain crystal sculptures; he made one of me as Electra and, as you can see, the role is well interpreted. My husband managed to acquire the seven-kilo sculpture as a present for my sixtieth birthday.

I gladly gave several guest performances at London's Covent Garden. Here I am Brünnhilde in the second act of *Götterdämmerung*, when Brünnhilde, after discovering Sigfried's infidelity, breaks into a vengeful rage of despair and ire.

Guest appearances on so-called TV "couch shows" come with the territory of my profession. Chairs also worked well on the Dick Cavet show. We had a very enjoyable chat for an audience of around 75 million. An opera singer would probably have to sing for a couple hundred years to reach as many people.

Carlos Kleiber, one of the greatest conductors, has one small flaw that irritates musicians—he is rather stingy with album recordings. We bumped into each other once in Mexico, where, at the line of my parasol, he fell to his knees.

With his millions of records sold and his open-air concerts for hundreds of thousands of people, Luciano Pavarotti has given opera singing a new dimension. Nowadays he sings everywhere except opera stages, which can no longer meet his financial demands.

This is an homage I will never forget: a gold ring with an engraved head of Isolde. It was given to me in 1968 by the standing room audience at the Vienna Opera—we got engaged! An artist could not receive a finer token of appreciation from her public, and to get it from the opera lovers of Vienna gives the gold an extra shine.

I'm hanging in Gripsholm Castle, painted by artist Lasse Jonsson. Opera fans, especially American tourists, think I look too "ordinary." For my part I think I look more or less like Birgit Nilsson.

This TV program was called "Star against Star"; and who wore her plumes more proudly than Zarah Leander! Lennart Swahn could hardly get a word in edgewise among these chatty prima donnas, but the show was pretty lively anyway. I met this fabulous woman in Vienna, also, where she really was the star she sang of.

My two priceless pillars of support and favorite pianists, American John Wustman and Dalecarlian Lars Roos. If you only knew how important the pianist is at a concert of Romantic music! It's actually wrong to call it "accompaniment" of songs; it's more like a dialogue, a collaboration in which the nuances of music, voice, and lyrics become one.

About every other year, West Karup's church becomes my music church, and music lovers make pilgrimages there from all over Sweden and even beyond. Here I'm making music with Gösta Winbergh and Lars Roos. Since the musicians perform for free, there is usually so much money left over that it's enough for a new thatched roof and other upkeep costs at the old homestead grounds in Båstad.

My faithful companion and husband, Bertil. We have circled the earth several times, and, since I ended my career in 1984, we've landed in sync and calmed things down a bit. We have the same sense of humor, are almost equally messy, and have the same eternal love for music.

"It is made for you, who have the whole world as your stage; therefore, it is yours," she said.

The mandate to follow the auction trail in Buenos Aires was easier said than done. For one thing, I was not fluent in Spanish. For another, the auctioneer spoke ten times faster than at any other auction I had ever attended. Also, the articles did not always come up in the order in which they were listed in the catalogue. One had to be 200 percent on one's toes.

One time a gentleman suddenly came up to me and asked nervously whether I realized that in two hours I was to sing Isolde at the Teatro Colón? I calmed him down, assuring him there would be an Isolde, but first I had to bid on something that would bring my performance to greater heights than ever. I succeeded in purchasing two beautiful diamond clips, and Isolde outdid herself that evening. Promises must be kept.

During one of my guest appearances in Buenos Aires I got to know a great opera lover, the Swedish ambassador, Torsten Björck, who came, as did I, from Skåne. When he was later ambassador in Lima, Bertil and I were invited to stop over on our way from Buenos Aires to San Francisco, which we gladly did. Torsten gave a great party in my honor and we passed many interesting and lovely days in his home. Some years later in San Antonio where I was singing Turandot, Torsten was in the audience. He had flown ten hours from Lima to attend one opera performance! He is a real friend and above all, an expert adviser when I go to an important affair requiring evening dress and the wearing of my decorations. He suggests where I place my medals and decorations to the best advantage. They must be as well placed as lovely tones.

In all, I was in Buenos Aires seven times. I sang Isolde in two different productions, between which lay fifteen years. In the second production, Jon Vickers, for whom I had waited fourteen years, was my Tristan. Rachel must have had much the same feeling when Jacob finally became hers. Vickers was a flawless, intensive Tristan with a very personal characterization.

I remember one episode during the premiere. At the dramatic meeting between Tristan and Isolde in act 1, we had a unique and unexpected guest onstage. A cat with black and white markings marched calmly from stage right, parked himself stage center and, after looking around carefully, began a painstaking cleansing after which he quietly left. It was really not easy to maintain concentration, especially as Brangäne, who had nothing to sing, turned her back to the audience and was shaking with laughter.

In Buenos Aires I sang two different productions of the *Ring.* I also managed to squeeze in a performance at a gala where President Ongania was present, and I gave some concerts for charity. During my guest appearance in 1965, I sang Salome and Turandot, the two bloodthirsty ladies who were always my trusted companions.

In *Turandot* a young singer I had never heard of by the name of Montserrat Caballé debuted as Liù. I immediately fell in love with this beautiful voice. What *piani* and *pianissimi!* And her fantastic phrasing! She seemed never to breathe. One day she was sad and said the conductor was not at all satisfied with her. I told her not to worry; her name would be remembered long after his was forgotten. Unfortunately, I never knew if this came to pass, as I never could recall the name of the conductor.

It is well known that Caballé easily falls into a faint, onstage as well as outside the opera. As she sang her last tone in the *Turandot* premiere she was supposed to thrust a knife into her heart and fall to the floor dead. Just at this moment she fainted, which actually fit in well, except the poor carriers of the corpse had to carry her all the way to her dressing room, where she soon came to. As the curtain calls began, Caballé was able to make it to the stage to receive her applause. The hairdresser had removed her wig, however, probably thinking she would not return to the stage. Of course, Caballé was wearing the standard nylon stocking-top over her hair. In her still rather dazed state, she went out to receive her ovation with the nylon stocking-top covering her hair. My poor colleague looked as though she was bald. I still wonder what Caballé thought when she later looked at herself in her dressing room mirror.

When the Buenos Aires public takes a singer to their heart, their admiration can be fiery, indeed, reckless and wild. At solo curtain calls there can be an absolute deluge of flowers; sometimes I waded up to my knees through them. When you finally manage to get out of the opera house and into a car, you notice missing buttons and anything else that could be pulled off your clothing. Once a number of my fans, who wanted to accompany me to the airport for my departure to Sweden, decorated their autos with Swedish flags. It had rained and was very windy; the flags, which they had obtained from the Swedish consulate, flapped wildly. I have no idea what the people at the consulate thought when the flags were returned dirty and in shreds.

But not all of the surprises were pleasant. On the day I arrived in Buenos Aires, hundreds of fans awaited me at the airport. As I went through customs many of them threw themselves at me, covering me with flowers and embracing me. It was impossible for me to move. I could not even raise my arms. Subconsciously I was hoping that nothing would happen to my purse, which I carried over my shoulder. My fear was justified: when I got to the hotel, my money and the jewelry I carried with me were gone! A pickpocket had mixed in with the fans and robbed me. I immediately called Swiss Air at the airport and discovered I was the third person to complain of being robbed on that day.

It was an unusually rainy and dreary day—and then to undergo this shock! I had to return to the airport, as only the police station in the district of the robbery could handle the complaint. There I ran into a pigheaded little policeman who claimed it was impossible that anyone at the Buenos Aires airport would steal from a passenger. He almost believed I had made up the story of the robbery. When I pointed out that most of the jewelry was not insured, he became a bit more human, but naturally I heard nothing from him. I was almost insane at the idea that someone else was wearing my jewelry, which included both gifts and the rewards of my own hard work. When I got back to the hotel, I called Bertil and told him of my misery. He was quiet for a moment, then said, "Yes, but they are just stones and you mustn't take it so seriously." He could always calm me down.

The seasons are, of course, at different times in Argentina than in Europe (when we have autumn, they have spring). With such a long, tiring trip to make, I was fair game for any and all kinds of germs. It was always the same: every time I came to Buenos Aires, I caught a cold. This was obviously quite a problem, as they had no cover in case I had to cancel a performance. It meant just cough, sing, and take antibiotics.

Our ear, nose, and throat doctor was Leo Forschner, a charming, older man who did everything he could for singers. He was born in Austria and married to an Argentinean. Both loved Wagner and through that we became good friends. The first time I consulted Dr. Forschner I was in such a bad state that he had to come to my hotel. He knocked on the door, but despite my "Come in," no one appeared for a long time. Then the door was carefully opened a crack, and at last he finally came in. When we got to know one another better, he explained why he was so hesitant. He was called once to a famous Swedish singer who in the Nazi period had great success in popular music. She received the doctor completely naked. He was uncertain whether this was the custom with all Swedish singers and wanted to be sure he did not compromise himself again. I could assure him that when Swedish opera singers call a throat doctor, they know in which organ the illness lies!

I ran into one very disagreeable person in Buenos Aires: Eduardo Arnosi, a teacher and also a music critic. Among other publications, he wrote for the English magazine *Opera* and later the American magazine *Opera News.* Before my departure for Buenos Aires I received a letter from Arnosi. He asked if I could bring with me my most recent recording, as he wished to play it over the radio. I fulfilled his wish. My next trip to Buenos Aires met with the same request, only for more recordings, including a complete *Ring.* I had the feeling that Arnosi, in asking singers to bring free samples of their artistry, was really completing his own private record collection. He was, after all, a critic, and most of the singers feared a reprisal if they did not heed his request.

Naturally, I took no recordings to him. I was hardly in the hotel before Arnosi was on the telephone. Rather shortly and sweetly I explained that I had no recordings for him. There followed several unpleasant telephone calls. Finally, I simply hung up when I realized he was on the end of the line. After a time I received an vituperative letter written on toilet paper! "Because it is the only paper you deserve," he wrote, gracefully scribbling his name. I had a feeling he would use the same type of paper when he had the opportunity to review me.

I have to tell about an Argentine singer who sang one of the Valkyries in *Walküre.* She was very sweet, lively and talkative, and she told me she was expecting a child—which was obvious. That was on Tuesday. On Friday of that week she sang again, jumping about the Valkyrie rocks with even more lightness in her spring. Her costume was suddenly a few sizes too large also. After the performance she told me, glowing, that she had given birth to a son in the night of the first *Walküre* performance. She called him Siegfried and I was named godmother.

I think often of my friends in Buenos Aires. One of my first fans there was a youngster, Carlos Baldonedo, who was in the dance school. In time he became a famous dancer and choreographer and ultimately head of the ballet in the Teatro Colón. I was very moved to learn he had dedicated two ballets to me.

In spite of the political unrest and the economic problems in the country, I have never met an Argentinean who wished to live elsewhere. They all find their country heaven on earth. True, things go on there with a kind of rusticity and the cracks in the walkways have certainly not become smaller. But there is a freedom and spontaneous love of life that is often missing in other lands.

My artistic life would surely have been poorer had I not experienced Argentina and the unforgettable Teatro Colón.

THE BATTLE OF THE HIGH Cs

It is sometimes said that life hangs on a silken thread. Worse than that! Life can hang on a very small dot over the musical staff, a dot not much larger than the head of a pin—a high C!

What good is it to a Puccini or Verdi tenor to have the most beautiful voice in the world, if he doesn't have a high C? His life is worth nothing, operatically speaking. Imagine how many sleepless nights have been brought on by Manrico's *stretta* in *Trovatore* or Rudolfo's high C in his aria from *La Boheme?* But it did not take long for the tenors in question to determine that life would be much more comfortable if the high C would be transposed to a B. Now honestly, when was the last time you heard the above-mentioned arias in their original key?

Not many are able in their sixties to do the nine high Cs that come one after the other in Donizetti's *Daughter of the Regiment.* The Spanish star tenor, Alfredo Krauss, has the ability to do this. And I must mention the Swedish tenor Einar Andersson, who has a phenomenal top. He was known as the "singing soccer player"; for him life really began with the high C. One time, at a piano rehearsal, he was feeling indisposed and he asked the conductor, Sixten Ehrling, to transpose the aria down a whole tone. Instead, he transposed the aria *up* a tone. Einar sang lightly and easily a high D! To Ehrling's question as to how he felt, Einar said, "Good. Now it feels as easy as back home on the farm."

Franco Corelli possessed one of the most fantastic tenor voices ever. In spite of his rather dark, dramatic timbre he had an unbelievable high voice. His life depended upon his high C. He could apparently sustain this tone forever. Whether it fit with any style or was in good taste is another matter.

The *Turandot* performances at the Metropolitan with Corelli and me are almost legendary. The audience was on the edge of their seats, full of anticipation, asking, "Who will win?" It was like a bullfight, except that the outcome was uncertain. When waiting for our entrances Corelli was pacing up and down like a caged lion, while I played the calm and collected one. I made it my habit to sit on a stool in the wings and pretend to read the *New York Times.* Someone once called my attention to the fact that the paper was upside down, which is fatal to appearing casual and cool. I believe that Corelli most often walked off with the prize for holding the C the longest, even if he claims otherwise.

But once, I remember clearly, I was victorious. I really felt in excellent form and planned to beat him at this game of holding on to high notes. I was successful. I noticed how Corelli always went to the apron of the stage for his high notes and slowly became blue in the face. This spurred me on and I sustained the high C we sang together until everything went black before my eyes. When my vision returned Corelli had disappeared. He left the stage and I had to end the act without my tenor. The conductor, Leopold Stokowski, who was over eighty and was debuting as opera conductor, noticed nothing.

When Rudolf Bing met up with his pet, Corelli, he discovered that Corelli, out of sheer frustration, had hit his fist so hard on the table that he had a laceration. Mrs. Corelli had already called for an ambulance. Bing tried to calm Corelli (there was still one act to go) and tempted him with the idea of getting revenge. In the next act, where I am transformed by his kiss from a block of ice into a passionate woman, he could bite me. Corelli's mood improved immediately at the very thought of planting an unforgettable kiss upon me. In the last moment, however, he lost his nerve and neither kissed nor bit. Bing had discreetly left the opera house, fearing the outcome of this plot. When I learned of Bing's attempt to pull off a coup against me, I sent the general manager the following telegram:

Must cancel next performance stop Serious bite injury stop Birgit

During another *Turandot,* a Saturday afternoon broadcast, I had just begun my difficult aria. Corelli stood below me on the stage proper and turned toward me. I was at the top of the stairs. Suddenly I saw him stick his hand into his waistband as though looking for something. I must admit that it broke my concentration. Finally he drew forth a little wad of something wrapped in plastic. He tore a hole into it and began to suck on what turned out to be a piece of sponge saturated with water. Corelli often had a problem with a dry throat. At the last second he tossed the sponge to a lady of the chorus, turned around, and blasted out a high C that shook the walls. This time he was the one who emerged victorious.

During a *Tristan* recording in Vienna the stormy meeting of Tristan and Isolde in act 2 had to be sung repeatedly. Solti with his fiery Hungarian temperament couldn't get his tempo fiery enough, and he repeated the passages over and over. In this section Isolde has two high Cs to sing. Altogether it was fourteen high Cs until Solti was finally satisfied. Just for fun I could not resist generously offering the extra high Cs for a future soprano in need. I didn't know how soon they would be needed. Only a few days later they were recording a Verdi opera with a well-known singer. In one aria there was a much-feared high C that the soprano missed over and over (rumors travel fast in Vienna). Eventually, understandably enough, she lost her nerve altogether. One says that the singer, as privately as possible, recorded the phrase in a lower key and the sound engineer took care of the rest with clever manipulation.

In defense of the singer, I have to reiterate that a high C is more difficult to sing in Vienna than in Stockholm, Milan, London, or New York, as the orchestra is tuned shamelessly high—almost a half tone higher than in other places. The Philharmonic refuses to change this, thereby obtaining orchestral brilliance at the expense of the struggling singers.

Kirsten Flagstad's voice became darker and more majestic over the years. It was hard to imagine that Flagstad had sung lyric roles in her younger years. When she was fifty-five, she was recording Isolde. Naturally she was concerned about the two high Cs in act 2. The producer, Walter Legge, suggested that his wife, Elisabeth Schwarzkopf should secretly help out with these tones. It soon became an open secret, discussed in all the music journals of the day. The two voices did not go together; the feather-light attack of Schwarzkopf did not harmonize at all with the monumental sound of Flagstad, and it didn't take an expert to tell the difference.

When only a beginner at the opera in Stockholm, I was cast in the demanding role of Lady Macbeth in Verdi's *Macbeth.* Fritz Busch conducted and his son, Hans Busch, did the staging. Just before coming to Stockholm Busch had conducted *Macbeth* in New York. There another singer had sung the high D-flat offstage for the actual Lady Macbeth in the Sleepwalking Scene. This he wanted to do in Stockholm. As I left the stage, another singer would stand in the wings and sing my high note. This made me very unhappy, as I wanted to sing the tone myself. But I spoke practically no German, which inhibited me from entering into a discussion with the conductor. A few singers were tried out for the high D-flat but not one of them had the note one hundred percent; some failed altogether. Had Verdi written the tone to be sung *forte*, there would have been no difficulty. But he asked for a finely spun thread of silken tone! Therefore he indicated a decrease in the dynamics, not just a *pianissimo* (*pp*), but still quieter (*ppp*), just to get the soprano's full attention. Hjördis Schymberg could have done the tone with bravura but one does not ask a star to sing a tone for a beginner.

On the morning of the premiere I was called unexpectedly to a lighting rehearsal with the stage director. I suddenly noticed Fritz Busch and forgot all of my reservations. I rushed to him and attempted to explain that if another singer cracked on my high tone *I* would be held responsible. Therefore I wanted to sing the confounded D-flat myself. "Can you do it?" he asked, astonished, as he had not even allowed me to attempt the D-flat in the rehearsals.

"You will hear it tonight," said I with the self-confidence of a girl from Skåne and thus revealed in advance the surprising success of the evening.

As already mentioned, my colleague Montserrat Caballé suffered from unexplained fainting spells. A few days before I was to sing a guest performance in Mannheim, Caballé had sung *Aida*. When I met Hans Wallat, the general music director, he said the guest performance had been a fantastic success with a singer by the name of Aballé as Aida. I asked, naturally, who Aballé might be and he said that it was Montserrat Cabellé who, just before the high C in the "Nile Aria," had fainted dead away so that there was no high C. So, she was rebaptized Aballé.

Luciano Pavarotti, great in every way, had a publicity manager with a rich imagination if not good judgment. He gave his client the title "King of the High Cs." When his colleague, Placido Domingo, was asked what he thought of the title, he answered that he took no exception to the title as he, himself, didn't have a high C. Well, it is probably better to be a king without a country than to sit in exile. However, Placido sells himself short here. As a member of the audience and as a colleague I have heard him sing countless wonderful high Cs. But this artist and singer, certainly one of the world's greatest, is a model of unpretentiousness and congeniality.

There is probably no tenor who can dynamically overpower the high C of a soprano in his natural voice. The soprano is an octave higher, has a brighter sound, and it carries better. Helge Roswänge, the famous Danish tenor, knew this. He was in his sixties when we sang *Turandot* together in Zurich. When we had to sing the high C together he stretched his mouth wide open and spread his arms dramatically—without, however, even attempting the high C. A totally successful effect. Everyone, even the critics, thought we both sang the C.

I saw once a telecast of Verdi's *Ballo* from the Metropolitan with Leontyne Price and "The King of the High Cs," that is, Pavarotti. In the second-act duet he placed himself, fully unmotivated, behind Leontyne Price and at the exact moment of their high C taken together, he ducked behind her lovely head. No one could say with any certainty whether he had sung the high C or whether the king had abdicated for a short time.

EMI wanted to record Verdi's *Aida* in Rome with, among others, Grace Bumbry, Franco Corelli, and myself; Zubin Mehta conducted. In the Triumphal Scene, Aida has a long sustained C that should soar out over the chorus and orchestra. This was always one of my favorite places. At the recording, shortly before my showpiece, I noticed Corelli move as closely as possible to the microphone and he sang the high C with me, even though it does not appear in his part. I left the stage and went into the recording room to gather up my things. The producer was astonished and ran after me to ask what had happened. I answered calmly that they obviously had another singer who could sing the part of Aida and I did not want to stand in anyone's way. The producer was alarmed and said if there was an altercation Corelli would probably refuse to continue recording.

"No, *I* am the one who is refusing to continue," I explained. "Corelli can go on in peace with his singing of Aida." The call came over the loudspeaker for the resumption of the recording. Instead I left the hall. The producer had to go back in and give the news that I had broken off the recording and was on my way back to my hotel. Corelli caught up with me on the street and offered a sincere apology—after which all complaints were forgotten. Corelli and I became good friends in the long run, and often a lovely bouquet of roses sent by Corelli decorated my apartment. When I appeared on Holmquist's television program *This is Your Life,* Corelli flew in from New York to surprise me. In this lovely gesture he was completely successful.

In Rome, a few days after the completion of a Decca recording of *Tosca,* the tenor singing Cavaradossi appeared relaxed, rested, and free of stress—and said he wanted to rerecord all of his high notes. This would not concern any of the other singers as the sound engineer could insert the new tones into the already finished recording. No one protested this highly unprofessional request of the "star."

When I was studying in the music academy in Stockholm, I did not have such easy high tones; some who heard me thought I was a mezzo-soprano. One day I was sitting alone at home on the farm trying unsuccessfully to get a grasp of how to produce a high C. My mother came in (she was then over sixty) and said calmly, "That's easy. There's nothing to it. Here's how it should sound—," whereupon she nailed a radiant high C. That was a lesson for me to live by, I believe. Even when I had difficulty with other notes at times, I could always, at three in the morning, if need be, belt out a high C.

My six cats on the farm in Skåne are as sensitive as tenors. They come running from every corner of the yard when their mealtime is announced with a high C.

BEAUTIFUL ITALY

Suddenly the white mountain tops of the Alps come into view. I am happy: after a long flight, Milan is near.

The loudspeaker crackles in the cabin and we hear the smooth voice of the captain, speaking from the cockpit, "Because of heavy fog in Milan we are forced to make our landing in Rome."

Well, someone has it in for me! That was all I could make of this. I had a strenuous trip from the States behind me during which I made a quick stop at my home to repack. It was now evening; according to my contract, rehearsals would begin the next morning at La Scala. Staying overnight in Rome was out of the question. There was nothing to do but jump in and go about the crazy business of making other travel arrangements, which travel delays always necessitate.

Having landed in Rome, I threw myself into a taxi. Thanks to the fast maneuvering of the Italian driver, I arrived in record time at the railway station to take the next, best train to Milan. The "next" train meant a two-hour wait and "best" meant one filled way over capacity. Those who have never traveled by train in Italy will find the picture impossible to imagine.

People sat on the floor with their bags and bundles and there was not the slightest chance to move forward or back. I had to use physical force to battle my way to a place to stand and where there was hardly room for my two large suitcases. I held on for dear life to a rope overhead.

There may be people who believe Italy to be full of gallant gentlemen who think it an honor to give a lady a place to sit. Think again! The varnish peels off very quickly. They have plenty of energy and perseverance when it comes to helping foreign ladies on the streets or when showering them with attention in every other way. But to offer a seat to a lady is unthinkable, even if she is in her ninth month!

I looked around and ascertained that 80 percent of the seats were occupied by young, so-called gentlemen. Perhaps they had to rest themselves after too much romantic dalliance. Who knows? In any case, this was a trip that would remain forever in my memory. Six hours I stood hanging onto the overhead cable with one arm and then the other.

I arrived in Milan at three in the morning, confused and half-dead from exhaustion. Nonetheless, the next morning at ten, I was at the opera: Teatro alla Scala, known to all opera lovers simply as La Scala. I announced myself to the porter and asked where the *Turandot* rehearsal was to take place. He leafed through a large blank notebook that had stamped on its cover "TURANDOT." "No, Signora, today is no rehearsal. . . . perhaps tomorrow," he added quickly, as he saw I was about to explode. I could have had a peaceful night in Rome instead of the torture of that train trip!

The same scene was played out for four days. "No, Signora, niente prova oggi, ma forse domani."

I had enough of the parroting of "perhaps tomorrow." I went to the management and asked, somewhat irritably, what was going on.

"Don't get excited. Calm down. Giuseppe di Stefano will be here in a few days. In the meantime, perhaps you can rehearse your staging together with the chorus," suggested the head of the opera, Antonio Ghiringhelli. Now Turandot is a role in which the protagonist is mostly standing at the top of a long staircase from where she flings out cascades of throat-breaking high notes. There is not much to rehearse concerning the staging. The stage director, Margarethe Wallman, was a former dancer and choreographer for whom not much existed outside ballet. And so I stood day in and day out up there on the top of the staircase, staying in one position until I thought I would grow moss.

At least I had a musical run-through with the conductor, Antonio Votto, otherwise, nothing happened. I had already sung the previous spring at La Scala, so perhaps I should have anticipated the muddle and confusion that prevailed now. But then I had been part of a German-Austrian ensemble and everything functioned in an orderly fashion. In the Italian ensemble nothing was in order. I have often said to myself that a premiere actually happening with an Italian company on a set date is an example of an impossibility. As usual, all the knots became untied at the last moment, thanks to the Italian talent for improvisation. But the cost is high in time, nerves, and money.

The days passed and there was no sign of my famous partner, di Stefano. My long wait gave me time to build up a mountain of antipathy toward the darling of La Scala. I decided to let him know exactly what I thought of him as soon as he *did* deign to appear. This appearance was at the first dress rehearsal! He came sauntering in as though he were right on schedule! And he had sung no more than ten bars before all my wrath was forgotten. He sang in a way that made your heart ache. He had a charm that could melt stone. And so . . . I melted!

This was not just any premiere but the opening of the 1958 season. The traditional day for the opening of La Scala is December 7. At that time I was the first non-Italian soprano to be given the honor of singing in the opening performance.

On the day of the premiere fog lay so thick over Milan that I could hardly breathe. To keep from collapsing, I forced myself to stop worrying about the fog. Perhaps I suffer from a kind of phobia, but I have experienced dangerous attacks when I have been in places with very high humidity, for example, in Bali, Taipei, Hong Kong, Bangkok, Rio, and Dakar. But vocal problems cannot, *must* not, exist on this great day at La Scala, also *my* great day!

The fog had actually crept into the auditorium, which was decorated with about ten thousand carnations, and it had dimmed the sparkle of the jewels worn by the beautiful—and above all—wealthy ladies. Their escorts wore white tie and tails, obligatory in 1958.

Turandot has nothing to sing in act 1, but appears for a brief time onstage to indicate with a gesture that all suitors who cannot answer her three riddles will be beheaded. After that I can follow the performance on the loudspeaker in my dressing room.

The reputation that the audience in La Scala has for being blasé is not exaggerated. I would not have believed, however, that they would have been so apathetic on such an evening. After act 1 there were only three curtain calls, which was almost scandalous! My heart sank. I was still having difficulty breathing. The ten-yard-long train was unusually heavy and hard to move. In addition, it got caught on a nail as I made my way up the staircase, almost causing me to fall backward. Finally, I ascended to the top of the stairs and could begin singing. The weak applause after the first act made one believe that it would be very difficult to bring the public to the point of enthusiasm. I was also not satisfied with myself; the voice seemed to disappear without my getting any reverberation.

But the day of miracles was evidently not past. Hardly had the final tone been sung when the aristocratic public jumped out of their seats screaming, jubilant, embracing one another, behaving like madmen.

There was a frenzy and thrill in the audience that astounded even those who made it a habit to observe the public's exuberance at performances. Not in my wildest fantasy had I dreamed of such a reception! The fog disappeared. The voice felt free and fresh. Giuseppe di Stefano sang a wonderful Calaf, and Rosanna Carteri was a deeply moving and lovely Liù.

The various branches of the press had much to do that evening. Among the many prominent members of the audience were President Gronchi, with his wife and two daughters; Prince Bernhard from Holland; Fosca Crespi, Puccini's daughter (who presented me with the Puccini Medal); Wally Toscanini (the daughter of the great maestro); Pierre Balmain, the fashion designer; and Erich Maria Remarque, with his wife, Paulette Goddard. The opening of the season at La Scala is a tremendous event.

I celebrated Christmas with a new opera friend, Bengt Svinhufvud, the former head of the airline ABA (later SAS) in Rome. It was a totally Swedish Christmas in his beautiful home; even though Bengt continued to live in Rome, his heart and soul still belonged to Sweden.

After the Christmas vacation, work went on without pause: in one month, eleven Turandots in Milan and a guest appearance in Zurich that turned out to be a real torture. Since the guest performance of *Tosca* with Jussi Björling, Sigurd Björling and myself during the Swedish Week in Zurich, I was often engaged there to sing Tosca, as well as Fidelio, Turandot, Isolde, and Brünnhilde in the *Ring*.

We had agreed that at some future date I would sing Amelia in *Ballo*. During my stay in Milan, the sympathetic head of the opera, Mr. Krahl, called and asked if I would agree to do an opera gala between my La Scala performances. We arranged—as I understood it—that I would sing *Ballo* on January 3, 1959. I went a day early to Zurich to have a costume fitting and a short rehearsal. The first costume turned out to be men's clothing and boots. I called their attention to the error, as that was certainly not Amelia's costume. "Surely you mean Leonora," said the seamstress.

Leonora??! Yes, she meant Leonora in Verdi's *Forza del Destino*. After I had convinced myself that this was not a nightmare, I hoped the earth would simply open and swallow me. When the director had spoken to me, he said *Forza del Destino*, which is not even in my repertoire, and I had heard *Ballo in Maschera*. He had used the German title, *Macht des Schicksals*—until then unfamiliar to me, as I only knew the Italian name.

Head over heels I rushed to the opera director, who was sitting comfortably in his office rubbing his hands together, self-satisfied at charging double admission prices for my sold-out gala performance. He was quiet for a while after hearing that I did not know the role of Leonora. Then he broke out in a hearty laugh and said, "I thought I had lived through everything that could go wrong in an opera house but this is something totally new!"

I suggested he get another guest and announce that I was ill, but he turned a deaf ear to this suggestion. The house was sold out because of my name and I was going to sing. Yes, but what? We agreed upon Tosca. But the conductor, Nello Santi insisted upon an orchestra rehearsal, as he had not conducted *Tosca* in some time.

"Oh, my, . . . an orchestra rehearsal will cost over a thousand francs," murmured the director, with a meaningful look at me. I volunteered to offset the cost of the rehearsal and he readily accepted the offer (he was Swiss, after all).

On the day of the performance the following notice was posted: Due to illness, *Tosca* will be presented tonight instead of *Macht des Schicksals.* Those reading the announcement must have wondered who was sick, as the roles were sung by the Verdi principals and the conductor was the same.

On this unlucky January 3, 1959, I worked around the clock, so to speak. I had to rehearse *Tosca* with the orchestra early in the day and sing the performance the same evening. After the performance I took the night train back to Milan, where on the following day, I had a matinee. One can easily see that because of this mix-up I did not close an eye.

Tired and exhausted, I got through the *Turandot* performance. How I managed it is still a puzzle to me. Now I had only Sunday to rest and recover, as Monday was the eleventh and final *Turandot* performance. Being able to rest on Sunday did wonders for me: on Monday I was in top form and one experience richer—as one says after making a mistake.

I fell in love with Italy, with the climate, the wonderful things to see, the food, and the people with their untroubled, carefree lifestyle. Rome became my favorite city.

To visit this wonderful city before it was choked with traffic and to be paid for going there—well, it seemed almost unfair. The Rome Opera was, however, not in the same class with La Scala where I appeared twelve or thirteen times a year. In Rome, my guest performances were more sporadic. My debut was in 1957 as Brünnhilde in *Die Walküre* with an ensemble from Vienna. There was another Swede along, Sigurd Björling, who was performing Wotan.

An audience with Pope Pius XII was arranged for the singers. We all gathered punctually, except for one singer, the one singing Fricka, who came storming into the ceremonial greeting late, with tears in her eyes. Her reason for being late was good: she had been to confession. In fact, she went to confession daily. Her list of sins was not so great that she had to go every day but she had fallen head over heels in love with her confessor. Only at her last confession did she reveal to him that she was Protestant.

At the word "confession," the eyes of the pope softened and her tardiness was also forgiven. He asked her what Wagner role was her favorite. "Venus," she replied, the tears still glistening in her lovely eyes. The Venus in *Tannhäuser*, known as one of the most sinful women in all opera literature! The pope closed the interview quickly and moved on to the next singer.

I had already sung at the lovely San Carlo Opera in Naples: Donna Anna in *Don Giovanni* and Venus in *Tannhäuser* in 1955 and 1956.

The conductor, Karl Böhm, was not in a good mood for the *Don Giovanni* performance—particularly when it came to my aria "Non mi dir." He was obdurately grim and disagreeable. I was either too fast or too slow in my tempo. No matter how I tried to change, he was not satisfied. I was singing then for the first time with Böhm and really tried to follow him like a shadow. That was a mistake: when one tried to subordinate oneself, he would become nervous and choppy in his tempi. If one simply took one's own tempo, that which was most natural, then he followed impeccably.

Böhm's stumbling block, however, was the orchestra, in whose vocabulary the word "discipline" did not exist. If some of the musicians during the rehearsal had nothing to play for a few bars they would sit there and converse loudly among themselves. If Böhm stopped the orchestra to repeat a section, it sounded like a henhouse; there was such complaining and cackling. It was the most talkative bunch of musicians I have ever seen. Finally Böhm exploded and left the orchestra sitting there as he departed, furious. But then the orchestra pulled themselves together. As though on command they played an "O sole mio" to die for. What conductor could resist such an apology? Not Böhm in any case: the silken tones were the perfect balm. Both the orchestra and Böhm continued, behaving like lambs.

When I returned to Naples in 1956 to sing Venus in *Tannhäuser*, I requested by telegram the same room in the same hotel that I had reserved the previous year. I arrived to find instead of a hotel a huge hole in the place where the hotel had stood. It had burned to the ground. I had to look for another hotel. Bertil was joining me and I had to let him know of a change of residence. But how? He was on the way to Naples after a stopover in Hamburg. At this point I had no idea where I would be staying and he knew nothing of these new events. Two days later he arrived at my hotel, sour as a lemon, at three in the morning. He had had to go to the police station to find out where I was staying. They did not believe he was just trying to locate me but were convinced his wife had left him because of abuse or some other heinous act. He was thoroughly cross-examined before he was given the address of my hotel.

In Naples I saw Maria Callas for the first time on stage. She was portraying Lucia in *Lucia di Lammermoor*. She was booed in act 1 and wildly cheered in the next—the gap between heaven and hell is very narrow in Italian opera. Her big aria was really phenomenal.

My next guest appearance in Naples was twenty years, later in 1976. It was in celebration of the fiftieth anniversary of the first performance of *Turandot* in 1926, with Toscanini conducting, and Rosa Raisa as Turandot.

The premiere was supposed to be on March 13 and the second performance on March 17. Three days between the first and second performances was very nice, not to mention necessary for someone like me who was not exactly dew-fresh. But luck was not with me. Quite by accident I read that the premiere had been rescheduled for March 15. As usual I was the last to know. Upon my demand to know why the date was changed, the director said, somewhat embarrassed, that it was impossible for the tenor to perform on that day as it was his unlucky day. My reaction was a flat-out veto. I said it so happened that the fifteenth was *my* unlucky day. The premiere was rescheduled for the thirteenth. Carlo Bergonzi sang his first Calaf, Maria Chiara was Liù and Franco Mannino (a pianist and composer) was the conductor. Nothing untoward happened; the thirteenth turned out to be a lucky day for everyone.

For my entrance in act 2 the opera fans had made a banner saying "Benvenuta Nilsson!" This was hanging on the balcony. There are many ways for the public to show their recognition and affection for an artist but this was the first time I was greeted with a banner.

Florence is known for its magnificent culture and I was always happy to return there. In 1956 I sang Brünnhilde in the *Ring*, and the following year, Isolde. As so often, I had in this performance my dear colleague Wolfgang Windgassen as Siegfried. He was not only the ideal partner; he always noticed any technical details that were not functioning. I had borrowed the costume of Brünnhilde from the Stockholm Opera. It closed at the back down to the waist with hooks and eyes. Apparently in the dry-cleaning the hooks had become softened: when I raised myself, awakening from the long sleep, I felt as though the top of my costume was falling off. Quite right—I felt as carefully as I could while I sang and realized all the hooks and eyes had opened! I broke out in a cold sweat at the thought of what could happen. Acting with one hand while keeping the other behind my back was no solution. What would I do when I had to embrace Siegfried? I had hardly grasped that thought when Windgassen placed himself behind me (which was not in the staging). And while continuing to sing his demanding music, remaining completely calm, he closed up the back of my costume, hook by hook! I cannot imagine anyone else who would have had the presence of mind to accomplish that. Other tenors are so self-involved, they wouldn't have even noticed if I had been singing in the "costume" of Eve.

The *Tristan* performance, part of the Maggio Musicale Fiorentino Festival in Florence in 1957, gained further luster from the presence of the Polish conductor, Artur Rodziński on the podium. He was very demanding, oversensitive, and given to endless rehearsing. In addition, he was a hypochondriac who traveled with enough medicine to stock a pharmacy. As soon as he arrived in a new place, he visited a number of doctors so that, according to Madame Rodziński's amusing version, they could convince him how healthy he was.

Rodziński did not give up until he had gotten everything out of the singers and the orchestra. Until then, I had not heard an orchestra play *Tristan* with such an ethereal sound as under Rodziński. When I resisted rehearsing on the day of the premiere, he became peeved with me. After the premiere, which proved to be a really wonderful performance, with newspaper headlines more than a foot wide, he wrote, "You are a naughty girl, but I love you."

In January 1956 *Tristan* was performed in Turin under the direction of Ferdinand Leitner, together with a concert performance broadcast over the radio. I arrived two days before the concert without my luggage, which had been lost. In spite of all effort, it appeared that my bag would not turn up before the concert. I went immediately to a dress shop where, for an agreed-upon price, they would make for me a white evening dress with a matching silk stole. The evening of the concert was upon us but my luggage as well as the new dress were conspicuous by their absence. I began to get really nervous. Then I had a call from the dress shop. The dress was finished but unfortunately they could not deliver it for the agreed-upon price, as it had taken more hours of work than anticipated. It was no small increase they were asking and as they knew I needed the dress because my luggage was lost, I assumed the price increase was a kind of blackmail. I was already at the fitting, standing there in my panties and bra, waiting for the dress to be brought in. I was outraged and shaking, but took a deep breath and lied as calmly as possible: "I think you can just keep the dress. My luggage arrived an hour ago. If you wish to give it to me at the agreed-upon price I will of course honor our agreement, provided that the dress is here and finished in twenty minutes." The dress was brought in as quickly as the wind. It was beautiful and put me in a victorious mood even before the concert.

A few days later I received a letter that made me extremely happy. The writer was none other than Kirsten Flagstad. She had heard the *Tristan* radio broadcast and wanted to tell me how much my Isolde had impressed her. Was this performance not in every way a victory?

For many years I had a standing offer from Verona that I was unable to accept because of my singing in Bayreuth. After Wieland Wagner's death I reduced the number of performances at Bayreuth, which in 1959 enabled me finally to realize my dream of singing in the famous Verona arena. I agreed to sing the first four performances of *Turandot.*

The feeling one has standing on that stage is indescribable. Before you is an audience of twenty-two thousand operagoers, seated on stone benches and holding lighted candles. The lighting of candles is a fantastic tradition. Someone told a conceited American tenor that the public lit the candles in his honor and I heard often about interviews in the States where he spoke of this unique honor.

This summer the temperature was 104°F, day in, day out. The dressing rooms were little stone lion cages from the times of the gladiators. When the costumes were brought into the dressing room there was hardly room for a hairdresser or a dresser. One had two choices: either you shut the door to the corridor and died of suffocation, or you left the door open and got the full attention of the male stage personnel. What was my decision? I was not ready to die. The second-act costume was of white lace. No doubt it appeared lovely and airy—but the underdress was of PLASTIC! It was horrible and the sweat poured off me in streams. Just standing, waiting for my entrance cue, I felt makeup melt away.

The acoustics of the arena were faultless. It was said in fact that the *Turandot* was heard throughout the entire city. Nota bene! Here there was no manipulation with amplification.

Molinari-Pradelli conducted the 125-piece orchestra. Gabriella Tucci sang the role of Liù, Ivo Vinco was Timur, and Plácido Domingo sang his first Calaf. What a wonderful singer and passionate actor he is! His kiss, which transforms Turandot from an ice block to a loving woman was so long that the public began to call out, "Basta, basta adesso!" In spite of a bad cold that caused his eyes to lose their sparkle, Placido was a fantastic Calaf.

But that cold did more than dim his eyes. Just before the next performance I came down with tonsillitis. My throat hurt so terribly that I could hardly swallow. For a singer to have a cold is bad enough, but to be ill in 104°F heat is catastrophic. I was successful, in any case, in getting through the remaining performances honorably. But in the future I was more careful in my behavior with tenors with colds.

Because of the inconvenient facilities, I declined future engagements in Verona. The director promised to make it heaven on earth: if I would come again he would even install air-conditioning in the lion cage. At that time I was all too well acquainted with the tendency of the Italians to forget their promises, so I wasn't tempted.

It was actually a great relief to get back to Bayreuth, costumed in real leather and singing in a mere 90°F in the shade.

In Macerata, a small town not far from the Adriatic, there is an arena built in the shape of a half-circle, dating from the nineteenth century. It was intended to be used as a sports arena and seated about six thousand people. Later it was used for big musical events such as operas and concerts. Poor management, however, led to less and less interest in the arena, and it was almost forgotten. But a new management came in determined to bring new life to the place by engaging internationally recognized artists. The first who came to mind was Franco Corelli, practically a native son, having been born in the neighboring town of Ancona, where he still spent many of his summers.

Corelli was only moderately interested as it would break up his vacation, but it was difficult to say no. Therefore he said he would accept their offer only if I could be persuaded to sing with him in *Turandot.* Corelli considered it totally unlikely that I would come to Macerata as I was declining Verona. In this way he would get out of singing in Macerata's arena. But he did not reckon with the cleverness of the new management. They offered me a princely salary; in addition, my husband and I would be domiciled in the Villa of the late Gigli. And of course we would be met at the Milan airport and taken by car to the villa. I fell for the huge fee, as well as the Gigli Villa, hook, line, and sinker, and I accepted the engagement.

When we arrived at the airport in Milan there was not a sign of the car to chauffeur us to Macerata. Naturally I was irritated and wanted to return immediately to Sweden. But Bertil, whose patience is greater than mine, suggested renting a car and driving in the direction of Macerata, at least to see where the Gigli Villa is located.

It was unbelievably difficult to find; we drove all over, often getting lost. I was all for turning around and heading back to Milan. Then there suddenly appeared before us the highest hill of Loreto with a villa similar to the description of Gigli's. At the end of the approximately quarter-mile driveway up to the villa we were halted by a large gate. After the porter held a conversation with someone from the house, we were found worthy and the gate was opened. As we stopped before the imposing edifice, three angry, barking sheepdogs ran up to the car and started nipping at the tires.

"We are going to turn around right now and return to Sweden," I cried out for the last time, as the owner of the villa came toward us, quieted the barking dogs, and welcomed us heartily. The owner of the villa!? I had thought the whole time that after the death of Gigli, the villa was bought by the town of Macerata and that we had been invited by the town officials to live there.

My mood was not improved when I realized we were to be quartered with total strangers. I had made it a rule never to live in a private residence when I was in engagement: I had to be completely free to come and go as I wished and to eat whenever and whatever I wanted. But Mr. and Mrs. Bartoloni and their three charming daughters were really a wonderful family. If one had to be housed privately there was no family better than these agreeable and considerate people.

They did everything possible for our comfort, and at the same time we had our freedom. Raffaelo Bartoloni was the owner of a ceramics firm in Treja and the Gigli Villa was his summer residence. The property consisted of a large park, pinewoods, and its own winery. Gigli's own sleeping quarters were opened up for us, an honor that until then had been accorded to no one. Otherwise they lived, uncrowded, in the remaining sixty-four rooms. (I wrote an American friend and boasted that I was sleeping in Gigli's bed and received a telegram with the terse question ". . . very well, but where is Gigli?")

In the days of the famous tenor there was a staff of sixteen-plus and an elevator operator. At the time of our visit the number of staff was considerably reduced. Gigli had installed a chapel with an altar, beautiful paintings, an organ, and church pews for the family and employees. He was in his naïve way very religious. Gigli's wife was obsessed with gambling; it was rumored that she had gambled away the greatest part of his fortune. In any case, the leather chairs in the game room were quite worn.

Gigli is buried in the place of his birth, Recanati. Over his grave rises a monument in the form of an Egyptian pyramid. It was my pleasure to place flowers on his grave not only in remembrance of the great artist but in gratitude for having had the privilege of knowing such an unusually good and generous human being.

Some years later I returned to Macerata, this time as soloist in an orchestra concert and we again lived with the hospitable Bartoloni family in Gigli's villa. We kept in touch, and when the daughters married we were invited to each of the weddings.

In 1960 I had the opportunity of appearing in Venice's wonderful Teatro La Fenice, a small residence theater seating 677. It was richly appointed in velvet, silk, crystal, paintings, and plenty of old theater dust. This guest performance was *Tristan und Isolde* in Wolfgang Wagner's production with singers from Bayreuth.

The abstract staging seemed a little out of place in the romantic setting offered by the Teatro La Fenice. Wolfgang Sawallisch conducted the Italian orchestra with great authority and musical finesse. It was like singing in a big jewel box with wonderful acoustics. It is painful to think this splendid example of theater architecture no longer exists.* A grateful public received the performance enthusiastically. It was in the middle of winter, very cold and damp, so a relaxing trip in a gondola was out of the question.

Parma is a city that has a bad reputation among singers. All too many artists have experienced being booed, and wild stories are told about how cruel the public can be. This story proves that the reputation is well deserved. A tenor was in Parma for a guest performance and was soundly booed. On the day after the performance the redcap at the rail station was helping him with his bags looked at the tenor and asked, "Were you singing at the opera last night?" The tenor, not without pride, said he had

*The Teatro La Fenice was destroyed by a fire on January 29, 1996. La Fenice was rebuilt in the style of the nineteenth century, reopening on December 14, 2003.

indeed sung the previous night. "Then you can carry this stuff yourself," said the redcap, as he dropped the luggage onto the platform.

The end of the 1970s found me on a concert tour of Italy. All too late I noticed I had a concert scheduled in Parma. I was really uneasy about what was awaiting me. After my last number, Isolde's "Liebestod" I expected to hear only booing. Out of fear that rotten tomatoes might even be awaiting me, I delayed going out to receive the applause—or whatever. The screams got louder and louder. The director of the opera quickly came to me and asked what the problem was, why did I not go out. I said that wild horses could not get me out in front of that booing public.

"Mamma mia . . . can't you hear that they are yelling *bis?*" This meant "encore"; they wanted to hear Isolde die again.

In fact, the public in Parma spoiled me. The Verdi Society received me with heartfelt warmth and presented me with a bronze bust of Verdi. There was also a documentary film of me shown, produced by the RAI in Rome. After all the spontaneous and warmhearted friendliness, I could unconditionally thank the citizens of Parma and say how much I loved their beautiful opera, the Parma ham, and the Parmesan cheese. The day before my departure two gentlemen from the opera house appeared with a whole ham and a large Parmesan cheese as farewell gift. Thank God, I had better luck with the redcap than the unfortunate tenor.

I would like to take you back to La Scala, my "home" theater in Italy.

It is a magical house and all the myths spun about it over the years are absolutely true. Without wanting to take anything away from its brilliance, I have to say the acoustics in La Scala are not the best—except for one spot, far left on the stage as seen from the auditorium. This place is not hard to find, as the boards are worn down from all the acoustic-conscious singers over the years seeking out this spot. If one is Italian *and* a tenor, there is no stage director in the world who can prevent his big aria from being sung on this favorable place. The fact that it might be sung in the dark, far from the other singers, and practically removed from the set is of no interest. Talk about "singing from the spot!"

The management of the opera consisted of a triumvirate: Antonio Ghiringhelli, the business manager; Francesco Siciliani, artistic director; and Luigi Oldani, who was responsible for everything else. Siciliani was a competent and congenial man who really understood voices (which is hardly the case with all heads of operas).

It was said that Dr. Ghiringhelli was very rich and that, after the war, he had personally taken on much of the expense of restoring La Scala. It was never quite clear to me what his duties were or whether he even had a great interest in the opera. His office was empty most days, and negotiations with the singers were handled by Oldani. Ghiringhelli also seldom attended a performance or even a rehearsal. No matter: he was a close friend of Maria Callas and Giuseppi di Stefano. Sometimes it happened that he appeared in my dressing room after a performance and regaled me with stories of his amorous escapades, which I'm sure he shared with others as well.

One day, before an *Aida* performance, the originally cast tenor became ill and Ghiringhelli telephoned me, asking if I would accept the alternate tenor. The one he named was a very good singer but very short and slight. Next to him I would look like a giant. When I expressed my concern about how we would look together, he wanted to know where the tenor would come to on me. "Doctor," I answered, "modesty forbids my being specific."

"Good," he said, "then we will find another."

And for the performance there was indeed a well-proportioned tenor of normal height.

From the German repertoire I sang at La Scala the *Ring* and Isolde, both in two different productions; in addition, Senta with Hans Knappertsbusch conducting, Fidelio with Karajan, Salome with Klobučar, and Elektra with Sawallisch. From the Italian repertoire I sang Turandot quite often and was given a second season-opening performance with Franco Corelli as Calaf and Galina Vishnevskaya as an unusually dramatic and intense Liù.

In addition I sang Lady Macbeth in a production by the Frenchman Jean Vilar. All the *Macbeth* sets were in black and white with a huge red blood spot in the background. Highly evocative! Giangiacomo Guelfi sang and acted Macbeth magnificently. The tenor role was sung by Bruno Prevedi, a wonderful singer who, in my opinion, was underestimated. The bass, Ivo Vinco, gave a strong portrayal of Banquo. Herman Scherchen was our maestro, reputed to be a competent but difficult conductor. But "all's well that ends well," and the result was an excellent performance. The sound of the La Scala chorus is unsurpassed by that of any other group, particularly in Italian opera. I took special pleasure in singing Lady Macbeth in the big ensembles with this marvelous chorus.

The *Aida* was less successful, at least in my opinion. The conductor was not exactly a Toscanini and had little understanding for the voice. The Nile Aria with its exposed and important high C is often a stumbling block for the Aida—it is probably the reason relatively few sopranos undertake the role. This high C lies particularly unfavorably: for several measures before the redoubtable tone, one has an up and down vocal line. The success of the high C is dependent upon a vocally light texture and a flowing tempo; the tone should be reached with, so to speak, the wind at your back. This conductor took such a slow, weighty tempo that one had the feeling of wading in snow up to the knees and against the wind. I felt I was never so near not making this high C and I was absolutely sure the audience would boo, as is often their habit. But I was lucky (maybe they felt sympathy for me). There was no booing, but also not much applause.

Some days later I went to Maestro Siciliani and requested to be released from the remaining *Aida* performances. He could see that my spirits were very low but didn't want us to make too hasty a decision. Given renewed confidence by his encouraging words, I decided to try again. As we neared the precarious high C in the second performance, the conductor again started to drag the tempo. I closed my eyes and in my imagination saw on the podium a conductor who carried me light as a feather to the high C. All difficulties were swept away and the remaining performances went easily. Through the power of suggestion and closed eyes I could summon a real musician instead of the woodchopper who was actually there. Naturally I was glad that I had not given up. I might never have found the courage to undertake the role of Aida again.

Along with the fantastic Giulietta Simionato as Amneris and di Stefano as Radames, there was a young bass singing the High Priest who impressed me very much. He was still new and unknown and had a wonderful vocal talent. He came into my dressing room one day and asked me for an autographed photo of myself. I requested in return a photo of him, "because in a few years you will be so famous that you will have no time to send me a photo." My prediction of his rise to fame was true. His name: Nicolai Ghiaurov.

The biggest problem I had at La Scala was, surprisingly, with a German ensemble, with whom everything usually worked perfectly. In December 1960 and January 1961, I was engaged to sing seven *Fidelio* performances with Karajan conducting and Paul Hager as stage director. We had rehearsed the staging for some time without Karajan's putting in an appearance. In fact, he arrived only four days before the premiere.

Usually there are one or two days free between the final dress rehearsal and the premiere. This is a given, as the singer needs this time for rest, especially before a strenuous role. Karajan changed this, however. Because of his "second job" in Berlin we had to rehearse day and night. That simply meant that I was singing the role of Fidelio about four times a day and I objected strongly.

My protest resulted in our having a meeting with Oldani in his office. I told it as it was: I was unable to sing every day up to the premiere and expect to be in form. Whereupon Karajan interjected that I would probably prefer to be at home, lounging around and collecting my money. I took no note of this impudence but suggested the premiere be moved to a slightly later date so that we could rehearse in the usual manner. At this Karajan jumped up as if stung by an adder and said he would have to be paid for any performances that were dropped! At this outburst I could not refrain from asking quietly who was the more concerned with money—he or I?

Now Karajan suggested that I mark the rehearsals; that is, sing with half-voice. I rejoined that, even though the suggestion came from him, I thought it unlikely that he would permit my marking in an opera such as *Fidelio* where the balance of voices is so important. Karajan kept silent. In the end I did mark the rehearsals but I was always unhappy about it.

The premiere was held on the date originally planned. The performances were all quite routine except one where Maestro Karajan put his shoulder to the wheel and brought the performance to the level all the others should have attained. This particular performance was attended by the La Scala conductor, Maestro Gavazzeni, who sat in the director's loge, on the side of the stage, right over the orchestra. Karajan gave a sterling example of how he could inspire singers and orchestra to unbelievably brilliant performance.

Although thirty-five years have passed, this performance lives in my memory. One has to ask, however, if it is justifiable to give one hundred percent artistically only when a colleague or competitor is in the audience.

Another opera performance with problems was *Elektra,* which was given in the summer of 1972 with Wolfgang Sawallisch conducting. He was full of enthusiasm for this, his first *Elektra.* Günther Rennert, head of the Munich Opera, was an inspiring stage director; and Rudolf Heinrich designed the sets. Ingrid Bjoner sang a splendid Chrysothemis, and Kerstin Meyer gave a fascinating study of Klytämnestra. Franz Crass sang Orest beautifully and the acting of Ragnar Ulfung, as Aegist, was unsurpassable. So distinguished an ensemble and yet something was not right. How could this be possible?

When I came to the first stage rehearsals, I found to my horror the entire stage covered with imitation stones, large and small, which made it impossible to stand feet flat on the floor. The role of Elektra is not only difficult to sing but requires her presence onstage from beginning to end. I explained that it was impossible to sing Elektra while constantly balancing myself on these stones, adding that even if I had the head of a goat I did not have their feet. To my great surprise I got no sympathy from the experienced stage director, Rennert, who resisted moving even the smallest stone. He claimed to have suffered two weeks of headache to plan the staging for the five servants (who appear in, at most, the first ten minutes of the opera). I could not resist suggesting that he might have taken ten minutes out of the two weeks he spent on the servants to think about how Elektra was going to negotiate the pebble-strewn stage. In other words, the atmosphere was "Elektric." Then I added, "You should not change a thing to accommodate me if you think another Elektra can overcome this problem. The excellent Danica Mastilović, who is following me, can try her luck. If she is able to manage, then I wish her well . . ."

With that I left the opera house, went to my hotel, and was fully prepared to leave Milan. I had barely gotten into the room when the telephone rang. Yes, they had agreed upon a change and they asked me please to come the following morning to see if it met my approval. They had erected a small platform that went between the stones at right angles across the stage. The stage gained a new dimension and the effect was in general more advantageous.

Danica Mastilović had been rehearsing on this rocky set before I first arrived and had stated her reservations about working on a floor of pebbles. Rennert answered her curtly, "If Nilsson can do it, so can you!" Mastilović was grateful to have her objections validated and happy that I was able to bring about a change in this insane set.

This story is important because it says something about contemporary opera staging and set design. When will the singers finally defend themselves against such extreme and unjust demands made upon them? A singer has to become an acrobat; if he doesn't, he'll be replaced by someone more willing to risk his neck. All to satisfy the whim of someone with little or no interest in the needs of the singer! Things have gone too far. So often one sees staging or settings that are horrible, adding nothing to the musical or dramatic elements of the work—flat-out misguided and wrongheaded. This can only be viewed as provoking the singers and the public for the designer's own gratification. Singing, which should absolutely have the most honored place in the opera, suffers when such egotistic self-indulgence is permitted by those in authority.

After the *Elektra* premiere, I received a lovely letter of appreciation from the stage director, Rennert, which pleased me very much.

As we all know, the summers of childhood were always happy, warm, and sunny. We just want to hold the beautiful hours in one's memory and (thank God) let the veil of forgetfulness fall over the rainy, cool, and unhappy days.

Although I had the help of my diary and the calendar to assist my recalling some of the days that remained shadowy, recalling the light of the Italian sun helped retrieve many memories. My longing for "La bella Italia" remains unchanged. I yearn for the sun, the warmth, the language, the culture, the people, the restaurants, and the narrow streets. I long to see again the view from the Monte Pincio in Rome and walk along the Arno in the evenings to see the rays of the setting sun turn the Ponte Vecchio into a golden bridge. It would be wonderful to see Venice again from a gondola or to take a boat from Naples to Capri just to sit and watch the fishermen. All that and much more of indescribably beautiful Italy fills me with the desire to return. Perhaps one of our greatest gifts is longing.

FANS, FANATICS, AND EXPERTS

When an artist speaks of a "fan" he is usually referring to an agreeable person in his life, an admirer, someone who respects him, someone devoted to him. *But* it can also happen that some fans become obsessed.

In the opera public there are many fans, and opera does not stand in the shadow of rock stars when it comes to admiration and idolization. The history of music is full of dramatic happenings when a fan's admiration gets out of control and results in tragedy. A well-known example is the riot that took place in the Grand Hotel in Stockholm on September 23, 1885, when the people wanted to greet the famous Christine Nilsson. In the course of the crowd's pressing forward, eighteen poor fans fell into the water and drowned. A concert of Franz Liszt in St. Petersburg was accompanied by similar drama, and the "witchcraft" of the violinist Sarasate was heard in the Wiener Musikverein only with the police controlling the crowd. Emotions can run high, and even boil over when the human voice casts its miraculous spell.

There is a feeling of great sympathy with a true "fan." He isn't living in a fantasy of false hopes; he is confident about his own artistic taste; and, while part of the crowd, he is not part of a herd mentality. A real fan knows that the artist cannot be disturbed if he is to give a good performance.

A true fan demands no special treatment but is most appreciative when he receives some friendly notice. Such friendliness does not cause him to take advantage with any ulterior motives.

There is also a special group of fans that I like the most. I had many such admirers and count many them among my close friends today. I am happy and grateful to have all these *real* fans. They belong to the happiest time of my life. I cannot name them all, and it would be unfair to single out any one in particular. But one thing is certain: every one of them has a special place in my heart.

Therefore, I'm sure no one will take it amiss if I do mention my oldest living fan, Dorothy Sivertson from Pasedena, California.

In the summer of 1954 I received my very first fan letter from America, and it was from Dorothy. She had heard me in a radio broadcast of *Salome* and was ecstatic. Her letter was so interesting and detailed that I answered it and so began a little exchange of letters. When I came to Los Angeles in 1956 to sing in the Hollywood Bowl, I met Dorothy. She was a musician and a passionate opera lover. Greatly to her regret, her husband and son did not share her great interest in music. She scrimped and saved in order to travel as often as possible to hear me sing. Once she came to Sweden to hear me and she also made trips to Vienna, Hamburg, and Copenhagen. Naturally she came to New York and Chicago as often as she could when I had appearances there.

Dorothy is a charming lady, and all my other fans who met her loved her. Over the years she has knit countless jackets, sweaters, and stoles for me. Today, Dorothy is about 90 years young and doesn't travel any longer, but we stay in close contact. In addition, we have a mutual interest: cats. She lives with her four feline companions for company.

There are, of course, other kinds of fans, the so-called name-droppers and "collectors" of artists. They are in the main "wannabe" experts whose interest in music is very superficial. For them it is important to be seen at the right premieres and to mingle with the stars, hoping to gain some advantage from such association. Presumably they are hoping that some of the brilliance of the stars will rub off on them. To impress anyone around them (and probably to impress themselves), they always use the first name of the artist when speaking of him. If the renown of the star declines, these "fame-parasites" disappear like greased lightning, moving on to enrich their image with new and more interesting victims.

They do not really admire the artist. They demand possession of him. It can be seen in their cold eyes. These "collectors" of artists are terribly exhausting and one has to get rid of them as quickly and as forcefully as possible. I am said to be sometimes brusque and resolute in my treatment of fans. In all such instances it is without exception these parasites who get my cold shoulder.

. . .

A fan often gives an artist flowers. In London and Stockholm they may take the flowers onto the stage. In all other houses that is forbidden; instead of bringing the flowers onto the stage they throw them from the parquet or the balconies. Ideally, these bouquets land on the stage apron and not in the orchestra pit. Liane, in Vienna, one of my favorite fans, was particularly good in tossing bouquets and most of the time I could catch them as they flew through the air. At the Teatro Colón in Buenos Aires the mountain of flowers was overwhelming. From every side it was raining flowers.

At the Metropolitan it was forbidden to throw flowers onto the stage, though occasionally this rule was broken. Supposedly, at times various items were stuck in with the flowers that could actually injure anyone catching the bouquet! Instead of tossing flowers, the fans tore up their programs into large confetti and those pieces of paper sailed down to the stage from the balconies. Naturally, all this confetti did not land on the stage but littered the orchestra pit and the front rows of the auditorium, much to the irritation of the cleaning staff. I think they would prefer to see flower tossing reinstated.

Now I want to speak about my most loyal fan, a pensioned officer from Uppsala. He was married and had ten grown children. It is no exaggeration when I say that I was the greatest joy of his later years. Whenever I sang at the Stockholm Opera, he sat in the third balcony with his field glasses. From there he saw and heard better than he would have from the parquet, or so he said. At every performance he sent me a large bouquet that was tied with ribbons of Sweden's colors. I made it a habit to roll up these ribbons and they have their place in my collection of souvenirs. Over the years the ball of ribbons has become larger than a soccer ball. Once a year at the Festival of Gröna Lund in Stockholm, I meet him. He makes it his habit to stand at the stage door in order to thank me personally for the concert. One day while making a stop in Copenhagen on my flight to New York, I received the sad news that my dear friend and fan had died. He was ninety years old.

At my next performance in Stockholm one of his sons visited me in my dressing room. He had promised his father to bring me, after his death, a letter and a box. The letter was a touching farewell and the box contained a beautiful gold bracelet with a very personal engraving. During the many years I had sent him (and other loyal fans) postcards from all corners of the earth, and I believe this gave him great pleasure.

Really, I should have lived in the nineteenth century. Then, prima donnas were showered with champagne, roses, and costly jewels. The walnut-size emerald that Christine Nilsson received during her guest appearance in Russia was definitely not of paste. And the laurel wreath given her by opera friends upon her opening of the Metropolitan season in 1883 was of genuine gold. In the final gala in 1966 at the old Met, it was my honor to wear this laurel wreath.

All right, I admit it: as far as jewelry goes, I have not been neglected. I recall an occasion in Frankfurt where I gave a guest performance of *Tosca.* There was an unexpected knock at my dressing room door, and a gentleman whom I had seen fleetingly a few times came into the room. I knew he was from a very rich and distinguished family. He opened a large package, which he had carried under his arm. There lay a gorgeous tiara decorated with diamonds. He asked if I would be so kind as to wear this tiara in the evening's performance. Tosca is a celebrated prima donna who, in act 2, appears in formal evening dress. Granted, a tiara is obligatory if you are true to the style of the time. But a tiara for the stage is made of glass stones. I was shocked at his suggestion to wear real diamonds on stage. When Tosca and Scarpia are struggling in the seduction scene, the tiara could be torn off. I explained to the gentleman what a risk it would be to wear this genuine diamond tiara on the stage, but he waved away my objections.

The hairdresser was informed and attached the tiara to my wig as securely as possible. German thoroughness demanded that she "skewer" me with about two dozen extra hairpins. After the performance the gentleman came to me beaming and thanked me for the wonderful evening. I had already placed the tiara back in its box and handed it to him with thanks for lending it to me. "Oh, no," said he, "of course the tiara now belongs to you." With that, he departed and I could only thank him profusely.

The most difficult and dangerous fans are the fanatics, and there is no telling where their inventiveness will lead.

For example, there was my fanatic admirer in Pittsburgh, an opera-loving lady who had one of the city's music critics as table companion at a dinner. On this occasion, this critic apparently expressed some unfavorable, if not unexpected, opinions about me. There ensued a very heated discussion. Finally she lost control, took a dessert plate, and struck him in the face. There was quite a scandal, what with the visit to the hospital for stitches—to say nothing of the money the court demanded she pay for causing him so much pain. The intense admiration of a fanatic can very quickly turn into equally intense hate. In the instance I am about to describe I had not shown sufficient appreciation for a gift from the fanatic. Suddenly, I received a stream of threatening letters. With the help of the police we discovered that these threats upon my life almost surely came from this fanatic. Sometime later I gave a concert in his hometown and it was decided best to have police protection during my visit to that city. Even though the situation was of a serious nature, I found the police protection a bit exaggerated. Could there be another solution to the problem? The thing was to simply go back to the cause of the problem. The fanatic was contacted and we met in the café at my hotel, at his importunate suggestion. I was quite calm and friendly while he, especially at the beginning, was noticeably nervous. Everything went well and we parted most agreeably. After this meeting the threatening letters stopped.

Another fanatic was a lovely young American from New York. A tragic case, she was an example of just how far from reality starry-eyed idolizing of an artist can lead. Over nine long years she caused me great uneasiness and distress. I tell this story, which I would prefer to forget, because it is an example of how fine a line there is between fantasy and reality and what all this can mean for the artist. I am convinced that this example is not unique in the world of famous artists.

Let us call her Miss N.

It began in the summer of 1968 in Bayreuth. Every morning on the day of my performance (the performances begin at 4 P.M.) there was a large bouquet of roses at my door. There was always a card, signed "L. Black," and the accompanying text appeared to be something taken from a novel. I told a friend about my fiery, unknown admirer and showed her the card. She understood immediately what was going on here and explained to me that I was dealing with a female admirer, not a male. The text was taken from a novel she had recently read. The book was "Of Lena Geyer," a novel whose plot was about a singer. The author was an American, Marcia Davenport, whom I had frequently met in New York. She was the daughter of the famous singer Alma Gluck, who was the source material for the main character. Marcia Davenport had not only written about the life of a phenomenal singer but had modeled it on the lives of two singers from the turn of the century; Alma Gluck and Lilli Lehmann, who were conflated in the book. The protagonist was a famous singer, beautiful and celebrated, to whom men of all ages were attracted. But she was also admired by a woman who followed her from city to city, country to country. The woman always sent her red roses and anonymous letters; she was always dressed in black and sat in the first row of the parquet for every performance.

The prima donna became so accustomed to the young, black-attired lady in the first row that she began to view her as a talisman. When the lady once did not appear because of illness, the singer was so unhappy that she refused to sing. At some point the singer wished to meet the young lady and invited her to her dressing room after a performance. The admiring lady quickly gained acceptance in the singer's social life and the two became inseparable until the death of the singer. That was it, a melodrama of the upper class. My friend's explanation made me uncomfortable and I tried in vain to find out who was sending the flowers.

Autumn found me again in the States, specifically, New York. Along with appearances at the Metropolitan I gave a number of concerts throughout the nation. But even when I performed outside of New York I received the red roses and a card signed "L. Black." By this time it had become a ritual.

After my first performance of the season at the Met, the head of Decca Records in New York, Terry McEwen, came to my dressing room. He had with him a lovely young lady, whom he introduced as Miss N. I thought nothing further of this until later in the week when I had a concert in Kansas City. After the concert, who should appear in my dressing room but this young lady. I had received the usual roses and card in Kansas City.

When I returned to New York, Mr. McEwen informed me that Miss N had bombarded him with letters and phone calls, begging him to introduce her to me.

When I met her again about a month later she was onboard the plane I was taking from New York to Vienna. There was no longer any doubt in my mind that this was the lady sending the roses. From Vienna I had to continue on to Stockholm to sing at the gala celebration at the Nobel presentation. Who was on the plane? Miss N! She had even managed to get the seat next to mine. I conversed with her and she told me she was a photographer's model in New York and also acted in a television soap opera. For the coming weeks she was on vacation and was traveling in Europe. A devotee of opera, she had hopes of becoming a singer. She would be staying at the Grand Hotel in Stockholm. Later I learned she had attended the Nobel Gala in the Concert House. With her natural charm—and her reference to her acquaintance with me—she gained entrance to the event.

Suddenly I received a call from the manager of the Grand Hotel. He had difficulty with a guest he said, a Miss N, who was paying her bills with rubber checks. She had assured him that I would cover the charges for her. He wanted to know if this was correct. I told him I had nothing at all to do with the young lady in question and that she would have to find another way of resolving her problem.

After the engagement in Stockholm for the Nobel gala I went directly to Munich, where I was doing a new production of Wagner's *Ring*. Miss N had already ensconced herself in the Hotel Vier Jahreszeiten. The day after my arrival, I met her by chance in front of the hotel and took the opportunity of very firmly advising her to be sensible and return to her work in New York. She said she did not mean to annoy me but only wanted to be my friend. I told her that I was accustomed to choosing my own friends and that she in no way qualified. In no uncertain terms, I begged her to leave me alone. After this encounter we never spoke to one another again.

But don't think for a moment that Miss N was discouraged by my brusque rebuff. No indeed; for nine years she followed me everywhere.

She managed to stay at the same hotel as I and somehow she was crafty enough to get the room next to mine. I felt as though I were being stalked. Occasionally I thought I could lose her by changing hotels; within a few hours, however, she would be lodged in the new hotel in a room next to mine. My accompanist, the excellent John Wustman, once had a serious talk with her, but she played the innocent and claimed I was actually following her!

When she followed me around the States, she was accompanied by various young men and she sat in the first row dressed in black. Her behavior had a horrible kind of devotion to it, but at the same time was derisive and taunting. I didn't want to give her the pleasure of making an open scandal, as that was probably what would have fulfilled her need to get into the tabloids and gossip columns. I kept silent about my suffering, but I sang.

As soon as I got to my hotel I made my unusual situation known to the manager, but only once did I succeed in getting her lodged on a different floor. Men always melted at her charm, and the rest she managed with subterfuge. She really thought that I, not she, was the crazy one. She was then about twenty-three or twenty-four and somewhat resembled Marilyn Monroe, even though Miss N was dark-haired and taller. But like Monroe, she had a perfect figure and was able to wrap the male hotel personnel around her little finger.

One day I read in the paper that she had won a long-drawn-out lawsuit and had received $200,000 dollars in damages. She was the model who had been photographed sitting on the hood of a General Motors automobile with a live lion. The lion had the bad taste to bite her in the thigh and she was awarded a large sum of money as a result of this accidental injury.

Now a life of luxury began for Miss N. She pretended to be some kind of VIP and made sure she reserved my favorite seat in the airplane, first row, left. She had expensive furs, wearing one and draping another over her arm. Different male escorts awaited her wherever she went. Photographers took pictures of her for the newspapers. She was interviewed and made clear that the reason for her many and long journeys was Birgit Nilsson, her very favorite singer.

I began to notice that things were disappearing from my hotel room: pictures, dresses, and lingerie. As some valuable jewelry belonged among the missing articles, I went to the police and answered clearly and definitely their question as to who I thought might be breaking into my room. The police could do nothing. I had no proof, and on the basis of mere suspicion they could not search the room of another hotel guest.

In Chicago, however, with the help of a good friend, I talked a police officer into searching her room. But all the drawers and pockets gave no clue. On the desk lay a half-finished letter to Ginger Rogers (Fred Astaire's sometime dancing partner), to whom she wrote she was on a trip traveling with her idol. You can say that again! The officer found the wardrobe of the lady quite disproportionate, consisting for the most part of very sexy negligees.

Eventually, I discovered how she got into my room. Behind the registration desk in American hotels, there are several keys to each room in the box for mail. She could easily ask for the key to my room, which, let us say, was number 427. Should the desk clerk happen to call her on this she could say, "Oh, excuse me, of course I meant 426," which was her room. Her own key she could have on her person, as most American hotel guests take their key with them. This was probably the reason she was so determined to get the room next to mine. She knew I was accustomed to leaving the hotel well in advance of my performance. She then had free access to my room where she looked up my appointments, coming engagements, and travel plans. It was as though she lived only for spying on me. She would have been as excellent candidate for FBI training.

In Chicago I was assigned a suite that had no adjoining room. I had also engaged a detective to watch my room while I was at the opera house.

The result of this police action netted nothing more than a lot of stinking cigarette butts in my bedroom, where he had obviously made himself at home watching television.

I didn't bother to close my curtains at night as I lived on the fifteenth floor and it was not possible for anyone to look into my room. Unfortunately I had not noticed that a fire escape with a tiny platform was outside my window. One evening someone tapped on my window and I saw a familiar face. It was one of Miss N's escorts. He was distraught and tried, unsuccessfully, to open the window. He begged to be let into my room. The door to the fire stairs locked behind him, he claimed, when he went out for a breath of air. (A strange place to get a breath of air.) The man said if I didn't feel comfortable letting him in, I could get my husband. I promptly called hotel security, who came and let him in. The court hearing brought no successful outcome for me. The police preferred to believe him, not me. It was easier that way.

Miss N had succeeded in getting her escort-accomplices to spy on me. How they must have laughed to see the detective blurred by the dense fog of his cigarette smoke! Sometimes I felt so helpless that I thought I would take leave of *my* senses.

In Washington a valuable emerald ring disappeared. I don't think this time she used any male assistance. Her escort this time was an internationally known politician. He was divorced and not yet remarried, a real catch for a young elegant lady.

In the autumn of 1973, Bertil and I, feeling greatly relieved, left for a trip to Australia. It was a wonderful feeling for me to be free of my constant hanger-on. I had no fear she would travel so far as Australia. The stalking had been going on now for five years. Yet since December 1968, on the street in front of her hotel in Munich, we had not exchanged one word.

The first thing we observed at the airport in Perth was a plane arriving from Hawaii. One of the first passengers at the baggage reception was—yes, indeed, Miss N! My reaction is difficult to describe. My strongest desire was simply to go back home. She was met at the airport by a gentleman. Then ensued the same pursuit from city to city, hotel to hotel. Sometimes we changed our reservation, but nothing helped; within a short time she was lodged in our hotel.

At this time I was giving concerts with Geoffrey Parsons as my accompanist and doing some orchestra concerts as well. The New York Philharmonic was on an Australian tour with Eric Leinsdorf as conductor. A young American conductor was also present to conduct a few of the many concerts and to jump in for Leinsdorf, should he become indisposed. Such measures are necessary when an orchestra is on a long tour. In Melbourne, the Philharmonic gave a farewell party to which Bertil and I were invited, as well as Melbourne's mayor and other honoraries.

Miss N had succeeded in ensnaring the rather well known young conductor and accompanied him to this party. As we entered, there she stood in the receiving line with him. I turned on my heel and went back to my hotel with Bertil. The situation was completely absurd but luckily the press took no notice of it.

In Sydney my most beautiful gold bracelet disappeared. It was my final concert and I was under stress from the packing and imminent departure. Instead of taking the trouble to put the bracelet in the hotel safe I hid it in between some of my lingerie in the wardrobe. When I returned from my concert the bracelet was gone.

We had planned on our way to Mexico to visit the Fiji Islands. In Sydney there was a strike at the airport and we reached our destination extremely late, in the middle of the night. It was a short but lovely time of relaxation on this undisturbed island. I enjoyed wading in the shallow water and gathering up lovely coral, using my skirt as a reticule. I enjoyed it, that is, until I was discovered by the photographer and music critic Albert Goldberg from Los Angeles. Then it was no pleasure at all. I prefer to be asked first before I am photographed.

In the hotel I was constantly disturbed by telephone calls that were dead at the caller's end, except for soft breathing. I was annoyed but didn't give it much thought, thinking that the person at the switchboard was having difficulty with the numbers.

After dinner on our first day there, some native dancing was performed in the hotel. At a table some distance from us sat a young couple hugging one another. The girl was in the traditional national costume. I looked, did a neck-wrenching double take and—yes!—it was Miss N! I nudged Bertil and asked him if he recognized the girl across the room. He had always laughed at me, accusing me of letting this Miss N business get to me. But the laughing stopped when he saw it was actually Miss N. Then even Bertil became disturbed. Because Bertil did not accompany me on all my guest performances (he had his own affairs to manage) he had viewed this pursuit of me as something humorous, not realizing what I was going through.

On the trip from the Fiji Islands, Miss N sat in my preferred seat, left side, first row. She was treated like the Queen of Sheba by the men around her as well as by the stewardesses. Before my concert in New York

I had a week free, and we planned to spend this time in Acapulco, Mexico. We decided it would be impossible to have any quiet at the Princess Hotel, where we had booked. Instead we reserved lodging at a simpler hotel and checked in as Mr. and Mrs. Bertilo. I informed my agent in New York about my new name and address. This, as well as I can recall, is the first time that we succeeded in escaping Miss N, but it was the first time I felt I could afford the luxury of being incognito. During my guest performances I had to be within reach of opera directors, journalists, and others, so that it was impossible to sail under a false flag.

The years were leaving their mark on Miss N. She was beginning to look the worse for wear, and her escorts were taking on a little in age as well as girth. She also appeared to have run through her $200,000 settlement.

I was singing less often in the United States. From 1975 to 1977 I was, for a variety of reasons, not in the States at all. At least once Miss N surfaced (in Stockholm during *Die Frau ohne Schatten*) and she succeeded in getting interviewed and photographed by one of the papers. More often I noticed her presence in the first row of the parquet at the Vienna Staatsoper, but the usual room next to mine at the Hotel Sacher was not available.

After all these years—nine, to be exact, without our having spoken a word to each other, she suddenly began to bombard me with letters and a host of photographs of herself. Her letters became more and more pathetic, and she wrote remorsefully about how mistaken she had been in trying to be my friend. She said she was tired of life and longed only to die. Miss N was obviously very unhappy.

During the festival in Vienna in 1977, she was again in the first row. I sang, with a break of only two days, Isolde and then Elektra. As we came back to the hotel after the *Tristan* the porter handed me a thick envelope addressed in her handwriting. Bertil advised me to read the letter the next day as he feared there might be something in it that would disturb my sleep. I did as he suggested. When I read the letter the next morning, I was horrified. If one could believe her letter, she had that night taken her own life.

It was a dramatic farewell letter in which she assured me I should not think I had anything to do with her decision to commit suicide. But if I had the courage to come to her and say goodbye, then she could die in peace: "seat number 12 in the first row will be empty tomorrow. Isolde's death potion means Tod! Tod unsbeiden! [Death! Death to us both!]"

With these words from *Tristan and Isolde* she closed her letter. The thick envelope contained a copy of her last will, which was signed and notarized. Several persons in the United States were to inherit her estate. But when I came to the next part of the will, my hair stood on end: her ashes were to be strewn over my farm in Svenstad! I awakened Bertil, who called the hotel desk and informed them of what might have happened. The hotel personnel had to break down her door, which was locked from the inside. She was found unconscious on the floor. She was taken immediately to the hospital, where an overdose of sleeping pills was pumped out of her stomach.

On the next day Bertil and I had to spend many hours at the police station. With the tendency of the Viennese for making scandal it was difficult for the police to believe that what lay behind this tragedy was nothing more than the story of a very sick lady. Maybe there was more to it than it seemed? When the chief of police saw how deeply upset I was, he closed the hearings.

After my last performance as Elektra in Vienna I went to Savonlinna in Finland to give an orchestra concert with Leif Segerstam conducting. The concert took place in the largest wooden church in the world (the builder got feet and yards mixed up!). I was lodged a little bit out of town in the woods in a bungalow that belonged to the hotel. I found a great burden lifted from me in not having to fear Miss N (her words in her letter, "Tod! Tod uns beiden" were more than a little creepy), but they said in Vienna she would have to be in the hospital at least ten days.

As I had two days free, before my usual summer concert in Gröna Lund in Stockholm, I decided to remain an extra day in Savonlinna in order to see the dress rehearsal of *Boris Godunov* with the formidable bass Martti Talvela.

As I returned to my hotel that evening accompanied by my friend, Bertil Hagman, then publicity manager of the Stockholm Opera, the desk clerk handed me a letter from the hospital, saying Miss N was taken again to the hospital, unconscious.

This was the last news and the final chapter in "The N Story." Some time later, friends in New York sent me a clipping from the *New York Times,* which noted that a well-known photo model was found dead in a Long Island hotel.

This gruesome story moves me even today. I have no explanation for her obsession with me. Perhaps she identified so strongly with me (she wanted to become a singer) that she eventually could not differentiate between dreams and reality. N was deeply psychologically disturbed, but her intelligence and beauty hid it from most people.

I have often asked myself why she traveled to Europe to live her life more or less in my presence. Was this my punishment because I had kept her at a distance? Or was it a cry for help? And, if so, how could I have helped her?

Her threat "Tod! Tod uns beiden" and her wish that I go to her to say farewell before she took her life was seen by the police to be obsessive behavior: she wished for me to accompany her in death in this way. One advised me to leave Vienna as soon as possible under police protection.

The reader will probably find this story as unreal as an old melodrama, but for me, it was gruesome reality.

Afterward I was full of self-recrimination. Why had I not taken a stronger stand? I believed and hoped that distancing myself so markedly would make her realize how impossible it was for her to force herself into my life. But a good friend who is a psychiatrist has said it was exactly my resistance that strengthened and spurred on her obsession. Like Isolde, in her hopeless love, her last thought was "Tod uns beiden!"

In another time this story would certainly have become an opera.

MAKING RECORDINGS

My very first gramophone recording was made in the spring of 1947.

I was to sing the Estrella's aria from Franz Berwald's *Estrella de Soria.* The recording, produced by the Swedish Radio with Sten Frykberg conducting the Radio Orchestra, was of course made on a 78-rpm disc. I believe another soprano, Inga Sundström, was originally to have sung the aria but she became ill. I was overjoyed to have the chance to make a recording and therefore dared not breathe a word to anyone that I was also ill.

I was alone in my little apartment in the old city, lying there with a high fever and a frightful sore throat. For several days I was hardly able to swallow. I was in despair. Somehow, though, I dragged myself out of bed, dressed myself warmly, and arrived punctually for the recording session in the auditorium of the Music Academy. I don't have a very clear memory of the event other than Sten Frykberg's being very polite and friendly. He was always so, and he is one of the most beloved and deeply missed influences of our musical lives. Out of this there came into existence a record of this horribly difficult aria.

Returning to my doctor a couple of days later, I told him that my skin was scaly and my eyes oversensitive to light. The doctor became hysterical and rushed me out of the examining room, which he was sure I had contaminated, and called out after me, "I'm giving you a prescription for a sulfate. You have scarlet fever!"

Other than a 78 rpm recording of Elisabeth's aria, "Dich, teure Halle" under the baton of Sixten Ehrling, I have nothing more to report on the "Gramophone front." The new technique, the LP record, was already at the starting gate. The music world was awaiting with great anticipation the day when an entire opera could be recorded on two or three discs instead of the dozens of 78s required. A Wagner opera required twenty or more heavy and breakable shellac records. Meanwhile, I had done various tape recordings for radio stations including those of Hamburg, Munich, and Cologne. Radio broadcasts became very popular after the war and were focal points of European musical life. These radio broadcasts were also important in building a career. During this time I taped a number of complete operas, oratorios, and arias.

Even more important for the singer's career was to make recordings with an internationally known record company. If the voice is warm, not very large, even in register, and not too expansive in the top, it is made for the microphone. If this is not so—as in my case—the voice can present a problem for the sound engineer. For a dramatic soprano such as mine, with great carrying power and expansion in the top tones, the standard instruction for high tones was "Please move back three steps!" In spite of the moving back and forth, there was a lack of overtones in the high voice because of the lowered volume. The true sound was compromised.

For an artist it is important to be able to adjust to various situations and different media—and above all to perform well in the recording studio. There are those who find little inspiration in making recordings. "It is like dry swimming," said a colleague who missed the audience's inspiration in the concert hall or opera house. Then there are those artists who are never better than when recording.

I definitely do not belong to that category. The opera stage has given me many wonderful hours. But I have repeatedly adjusted myself to the studio, even though the particular stress I feel before the microphone never lets up. It can be very nerve-wracking to stand in that soundproof room awaiting the green light—and then instantly get into the mood for a passionate love scene.

I am grateful that my first experiences in the recording studio were very positive and my attitude toward making recordings was put in proper perspective. This was due to the powerful musical director Walter Legge, producer of the classical recordings of the international firm HMV (His Master's Voice). He was married to the lovely and famous singer Elisabeth Schwarzkopf, who had in him a strict, demanding teacher and knowledgeable adviser. He offered me not only an exclusive contract for certain arias and duets but guaranteed me all three Bünnhildes in Wagner's *Ring* within an agreed-upon time period. This contract offered me a great opportunity and I signed it most happily.

. . .

The first recording of German and Italian arias was made in London in 1957. The orchestra was conducted by the general music director of the Hamburg Opera, Leopold Ludwig. The second recording, of German arias exclusively, was conducted by Hans Walberg.

As we finished the last of these recordings, Legge asked if I could remain another day and record two Beethoven songs with none other than Otto Klemperer. He had just completed Beethoven's Ninth Symphony with the young, promising Aase Nordmo-Løvberg, from the Stockholm Opera, as soprano soloist. There was still some room on the record and Legge thought I should complete it with the Beethoven songs.

I had never sung these songs, but the night was long. I began immediately to study them and continued well on into the morning. One song "Die Trommel gerühret" was about a young girl who dreams of going off to war with her beloved and conquering the enemy.

Since his stroke, Klemperer was partly paralyzed but he remained a lion on the podium. And his well-known amorous inclinations had not suffered. As he lifted his baton at our rehearsal, he asked me, "Are you married?" When I answered in the affirmative, he replied, "Too bad."

So the rehearsal began and continued without any difficulties, until I came to the sentence "Die Feinde schon weichen, wir schiessen darein" (The enemy is weakening, we're shooting at them). I sang instead, "Die Feinde schon weichen, wir *scheissen* darein" (The enemy is weakening, we're shitting on them). The German-speaking members of the London Philharmonic Orchestra erupted in laughter and I, red with embarrassment, had to begin the song all over again.

Afterward, Walter Legge said it was finally clear to him why for two hundred years, Sweden had not been involved in a war: "Who wants to battle an enemy that uses such ammunition?"

The work with Legge was unique. He had an unbelievably good ear and gave me valuable advice and counsel. His musical finesse—which I often recognized in Schwarzkopf—opened a new world to me.

While I waited for the date for the *Ring* to be set, I recorded a duet album with the formidable Wagner singer Hans Hotter. We sang the final duet between Wotan and Brünnhilde from act 3 of *Die Walküre* as well as the duet between Senta and the Dutchman from *Der Fliegender Holländer.* The recording received very good notices and has since been transferred to a CD.

I was beginning to become impatient about the promised *Ring.* I noticed soon there were difficulties. As the time period for the recording of the "Ring" had passed, I asked Legge to release me from the contract. I had received an offer from Decca to record *Tristan und Isolde* with Jon Vickers as well as the three Brünnhildes in the *Ring*. But Legge was reluctant to release me. While I was in San Remo for a few days vacation, he appeared and tried to talk me into staying with the English company Columbia, a sister firm and prestigious label of HMV. If two lives had been granted me I would have gladly stayed with Legge, waiting for the right time for the *Ring* to present itself. But I had the feeling that the professional singer's life is relatively short. I was about forty and wanted to use my time well. It ended with my being released from the contract with compensation, as stipulated in the contract, in case the *Ring* recording did not come to pass within the agreed-upon time. Now I was free to work with whomever I wished. Since then I have never signed an exclusive rights contract—which is really nothing more than a limitation on the freedom of the artist.

My first recording with Decca was Isolde's "Liebestod" and scenes from act 1 of *Tristan* with the wonderful mezzo-soprano Grace Hoffman as Brangäne. In addition to her beautiful voice, she had another talent: she could warm up her voice while simultaneously studying the financial page of the paper.

The conductor was the great Wagner master, Hans Knappertsbusch. "Kna," as he was called in the opera world, was known for hating to rehearse. But he was able to inspire musicians to great performances through his personality alone. Often he surpassed the well-rehearsed Wagner performances of other conductors.

Kna put his heart and soul into our first recording. In making recordings we are sometimes required to repeat a particular scene three or four times. This was not possible with Knappertsbusch. The producer succeeded by diplomatic persuasion to get the *Tristan* scene repeated, but that was it, and Knappertsbusch was visibly irritated. Kna also never went into the control room to hear the playback; rather he waited impatiently outside for notification from the producer that he could be on his way. Seen from this side, perhaps Knappertsbusch was not the ideal conductor for recordings. He preferred the ocean waves of the opera performance to the dry swimming of the studio.

In the summer of 1959 I recorded both *Don Giovanni* and *Turandot*. In *Giovanni*, which was recorded in Vienna, I sang the role of Donna Anna. The *Turandot* was recorded in Rome at the Academy of Saint Cecilia. Erich Leinsdorf conducted both recordings for the American label RCA. Leinsdorf (like Georg Solti) had worked with Toscanini as coach.

Leinsdorf was an experienced and intellectual conductor. His feelings were not given free rein; everything was under cool control. Above all, his rehearsals, which could smack of the schoolroom, were very interesting and educational.

I greeted the *Turandot* recording with joy and great expectations. Jussi Björling was to sing Calaf for the first time and Renata Tebaldi was Liù. I admired Tebaldi very much. She had one of the most beautiful voices I had ever heard. I knew that both Jussi and Tebaldi would sing like angels, but one thing really surprised me. I take it as a given that one comes to a recording session in total control of the role one is to sing, at least with the score in hand. Perhaps it was merely nerves, I can't say, but Tebaldi was astonishingly uncertain. In addition to the conductor, two coaches were necessary to get her on the right pitches and to sing in rhythm. Even then she was sometimes off the mark. For this reason, much valuable time was spent on this relatively easy part, creating an impatient and stressful atmosphere among the other singers. Jussi knew his role perfectly. It was, as ever, a special joy for me to be able to blend my voice with his.

The heat in Rome, particularly in the recording studio, could be unbearable. There was no air-conditioning. After a few hours of recording in a room packed with soloists, chorus, and orchestra one had the feeling there was no oxygen at all. Today, recording under such conditions would be unthinkable.

As I have recalled the frightful heat, I must in fairness summon another memory of this time. The mild evenings in Rome were wonderful. Jussi and Anna Lisa invited me to join them in one of their favorite restaurants in Trastevere. There I had fresh figs for the first time. Melon, figs, and ham: heavenly! A dark, mild, soft-as-silk evening in Rome in a cozy restaurant garden is something I often find myself longing for. A great dinner at the summer residence of the famous singer Tito Gobbi belongs to the experiences I now and again retrieve from my treasure chest of memories.

Plans for the following year included another meeting with Jussi and Anna Lisa in Rome. Decca planned to record *Ballo* with Georg Solti as conductor. Jussi had specifically requested that I sing Amelia, which pleased me immensely. Because of rehearsals in Bayreuth, I was unable to be in Rome at the beginning of the recording sessions. Therefore it was decided to record first the scenes between Björling and Simionato, who sang Ulrica. Arriving late in the evening at my hotel in Bayreuth, I received a phone call telling me the recording had been canceled and I should remain in Bayreuth. I demanded to speak with John Culshaw, who informed me in no uncertain terms that Jussi had appeared at the session drunk and was not musically prepared.

This was shocking news, and there seemed something very strange about it to me. Jussi was always on top of his roles musically, and when Anna Lisa was along she took very good care of him. Some time later I spoke with a Decca official who was in Rome at that time. *His* version of the story was quite different: Solti requested Björling's presence at a number of rehearsals and Jussi had protested because it was so terribly hot. He had sung the part in former times with Solti's own teacher, Toscanini, and was confident that he knew how to sing the role. In the unusual heat he wanted to husband his resources and thus be able to do his best work for the recording. Solti did not give an inch and Jussi reportedly told Solti: "Go home and study your orchestra score. I know my part."

"Thank you all very much. I want to inform you that the recording is finished," said Solti as he slammed his score shut.

This incident had to do not only with the high temperature but the volatile temperament of two great artists. One said that Jussi later apologized and wanted to go on with the recording, but Solti was adamant.

Two months later Jussi was dead. The recording was resumed in 1962 with Carlo Bergonzi in Jussi's role.

What has irritated me even more was that Culshaw, a few years later, put out a book in which he repeated the lies about Jussi and other colleagues involved in the canceled recording. About me he wrote, among other things: "when Birgit got to Rome and was informed that the recording had been cancelled she went immediately to the paymaster and demanded her salary." Not only had I *not* gone to Rome after I received the phone call to stay in Bayreuth, but the paymaster to whom I supposedly rushed was a Mr. Rosengarten of Badenerstrasse in Zurich. This man resembled no one more than Fafner in *Rheingold,* who hung onto his money as long as possible before opening his purse. His cashier said point-blank that payment would be made when the exchange was to the advantage of Mr. Rosengarten and company. My husband, Bertil, who was a veterinarian, said that getting your fee out of Rosengarten was as difficult as getting a foal out of a mare.

The crowning blow was that I received a request from the publisher to write a forword for Culshaw's book! I accepted but with the stipulation that I would have guaranteed in writing that nothing could be changed and that my article would appear in full. I heard nothing more.

Two months later a full recording of *Tristan* was to be made in Vienna with Solti conducting. I tried to put out of my mind the sad events connected with Jussi and Decca and dedicate myself optimistically to the difficult work ahead. We all had hoped that Jon Vickers, the great Canadian tenor, would keep his promise and attempt recording *Tristan,* but again he felt he was not yet ready. It would be fourteen years before we sang *Tristan und Isolde* together. I remember I gave him an Isolde photo with the inscription, "I waited for my Tristan as long as Jacob waited for Rachel but it was well worth it."

And so Decca had to engage another tenor. The choice fell to the excellent singer and good colleague, Fritz Uhl, from Munich. He was singing Tristan for the first time and did so nobly. Kurwenal was sung by the young Finnish baritone Tom Krause, who was fresh out of the conservatory in Vienna. His voice promised much and he has since more than fulfilled his potential. Brangäne was the American mezzo Regina Resnik, a very intelligent singer and superb artist. She had a great sense of humor that often lightened up the tense atmosphere. Arnold van Mill was King Marke.

In recording such a demanding role as Isolde, the singer needs all the help and support a producer can give her. I was naïve enough to believe all producers were as competent as Walter Legge. Did I have a lot to learn! John Culshaw, at that time new to the business, appeared to be shy and self-conscious. He always wore a smile, which had no particular meaning. "Very lovely, indeed" was his stock comment. But what use is "Very lovely, indeed" to one recording Isolde? How I missed Walter Legge!

For this recording, Georg Solti was our port in the storm. He would not put up with anything smacking of prima donna egotism and he was unsparing with his own energies. He asked much of everyone but demanded even more of himself. There were singers who refused to sing with him. As for myself, I liked working with him. I have nothing against being treated like a schoolgirl as long as the teacher brings out the best in me. With the Vienna Philharmonic and Solti there was always one problem or another. Any cooperation between them was short-lived. When two such combustible elements interact, an explosion is inevitable.

During the first days of the recording sessions Solti was unusually tense. After half an hour he looked as though he had showered in his clothing. He was like a Fury. I see him now, as he conducted then: with the sleeves of his sweater pushed up over his elbows, stomach and navel naked, and shorts that prevented far too much being revealed, as his pants were about to fall down around his knees. "Take it easy, Birgit—relax," he would say, taking me by the wrist, which after a week bore five blue fingerprints.

He reveled in waves of sound and the orchestra could not play loudly enough for him. During one such rehearsal he repeated again and again a particular passage. Resnik and I sat onstage awaiting our entrance. At last the orchestra sound swelled to almost unbearable loudness and Resnik and I agreed at the seventh big crescendo to fall from our chairs as though struck by lightening. We created quite a stir, lying there like two dead fish—with the laughing orchestra totally on our side. Even against his will, Solti had to join in the laughter. After this release of tension, the rehearsal proceeded with everyone more relaxed.

Personally, Solti is an extraordinarily friendly and amusing man. He is a wonderful host and I was often invited to his various residences. It was a special honor for Bertil and me to be invited by Prince Charles to the celebration of Solti's eightieth birthday held in Buckingham Palace.

For some time Decca had been planning to record, for the first time, the entire *Ring*. It was an enormous project and would require a huge organization to be set in motion. It necessitated not only a large number of famous artists but also an orchestra of 125 musicians and a chorus of 130 singers.

Nothing was spared to make this dream a reality. New "original" instruments (steerhorn) were procured (even in Bayreuth the roar of the steerhorn was represented by the trombones). Not only LPs but also stereo technology had improved immensely; every sound effect that was necessary or thought to be necessary could be reproduced naturally. Because of these possibilities, some things were overdone. For example, in *Das Rheingold*, for the clinking of the gold bars that the dwarfs carried in for Freia's ransom, the producer insisted on having the sound of *genuine* gold bars clinking together. Every bank in Vienna was canvassed about the possibility of borrowing gold bars but no bank felt any need to contribute to this clinking of real gold. Even in Vienna, music sometimes has its limits.

For the forging of the gold by the dwarfs they had made eighteen anvils of different sizes with eighteen hammers, also of various sizes. Forty youths from the Vienna Boys' Choir were to accompany this hammering with dwarflike cries. Eighteen members of the Philharmonic were given the formidable task of forging the gold in absolute rhythm. In an actual performance, the effect of forging is not usually noticed as the scene with the dwarfs doesn't take place onstage. Besides, conductors prefer to let the music speak without mixing in the other elements of sound. In the Decca recording the eighteen anvils were given prominence—indeed, were a highpoint—of *Rheingold.* Culshaw writes in his book *Ring Resounding* that he credits the forging on the anvils along with the fake thunder (produced by an eighteen-foot metal plate and specially manufactured bass drums) for the tremendous sale of the recordings and the setting of a new standard for the quality of stereo records. If all these effects did not come through fully, the listener was advised to get a better stereo player to appreciate the recording fully.

Mr. Mauritz Rosengarten of Zurich had a financial interest in Decca. He had to take care of all business matters having to do with the *Ring.* Now, anyone who ever had anything to do with Mr. Rosengarten would find it difficult to understand how he had been talked into financing this project. Almost everyone thought of the recording of the *Ring* as a fantastic project, but they never believed it would sell. Rosengarten knew little about music, least of all about Wagner. He never thought like a businessman; he was simply greedy. When he was negotiating a contract, he used the starvation method: he would sit all day like a cat before a mouse hole, waiting for the artist in question to become so exhausted he would sign anything. Karajan liked to say that after one shook hands with Rosengarten it was a good idea to count one's fingers.

But deep down, there must have been a heart beating and not merely an adding machine clicking. Or did he possess a sixth sense that allowed him to smell a good deal from afar? Against all bets the *Ring* proved to be a great merchandising success.

Rosengarten had met Georg Solti in Zurich in 1946. Solti, after his escape from Hungary, was working as a nightclub pianist. Rosengarten made a contract with Solti that tied him exclusively to Decca.

"There was something about Solti that made me believe he would have a great future," said Rosengarten in an interview.

The recording of the *Ring* began in 1958 with *Das Rheigold.* The wonderful Kirsten Flagstad was about to end her long and glorious career. The "Decca Boys" as Flagstad called the team, talked her into taking part in the *Ring* and, finally, she declared herself willing to sing the role of Fricka in *Rheingold.*

I had no role in *Rheingold,* but at the time of this recording I was making guest appearances in Vienna. One day at the Hotel Imperial I had the good fortune to meet my idol. Flagstad recognized me and said she had been at the previous evening's performance of *Don Giovanni* at the Staatsoper. She congratulated me upon my Donna Anna. Of course, I was thrilled to receive her praise. I overcame my speechlessness just long enough to thank her for having written me a most friendly letter after hearing a radio broadcast of *Tristan* in which I sang Isolde. In spite of her sixty-three years, she looked amazingly young. Her skin was as smooth and as fresh as a peach. She seemed uncomplicated and down-to-earth, exactly like the simple Norwegian girl she was. It is no wonder the Decca Boys idolized her.

A few days later I met Set Svanholm, who sang Loge in *Das Rheingold.* He was also staying at the Imperial and had come directly from a rehearsal with Solti. He seemed a little downcast. No wonder: he explained that he thought he knew the role of Loge but over time some minor errors had crept in that Solti immediately called to his attention.

I was not surprised to hear that Solti could find fault even with the former high school teacher and future director of the Stockholm Opera. All of his colleagues looked upon Svanholm as a phenomenal musician and a perfectionist.

The second recording, *Siegfried,* came four years later. Culshaw had, with Solti's approval, engaged a tenor with a fantastic voice but who would be singing Siegfried for the first time. He was assigned to the best-known coaches but to no avail. He was unable to master the enormous role.

The excellent and well-disciplined Wagner specialist, Wolfgang Windgassen, already had a long career behind him. Precisely because of the length of his career, it was presumed he would be no sensation. But even though he received the offer at the last moment, he put his pride aside and came onboard, as he had not yet recorded *Siegfried.*

When I arrived in Vienna, Solti and Windgassen were already in rehearsal. Windgassen had a very beautiful voice, more lyric than dramatic, with a light delivery. He was able to sing Siegfried one day and Tamino in *Zauberflöte* the day after, which is not usual for a Wagner tenor. Because of his lighter-weight voice he had developed over the years an unnoticeable system of saving the voice: high sustained tones were shortened by staying with the beginning and end consonants as long as possible; consequently the sung vowel became shorter and saved his voice. He also took care to make the most of the German text. If the long note had only one vowel it would be shortened and supplanted with a light rest. If you didn't have the score in front of you, this trick passed unnoticed—except by Maestro Solti. I had never seen Windgassen so flushed and bathed in sweat as he was in these rehearsals. His voice-saving system was by now second nature to him and it was almost impossible for him to sing the correct note values. But Solti was not satisfied until every detail was correct. And Windgassen never sounded so marvelous!

According to Wagner's original score, Siegfried appears in act 1 accompanied by a bear, which one does not see on the stage. This bear had most certainly been in hibernation since Wagner's day, but not so in the Decca version. The bear became a major player and his roar has been immortalized on the recording.

But how does one make a bear roar on command? Believe it or not, after serious research at the London Zoo they came upon the idea of putting a male and female bear in adjoining cages. When the female bear got honey the male bear, offended, let out a booming roar. All went as planned and the Decca Boys went back to Vienna with the genuine bear growl in their luggage! Unfortunately, it was too much of a good thing. Solti almost had a heart attack when he heard the playback. The bear roar drowned out the entire orchestral! Mother Nature lost; the bear sank into oblivion.

I cannot resist asking myself whose roar was greater: that of the bear or that of Rosengarten when he received the bill for this foolishness.

A recording session encompassed three hours with a break of twenty minutes halfway through.

Before the break Solti suggested that he rehearse with the orchestra alone. Sometimes he was not satisfied and he continued rehearsing with them after the break. Such was the case in the last part of *Siegfried.*

If the recording was not approved, then three hours were wasted. I began to get nervous as we were assured of at least two repetitions at our disposal. Time passed and eventually there was only time for one take. If we were not good enough, the entire recording session would be lost! That was so terrible for me to contemplate; it was as though I had to pay for the wasted time. But finally we recorded.

We were as tense as strung bows and flung our scores aside. Windgassen was fantastic and Solti was afire. Whether one believes it or not, the entire end scene of *Siegfried* went perfectly without repetitions or splicing. The scene was incredibly intense! "Marvelous," cried Solti, and with that we saved Rosengarten a lot of money.

Götterdämmerung was to be recorded in 1964, the longest, most difficult, and most important opera of the *Ring*. For this the Decca engineers had devised a new sound mixer that cost as much as the entire recording. Confronting this monster for the first time, I felt as though I had been transported to the control room of Cape Canaveral. The sound mixer had all imaginable refinements. In a split second interesting effects could be created. I had the feeling anything was possible. But with the microphone the time-honored rule held: three steps back for the high notes. Even the most advanced technique in recording had its limits.

Meanwhile, Solti and the Vienna Philharmonic were getting along better. The orchestra played as only the Philharmonic can through its tradition of playing under Gustav Mahler, Richard Strauss, Furtwängler, and Knappertsbusch. The more than one hundred musicians sounded like one superb instrument. A small diminuendo or the building of a crescendo was as natural to them as breathing. Each player felt what the other wanted and the rich, luxurious tone they achieved is the hallmark of the orchestra.

The cast of the *Götterdämmerung* was unsurpassed. Christa Ludwig, who sang Waltraute, was a phenomenal artist who brought every role to life through her thorough characterization and wonderful voice. Gottlob Frick sang Hagen with an incomparable bass, black as night. Wolfgang Windgassen was again a fantastic Siegfried. The siblings, Gutrune and Gunther, were nobly cast with Claire Watson and Dietrich Fischer-Dieskau. And, last but not least, Gustav Neidlinger was Alberich. In this role he excelled everyone whom I have ever seen or heard. The remaining parts were richly cast with stars from the opera world. Georg Solti and John Culshaw took Wagner's words to heart when he said, "In my operas every role is a major role."

The first act of *Götterdämmerung* was recorded in the spring, acts 2 and 3 in the fall. It was decided to produce a documentary for the BBC with Humphrey Burton as producer. The film was to chronicle the recording of the last two acts. It was nearly impossible not to stumble over the intrigues that like snakes, coiled themselves around everything. One dare not let the conductor out of sight. And the cameras demanded one's attention as well; out of the corner of your eye, you were always aware of their presence.

Sometimes the Decca Boys wanted to play some prank on me—as, for example, with the recording of *Salome*. Just at the moment when the last tone was sung in the scene where Salome kisses the severed head of John the Baptist, there appeared before me a huge head on a platter. I nearly fainted in horror. But the bloody, disgusting-looking head proved to be a delicious cake covered over with marzipan. All the soloists, orchestra members, and technical crew fell upon this delicacy like starving cannibals.

As the recording of *Götterdämmerung* came to an end, I had no idea that further pranks would be tried, particularly as the cameras were running. But I was in for a surprise. After the long and strenuous singing leading up to the end scene, the climax of the opera, all of us spurred ourselves on to even greater artistic heights. As I spiritually called to Grane, my faithful horse on whose back I would ride into the flames of blazing Valhalla, there serenely marched into the recording studio a real, live horse. It was apparently totally undisturbed by my *fortissimo* singing and the orchestral flares depicting the downfall of Valhalla. The horse seemed to find this all quite normal. No doubt a Wagner fan.

The last opera of the *Ring* to be recorded was *Die Walküre,* in 1965. The reason that *Siegfried* and *Götterdämmerung* were recorded before *Walküre* was that the American label RCA (who worked closely with Decca) had already issued this opera in 1962 with me as Brünnhilde. For commercial reasons it made good sense to delay the issuing of *Walküre.*

The conductor of the RCA recording was Erich Leinsdorf, with Jon Vickers singing a superb Siegmund. Gré Brouwenstijn was Sieglinde; George London, a great actor and singer, sang Wotan; Rita Gorr sang Fricka; and David Ward, Hunding. It was an especially good recording.

I remember one episode in connection with this recording. When I arrived in London and found that Rita Gorr was to sing Fricka instead of the already contracted Grace Hoffman, I was astonished. I called Grace in Stuttgart and asked if she were ill. She said she was fine and only waiting to hear when she was expected in London. When I told her Rita Gorr was in London and was to take over the part of Fricka, Grace was shocked. She immediately called her agent, the ordinarily reliable Alfred Dietz. He knew the whole story but had not breathed a word of it to Grace. He advised her, in order not to compromise future engagements, not to make any fuss. Mr. Dietz was also Rita Gorr's representative, so obviously he was suffering no loss of income. In answer to my inquiry, the producer said they did not want Hoffman for this recording. I asked further if she was being reimbursed for what was openly a breach of contract and my answer was a shrug of his shoulders.

I decided then to strike. I won George London over and we refused to sing until we were assured that Grace would be compensated. This created great alarm as every hour lost cost a tremendous amount of money. Quickly, RCA in New York was consulted. They promised Grace Hoffman another contract for a recording but no money was to be got out of them. I advised them to sleep on this decision as George London and I had all the time in the world to wait. *That* hit home. Immediately came a telegram that authorized Grace Hoffman's fee. George and I enjoyed our victory.

This did not mean we had anything against Rita Gorr. On the contrary, she was a splendid singer and as lovely a colleague as Grace Hoffman. It was the shameful way RCA had of simply ignoring an existing contract, assuming the singer had no recourse. In such situations artists must stick together. Even the most powerful executive has his Achilles' heel.

It was later revealed that the conductor, Leinsdorf, had rejected Hoffman. Earlier, when making a recording with him, she had asked him if he could make his beat clearer for her. Leinsdorf never forgot this and held it against her. Hardly had Grace received her check from RCA when she received a call from Dietz asking for his commission!!!

The cast of the *Walküre* in the Decca set was also not bad. What more can one say about James King and Régine Crespin as the "Wälsungenpaar," Sieglinde and Siegmund? Or about the fantastic Gottlob Frick as Hunding? Hans Hotter was already a legend as Wotan. Christa Ludwig sang Fricka. She had an unusually beautiful mezzo-soprano voice, but she dreamed of singing dramatic soprano roles. She confided to me that she would give a year of her life to sing one of my big roles such as Isolde, Elektra, or Brünnhilde.

Christa Ludwig had a good friend in Vienna, a Doctor Kürsten, who was a famous throat doctor. She asked him to look at our vocal cords and make a comparison. I thought this would be interesting and agreed to it. He said our cords were as different as day and night. While mine were meant for long, sustained phrases, hers were ideal for phrases with movement and coloratura passages. In other words: if I were to try to sing coloratura repertoire, the voice would lose its placement and I would face an early vocal demise. And the same would be Ludwig's fate should she risk singing the heavy, sustained phrases that were so typical of the repertoire she dreamed of singing. Granted, Christa Ludwig undertook a few excursions into the dramatic soprano realm, but she apparently accepted that Dr. Kürsten was right when he advised her to remain with the mezzo-soprano roles.

. . .

An unforgettable moment in the recording of *Walküre* was singing Brünnhilde's beautiful phrase in act 3: "Der diese Liebe mir ins Herz gelegt" (He who put this love in my heart). This phrase must absolutely be sung bel canto, with the voice floating over the orchestra like a feather on water. Of course Solti was aware of this and inspired me with encouraging gestures. This made everything a conscious effort, and when I feel I'm being asked to give more than I can, my throat just closes up. And exactly that happened: the voice relaxed and had a vibrato I didn't like. Again and again we recorded the phrase but without the desired result. Finally I got up nerve enough to ask Solti not to look at me when I sang. He understood completely and said he would focus his attention on the violins. It went beautifully.

In reviewing the cast of the various *Ring* recordings I find at least seven singers who sooner or later donned the mantle of Brünnhilde: Kirsten Flagstad, Anita Wälki, Berit Lindholm, Gwynneth Jones, Helga Dernesch, Régine Crespin, and myself.

Even though we occasionally did not see eye to eye, the teamwork between singers and the Decca staff was basically very good. In addition to the engineer, Gordon Parry, and the producer, John Culshaw, there were James Brown, Erik Smith, and Christopher Raeburn. They were all cheerful, able, and helpful young men.

After a day of hard work in the studio some of the singers got together now and then with Solti and some of the Decca staff. If the recording session had been unusually good, we had champagne. The atmosphere was congenial and there were always a few amusing anecdotes to enjoy. Erik Smith (the son of the conductor Hans Schmidt-Isserstedt) was a most congenial young man, who would later produce many of my recordings. With Christopher Raeburn as producer I recorded *Tosca*, as well as an album of arias and Scandanavian songs, with Bertil Bokstedt conducting. (This is, incidentally, one of my favorite recordings.) When Raeburn celebrated his sixtieth birthday, I was invited as a surprise guest; he had no idea I was to be there and he seemed quite moved. The camaraderie that grows out of making recordings affords one a lifetime of memories.

But, the efforts of all involved notwithstanding, I have to admit I am not wholly satisfied with the Decca recordings. I have to agree with the music lovers and critics who say "the balance between the orchestra and the singers finds the singers at a great disadvantage."

We were often covered by the enormous volume of the orchestra, far, far too often. Throughout, the orchestra was too loud. Of course, one should hear every instrument and the special effects—but not at the cost of hearing the singers! Perhaps the motto for the recordings was the comment attributed to Richard Strauss during an *Elektra* rehearsal: "Play louder, please. I can still hear the singers." (Maybe the singers on that occasion were very bad?)

During the period of the loud orchestra and special effects, *Salome* was also recorded by Decca. On the album cover the producer, John Culshaw, is quoted as saying, "Never before has one been able to hear the triangle in a performance. Here for the first time you can hear this instrument." I have nothing against the public's hearing the triangle, but I ask myself whether the voice of Salome is not at least as important. It is always lovely to hear one's voice praised but it is a bit disappointing to hear that the sound is better live than on the recording. Or worse: that the voice sounds better on some pirated recordings than on takes from the studio.

I had many discussions with John Culshaw and the sound engineer, Gordon Parry, about this. Mr. Parry explained that in the orchestra sat a hundred prima donnas who wished to be heard. I looked at him as sweetly as possible and said it was unlikely that Decca had told any orchestra member what they had told me, namely, that a *Ring* recording without Nilsson was unthinkable.

Possibly the Decca Boys were so taken with the idea of getting in *all* of the effects previously unheard that they temporarily forgot that opera is actually *singing* with orchestral accompaniment.

Later, in transferring the recording to CD, the balance was changed. Despite the hundred prima donnas, the opera was restored to its original form. I was very happy with the result, even though it took twenty-five years for my criticism to be validated.

It was quite exciting to have been there in those years of experimentation and seeking new paths in recording sound. These recordings are, in their way, unique and of great historical value. Today, no record company can afford such an extravagance as that seven-year project in Vienna.

I want to add this thought to what among musicians is called "the truth of the microphone."

In the last few years there has arisen debate between listeners and the producers of recordings about which is better: a live recording or a studio recording. The discussion revolves around the *truth* of the microphone.

Above all, music critics prefer a live recording. They are suspicious of the faithfulness of the studio recording. It is not only whether a rather small voice can be made the size of Placido Domingo's, or that here and there a few fresh tones are supplemented. It is about much more. In Igor Stravinsky's acerbic words: a studio recording differs from a live recording as much as a painted corpse differs from a living being!

I have to admit that in the studio I miss the inspiration given me by the audience. It was at first very hard to get used to the cold, unfriendly microphone that not only registered every little blemish but even enlarged it. After the first hearing of the tape, one concentrates on improving the less advantageous tones. The music is not heard overall as a complete performance. Instead, small details are listened to neurotically and criticized until, to a large extent, the artistic integrity and inspiration is lost.

I personally prefer live recordings. What they lose in technical perfection they gain in vitality and spontaneity. A studio version cannot escape the danger of substituting a lovely collage for a true interpretation. The CD technique is especially criticized for its cold, sterile reproduction (recent improvements notwithstanding).

Conductors have often selected record-making as their principal career advancement. Fat recording contracts have great professional significance for conductors and musicians. The success of their careers often stands in direct proportion to the purchase of their recordings. Karajan quickly discovered this advantage and his recording schedule was hectic; indeed, he was one of the first to specialize in studio recording. Leopold Stokowski experimented a great deal with the possibilities of studio recording. For instance, he did not shy away from changing to his liking the traditional seating of the orchestra. He placed the first violins directly in front of him, celli and basses far to the back. Leonard Bernstein made a career by cleverly switching between Broadway and Lincoln Center, between musicals and classical music, and between live concerts and recordings. Toward the end of his career he made almost all this recordings at concerts with an audience—perhaps like the circus horse who needed the smell of sawdust for inspiration.

Great conductors may have totally different attitudes toward performance. Because of their extraordinary quality and their rarity, the concerts and opera performances of Carlos Kleiber are almost viewed as cult events. This makes every concert a performance of historical significance.

The master conductor Sergiu Celibidache was legendary for his uncompromising refusal to put even the smallest work on record or to have it filmed for television. Neither were his concert performances ever immortalized for the public. Did this have to do with his seven memorable years as chief conductor of the Swedish Radio Orchestra, when every concert was broadcast and some televised? He had a philosophical explanation for this inconsistency. Celibidache thought that music had the greatest meaning in the moment it was played, while all mechanical repetitions were merely copies. Glenn Gould went to extremes in the other direction: for decades he refused to play before an audience and limited himself exclusively to studio recordings done with endless repeats and splicing. In his last years he avoided the famous Studio 2 of CBS in New York and required the engineers to haul all their apparatus to Toronto—where he wished to record only at night.

The Canadian critic, Robertson Davies, believes there cannot be a splendid performance without the inspiration of the audience. Often there is some spark that ignites the fire of a fantastic performance. And if there are a few less than wonderful tones, well, this is no reason that the otherwise beautiful performance should not be recorded for the future. Of course, some artists will not let the smallest mistake pass even when everything else is magnificent. Arturo Toscanini was known for such an attitude, blocking the issue of some of his most beautiful recordings.

The recording companies accept either method. They are ready to bring out a genuine recording or take the opportunity to fabricate something beautiful. I know for certain that there are many live recordings that are genuine as well as beautiful.

Sound recording is a science that is constantly changing, putting the artists in ever-new situations. The new digital technique holds practically boundless possibilities for manipulating tone quality: the computer divides sounds into ones and zeros, then combines them with something completely different, making tones out of tones. In connection with this I heard a memorable example that could easily have come out of a science-fiction novel: There was this singer who thought he recognized his voice on the loudspeaker of a department store—or *was* it his voice? The voice was distorted and accompanied by the artificial background music that engulfs public places with an undifferentiated tone soup. But the singer was pretty sure it was his voice and sued the department store for theft. Someone had used his voice without getting his permission or reimbursing him.

He was within his rights yet *not* within his rights. The department store, which had purchased a tape of background music, countered that the singer had provided the basic material—namely, a number of tones—but it was the technicians who had assembled them into a new work of art. The lawyers were of the opinion that he was a partial owner of something that had been turned into another entity. The case is now being handled by cultural organizations under the umbrella of the United Nations. It is considered a precedent-setting case. The question is whether artists can claim to have sole rights to their digitally processed tones. The technicians, after all, have produced something entirely different and artistically equally valuable! Photographers are suffering a similar fate: they are "delivering" the basic material for the manipulation of digital imagery.

Protective measures are being developed. There are technical means by which an artist can code his tones, creating a kind of fingerprint that could be referred to in a dispute over artistic ownership. If I understand it correctly, this works by means of a search that uncovers suspect tones and subsequently identifies who produced the tones and has artistic rights. Bootleg copies are the bane of the music industry; they affect the artist personally, not just economically. Some time ago I received a list of all pirated recordings that were made from my live opera and concert performances. It comprised twenty-seven tightly spaced pages. This doesn't make me terribly happy. The moral rights as well as the artistic rights of artists to their output has never been very clear. After his opera performances Mozart stood nervously at the door of the orchestra pit, collecting the orchestra parts so that they could not be copied or stolen. This annoying problem for artists has yet to find a satisfying solution.

BERTIL, MY NUMBER ONE ADMIRER

Once I met the enormous little god Cupid. He was dressed as the warm hearted Johannes Norrby, the soul and benefactor of Stockholm's musical life and the director of the Concert House. Cupid's arrow was shot off under rather unusual circumstances, but his aim was certain. It happened like this:

Johannes Norrby organized my first public concert at the city hall in Stockholm, and on the strength of that success I was engaged as soloist with the Concert Society, with Tor Mann conducting. The concert was on January 11, 1945, during my first year in the opera school. The critics thought Norrby rather courageous to engage so young and inexperienced a singer for such an important concert; he was hailed again and again in their reviews.

My Christmas vacation had been spent with my parents in Skåne. It was agreed that I would return to Stockholm on January 8, but Johannes Norrby called and requested that I come a day earlier. I was unhappy, since on that very day I was planning to attend a big party where I would see all my old friends. Norrby was very understanding but still would not give in. I had no choice but to go.

In the train I purposely sought out a window seat across from an elderly lady. She appeared serious and tight-lipped enough that I had no fear of one of those tiring conversations with questions about any- and everything. I had just had my first experience with such obtrusiveness during a train trip (and on the trip home from a concert in Borås I was subjected to an exhibitionist, which gave me a real shock). I always tried to avoid any contact with strangers while traveling. I preferred to sit alone, quiet as a mouse, when I traveled. This rested my voice while I relaxed, read, or prepared for my work. This time I was lucky. Not a peep out of the lady across from me.

About halfway to Stockholm I began to feel hungry and I went to the dining car. On the way back I ran into a schoolfriend from home and sat with her awhile talking about old times. While we talked, I noticed a young, blond man who stood in the door of the compartment and stared at me. I remember saying to my friend that I had apparently won an admirer. The young man continued to stare at me, devouring me with his eyes. In return he received from me a definitely uninviting glance, at which he withdrew and I gave him no more thought.

But as I returned to my compartment I could hardly believe my eyes. The tight-lipped woman had disappeared. And who lay stretched out across the seats, napping? The young admirer!

I went ahead studying my arias and hoped he would have a nice long sleep—which was, as it turned out, wishful thinking. It wasn't long until he woke up and proceeded for a time to look at me and my music. He then came out with what seemed to me an unbelievably stupid question, "Is that difficult?"

"No, not at all when you know what it means," I answered coolly, probably sounding rather self-important.

He wasn't about to remain silent; indeed he continued to speak. All at once I found him not at all uninteresting, in fact, quite pleasant to talk to. After a while we seemed to have a certain rapport that made it seem as though we had known each other for a long time. He even came from the same area as I—from Kristianstad—which made conversation easier. I have never been very good at drawing people out. He, on the other hand, was a master of the art. I noticed he had a notebook on which "Medizin" was printed, and I suggested he might be better off busying himself with his papers rather than conversing with me. But he was very ingratiating and before I knew it he had got my telephone number out of me.

"I'll call you when I'm finished with this," he said, waving his notebook as we parted company on the railway platform.

Either he was a slow learner or he had forgotten about our meeting, as it was three months before I heard from him. By then the entire thing had slipped my mind and I had no real desire to meet him again. I said I had a lot of work to do. But he didn't allow me to get away with that and soon called again. How about a little walk in the park this Sunday? I dressed up especially nice and when I opened the door, he didn't recognize me. He thought he had rung the wrong bell. Many walks in the park resulted from this and I soon realized I couldn't manage without him. Every parting was difficult and I longed more and more for Bertil Niklasson.

We were both very busy with our work. Bertil had his last year of veterinary school before him and I had, along with my studies at the opera school, a string of offers for concerts outside Sweden. I made an important discovery: everything becomes easier when you have someone with whom you can share your thoughts and problems.

In the summer of 1945, fresh out of school, Bertil entered upon his first position as assistant veterinarian. This position was in Varberg, not very far from Båstad. There was much commuting between Varberg and Båstad that summer. Bertil was eager to have me accompany him on all of his trips and we rushed around from morning till night. He drove very fast in order to get everything done and I lived in fear that his old DKW would break down. Sometimes I was able to assist when he operated, which I didn't care for all that much—but what one will do when in love!

My parents liked Bertil immediately and accepted him naturally "as family." My father, Nils, was in his element having someone with whom to discuss diseases of animals. Nils was reputed to be an excellent quack, tending to his own animals as well as those of his neighbors. The future son-in-law served well as an adviser.

Bertil, of course, knew a lot more about animal diseases than he did about opera. He liked to say that he married me *in spite of* my being an opera singer, but I believe it was my French omelet with steamed mussels that he fell for. This led to our engagement in Nice and to getting married in the Swedish Church in Copenhagen—much to the disappointment of relatives and friends who were looking forward to a magnificent wedding, as is the custom in Skåne.

One can hardly say that our mutual interests brought us together. But even though we had such different professions, Bertil never tried to influence me to abandon my career. In those days it was usually expected that a woman, once married, would put aside any plans for a profession and devote herself to household tasks: cooking, cleaning, having children. Bertil was different. Fortunately, he was not one of these old-fashioned pashas. He gave me the courage to fight when I experienced difficulties. I think he believed in my future as a singer more than I did. He created a place for himself in my world in that he listened to music, learned about it, and came to enjoy it. Bertil is living proof that one can develop a musical ear.

I remember receiving a recording on which various soloists of the opera were introduced by each singing an aria. I was represented on the recording singing the "Dich, teure Halle" from *Tannhäuser* and had just put the recording on when Bertil came in. He didn't know the recording existed and asked who was singing. I answered with a question as to how he liked the singer. "Well, I must say that you have some real competition here," he said.

Not bad for a beginner! I tend to believe, however, that he recognized my voice immediately. Today he is almost an expert. In any case, Bertil has a fine ear and has a very definite taste. When he would go with me to some of the competitions where I was a member of the jury, I used to say it would be much simpler—and cheaper—if they would let Bertil be the jury. It usually produced the same result.

During my career I always tried not to take my work home with me. I tried as far as possible to relax by doing something completely different. By the same token I avoided, when possible, warming up or practicing when Bertil was around. Eternal vocalizing and running scales could kill any marriage, or at least destroy your spouse's nerves. Even carpenters or builders get jittery when people like me are around. We once had bricklayers working on the farm. I was alone at home and took the opportunity to warm up my voice. As I was totally alone, I let myself go, uninhibited. The mason's helper was not from our region and therefore didn't know me. When he heard the noise, he was frightened half to death. He let his mortar and water pail fall to the ground and rushed, white as a sheet, to the master mason who was working in the barn: "Come quick! Something terrible has happened to the woman in the house. She is screaming and howling like a madwoman!" The master mason quieted him down and said he should not worry, the screaming was so to speak, the woman's profession.

"Horrible, to have a wife with such a voice," sighed the worker. No one could have pitied Bertil more.

A young man who was married to a singer asked Bertil once how much I practiced and what vocalises I used. "You're asking the wrong person," answered Bertil truthfully, "I have never heard Birgit practicing." I'm sure the young man didn't believe him.

But it was so. Neither of us tried to interfere in the career of the other or to put difficulties in the way. When Bertil after a few years had the feeling he wanted to leave veterinary practice and run his own business, he was certainly permitted to decide for himself without my trying to influence him. Fortunately, I saw early on that Bertil did not wish to become "Mr. Nilsson," traveling around with me as an appendage and luggage carrier. He was always too energetic and enterprising to live through the fame of his wife—or on her earnings. He insisted upon standing on his own two feet.

Naturally it would have been wonderful and less stressful for me had I not had to be alone so often. I would have loved having him there to "run interference" and smooth the path for his singing wife. But when I am really honest—and one should always be—I don't think it would have been very smart. Many problems can arise between a hardworking singer and her husband who doesn't know quite what to do with his life. I cannot imagine demanding from someone that for my benefit he give up his interests, his dreams, and his goals in life. That would be sacrificing his very integrity. I would have had a quite guilty conscience.

Bertil was of the same opinion. He never waggled his forefinger at me or forbade my undertaking anything. And when I went to him with concerns or worries he did everything he could to help me—and I mean *everything!* He is wonderful in resolving problems where I am more apt to lose interest and perspective. Besides, Bertil is the most well-balanced person in the world and he has a great sense of humor. Oh, I, too, have a sense of humor, but I am "blessed" with an equal amount of temper.

There is one particular characteristic I must praise him for: he never spoiled me, never put me on a pedestal and worshiped at the feet of the great Diva. Instead, he treated me as a woman. This down-to-earth perspective actually normalized the sometimes artificial existence of an opera star. It is wonderful and very comfortable not to have to live up to one's public image all the time.

I also have to add that Bertil is very sloppy, forgetful, and absent-minded—none of which have improved with time. Our wedding anniversary he always forgets. My birthday is easier to remember, as it falls on the same day as Norway's National Day. He also forgets his own birthday. As to the messiness, that is a lost cause. I am also thoroughly careless but next to Bertil I seem compulsive.

As I was recently going through my papers I came across a poetic work of Bertil, which I received many years ago in New York. I offer it here gladly as the chaotic elements in his life are so realistically described that it makes me really homesick:

Good morning, Thursday morning, horrible morning
Frost and wind, gloomy and dry, TV kaput.
Flies in the kitchen, weeds in the garden, leak in the swimming pool.
Putte [the car] in the shop, and Petterson
Battling the rust on the roof.

It goes bad with me; yesterday, so what?
Stomach up and down
Headache, cannot breathe, rheumatic shoulder
Throat worn out, back stiff, head abuzz
Dust behind the ear, feet black, nails too.

Sit and wait for a call from Småland
Should ring at eight or shortly after
Devil take it, the line stays still!
Customer is K.F. von Växsjö, sly as they come.
Shop never again at Konsum in the City.

Over the weekend, travel to Stockholm
Petter and Sten drive Putte
I choose to take a sleeping car.
Two weeks paint and repair
So long till the house is as pretty
As the Maiden in May.

As my career slowly drew to a close I noticed that Bertil was nervous about how I would handle the transition into a new life.

He often asked how I was going to keep busy and how I imagined my life when I was no longer performing. In other words: he was terribly afraid that I would be unbearable, sitting at home weeping and feeling sorry for myself, missing the spotlight and the ovations of former days. I gave him the plain, unvarnished truth: I hadn't the foggiest idea. Planning and looking ahead have never been strong qualities with me—which is not a disadvantage really; things seldom turn out as you think they will. My career had lasted longer than I ever dreamed it would. In any case, I have never complained or shed tears over the "past greatness." Life has so many things to offer. It is exactly as the Marschallin in *Der Rosenkavalier* says: "Everything has its right time."

Just so: everything *does* have its right time. To my great pleasure I was able to acquaint myself with the upcoming generation of singers and, to a degree, smooth the way for those I believed truly talented. As usual I had many irons in the fire and often wished to have more time for myself. At the same time I feared I would be bored if I had as much free time as I dreamed of. All this extra time had given me a new dimension. It is beautiful to grow old together without having the feeling of being put on the shelf. We both have indulged ourselves in our childish desires, and we are always curious about life and the world.

As I sit here wrapped in memories, I ask myself a question I can never answer: What would my life have been if Cupid, disguised as Johannes Norrby, had not commanded me to appear one day early in Stockholm? I would not have been on the train and never would have met my beloved, clever, protective, helpful, funny, sloppy, and wonderful husband. To think how empty my life would have been!

Afterword

BY PEGGY TUELLER

The setting sun is casting sharp shafts of light far into the sky as I write. Reflections of the bright orange colors dance on the ripples of the Hudson River. In my mind's eye I see in the midst of this fiery vista a mighty Valkyrie, with arms outstretched. I am filled with many warm and wonderful memories and, at the same time, with an overwhelming sense of loss. I have just finished reading the English translation of *La Nilsson: My Life in Opera.* It is May 2006, and I have an almost uncontrollable urge to place a phone call to Sweden to reminisce and laugh with Birgit about the things she recalls in her book. But, of course, this is impossible because she left us in December on Christmas Day 2005. It is inconceivable.

At the time her book was first published in Swedish and later translated into German, Birgit was very much alive. Now that the English translation is being prepared for publication, Birgit's husband, Bertil Niklasson, feels that her book requires a concluding section, and he has asked me to write one. I thank Bertil for this honor.

From 1963 to 1975 I served as secretary to Paul Jaretzki, Robert Herman, Goren Gentele, and Schuyler Chapin at the Metropolitan Opera. During those years I came to know many famous singers, but Birgit and I had a special affinity from the moment we met. Perhaps it was because we were both farmgirls who aspired to other lives, but I believe the thing we shared the most was our sense of humor.

I really came to know Birgit during my first tour with the Met. We were in Atlanta, and my boss at the time, Artistic Administrator Robert Herman, made arrangements for him, Birgit, and me to dine together in a very nice Swiss restaurant in the motel where we were all staying. At the last minute Bob was summoned to the theater to tend to an emergency, so Birgit and I went to dinner together. We were barely seated when a roving accordion player headed toward our table. "Brace yourself," says Birgit, "I met him last night, and he can't play 'Come to Jesus' in Whole Notes!" He greeted Birgit and immediately inquired what I did with the Met. I was about to explain that I was with the administration, when Birgit piped up, "Oh, she's a singer." Very impressed, the accordionist then asked me what roles I performed. " Mostly Wagnerian," I replied, happily going along with the farce. Even more impressed, he asked for my name. I said the first artist that popped into my mind, "Kirsten Flagstad." "Oh, Miss Flagstad," he gushed, "I'm so pleased to meet you. I see you often on television." (That would be highly unlikely, as Flagstad was deceased, but I surmised he thought that I was Dorothy *Kirsten,* who at that time was appearing on television). I glanced at Birgit. She looked like she was holding walnuts in both cheeks. The next thing we knew, he had produced the restaurant's postcard, on which he wanted our autographs. Birgit signed first, and then I turned it over. At least he would have one legitimate signature when he discovered a joke had been played on him. However, nothing would do but that we sign side by side. So in my best flowing hand I wrote, "Best wishes, Kirsten Flagstad." By this time I thought we were both going to explode. When he finally wandered away, Birgit said in her very distinctive voice, "That's the first and the last time those two signatures will ever been seen together!" We dissolved into hopeless giggles, and that, as they say, was the beginning of a beautiful friendship.

To know Birgit was to revel in her razor-sharp, split-second comebacks. One that comes immediately to mind occurred on the tour just mentioned. In Memphis, the Corps de Ballet always threw a party for the entire company. The opera stars rarely attended these fetes, but Birgit thought it would be fun, so she, Bob, and I arrived at the designated suite. We asked Birgit to stand in front of us and knock. Paul Franke, one of the Met's accomplished comprimario tenors, opened the door and exclaimed, "My God!" to which Birgit replied without missing a beat, "Please, call me Birgit." The lady had a wonderfully subtle way of communicating that she was very well aware of her worth, but I never knew her to flaunt it egotistically to anyone.

I could go on endlessly recalling moments when Birgit's sense of humor put people in their places, but I will relate just one of my favorite instances. Birgit made it very clear in this book of recollections that she was highly uncomfortable in Herbert von Karajan's pitch-dark production of *Die Walküre* at the Met. What she didn't mention is that von Karajan, who was a short man, had himself bathed in a bright spotlight on the conductor's podium, which he insisted the management make higher, so he was visible to the audience from the waist up. (After the *Walküre* premiere, the Met management received complaints from patrons in the upper tiers who found this strange exhibition extremely distracting.) One day I happened to be in the auditorium during a rehearsal when von Karajan stopped the proceedings to complain that there was a draft on the back of his neck. He requested that the air-conditioning be turned off. From the dark expanse of the stage came Mme. Nilsson's clarion voice, "Maestro, you must realize that those who insist on standing in high places must expect a strong wind!" While on the subject of this particular production of *Die Walküre,* I think it is safe to reveal here that I am the culprit who presented to Birgit in her dressing room, just prior to the premiere, the miner's helmet complete with gas lamp, reflector lights, and Brunnhilde wings. I believe the reasoning behind this gift is, by now, self-explanatory.

As Birgit and von Karajan had an ongoing one-upsmanship, I couldn't resist superimposing on one of Birgit's *Salome* publicity photos the maestro's head on Jochanaan's platter. I framed it and presented it to her as a joke, so you can imagine my surprise when I saw that she included it in her book *My Memoirs in Pictures.* In the copy of the book she gave me, she inscribed: "To Peggy Lou, who contributed the most appreciated picture." (Incidentally, she insisted on addressing me by both my given names, while I always referred to her as Super Madam). If anyone reading this possesses the picture book, the doctored photo appears on page 98.

It becomes apparent in Birgit's recounting of the significant events throughout her career that she was very strong, both physically and mentally. However, she did not mention a major episode at the Met that fully demonstrates her extraordinary determination and personal resolve. Four days before the premiere of the long-awaited new production of *Götterdämmerung,* Birgit suffered a very serious shoulder dislocation and severe facial and body bruises when some steps came apart under her during a dress rehearsal. She was rushed to the hospital in an ambulance, as her colleagues and Metropolitan Opera employees stood onstage in horrified silence. For three days she lay in her hospital bed black-and-blue, plagued with a throbbing headache, her helpless right arm strapped to her chest. As she left the hospital twenty-four hours before the premiere, no one believed that she could walk, much less move about a dark and crater-filled stage. Eager patrons and fans from all over the world who had flown to New York for this prestigious event were praying for a miracle that would allow her to perform. The stage director and the Met management made it clear that she could disregard all the staging, if she could simply find the strength to sing. Birgit was not at all sure she had the stamina to survive the five and a half–hour opera. When she left the hospital, she insisted on walking up and down the sidewalk several times before entering her hotel. She informed the Met management that she would let them know at 10:30 A.M. the next day if she had recouped enough vitality to take on Brunnhilde that night. At exactly 10:30 A.M. she telephoned the Met to say that she would sing with her arm in the sling. One-sleeve costumes and capes were quickly devised, her black-and-blue face was camouflaged with stage makeup—and right on cue she made her entrance over the rough and raked stage to a thunderous ovation. She kept exactly to the original staging, going through dark passageways for entrances on precarious stairs and making exits by even riskier means. As the curtain came down after the last note, stagehands, management, and performing colleagues broke into cheers and applause for the courageous lady who had just done the impossible. When she stepped in front of the curtain, a tremendous roar greeted her from four thousand incredulous and adoring people. A blizzard of confetti came from the upper reaches of the theater, along with flowers thrown from everywhere. In his review of the performance Harold Schonberg of the *New York Times* wrote: "Nilsson the Indestructible sang magnificently. She was white hot and the soprano seemed eager to show the audience that a little thing like a dislocated shoulder and perhaps a few bent ribs meant nothing to her, a real Valkyrie. She continues to be a marvel and one can do no more than stand off and admire her with awe."

In her book Birgit did not reveal one of her major achievements. It all began when I invited her to give a Master Class at Manhattan School of Music (MSM), where I served as vice president for administration under John Crosby's tenure as president. Birgit's own miserable and damaging experiences with voice teachers had turned her completely off the subject of teaching. In response to my pleadings, she was quite explicit in informing me that she had no intention whatsoever of telling young people how they should sing. It seemed unconscionable to me that the students in the MSM voice department, known for its excellence, should be deprived of the opportunity of meeting this legendary artist. So I came up with an idea to which Birgit finally agreed. With the proviso that there would be no individual coaching, she would meet with the students and answer any questions they would like to ask. And ask they did! The ecstatic students had many queries, but it turned out that one, in particular, reversed her stance on teaching. "Madame Nilsson," the student asked, "what does it feel like when you sing a high C?" She thought for quite a long time, and then proceeded to give a detailed lesson in vocal technique. I believe this was as much a revelation to Birgit as it was to the students, because she realized at that moment she was quite capable of communicating to young singers the proper way to produce sounds. Thankfully, that was the beginning of ten years of her Master Classes at MSM. And what classes they were! At every one, Birgit appeared on stage in four-inch heels, effervescent and fully prepared to meet the challenge, all fears behind her. She was an ideal teacher: firm, but kind, and one who could immediately identify a problem and offer solutions. She had many humorous and colorful ways to demonstrate how to sing musically as well as beautifully. Among the students who benefited from her wisdom were Lauren Flanigan, Susan Graham, Andrea Gruber, and Dawn Upshaw.

Teaching voice is hard work, and after her eighth year Birgit told me on the way to the airport that she thought this would be her last year. This came as a complete surprise, and as soon as I had recovered from the shock, I pointed out that through her generosity, donors, and ticket sales, we had built up a Nilsson Scholarship Fund of $100,000. (Birgit could have commanded a huge fee, but insisted on only being reimbursed for her hotel and airfare expenses). I asked her if she would consider teaching another two years, at the end of which we could have an impressive fund-raising gala on the tenth anniversary of her Master Classes at Manhattan School of Music, where she would serve as mistress of ceremonies. She agreed. I immediately began asking prestigious artists if they would perform and donate their services for the Birgit Nilsson Scholarship Fund. Those whose schedules allowed enthusiastically agreed. At the same time, Tony Newman, vice president for development, began selling $10,000 tables for a dinner at which Henry Kissinger would present Birgit with a special music box. Among the performing artists were Mignon Dunn, Susan Graham, Sherrill Milnes, and Dolora Zajick. Of course, Birgit reigned supreme as mistress of ceremonies. November 3, 1991, was a night to remember at MSM. When Tony Newman and I left the school in 1992, the Birgit Nilsson Scholarship Fund exceeded $200,000.

It is not unusual for highly gifted individuals to be complex, and Birgit was no exception. On the one hand, she was absolutely secure and certain of her artistic convictions. On the other, she could not bring herself to ask anyone for anything. For example, in 1975 she was scheduled to sing several *Walküre* Brünnhildes at the Met. She learned after her arrival in New York that the artist scheduled to sing Sieglinde was unable to appear in that production. Birgit casually mentioned to me that she would really like to sing Sieglinde at the Met, whereupon I urged her to immediately make this known to the Met management. Rather timidly, she asked me if I would mind bringing it to their attention. I did, and as a result she sang Sieglinde in the premiere and in three subsequent performances in which Berit Lindholm and Rita Hunter shared the role of Brünnhilde. A composite photograph, in which Birgit appears as both Brünnhilde and Sieglinde, hangs on my wall. On it she wrote: "Thank you for letting my sister sing at the Met. She was thrilled."

A keen observer will have discovered that there is no portrait or picture of Birgit Nilsson in the Artists' Gallery in the Metropolitan Opera House, which to any serious opera enthusiast is a grievous omission. Birgit's answer when questioned about this was "No one at the Met has asked me for one." She would go to any length to avoid feeling obligated to anyone.

Birgit's proudest moments were the many occasions during which she was honored by royalty and heads of state. Her numerous medals were always prominently displayed on her evening gowns at gala events.

On May 23, 2006, the Metropolitan Opera Guild presented a program in Lincoln Center's Alice Tully Hall celebrating Birgit Nilsson's life. The program was entitled "Birgit Nilsson: A Force of Nature." This sold-out event was hosted by the charming and articulate Dame Gwynneth Jones. Irene Dalis, Mignon Dunn, Lauren Flanigan, Evelyn Lear, Thomas Stewart, and Edgar Vincent joined Dame Gwynneth in recalling fond memories of Birgit on- and offstage. They introduced a number of carefully selected video clips of Birgit singing the roles of Lady Macbeth, Isolde, Brunnhilde, Salome, Turandot, Leonore in *Forza del Destino,* Eva in *Meistersinger,* and the Swedish folk song, "When I Was Sixteen," which she often included in her recital programs. The audience was also treated to a recording session of *Götterdämmerung* with Sir Georg Solti conducting, when a horse (Grane, we assume) comes ambling back and forth. Birgit's expression on this occasion was priceless, as it was when she was surprised by Franco Corelli on the Swedish television show *This is Your Life.* A delightful clip of her televison interview with Dick Cavett was also shown. At the end of this unforgettable evening, there was no doubt in anyone's mind that those who knew and worked with Birgit Nilsson had a profound respect for her consummate artistry. They loved her equally for her down-to-earth approach to life and, above all, for her matchless sense of humor.

Birgit detested farewells. To my knowledge, she never sang an acknowledged farewell performance. She certainly would not be pleased if I belabored her final farewell here. Instead, I shall paraphrase the sentiment she expressed at the conclusion of her chapter on Bayreuth. As she left Bayreuth for the final time, she was presented with the casket that held Isolde's magic potion. If Birgit's wish had been granted, that casket would have contained a few drops of something to give eternal youth. If only that had been the case! Then all of us would have had the unsurpassed joy of hearing Birgit Nilsson simply begin all over again.

Career Milestones

1918	Born May 17, 1918, in Västra Karup.
1939(?)	First voice lessons with Music Director Ragner Blennow in Ästorp.
1941–46	Stockholm Royal Academy of Music (study as vocal soloist and at the Opera School.
1946	Royal Opera, Stockholm, *Der Freischütz,* with Leo Blech, conductor.
1947	Breakthrough as Lady Macbeth in new production of Verdi's *Macbeth,* Stockholm Opera, with Fritz Busch, conductor.
1948–58	Permanent member of Stockholm Opera.
1948–81	Guest contract with Stockholm Opera.
1951	First engagement outside Sweden. Berlin concert, with Leo Blech, conductor. Glyndebourne, as Elettra in Mozart's *Idomeneo,* with Fritz Busch, conductor.
1953	Debut in Bayreuth's Festspielhaus as soprano soloist in Beethoven's Ninth Symphony, with Paul Hindemith, conductor.
1954–82	Guest appearances at the Vienna State Opera.
1954	First performance with Munich Opera (Prinzregentin Theater) as Aida.
1954	Elsa in *Lohengrin* in Bayreuth, with Eugen Jochum and Joseph Keilberth, conductors.
1954	New production of *Salome,* Stockholm Opera, with Sixten Ehrling, conductor.
1955	Debut at Teatro Colón in Buenos Aires as Isolde, with Fritz Rieger, conductor.
	American debut in Hollywood Bowl Concert, with William Steinberg, conductor.
1956	Debut at San Francisco Opera, with Hans Schwieger, conductor.
	Debut at Chicago Opera as *Walküre* Brünnhilde, with Georg Solti, conductor.
1957	First Turandot, with Stockholm Opera, Herbert Sandberg, conductor.
1957–70	Bayreuth performances as Ortlinde, Third Norn, and the three Brünnhildes, with Hans Knappertsbusch, Rudolf Kempe, Karl Böhm, and Berislav Klobučar, conductors.
1957	Covent Garden debut as Brünnhilde in the *Ring.* New production, with Rudolf Kempe, conductor.

1958	La Scala debut as *Walküre* Brünnhilde and as Turandot opening the season, with Herbert von Karajan, conductor.
1959–83	Guest performances at the Metropolitan Opera in New York. Debut as Isolde, with Karl Böhm, conductor.
1964	Guest performance with La Scala in Moscow as Turnadot.
1965	Debut as Elektra, Stockholm Opera, with Berislav Klobučar, conductor.
1967	New production of *Walküre* at the Metropolitan Opera in New York with Herbert von Karajan, conductor. My 100th Brünnhilde.
1968	New production of *Turandot* in Paris, with Georges Prêtre, conductor.
1968	New production of *Tosca* at the Metropolitan Opera in New York, with Molinari Pradelli, conductor.
1971	*Aida* in Göteborg, with Sixten Ehrling, conductor.
1973	Three concerts in Sydney, Australia, dedicating the new opera house, with Sir Charles Mackerras, Lorin Maazel, and Geoffrey Parsons, conductors.
1975	Last new role, Dyer's Wife in Strauss's *Die Frau ohne Schatten,* Stockholm Opera, with Berislav Klobučar, conductor.
1976	My 200th performance of Isolde, with Karl Böhm, conductor. Performance at Vienna State Opera.
1976	Thirty-year Jubilee in the opera, Stockholm Opera, performing Isolde, with Silvio Varviso, conductor.
1983–93	Master class at the Manhattan School of Music in New York City.
1984	Concert tour in Germany with Leif Segerstam. Last public performances.

Honors and Awards

1954 Court Singer, Stockholm
1958 Gold Medal from Teatro Liceos, Barcelona, Spain
1960 Royal Medal "Litteris et Artibus" Stockholm
1960 Honorary Member of the Royal Academy of Music, Stockholm
1966 Sonnings Music Prize, Denmark
1967 Gold Medal for "The Advancement of the Art of Music" from the Royal Academy of Music, Stockholm
1968 Awarded title of Austrian Court Singer
1968 Honorary member of the Vienna State Opera
1970 Honorary doctorate from Andover University, Andover, Mass.
1970 Honorary member of the Royal Academy of Music, London
1970 Awarded title of Bavarian Court Singer, Munich
1972 Royal Medal "Ingenio et Arte," Denmark
1974 Commander of Vasaordens Class I, Stockholm
1975 Commander of St. Olavsordens Class I, Norway
1981 Order of "Illis Quorum" Size 18 with Chain, Stockholm
1981 Gold Medal from the Royal Opera, Stockholm
1982 Honorary Doctorate from Manhattan School of Music, New York
1982 Honorary Doctorate from Michigan State University, East Lansing, Mich.
1982 Awarded "Swedish-American of the Year," New York
1988 Distinguished Service Cross, First Class, from Niedersachsen, Germany
1991 Commander of Arts and Letters, France
1994 Award of the American-Swedish Foundation, New York
1997 Honorary Doctorate from the Sibelius Academy, Helsinki, Finland

Discography

Adam

O Holy Night

Stockholm August 1963	Leven, organ	45: Decca CEP 5517/SEC 5517
Stockholm February 1977	Bondeman, organ	LP: Swedish Society SLT 33256

Adams

The Holy City

Stockholm February 1977	Bondeman, organ	LP: Swedish Society SLT 33256

Bach

Ave Maria, arranged by Gounod

Stockholm August 1963	Leven, organ	45: Decca CEP 5517/SEC 5517 CD: Bluebell ABCD 3001
Stockholm February 1977	Bondeman, organ	LP: Swedish Soceity SLT 33256

Bartok

Bluebeard's Castle

Stockholm February 1953	*Role of Judith* Sönnerstedt Stockholm RD Fricsay *Sung in German*	LP: Swedish Radio SRLP 1377 *A version on HRE 225, also sung in German with the same soloists but from Danish Radio in 1953 and conducted by Frissholm, is probably identical to the Stockholm performance*

Beethoven

Ah perfido!

London May 1958	Philharmonia Wallberg	LP: Columbia 33 CX 1629/SAX 2284 LP: EMI 1C 187 00786-00787 CD: EMI COM 763 1082
London May 1963	Covent Garden Orchestra Downes	45: Decca CEP 5533/SEC 5533
Vienna 1972	VSD Leitner	LP: DG 2721 138/2721 206/2538 098

Egmont, Klärchen-Lieder (Die Trommel gerühret; Freudvoll und leidvoll)

London November 1957	Philharmonia Klemperer	45: Columbia SEL 1609 LP: Columbia 33 CX 1575 LP: EMI ED 29 02531/EX 29 03793 CD: EMI CDC 747 1882/CDM 763 3582

Die Ehre Gottes aus der Natur

Stockholm February 1977	Bondeman, organ	LP: Swedish Society SLT 33256

Fidelio

Cologne January 1956	*Role of Leonore* Wenglor, Hopf, Unger, Schöffler, Frick, H. Braun WRD Orchestra and Chorus Kleiber	LP: Rococo 1014 LP: Centra LO 68 CD: Hunt CDLSMH 34048
New York February 1960	*Role of Leonore* Hurley, Vickers Anthony, Tozzi, Uhde, Czerwenka Metropolitan Orchestra & Chorus Böhm	LP: Melodram MEL 045
Milan December 1960	*Role of Leonore* Lipp, Vickers, Unger, Hotter, Frick, Crass	LP: HRE Records HRE 388

	La Scala Orchestra and Chorus Karajan	
Milan December 1960	*Role of Leonore* Lipp, Vickers, Unger, Hotter, Frick, Crass La Scala Orchestra and Chorus Karajan	LP: HRE Records HRE 388

Fidelio/concluded

Vienna March and June 1964	*Role of Leonore* Sciutti, McCracken, Grobe, Krause, Böhme, Prey Vienna Opera Chorus VPO Maazel	LP: Decca MET 272–273/ SET 272–273 *Abscheulicher* CD: Decca 421 3232
Rome March 1970	*Role of Leonore* Donath, Spiess, Unger, Vogel, Crass RAI Rome Chorus and Orchestra Bernstein	CD: Hunt CDLSMH 34049

Other recordings of the opera may be preserved; Metropolitan Opera broadcasts with Nilsson in the role of Leonore also took place in January 1963 and January 1966

Fidelio, excerpt (Abscheulicher!)

London May 1958	Philharmonia Wallberg	LP: Columbia 33 CX 1629/SAX 2284 LP: Angel 35715/60353 LP: EMI 1C 187 00786-00787 CD: EMI CDM 763 1082
Stockholm January 1961	Stockholm RO Grevillius	CD: Bluebell ABCD 055
London June 1963	Covent Garden Orchestra Downes	LP: Decca LXT 6077/SXL 6077

Missa Solemnis

Stockholm March 1948	Soprano soloist Tunnell, Bäckelin, S. Björling Stockholm Philharmonic Chorus & Orchestra Kleiber	LP: Discocorp IGI 366

Berwald

Estrella de Soria, excerpt (Estrella's aria)

Stockholm April 1947	Stockholm RO Frykberg	CD: Bluebell ABCD 055 *Earliest extant recording of Birgit Nilsson*

Catalini

La Wally, excerpt (Ebben? Ne andro lontana)

Sweden 1978–1979	Roos, piano	LP: Bluebell BELL 109

Coates

Bird Songs at Eventide

Sweden 1978–1979	Roos, piano	LP: Bluebell BELL 109

Eriksson

Stora och underbara äro dina verk

Stockholm February 1977	Bondeman, organ	LP: Swedish Society SLT 33256

Franck

Paris angelicus

Stockholm August 1963	Leven, organ	45: Decca CEP 5517/SEC 5517
Stockholm February 1977	Bondeman, organ	LP: Swedish Society SLT 33256

De Frumerie

När du sluter mina ögon

Stockholm September 1974	Parsons, piano	CD: Bluebell ABCD 009 *Previously issued by Bluebell on LP*

Som en väg

Stockholm September 1974	Parsons, piano	CD: Bluebell ABCD 009 *Previously issued by Bluebell on LP*

Gounod

O civine redeemer

Stockholm February 1977	Bondeman, organ *Sung in Latin*	LP: Swedish Society SLT 33256

Grieg

Den store hvide flok

Stockholm February 1977	Bondeman, organ	LP: Swedish Society SLT 33256

En droem

Stockholm September 1974	Parsons, piano	CD: Bluebell ABCD 009 *Previously issued by Bluebell on LP*
Sweden 1978–1979	Roos, piano	LP: Bluebell BELL 109

En svane

New York May 1961	Taubman, piano	LP: RCA LM 2578/LSC 2578 CD: RCA/BMG 09026 618792/ 09026 618272
Vienna April 1965	VPO Bokstedt	LP: Decca LXT 6185/SXL 6185
Stockholm September 1974	Parsons, piano	CD: Bluebell ABCD 009 *Previously issued by Bluebell on LP*

Et haab

Sweden 1978–1979	Roos, piano	LP: Bluebell BELL 114

Fra Monte Pincio

Vienna April 1965	VPO Bokstedt	LP: Decca LXT 6185/SXL 6185

Jeg elsker Dig

New York May 1961	Taubman, piano	LP: RCA LM 2578/LSC 2578 CD: RCA/BMG 09026 618792/ 09026 618272

Sweden 1978–1979	Roos, piano	LP: Bluebell BELL 109

Mens jeg venter

New York May 1961	Taubman, piano	LP: RCA LM 2578/LSC 2578 CD: RCA/BMG 09026 618792/ 09026 618272
Stockholm September 1974	Parsons, piano	CD: Bluebell ABCD 009 *Previously issued by Bluebell on LP*

Og jeg vil ha mig en hjertenskjaer

New York May 1961	Taubman, Piano	LP: RCA LM 2578/LSC 2578 CD: RCA/BMG 09026 618792/ 09026 618272
Stockholm September 1974	Parsons, piano	CD: Bluebell ABCD 009 *Previously issued by Bluebell on LP*

Vaaren

Vienna April 1965	VPO Bokstedt	LP: Decca LXT 6185/SXL 6185

Gruber

Silent Night, Holy Night

Stockholm August 1963	Leven, organ	45: Decca CEP 5517/SEC 5517
Stockholm February 1977	Bondeman, organ	LP: Swedish Society SLT 33256

Händel

Joy to the World

Stockholm February 1977	Bondeman, organ *Sung in German*	LP: Swedish Society SLT 33256

See the Conquering Hero

Stockholm February 1977	Bondeman, organ	LP: Swedish Society SLT 33256

Hopkins

We Three Kings of Orient Are

Stockholm February 1977	Bondeman, organ	LP: Swedish Society SLT 33256

Liebermann

Penelope. excerpt (Penelope's aria)

Stockholm April 1959	Stockholm Opera Orchestra Ehrling *Sung in Swedish*	CD: Bluebell ABCD 055

Lilliebjörn

Fjorton ar tror jag visst att jag var

New York October 1983		Unpublished video recording of Met centennial gala

Lindblad

En ung flickas morgonbetraktelse

Sweden 1978–1979	Roos, piano	LP: Bluebell BELL 114

Frederick Loewe

My Fair Lady, excerpt (I could have danced all night)

Location uncertain 1960	Orchestral ensemble	LP: Decca MET 201–203/ SET 201–203 LP: Decca D247 D3 CD: Decca 421 0462 *Part of the gala sequence included in Karajan's recording of Die Fledermaus*
New York November 1967	Wustman, piano	CD: Melodram MEL 18027
Sweden 1978–1979	Roos, piano	LP: Bluebell BELL 109

Marchesi

La folletta

New York November 1967	Wustman, piano	CD: Melodram MEL 18027

Melartin

Gib' mir dein Herz

New York November 1967	Wustman, piano	CD: Melodram MEL 18027

Morgonsdång

New York November 1967	Wustman, piano	CD: Melodram MEL 18027

Tjugo år

Stockholm September 1974	Parsons, piano	CD: Bluebell ABCE 009 *Previously issued by Bluebell on LP*
Sweden 1978–1979	Roos, piano	LP: Bluebell BELL 109/BELL 114

Mendelssohn

Hark the Herald Angels Sing

Stockholm February 1977	Bondeman, organ	LP: Swedish Society SLT 33256

Mozart

Don Giovanni

Vienna June 1959	*Role of Donna Anna* L. Price, Ratti, Valletti, Siepi, Corena, Van Mill Vienna Opera Chorus VPO Leinsdorf	LP: RCA RE 25028–25031/ SER 4528–4531 LP: Decca D10 D4 *Excerpts* CD: Decca 421 8752
Prague February and March 1967	*Role of Donna Anna* Arroyo, Grist, Schreier, Talvela, Fischer-Dieskau Prague National Chorus & Orchestra Böhm	LP: DG 271: 006/2740 108/2740 119 LP: DG 2740 205/2740 222 CD: DG 429 8702/435 3942 *Excerpts* LP: DG 2537 014/2538 098/2721 206

Don Giovanni, excerpt (Or sai chi l'onore)

London May 1958	Philharmonia Wallberg	LP: Columbia 33 CX 1629/SAX 2284 LP: Angel 35715/60353 LP: EMI 1C 187 00786-00787 CD: EMI CDM 763 1082

Nielsen

Aeoleblomst

New York November 1967	Wustman, piano	CD: Hunt CDLSMH 34049 CD: Melodram MEL 18027
Sweden 1978–1979	Roos, piano	LP: Bluebell BELL 114

Den forste laerke

New York November	Wustman, piano	CD: Hunt CDLSMH 34049 CD: Melodram MEL 18027

Nordqvist

Det var en gång

Sweden 1978–1979	Roos, piano	LP: Bluebell BELL 114

Peterson-Berger

Aspåkerspolska

Sweden 1978–1979	Roos, piano	LP: Bluebell BELL 109

Visa i svensk folkton

Sweden 1978–1979	Roos, piano	LP: Bluebell BELL 114

Piccini

Alessandro nelle India, excerpt (Se il ciel mi divide)

New York November 1967	Wustman, piano	CD: Hunt CDLSMH 34049 CD: Melodram MEL 18027

Puccini

La fanciulla del West

Milan July 1958	*Role of Minnie* Carturan, Gibin, Ercolani, Sordello, Zaccaria La Scala Chorus and Orchestra Matacic	LP: Columbia 33CX 1631–1633/ SAX 2286–2288 LP: Angel 3593/SIC 6074 LP: EMI SLS 5079 CD: EMI CXS 763 9702

Gianni Schicchi, excerpt (O mio bambino caro)

Sweden 1978–1979	Roos, piano	LP: Bluebell BELL 109/BELL 114

Tosca

Philadelphia April 1963	*Role of Tosca* Tagliavini, Vinay Philadelphia Opera Association Chorus & Orchestra Moresca	CD: Melodram CDM 270112
Rome June 1966	*Role of Tosca* Corelli Fischer-Dieskau Santa Cecilia Chorus & Orchestra Maazel	LP: Decca MET 341–342/SET 341–342 CD: Decca 440 0512 *Vissi d'arte* CD: Decca 421 3152/421 3232
New York February 1969	*Role of Tosca* Domingo, Dooley Metropolitan Opera Chorus & Orchestra Schick	CD: Nouva Era NE 2286–2287 *Excerpts* CD: Memories HR 4275–4276

Another recording of the opera may be preserved; a Metropolitan opera broadcast with Nilsson in the title role took place in April 1963.

Tosca, excerpt (Vissi d'arte)

Philadelphia January 1962	Philadelphia Orchestra Stokowski	LP: Melodram MEL 228
Stockholm January 1961	Stockholm RO Grevillius	CD: Bluebell ABCD 055
Moscow September 1964	Tonini, piano	LP: HRE Records HRE 340 CD: Legato LCD 147
New York November 1967	Wustman, piano	CD: Hunt CDLSMH 34049 CD: Melodram MEL 18027
Sweden 1978–1979	Roos, piano	LP: Bluebell BELL 109

Turandot

Milan December 1958	*Role of Turandot* Cateri, Di Stefano, Modesti La Scala Chorus and Orchestra Votto	LP: Cetra LO 84 Also issued on LP by Ed Smith
Rome 1960	*Role of Turandot* Tebaldi, Björling, Tozzi Rome Opera Chorus and Orchestra Leinsdorf	LP: RCA RE 25020–25020/LSC 6149 SER 4520–4522/SER 5643–5645 LP: RCA 26–35116 CD: RCA/BMG RD 85932
New York March 1961	*Role of Turandot* Moffo, Corelli, Giaiotti Metropolitan Opera Chorus & Orchestra Stokowski	LP: HRE Records HRE 299 CD: Metropolitan Opera MET 16 CD: Memories HR 4535–4536 *Also issued on LP by Metropolitan Opera*
Vienna June 1961	*Role of Turandot* L. Price, Di Stefano, Zaccaria Vienna Opera Chorus VPO Molinari-Pradelli	LP: Morgan MOR 6101 LP: HRE Records HRE 321
Milan July 1964	*Role of Turandot* Vishnevskaya, Corelli, Zaccaria La Scala Chorus and Orchestra Gavazzeni	LP: Edizione lirica EL 003 CD: Nuova Era 013.6318–6319 *Excerpts* CD: Memories HR 4275–4276
Rome 1965	*Role of Turandot* Scotto, Corelli, Giaiotti Rome Opera Chorus and Orchestra Molinari-Pradelli	LP: EMI AN 159–161/SAN 159–161 LP: Angel 3671 LP: EMI SLS 921/EX 29 02863 CD: EMI CMS 769 3272 *Exceprts* LP: EMI ASD 2403/ESD 100 3821 LP: EMI 1C 187 00786–00787
New York December 1966	*Role of Turandot* Freni, Corelli, Giaiotti	LP: GOP Records GFC 17

	Metropolitan Opera Chorus & Orchestra Mehta	

Other recording of the opera may be preserved; Metropolitan opera broadcasts with Nilsson in the role of Turandot also took place in February 1962 and January 1965.

Turandot, excerpt (In questa reggia)

Stockholm August 1961	Stockholm RD Grevillius	CD: Bluebell ABCD 055
Moscow September 1964	La Scala Orchestra Gavazzeni	LP: HRE Records HRE 340 CD: Legato LCD 147
New York 1966	Bell Telephone Orchestra Voshees	LP: HRE Records HRE 379 CD: GOP Records GOP 736 *Broadcast in January 1967*

Turandot, excerpts (Straniero ascolta; Principessa di morte)

Moscow September 1964	Prevedi, Gullino La Scala Chorus and Orchestra Gavazzeni	LP: HRE Records HRE 340 CD: Legato LCD 147

Rangström

Bön till natten

Vienna April 1965	VPO Bokstedt	LP: Decca LXT 6185/SXL 6185

En gammal dansrytm

Vienna April 1965	VPO Bokstedt	LP: Decca LXT 6185/SXL 6185

Flickan under nymånen

Stockholm September 1974	Parsons, piano	CD: Bluebell ABCD 009 *Previously issued by Bluebell on LP*
Sweden 1978–1979	Roos, piano	LP: Bluebell BELL 109

Melodi

Vienna April 1965	VPO Bokstedt	LP: Decca LXT 6185/SXL 6185

Sköldmön

Vienna April 1965	VPO Bokstedt	LP: Decca LXT 6185/SXL 6185
Stockholm September 1974	Parsons, piano	CD: Bluebell ABCD 009 *Previously issued by Bluebell on LP*

Runbäck-Wikander

Friday

Stockholm February 1977	Bondeman, organ	LP: Swedish Society SLT 33256

Schubert

An die Musik

New York April 1961	Taubman, piano	LP: RCA LM 2578/LSC 2578

Auflösung

New York November 1967	Wustman, piano	CD: Hunt CDLSMH 34049 CD: Melodram MEL 18027 CD: Memories HR 4275–4276

An dem Unendlichen

New York April 1961	Taubman, piano	LP: RCA LM 2578/LSC 2578
New York November 1967	Wustman, piano	CD: Hunt CDLSMH 34049 CD: Melodram MEL 18027 CD: Memories HR 4275–4276

Die junge Nonne

New York November 1967	Wustman, piano	CD: Hunt CDLSMH 34049 CD: Melodram MEL 18027 CD: Memories HR 4275–4276

Nur wer die Sehnsucht kennt (Mignon)

New York April 1961	Taubman, piano	LP: RCA LM 2578/LSC 2578

Seligkeit

New York November 1967	Wustman, piano	CD: Hunt CDLSMH 34049 CD: Melodram MEL 18027

Sibelius

Demanten på marssnön

Vienna April 1965	VPO Bokstedt	LP: Decca LXT 6185/SXL 6185

Den första kyssen

New York April 1961	Taubman, piano	LP: RCA LM 2578/LSC 2578
Stockholm September 1974	Parsons, piano	CD: Bluebell ABCD 009 *Previously issued by Bluebell on LP*
Sweden January 1975	Solyom, piano	LP: Bis BISLP 15 CD: Bis BISCD 15

Flickan kom ifrån sin älsklings möte

Vienna April 1965	VPO Bokstedt	LP: Decca LXT 6184/SXL 6185
Sweden January 1975	Solyom, piano	LP: Bis BISLP 15 CD: Bis BISCD 15
Sweden 1978–1979	Roos, piano	LP: Bluebell BELL 109

Höstkväll

Vienna April 1965	VPO Bokstedt	LP: Decca LXT 6185/SXL 6185
New York November 1967	Wustman, piano	CD: Hunt CDLSMH 34049 CD: Melodram MEL 18027

Illalle

Sweden January 1975	Solyom, piano	LP: Bis BISLP 15 CD: Bis BISCD 15

Im Feld ein Mädchen singt

Sweden January 1975	Solyom, piano	LP: Bis BISLP 15 CD: Bis BISCD 15

På verandan vid havet

Sweden January 1975	Solyom, piano	LP: Bis BISLP 15 CD: Bis BISCD 15

Säv säv susa

New York April 1961	Taubamn, piano	LP: RCA LM 2578/LSC 2578

Vienna April 1965	VPO Bokstedt	LP: Decca LXT 6185/SXL 6185
New York November 1967	Wustman, piano	CD: Hunt CDLSMH 34049 CD: Melodram MEL 18027
Sweden January 1975	Solyom, piano	LP: Bis BISLP 15 CD: Bis BISCD 15

Se'n har jag ei frågat mera

Sweden January 1975	Solyom, piano	LP: Bis BISLP 15 CD: Bis BISCD 15

Svarta rosor

New York April 1961	Taubman, piano	LP: RCA LM 2578/LSC 2578
Vienna April 1965	VPO Bokstedt	LP: Decca LXT 6185/SXL 6185
Sweden January 1975	Solyom, piano	LP: Bis BISLP 15 CD: Bis BISCD 15
Sweden 1978–1979	Roos, piano	LP: Bluebell Bell 109

Till kvällen

Stockholm September 1974	Parsons, piano	CD: Bluebell ABCD 009 *Previouly issued by Bluebell on LP*

The Tryst

New York April 1961	Taubman, piano	LP: RCA LM 2578/LSC 2578

Var det en dröm?

New York April 1961	Taubman, piano	LP: RCA LM 2578/LSC 2578
Vienna April 1965	VPO Bokstedt	LP: Decca LXT 6185/SXL 6185
Stockholm September 1974	Parsons, piano	CD: Bluebell ABCD 009 *Previously issued by Bluebell on LP*
Sweden January 1975	Solyom, piano	LP: Bis BISLP 15 CD: Bis BISCD 15
Sweden 1978–1979	Roos, piano	LP: Bluebell BELL 114

Våren flyktar hastigt

Vienna April 1965	VPO Bokstedt	LP: Decca LXT 6185/SXL 6185
Stockholm September 1974	Parsons, piano	CD: Blueball ABCD 009 *Previously issued by Bluebell on LP*
Sweden January 1975	Solyom, piano	LP: Bis BISLP 15 CD: Bis BISCD 15

Sieczynski

Wien, du Stadt meiner Träume

Stockholm September 1974	Parsons, piano	CD: Bluebell ABCD 009 *Previoulsy issued by Bluebell on LP*
Sweden 1978–1979	Roos, piano	LP: Bluebell BELL 109

Sjögren

Jeg giver mit digt till vaaren

Sweden 1978–1979	Roos, piano	LP: Bluebell BELL 109/BELL 114

Stenhammar

Adagio

Sweden 1978–1979	Roos, piano	LP: Bluebell BELL 114

Flickan knyter i Johannesnatten

New York November 1967	Wustman, piano	CD: melodram MEL 18027

I skogen

Sweden 1978–1979	Roos, piano	LP: Bluebell BELL 109

Richard Strauss

Elektra

Vienna December 1965	*Role of Elektra* Rysanek, Resnik, Windgassen, Wächter Vienna Opera Chorus VPO Böhm	LP: HRE Records HRE 314 CD: Legato SRO 833

Vienna June, September and November 1966 and February and June 1967	*Role of Elektra* Collier, Resnik Stolze, Krause Vienna Opera Chorus VPO Solti	LP: Decca MET 354–355/ SET 354–355 CD: Decca 417 3452 *Exerpts* CD: Decca 421 3232
New York February 1980	*Role of Elektra* Rysanek, Dunn, Nagy, McIntyre Metropolitan Opera Chorus & Orcestra Levine	Unpublished video recording

Other performances may be preserved; Metropolitan opera broadcasts with Nilsson in the role of Elektra took place in December 1966 and February 1971.

Elektra, excerpts (Ah! Das Gesicht! . . . Ich kann nicht sitzen; closing scene)

Vienna September 1975	Rysanek VPO Böhm	LP: Legendary LR 101

Die Frau ohne Schatten

Munich September 1976	*Role of Färberin* Bjoner, Varney, King, Kohn, Fischer-Dieskau Bavarian State Chorus & Orchestra Sawallisch	CD: Legendary LRCD 1029 *Previously issued by Legendary on LP*
Vienna October 1977	*Role of Färberin* Rysanek, Hesse, King, Berry, Wimberger Vienna Opera Chorus VPO Böhm	LP: HRE Records HRE 322 LP: DG 415 4721 CD: DG 415 4722

Salome

Vienna October 1961	*Role of Salome* G. Hoffman, Stolze, Kmennt, Wächter VPO Solti	LP: Decca MET 228–229/ SET 228–229 CD: Decca 414 4142 *Closing scene* LP: Decca LXT 6261/SXL 6261

Another performance may be preserved; a Metropolitan opera broadcast with Nilsson in the role of Salome took place in March 1965.

Salome, excerpt (closing scene)

Stockholm 1954	Berström, Hendriksen Stockholm Opera Orchestra Ehrling *Sung in Swedish*	CD: Legato SRO 833 *This excerpt begins at Es ist Kein Laut zu vernehmen*
New York April 1972	Metropolitan Opera Orchestra Böhm	LP: DG 2530 260/2721 206

Früling (4 letzte Lieder)

Stockholm January 1970	Stockholm RO Segerstam	CD: Bluebell ABCD 009 *Previously issued by Bluebell on LP*

September (4 letzte Lieder)

Stockholm January 1970	Stockholm RO Segerstam	CD: Bluebell ABCD 009 *Previously issued by Bluebell on LP*

Beim Schlafengehen (4 letzte Lieder)

Stockholm January 1970	Stockholm RO Segerstam	CD: Bluebell ABCD 009 *Previouly issued by Bluebell on LP*

Im Abendrot (4 Jetzte Lieder)

Stockholm January 1970	Stockholm RO Segerstam	CD: Bluebell ABCD 009 *Previously issued by Bluebell on LP*

Allerseelen

Sweden January 1975	Solyom, piano	LP: Bis BISLP 15 CD: Bis BISCD 15

Befreit

Sweden January 1975	Solyom, piano	LP: Bis BISLP 15 CD: BiS BISCD 15

Cäcilie

New York April 1961	Taubman, piano	LP: RCA LM 2578/LSC 2578
Sweden January 1975	Solyom, piano	LP: Bis BISLP 15 CD: Bis BISCD 15

Freundliche Vision		
New York November 1967	Wustman, piano	CD: Hunt CDLSMH 34049 CD: Melodram MEL 18027 CD: Memories HR 4275–4276
Kornblumen		
New York November 1967	Wustman, piano	CD: Hunt CDLSMH 34049 CD: Melodram MEL 18027 CD: Memories HR 4275–4276
Morgen		
Stockholm September 1974	Parsons, piano	CD: Bluebell ABCD 009 *Previously issued by Bluebell on LP*
Die Nacht		
Stockholm September 1974	Parsons, piano	CD: Bluebell ABCD 009 *Previously issued by Bluebell on LP*
Ruhe, meine Seele		
Sweden January 1975	Solyom, piano	LP: Bis BISLP 15 CD: Bis BISCD 15
Ständchen		
Sweden January 1975	Solyom, piano	LP: Bis BISLP 15 CD: Bis BISCD 15
Wiegenlied		
New York November 1967	Wustman, piano	CD: Hunt CDLSMH 34049 CD: Melodram MEL 18027 CD: Memories HR 4275–4276
Stockholm September 1974	Parsons, piano	CD: Bluebell ABCD 009 *Previously issued by Bluebell on LP*
Sweden January 1975	Solyom, piano	LP: Bis BISLP 15 CD: Bis BISCD 15
Zweignung		
New York November 1967	Wustman, piano	CD: Hunt CDLSMH 34049 CD: Melodram MEL 18027 CD: Memories HR 4275–4276
Stockholm September 1974	Parsons, piano	CD: Bluebell ABCD 009 *Previously issued by Bluebell on LP*
Sweden January 1975	Solyom, piano	LP: Bis BISLP 15 CD: Bis BISCD 15

Söderman

Den hvide roede rose

Sweden 1978–1979	Roos, piano	LP: Bluebell BELL 114

Verdi

Aida

Rome June and July 1965	*Rome of Aida* Bumbry, Corelli, Sereni Rome Opera Chorus & Orchestra Mehta	LP: EMI AN 189–191/SAN 189–191 LP: Angel 3716 LP: EMI SLS 929 CD: EMI CMS 763 2292 *Excerpts* LP: EMI ASD 2543 LP: EMI 1C 187 00786–00787 CD: EMI COM 764 0352/CD-EMX 2174

Another performance of the opera may be preserved; a Metropolitan opera broadcast with Nilsson in the role of Aida took place in March 1965.

Aida, excerpt (Ritorna vincictor)

London May 1957	Philharmonia L. Ludwig	45: Columbia SEL 1584 LP: Columbia 33 CX 1522 LP: Angel 35540 LP: EMI 1C 187 00786–00787
Walthamstow April 1963	Covent Garden Orchestra Pritchard	LP: Decca LXT 6068/SXL 6068 LP: Decca 411 8851

Aida, excerpt (Fu la sorte dell' armi)

Walthamstow April 1963	G. Hoffman Covent Garden Orchestra Pritchard	LP: Decca LXT 6068/SXL 6068

Aida, excerpt (O patria mia)

London May 1957	Philharmonia L. Ludwig	45: Columbia SEL 1584 LP: Columbia 33 CX 1522 LP: Angel 35540 LP: EMI 1C 187 00786–00787
Stockholm August 1961	Stockholm PO Grenvillius	CD: Bluebell ABCD 055

Walthamstow April 1963	Covent Garden Orchestra Pritchard	LP: Decca LXT 6068/SXL 6068

Aida, excerpt (O ciel! Mio padre!)

Phiadelphia January 1962	G. London Philadelphia Orchestra Stokowski	LP: Melodram MEL 228
Walthamstow April 1963	Ottolini, L. Quilico Covent Garden Orchestra Pritchard	LP: Decca LXT 6068/SXL 6068

Aida, excerpt (La fatal pietra . . . O terra addio)

Walthamstow April 1963	Ottolini Covent Garden Orchestra Pritchard	LP: Decca LXT 6068/SXL 6068

Un Ballo in maschera

Rome July 1960 and July 1961	*Role of Amelia* Stahlman, Simionato, Bergonzi, MacNeil, Krause Santa Cecilia Chorus & Orchestra Solti	LP: Decca MET 215–271/SET 215–217 CD: Decca 425, 6552 *Excerpts* LP: Decca LXT 6013/SXL 6013 LP: Decca 414 8854 CD: Decca 421 3232
New York January 1963	*Role of Amelia* Dobbs, Maderia, Tucker, Merrill, Reitan Metropolitan Opera Chorus & Orchestra Santi	LP: Hope Records HOPE 236

Un Ballo in maschera, excerpt (Ecco l'orrido campo)

Munich Date uncertain	Bavarian RO Erede	LP: Melodram MEL 653
London May 1957	Philharmonia L. Ludwig	45: Columbia SEL 1606 LP: Columbia 33 CX 1522 LP: Angel 35540 LP: EMI 1C 187 187 00786–00787

Don Carlo, excerpt (O don fatale)

Walthamstow April 1962	Covent Garden Orchestra Quadri	LP: Decca LXT 6033/SXL 6033

La Forza del destino, excerpt (Madre, pietosa vergine)

Walthamstow April 1962	Covent Garden Orchestra Quadri	LP: Decca LXT 6033/SXL 6033 LP: Decca 411 8851

La Forza del destino, excerpt (Pace, pace, mio Dio!)

London May 1957	Philharmonia L. Ludwig	45: Columbia SEL 1606 LP: Columbia 33 CX 1522 LP: Angel 35540
Stockholm January 1961	Stockholm RD Grevillius	CD: Bluebell ABCD 055
Walthamstow April 1962	Covent Garden Orchestra Quadri	LP: Decca LXT 6033/SXL 6033

Macbeth

Rome July 1964	*Role of Lady Macbeth* Prevedi, Taddei, Foiani Santa Cecilia Chorus & Orchestra Schippers	LP: Decca MET 282–284/ SET 282–284 CD: Decca 433 0392

Macbeth, excerpt (Vieni t'affretta / Or tutti sorgete)

Walthamstow April 1962	Covent Garden Orchestra Quadri	45: Decca CEP 5525/SEC 5525 LP: Decca LXT 6033/SXL 6033 LP: Decca 411 8851 CD: Decca 421 3232
Moscow September 1964	Tonini, piano	LP: HRE Records HRE 340 CD: Legato LCD 147
New York 1966	Bell Telephone Orchestra Voshees	LP: HRE Records HRE 379

Macbeth, excerpt (La luce langue)

Walthamstow April 1962	Covent Garden Orchestra Quadri	LP: Decca LXT 6033/SXL 6033 LP: Decca 411 8851 CD: Decca 421 3232

Macbeth, excerpt (Una macchia è qui tutt' ora)

Walthamstow	Covent Garden	45: Decca CEP 5525/SEC 5525
April 1962	Orchestra	LP: Decca LXI 6033/SXL 6033
	Quadri	LP: Decca 411 8851
		CD: Decca 421 3232

Nabucco, excerpt (Ben io t'invenni / Anch' io dischiuso / Salgo già)

Walthamstow	Covent Garden	LP: Decca LXT 6033/SXL 6033
April 1962	Orchestra	LP: Decca 411 8851
	Quadri	

Requiem

Boston	*Soprano soloist*	LP: RCA LSC 7040
1965	Chookasian, Bergonzi,	LP: RCA RE 5537–8/SER 537–8
	Flagello	
	Pro Musica Chorus	
	Boston SO	
	Leinsdorf	

Wagner

Die Feen, excerpt (Weh mir! So nah die fürchterliche Stunde / Ich häufe selbst die Schrecken an)

London	LSO	LP: Philips 6500 294
1972	C. Davis	

Der fliegende Holländer, excerpt (Traft ihr das Schiff im Meere an)

London	Chorus	LP: Columbia 33 CX 1522
May 1957	Philharmonia	LP: Angel 35540
	L. Ludwig	LP: EMI 1C 187 00786–00787
		CD: EMI CDM 763 1082
London	Alldis Choir	LP: Philips 6500 294
1972	LSO	
	C. Davis	

Der fliegende Holländer, excerpt (Wie aus der Ferne / Willst du des Vaters Wahl nicht scheltern?)

London	Hotter	LP: Columbia 33 CX 1542/SAX 2296
May 1957	Philharmonia	LP: Regal SREG 2068
	L. Ludwig	LP: EMI SXLP 30557
		CD: EMI CMS 764 0082

Götterdämmerung

Munich	*Role of Brünnhilde*	LP: Melodram MEL 425
September 1955	Rysanek, Malaniuk,	
	Aldenhoff, Uhde,	
	Frick	
	Bavarian State	
	Chorus & Orchestra	
	Knappertsbusch	
Bayreuth	*Role of Brünnhilde*	LP: Melodram MEL 609
August 1960	Bjoner, G. Hoffman,	
	Hopf, Stewart,	
	Frick, D. Kraus	
	Bayreuth Festival	
	Chorus & Orchestra	
	Kempe	
Vienna	*Role of Brünnhilde*	LP: Decca MET 292–297/SET 292–297
May, June,	Watson, C. Ludwig,	LP: Decca D100 D19/RING 1–22
October and	Wingassen, Frick,	LP: Decca 414 1001/414 1151
November 1964	Fischer-Dieskau,	CD: Decca 414 1002/414 1152
	Neidlinger	*Excerpts*
	Vienna Opera Chorus	LP: Decca LXT 6220/SXL 6220
	VPO	LP: Decca LXT 6261/SXL 6261
	Solti	LP: Decca GRV 24/417 1811
		CD: Decca 421 3132
Bayreuth	*Role of Brünnhilde*	LP: Philips 6747 037/6747 049
July and	Dvorakova, Mödl,	CD: Philips 412 5882/420 3252
August 1967	Windgassen,	*Excerpts*
	Stewart, Greindl	LP: Philips 6575 503/6575 504
	Bayreuth Festival	LP: Philips 6833 083
	Chorus & Orchestra	
	Böhm	

Other performances may be preserved; Metropolitan opera broadcasts with Nilsson in the role of Brünnhilde took place in January 1962, December 1963, and March 1975.

Götterdämmerung, excerpt (Starke Scheite schichtet mir dort)

Philadelphia	Philadelphia Orchestra	LP: Melodram MEL 228
January 1962	Stokowski	

Lohengrin

Bayreuth	*Role of Elsa*	LP: Cetra LO 77
August 1954	Varnay, Windgassen,	LP: Melogram MEL 541
	Adam, Uhde,	CD: Laudis LCD 44035
	Fischer-Dieskau	CD: Melodram MEI 36104
	Bayreuth Festival	*Excerpts*
	Chorus & Orchestra	LP: Gioielli della lirica GML 20
	Jochum	CD: Memories HR 4275–4275

Lohengrin, excerpt (Einsam in trüben Tagen)

London	Philharmonia	LP: Columbia 33 CX 1522
May 1957	L. Ludwig	LP: Angel 35540
		LP: EMI IC 187 00786–00787
		CD: EMI CDM 763 1082
London	Covent Garden	LP: Decca LXT 6077/SXL 6077
June 1963	Downes	LP: Decca GRV 24

Parsifal, excerpt (Die alles hab' ich nun geträumt / Ich sah das Kind . . . to end Act 2)

London	Brilioth, Bailey,	LP: Philips 6500 661
1974	Covent Garden Orchestra	
	Segerstam	

Reinzi, excerpt (Gerechter Gott!)

London	LSO	LP: Philips 6500 294
1972	C. Davis	

Siegfried

Bayreuth	*Role of Brünnhilde*	LP: Melodram MEL 608
July 1960	Siebert, Höffgen,	
	Hopf, H. Kraus,	
	Uhde, O. Kraus,	
	Roth-Ehrang	
	Bayreuth Festival	
	Orchestra	
	Kempe	
Vienna	*Role of Brünnehilde*	LP: Decca MET 242–246/SET 242–246
May, October	Sutherland	
and November	Höffgen, Windgassen,	LP: Decca D100 D19/RING 1–22
1962	Stolze, Hotter,	LP: Decca 414 1001/414 1101
	Böhme, Neidlinger	CD: Decca 414 1002/414 1102
	VPO	*Excerpts*
	Solti	LP: Decca LXT 6142/SXL 6142

Bayreuth July 1966	*Role of Brünnhilde* Köth, Soukupova, Windgassen, Wohlfahrt, Adam, Böhme, Neidlinger Bayreuth Festival Orchestra Böhm	LP: Philips 6747 037/6747 048 CD: Philips 412 4832/420 3252

Tannhäuser

Naples March 1956	*Role of Venus* Rysanek, Lustig, Terkal, Cordes, Frick San Carlo Opera Chorus & Orchestra Böhm	CD: Melodram MEL 37073
Berlin 1968	*Roles of Elisabeth and Venus* Windgassen, Laubenthal, Adam, Fischer-Dieskau Deutsche Oper Chorus & Orchestra Gerdes	LP: DG SLPM 139 284–139 287 LP: DG 2711 008/2740 142 *Excerpts* LP: DG 2721 2C6/2537 C16/2638 098

Another performance may be preserved; a Metropolitan opera broadcast with Nilsson in the roles of Elisabeth and Venus took place in March 1966.

Tannhäuser, excerpt (Dich teure Halle)

London May 1957	Philharmonia L. Ludwig	LP: Columbia 33 CX 1522 LP: Angel 35540 LP: EMI 1C 187 00786–00787 CD: EMI CDM 763 1082
Stockholm March 1959	Stockholm PO Grevillius	CD: Bluebell ABCD 055
Stockholm 1959	Stockholms Opera Orchestra Ehrling	LP: HMV (Sweden) ALPC 1
London June 1963	Covent Garden Orchestra Downes	LP: Decca LXT 6077/SXL 6077 LP: Decca GRV 24

New York 1966	Bell Telephone Orchestra Voshees	LP: HRE Records HRE 379 CD: GOP Records GOP 736 *Broadcast in January 1967*

Tristan und Isolde

Florence May 1957	*Role of Isolde* G. Hoffmann, Windgassen, Neidlinger, Rohr Maggio Musicale Chorus & Orchestra Rodzinski	LP: Cetra DOC 20
Bayreuth July 1957	*Role of Isolde* G. Hoffman, Windgassen, Hotter, Van Mill Bayreuth Festival Chorus & Orchestra Sawallisch	LP: Melogram MEL 575
Vienna September 1960	*Role of Isolde* Resnik, Uhl, Krause, Van Mill Vienna Opera Chorus VPO Solti	LP: Decca MET 204–208/SET 204–208 LP: Decca D41 D5 CD: Decca 430 2342 *Excerpts* LP: Decca LXT 6178/SXL 6178 CD: Decca 421 3232/421 8772 CD: Decca 440 0692 *Original LP issue contained a bonus LP of rehearsal extracts*
Bayreuth July 1962	*Role of Isolde* Meyer, Windgassen, Wächter, Greindl Bayreuth Festival Chorus & Orchestra Böhm	LP: Melodram MEL 525
Bayreuth July and August 1966	*Role of Isolde* C. Ludwig, Windgassen, Wächter, Talvela Bayreuth Festival	LP: DG KL 512–516/SKL 912–916 LP: DG LPM 139 221–139 225/ SLPM 139 221–139 225 LP: DG 2713 001/2740 144/415 3951 LP: Philips 6747 244-3

	Chorus & Orchestra Böhm	CD: DG 419 8892 CD: Philips 434 4202/434 4252 *Excerpts* LP: DG SLPEM 136 433/135 118 LP: DG 2705 015/2721 112/2721 115 LP: DG 2721 206/2535 243/2536 037 LP: DG 2537 001/2538 098/2538 245 LP: DG 410 8551 LP: Philips 6833 195 *Original LP issue continued rehearsal extracts not involving Nilsson, but Philips LP 6701 048 did contain Liebesnacht rehearsal*
Bayreuth August 1966	*Role of Isolde* C. Ludwig, Windgassen, Wächter, Talvela Bayreuth Festival Chorus & Orchestra Böhm	CD: Frequenz CML 3 *Excerpts* CD: Curcio-Hunt OPV 16 CD: Memories HR 4275–4276 CD: Memories HR 4424–4425
Orange July 1973	*Role of Isolde* Hesse, Vickers, Berry, Rundgren New Philharmonia Chorus Orchestre National Böhm	LP: HRE Records HRE 359 CD: Rodolphe RPC 32553–32555
New York January 1974	*Role of Isolde* Wilma, Vickers, Dooley, Plishka Metropolitan Opera Chorus & Orchestra Leinsdorf	LP: ERR Records ERR 147 *Source of this recording is not a Metropolitan opera broadcast*

Other performances may be preserved; Metropolitan opera broadcasts with Nilsson in the role of Isolde also took place in March 1961, February 1963, and December 1971.

Tristan und Isolde, excerpt (Weh, ach wehe, dies zu dulden . . . der Trank ist's, der mir taugt)

Vienna	G. Hoffman	LP: Decca LXT 5559/SXL 2184

September 1959	VPO Knappertsbusch	LP: Decca JB 58
New York October 1983	Metropolitan Opera Orchestra Levine	Unpublished video recording of Metropolitan centennial gala *Beginning only at Wie lachend sie mir Leider singen*

Tristan und Isolde, excerpt (Tristan! Geliebter! . . . Liebesnacht)

Milan April 1959	Rössel-Majdan, Windgassen La Scala Orchestra Karajan	CD: Hunt COKAR 224 *Beginning only at Sink hernieder, Nacht der Liebe*
New York January 1960	Dalis, Vinay Metropolitan Opera Orchestra Böhm	CD: Melodram CDM 26519
New York April 1981	Dunn, Vickers Metropolitan Opera Orchestra Levine	Unpublished radio broadcast *Beginning only at Sink hernieder, Nacht der Liebe*

Tristan und Isolde, excerpt (Mild und leise)

London May 1957	Philharmonia L. Ludwig	LP: Columbia 33 CX 1522 LP: Angel 35540 LP: Columbia (Germany) SHZE 154 LP: EMI 1C 187 00786–00787 CD: EMI CDM 763 1082
Vienna September 1959	VPO Knappertsbusch	LP: Decca LXT 5559/SXL 2184 LP: Decca JB 58/GRV 24 CD: Decca 414 6252/433 3332/433 3402
Vienna May 1962	VPO Knappertsbusch	Unpublished video recording

Die Walküre

Bayreuth July 1954	*Role of Ortlinde* Varnay, Mödl, Milinkovic, Lorenz, Hotter, Greindl Bayreuth Festival Orchestra Keilberth	LP: Melodram MEL 547 CD: Melodram MEL 36102

Bayreuth August 1957	*Role of Sieglinde* Varnay, Milinkovic, Vinay, Hotter, Greindl Bayreuth Festival Orchestra Knappertsbusch	LP: Estro Armonico EA 032 LP: Discocorp IGI 292 LP: Cetra LO 59/DOC 48 LP: Melodram MEL 577 CD: Music and Arts CD 254 CD: Laudis LCD 44071/154 021
Walthamstow September 1961	Role of Brünnhilde Grouwenstijn. Gorr, Vickers, G. London, Ward LSO Leinsdorf	LP: RCA LD 6706/LDS 6706 LP: Decca 7BB 125–129 CD: Decca 430 3912 *Excerpts* LP: RCA RB 6658/SB 6658 LP: Decca SDD 430/GRV 24
Vienna October and November 1965	*Role of Brünnhilde* Crespin, C. Ludwig, King, Hotter, Frick VPO Solti	LP: Decca MET 312–316/SET 312–316 LP: Decca D100 D19/RING 1–22 LP: Decca 414 1001/414 1051 CD: Decca 414 1002/414 1052 *Excerpts* LP: Decca SET 390 CD: Decca 421 8872
Bayreuth July and August 1967	*Role of Brünnhilde* Rysanek, Burmeister, King, Adam, Nienstedt Bayreuth Festival Orchestra Böhm	LP: Philips 6757 037/6747 047 CD: Philips 412 4782/420 3252 *Excerpts* LP: Philips 6575 501/6575 504 LP: Philips 6833 083
New York March 1969	*Role of Brünnhilde* Crespin, Veasey Vickers, Adam, Talvela Metropolitan Opera Orchestra Karajan	CD: Nouva Era NE 2405–2408 CD: CDKAR 217 *Excerpts* CD: Memories HR 4275–4276

Other performances may be preserved; Metropolitan opera broadcasts with Nilsson in the role of Brünnhilde also took place in December 1961, February 1965, February 1968, December 1972, and March 1975.

Die Walküre, Act 1

Hamburg	*Role of Sieglinde*	LP: HRE Records HRE 347

[Date uncertain]	Svanholm, Greindl NDR Orchestra Schmidt-Isserstedt	

Die Walküre, excerpt (Der Männer Sippe)

Hamburg 1953	NDR Orchestra Sandberg	LP: Melodram MEL 653
London June 1963	Covent Garden Orchestra Downes	LP: Decca LXT 6077/SXL 6077 LP: Decca GRV 24

Die Walküre, excerpt (Du bist der Lenz)

Hamburg 1953	NDR Orchestra Sandberg	LP: Melodram MEL 653
London June 1963	Covent Garden Orchestra Downes	LP: Decca LXT 6077/SXL 6077 LP: Decca GRV 24

Die Walküre, excerpt (Schläfst du, Gast? . . . to end Act 1)

London 1974	Brilioth Covent Garden Orchestra Segerstam	LP: Philips 6500 661
New York February 1975	Vickers Metropolitan Opera Orchestra Ehrling	LP: ERR Records ERR 141 *Source of this recording is not a Metropolitan opera broadcast*

Die Walküre, excerpt (War es so schmählich? . . . trotzt' ich deinem Gebot)

Hamburg 1953	S. Björling NDR Orchestra Sandberg	LP: Melodram MEL 653

Die Walküre, excerpt (War es so schmählich? . . . to end of opera)

London May 1957	Hotter Philharmonia L. Ludwig	LP: Columbia 33 CX 1542/SAX 2296 LP: Regal SREG 2068 LP: EMI SXLP 30567 CD: ENI CMS 565 2122

Die Walküre, excerpt (Siegmund, sieh' auf mich)

Milan April 1958	Suthaus La Scala Orchestra Karajan	CD: Hunt CDKAR 223

Die Walküre, excerpts (Kehrte der Vater nun heim; Schützt mich in höchster Not; Nicht sehre die Sorge um mich; Fort denn eile)

Bayreuth August 1965	Rysanek, King, Adam, Talvela Bayreuth Festival Orchestra Böhm	CD: Legato SRO 833

Der Engel (Wesendonok-Lieder)

New York April 1961	Taubman, piano	LP: RCA LM 2578/LSC 2578
London 1972	LSO C. Davis	LP: Philips 6500 294

Stehe still (Wesendonok-Lieder)

London 1972	LSD C. Davis	LP: Philips 6500 294

Im Treibhaus (Weserdonok-Lieder)

London 1972	LSO C. Davis	LP: Philips 6500 294

Schmerzen (Wesendonok-Lieder)

London 1972	LSO C. Davis	LP: Philips 6500 294

Träume (Wesendonok-Lieder)

New York April 1961	Taubman, piano	LP: RCA LM 2578/LSC 2578
London 1972	LSO C. Davis	LP: Philips 6500 294

Weber

Der Freischütz

Munich 1968	*Role of Agathe* Köth, Gedda, Berry, Crass Bavarian State Chorus & Orchestra Heger	LP: EMI 1C 165 28351–28353 *Excerpts* LP: EMI 1C 063 29023

Der Freischütz, excerpt (Leise, leise)

London May 1958	Philharmonia Wallberg	LP: Columbia 33 CX 1629/SAX 2284 LP: Angel 35715/60353 LP: EMI 1C 187 00786–00787 CD: EMI CDM 763 1082/CD-CFP 4561
London June 1963	Covent Garden Orchestra Downes	LP: Decca LXT 6077/SXL 6077

Oberon

Munich March and December 1970	*Role of Rezia* Hamari, Domingo, Grobe, Prey Bavarian Radio Chorus & Orchestra Kubelik	LP; DG 2709 035/2726 052 CD: DG 419 0382 *Excerpts* LP: DG 2538 098/2721 206

Oberon, excerpt (Ozean, du Ungeheuer)

London May 1958	Philharmonia Wallberg	LP: Columbia 33 CX 1629/SAX 2284 LP: Angel 35715/60353 LP: EMI ASD 3915/1C 187 00786–00787 CD: EMI CDM 763 1082
Stockholm August 1961	Stockholm PO Grevillius	CD: Bluebell ABCD 055
London June 1963	Covent Garden Orchestra Downes	LP: Decca LXT 6077/SXL 6077

Wennerberg

Man borde inte sova

Sweden 1978–1979	Roos, piano	LP: Bluebell BELL 114

Wiklund

Silkesko över gylden Laest

New York November 1967	Wustman, piano	CD: Melodram MEL 18027

Miscellaneous

I rosens doft

Stockholm December 1975	Oestman, piano	LP: Swedish Society SLT 33243

The Golden Ring: TV film of the making of Decca's Solti Ring

Vienna 1965	Watson, Windgrassen, Fischer-Dieskau, Frick VPO Solti	VHS Video: Decca 071 1533 Laserdisc: Decca 071 1531

German language version of the above

Vienna 1965	Watson, Windgassen, Fischer-Dieskau, Frick VPO Solti	VHS Video: Decca 071 0023

Index